BE YOUR
OWN BOSS

BE YOUR OWN BOSS

*A Step-by-step Guide
to Financial Independence
Through Your Own
Small Business*

DANA SHILLING

WILLIAM MORROW AND COMPANY, INC.

New York   1983

Library of Congress Cataloging in Publication Data

Shilling, Dana.
   Be your own boss.

   Bibliography: p.
   Includes index.
   1. New business enterprises.   2. Small business.
I. Title.
HD62.5.S54   1983   658'.041   82-14180
ISBN 0-688-01572-7

Printed in the United States of America

First Edition

1   2   3   4   5   6   7   8   9   10

BOOK DESIGN BY BERNARD SCHLEIFER

Contents

Contents

Contents

Contents

Contents

Introduction

WHEN I STARTED my business I read every book I could find about starting a business. I was alternately disappointed and furious to find very little useful information. Many of the books wasted twenty or thirty pages of large print on quizzes intended to show whether or not you have the "entrepreneurial character." I don't think a series of stupid questions about whether you would take a tuba or a Bible to a desert island will contribute anything to your profits. Certainly there are some people who are natural employees—I'm one of them—but for the purposes of this book we will assume that anyone who wants to start a business is qualified to do so, and is entitled to practical help and not blather.

Although I may slide in an inspirational word here and there, I try to avoid twenty-five-hundred-word chunks of sweetness and light. I'll stick to practicalities: tax breaks and choosing call brands for your bar. Take it as stated that starting a business is hard, often discouraging, and that just because it's very dark *doesn't* mean that dawn is imminent. You can't be paranoid if you own your own business. By this I do not mean that trusting people will succeed and suspicious ones fail. What I do mean is that even your darkest imaginings, as you wake up at 3 A.M. and can't get back to sleep, will be surpassed. You won't believe some of the things that will go wrong, and you won't be able to predict them. If you're prepared to go through all this, you'd better believe in what you're doing. All businesses yield anxiety. A routine business, one which piques your greed but not your imagination, never yields joy.

That's why I don't devote any space to the question of what kind of business to go into. I went to one business start-up seminar and asked a nice young woman what kind of business she owned. She said she wanted some information before getting started—fair enough—and that she thought she might go into some kind of retail business. I pity her. Life is hard enough if you know you want an eight-hundred-square-foot store within three blocks of a major commuter railroad station in order to sell cosmetics made with cucumbers to a potential market of women in the eighteen to thirty age bracket. If your ideas are not immediate, specific, and about to be confirmed by reality, you don't have a snowball's chance in hell.

Most books about starting a business assume that you're a traditional business person: that is, within the bounds of your ethics, you don't particularly care what you do to make money. You won't sell heroin to schoolchildren, nor will you sell cans you know to be infected with botulism, but selling bath towels is as good as selling frozen Thai food which is as good as running a limousine service. This seems to me a singularly joyless way to do business. If you don't have any feeling for, or belief in, your service or product, the only fun you'll get will be counting money or beating someone out of something on a deal. But if you believe in your special formula for fuchsia eyeshadow, or that you give markedly better plumbing service, you have the satisfaction of giving customers something they can't get anywhere else. When your psychic income is high, you can accept a lower level of cash income. Unconventional business aims can be coupled with unusual financing and business techniques.

Most other books about starting a business assume a conventional business: high capitalization, immediate incorporation, heavy borrowing, high technology, and a hierarchical structure. Therefore, these books spend a lot of time on financial statements and business plans—which are needed for disclosure to stockholders and for borrowing large sums of money from banks. I have nothing against disclosure, or against borrowing, but I treat those topics very lightly here. First of all, you can get that information elsewhere. Second of all, you have a lot of other problems before you reach that stage. A major national corporation just calls an office decorator when it needs to furnish a new office. You probably can't afford to buy furniture in an office furniture store; you may not even be able to afford a thrift shop; so I include hints for improvising furniture. It's the big corporations that have given us our high standard of living—but they have also contributed to the high inflation rate, high unemployment, pollution, and waste. At any rate, it was a lot easier to become a robber baron during the period of industrialization than it is today. You may hit upon some invention as dramatic—and as wealth-producing—as the microchip and the minicomputer. But don't count on it.

Books are still being written to preach the doctrine of leverage: that is, you invest a little money of your own, borrow a large chunk of money, and chortle at the amount by which your profit exceeds your investment. When this tactic was called "buying on margin" in the pre-1929 stock market, it created some millionaires, many paupers, and creamed the economy. Today, there are additional problems. First, who's going to lend money to a speculative enterprise when there isn't enough credit to meet the demand of established, credit-worthy enterprises? Second, even if you could borrow the money, leverage is plausible when you earn a ten-percent profit on money you borrowed at five percent. When the interest rate is twenty percent and the rate of profit has stayed the same, or been eroded by high prices, you're in trouble. And the more money you borrow, the deeper the trouble.

As the OTB (Off-Track Betting) slogan advises, don't gamble more than you can afford to lose. There's a strong possibility that your business will fail. If you are prepared, both psychologically and with bucks in the cookie jar, for this eventuality, you will survive. If you pay off all your debts in full, your credit rating will be unimpaired, and your memory book will be full of priceless (or at any rate expensive) recollections. You can start again when you raise more money, or try a different kind of business altogether.

With luck, planning, and a pathological dread of spending money, you may be able to finance the entire operation yourself. This is the best possible outcome. You take all the risks and keep all the profits. If you can't do this, the conventional wisdom is that you should turn to equity investors—either partners, limited partners, or stockholders. After all, a hundred percent of zero is zero, and fifty percent of a prosperous business is better than a sharp stick in the eye. But then you're betting on yourself to lose. If you go broke, your partners and stockholders can't demand that you repay their losses. That'll show *them*. But if you make it big, isn't it a shame to see all those millions going to someone who shelled out a measly few bucks? I think it's better to decide the amount you can borrow and be reasonably sure of repaying. You budget the interest as one of your costs of doing business—and keep all the profits. The situation is different if the business is a genuine collaboration between people, all of whom contribute skills and money, or if you want to share the profits with the workers who made the profits possible. But I think a debt relationship is more straightforward, and saves money in the long run, when all a person contributes is money.

Fortunately, undercapitalization is a challenge to your wit and stamina. You'll learn how to make cheap black-on-white line work look expensive, you will learn how to splice machinery together with twine and chewing gum, you'll find twelve sequential uses for a used packing carton. If you manage cannily and plow the profits back into the business, growing from a one-person operation, hiring your first employees, opening branches, or integrating your business vertically, you may have the satisfaction of building a large business from nothing. You can avoid building an ugly conventional business, one with a paramilitary hierarchy of "line" and "staff," with a proletariat of typewriter-pounding females. You can collect information and write reports only when the information is needed, not because someone else's dumb routine demands it. Many established businesses are like dinosaurs: it takes the brain two years to discover that the dinosaur has died. (Chrysler comes to mind in this connection.) The business you build yourself can have a more efficient nervous system.

Owning a business has done little for my own nervous system. The sleepless nights, the daily hassles—nonetheless, it really is worth it. I've lost a moderate amount of money, but I haven't missed any meals. I haven't had to commute, go to an office, play office politics, or flatter anyone. I've had the chance to do something myself, in my own way, and can point with pride to something I believe in. So I have a positive motive for being in business for myself and in encouraging you to try.

I also have a negative motive. During my brief career as an employee, I saw a lifetime's worth of inefficiency, stupidity, ass-kissing, and gross time-wasting. I never saw any traditional corruption; if any embezzlement or bribery went on around me, it's news to me. But it bothered me that the clients and/or the taxpayers were subsidizing this slapstick. Wasp, Wasp & Token (which I occasionally refer to in the chapters that follow) is a composite of various places I've worked. Names have been changed to protect me from libel suits. I include these anecdotes so you can learn, relatively painlessly, from the stupidity and inefficiency of others. I also try to mention some of the more stupid things I did myself, so at least you can make different mistakes.

By the way, the names of parts and industrial processes that you'll find in later chapters are entirely imaginary, though some of the names are real words that mean something else. The principles of budgeting, time scheduling, and quality control apply to the fabrication of any product or the delivery of any service. The focus of this book is on offices—whether at home or away—because all businesses have some kind of record-keeping, bill-sending capacity; some service businesses, especially those concerned with words, have nothing else. But I've also tried to provide specific information for retailers, restaurateurs, crafts people, and others. You are at liberty to skip the sections that don't apply to your business. They won't be on the exam.

All start-up businesses have some things in common. Money required inevitably exceeds money available. Time follows the same law. Try to ration your consumption of success stories: reading about the ten million dollars earned in a month on an investment of a dollar ninety-eight will only frustrate you. Studying other people's experience to gain ideas and see what worked and what didn't is very helpful. But descending into a sink of one-upmanship is not. Parents of new babies find that the exploits of their own beloved infants are sneered at. All the *other* babies in the family sat up at one month, walked by six months, and did calculus by the age of two. Similarly, if you seem vulnerable or hesitant about your business, plenty of people will be glad to tell you about *their* fabulous success and *your* imminent failure. Avoid such people.

All these stories are told in retrospect, of course, when the outcome is known. If you have a daring idea and it succeeds brilliantly, you will have been a genius all along. If the same idea fails miserably, you will have been a turkey all along. And perhaps ten years later someone else with more money, better management, or simply a more hospitable climate will make a go of your ridiculously impractical idea. It's like the Saturday morning serial. All the kids in the audience know that the hero will get out of the cave infested with cobras and man-eating lions. The *hero* doesn't know if he'll get out or not. The hero's reactions demonstrate his bravery, and perhaps his stupidity in getting into this mess in the first place. The day you decide to enter a business, you enter into the world of Buck Rogers and Ming the Merciless (your bank manager). You must be brave but not foolhardy, optimistic but not delusional, patient but not hidebound. Naturally this combination of qualities is rarely found and hard to attain.

To be realistic, I think you have to be prepared to hang in for at least three years, with some form of alternate income, before the business is self-sustaining and pays you an income. After that it should be gravy. You may break even much sooner—even immediately—but I think you need three years' worth of money in the bank and gravel in the gizzard to make starting a business worthwhile. If you need an assured source of income, or nights of unbroken sleep, before then, I think you're better off doing something less risky.

Being an employee, after all, has a great deal to recommend it—a steady salary, sometimes quite a generous one, health insurance, perhaps a pension or stock plan, freedom from isolation, sharing ideas with co-workers. Yet, it's hard to become really uproariously, obscenely rich as an employee. You can make your points strongly, express your ideas forcefully, but still and all it's not your company. You can get an MBA, be very creative, and work very hard, but you know damn well you'll never be the president of IBM. If you start your own business, you start at the top. By the same token, you'll never get a promotion, but perhaps you can get a substitute thrill when you start making money.

When you own a business, you have fistfuls of bills to pay and customers at your throat and on your case, but you at least have control over your own product and have customers to bill and suppliers to scream at.

In a *New Yorker* cartoon, a very small fish, about to be eaten by a medium-sized fish, thinks despairingly, "There is no justice." The medium-sized fish thinks, "There is some justice," as it is eaten by the largest fish, who thinks, "The world is just." The following pages are intended as an invitation for you to get higher in that food chain. I hope you will find a good part of the practical information you need. My assumption is that all my readers are intelligent and know their own minds, but do not have technical accounting or legal information at their fingertips, and can use some practical help with matters such as billing and paperwork.

Although I have tried to be as specific as possible, such things as prices, addresses, and laws are subject to change. Please don't rely on specific data in this book without checking. I try to include a detailed discussion of common legal questions, but this is not a substitute for individual advice from a knowledgeable lawyer who understands your particular situation. I don't think you should do without a lawyer and an accountant—but not all members of these professions know enough about business start-ups to help you. If you understand the issues involved so that you become an informed and active client, I think you have a better chance of benefiting from the professional advice you get. Professional advisers literally give you advice. You have to make the decisions.

When you get to the end of your rope—or your shoestring—make a knot and hang on.

CHAPTER ONE

Money—How Much Do You Need?

UNFORTUNATELY, no matter how successful your business will ultimately be, you have to face the planning period (when there's still time to say the hell with it and get a job) and the start-up period (when you're committed to running the business, but you have yet to start the assembly line, put the first Le Creuset pot on the shelves, or cook your first quiche).

The planning period is a good time to start living below your income—inviting your friends over for a potluck dinner and conversation rather than going out to dinner and the theater; buying your clothes at factory outlets and the Salvation Army; selling your car and either doing without one entirely or buying a squat, tank-like vehicle with good fuel economy, lots of cargo space, and no collision insurance. You're setting yourself up for several years of poverty, so you might as well get used to it.

Some of the information in this chapter applies across the board; much of it assumes that you plan a factory/retail store/restaurant/bar or other business outside your home. If you plan to run your business from your home or an office, you can skim this material and turn to Chapter Three, "The Office and Its Alternatives," for immediately usable information. If you do need a place of business, though, there are three ways to do it: buying an existing business, taking over a fully stocked business location without buying a going business, and furnishing and equipping (or building, furnishing and equipping) space. Once that's out of the way, you'll need an inventory of things to sell or components to assemble into things to sell. When you know what to buy, compiling your start-up budget is reasonably easy, if heartbreaking.

Buying an Existing Business

The normal term is "buying a going business," but if the business were going, it would probably not be for sale, n'est-ce pas? The ideal situation would be to find a seller who, disgusted with the materialism he had to espouse in order to build a thriving business, is about to retire to a Trappist monastery. Another example: the huge income thrown off by the business, cannily invested in grain futures, will enable the owner to live in luxury on a yacht, so she doesn't want to be bothered anymore. These scenarios rank with the apocryphal used car owned by a little old lady who only drove it to church on Sunday.

The reason the current owner gives for selling the business is not necessarily the whole story. Probably, the owner wants to bail out before the ship sinks—and you may, or may not, be able to install a superior bilge pump. Maybe your superior management skills, detailed records, and brilliant buying will turn the corner. Maybe not.

If you want to go this route, businesses for sale are advertised in newspaper classified ads under "Business Opportunities" (often a euphemism), in trade publications, and in the *National Buying Guide,* free copies of which can be obtained by writing to 5400 Wilshire Boulevard, Los Angeles, CA, 90017. The *Wall Street Journal* traditionally has its greatest concentration of business-for-sale ads on Thursdays.

The advantage of buying an existing business is that you know in advance what you're buying and can budget the purchase fairly accurately. You also get something called "goodwill"—the propensity of people to buy at that particular store, or to use that product— and will pay quite a bit for it. There can also be ill-will—people can have a firm belief that a store is dirty, or that a restaurant serves bad food. These beliefs are very hard to change.

Location, location, and location are indeed primary. Consider your needs: a factory doesn't have to attract consumer foot traffic, but it must have ample power sources, loading docks, and be accessible to cargo ships, UPS, the highway system, or whatever the shipping method is. A store or restaurant may, against all odds, draw people to an out-of-the-way location (where rents will be gratifyingly lower) by sheer excellence or fashion (which, unfortunately, is transitory). Normally, however, such a business has to be located where many people will pass it (a downtown business district, a shopping mall, a residential area, near the commuter train). It must also be located in a place where people *expect* to buy whatever you're selling. A Bible store opened in the heart of Times Square—surely a location most in need of blessing, but one where Amen sticks in the throat. I don't think they do a land-office business.

If you want to open a bar, or a restaurant serving liquor, the location must have a liquor license already, available for transfer to you as the new owner—or you must be able to transfer to an existing license you already own or buy separately to the new location. You must check the licensing situation in advance because sometimes liquor control authorities decide that a particular area is a "problem area" and additional liquor licenses should not be granted. Or local regulations may forbid the sale of liquor within a particular distance from a church or school.

The business location must include the facilities you need (ten telephone lines, six gas ranges) or at least be suitable for installing them. Check the equipment—or have a professional inspection—to make sure it has at least three years of useful life remaining before its probable demise. If the equipment is moribund, forget about that location, or demand that the rent and/or sales price be lowered, or set aside a reserve for replacements as needed.

The location must be zoned to permit whatever it is you want to do. The former owner may have gotten away with it, due to some combination of luck, connections, and out-and-out bribery. Moral problems aside, you can't count on getting the same arrangements.

For your own good, I hope you have a lawyer. Ask your lawyer to verify that the zoning is acceptable and a liquor license will be available if you need one. If you don't have a lawyer, ask the seller's lawyer, who will usually be truthful on these points. If neither of you has a lawyer, call up City Hall and ask which agency handles zoning, which alcoholic beverage control. Then call the agency in general terms. There is an argument against identifying yourself and giving them the chance to refuse automatically.

Consider the neighborhood. If it is becoming fashionable, you have at least a few good years. If it is becoming a burned-out slum, with shopkeepers and residents fleeing as soon as they can, you may have some clue as to why the present owner wants to sell. Although banks swear they have ended the practices of the bad old days, red-lining still continues. If the bank has given up on your neighborhood, it will be hard to get bank loans and trade credit. Suppliers may hesitate to deliver to neighborhoods where they expect (or fantasize) armed marauders lurk. You may have to pay cash for merchandise, not because your credit rating is bad, but because the neighborhood is considered unstable. On the other hand, a so-called bad neighborhood has nowhere to go but up, whether by gentrification or by the efforts of its existing population.

Consider the competition. A new store or two new restaurants nearby, or a decline in sales because the customers switched from American components to Japanese components, may also explain the gleam in the current owner's eye.

Sometimes the business owner owns, and wants to sell you, the building. This has its own problems of valuation (usable floor space, energy efficiency, and so on). In urban areas, the more usual case is for businesses to use rented premises. If this is true, first find out if the lease can be sublet or assigned at all: it may have a provision that the lease ends as soon as the business currently occupying the space is sold. If the lease is transferable, find out how long it has to run, and what the landlord is likely to do when it's up. It is embarrassing to have to hold the "Going Out of Business—Lost Our Lease" sale right after the gala opening sale.

Consider security. A working alarm system is a plus. Architectural details that make it hard to install alarms are demerits. If gates are needed, it's a plus if they're already in place. Skylights are charming, but attractive to drop-in burglars. A large show window highlights your goods—and invites forced entry. You'll need a secure fire exit—and some way to keep intruders out. If you need a safe, a built-in is nice. If you think a camera for surveillance is necessary, see if it has been installed; if not, see if the sight lines are appropriate. A dummy camera has the same effect, at lower cost, as a real camera, although it doesn't furnish any evidence if a crime does occur. Stand at the checkstand (the cash register area) and see if you can observe customers—and shoplifters—from that vantage point.

The sale of the business will include some, or all, of these items:

- Leases
- Leasehold improvements such as built-in furniture or equip-

ment, improved lighting, air conditioning, carpeting installed
by the tenant
- Furniture and equipment
- Company cars and/or delivery trucks
- Inventory
- Accounts receivable
- Insurance policies
- Goodwill (including tangible items such as customer lists and
  prospect files)

Be sure you understand which of these are included in the sale.
Are you buying the accounts receivable? If you are, you'll have
extra income, but at the financial and psychic cost of collecting the
money. The owner may be willing to guarantee the collectability of
the accounts receivable by depositing, say, thirty-five percent of the
value of the receivables in an escrow account for sixty to ninety
days, retrieving the money as the accounts are collected. If s/he
does this, the business is more valuable, and the asking price will go
up proportionately.

You may assume that the lovely equipment you admire so much
is part of the deal; but the walk-in freezer may already have been
sold, or may be about to be repossessed by the seller, or levied upon
by an anxious creditor. The carpeting for which the seller is asking a
premium price may belong to the landlord, not the tenant-seller.
Take nothing for granted. Not everyone is honest, and not all honest
people are efficient.

Apropos of sales, when you buy the business you will probably
buy over fifty percent of its assets and inventory, so this will be a
"bulk sale." Alert your lawyer to this fact, so the local Bulk Sales
Act formalities can be taken care of. The Bulk Sales Act gives you
the right to get a sworn list of creditors, detailing how much the
seller owes each of them (which keeps you from suffering awkward
moments later when surprise creditors show up), a description of
what property is included in the sale, and how much the owner
paid for each item (which prevents the owner from overstating
values, but remember that inflation strikes, and some items really
do appreciate).

There are several methods for valuing an existing business. Naturally, the seller will stress a method that produces a high value and
price; you will incline toward a lower price.

This discussion assumes that you will be paying in money (not stock or property), and buying all assets of a business, and that you and the buyer are not related by blood or commercial interest. There are many sophisticated options like stock-for-stock swaps, mergers, consolidations, recapitalizations, sale-leasebacks, intra-family gift-leasebacks, but it's highly unlikely you will have to deal with any of these. In any event, none of it is covered in this book, though an abbreviated discussion of the tax consequences of simple sales can be found in Chapter Six, and Chapter Eleven discusses the process from the seller's point of view.

The Bank of America suggests that you start by finding the business' liquidation value: the amount you would get by selling off all the assets and paying off all the debts. Liquidation value can be calculated indirectly by weighting different items to correspond to their present value. Assign these values:

- 80% of the accounts receivable which are less than 90 days old
- 0% of any account for which more than 10% of the sum is more than 90 days past due; write these off as uncollectable
- 50% of the value of raw materials and finished goods in inventory; write off all goods in process
- 40% of the current market value of machinery and equipment
- 40% of the current market value of any land owned by the seller and included in the sale
- 25% of the current market value of any buildings owned by the seller and included in the sale.

Next, figure out the amount you would earn by investing the liquidation value. The very conservative will compute the amount earned by a savings account; the merely conservative will consider the earnings of T-bills or municipal bonds; the less conservative will compute the return of more volatile investments like money market funds or Ginnie Maes.

Add this investment return to the salary you could reasonably be expected to earn if you got a job instead of buying the business. The total is the amount you would earn each year if you gave up on entrepreneurship and invested the money. Unless the psychic rewards are very great, you don't want to get less from owning a business than you would from a passbook and a nine-to-five stint.

Now find the business' net profit (after expenses, but before the owner's draw) for the last few years. The problem with this is that you'll have to use the owner's figures, and his/her records may be inaccurate or deceptive. The very cynical will discount those figures; the percentage depends on the depth of the cynicism. You may also want to weight the annual income so that recent figures are given more importance. For example, if you are given income figures for the last five years, multiply the most recent figure by five, the next most recent by four, the next by three, and so on. Add up the weighted figures and divide by 15 ($5 + 4 + 3 + 2 + 1$); the average is the "most likely" annual income. This is also a good time to analyze the trend of earnings, whether they have been rising or falling, and what can be done to improve them.

Subtract your "salary" and "investment return" from the average net earnings. If the result is negative, unless you can turn the business around, you are buying a dead horse. If the result is positive, it is the business' "added earning power." Finally, multiply the business' added earning power by a goodwill factor (or fudge factor)—perhaps 1.5 for a new business or a personal service business (where the customers have a relationship with the business owner, and may not choose to deal with a successor). The factor might be 3 or 4 for a small business with a low capital requirement (not too high, because it's not too hard to start a competing business from scratch), 5 to 7 for a well-established business that is sensitive to changes in the economy; as much as 10 for a stable business selling a necessity (so that demand doesn't change much if incomes fall). The price of the business should be its net worth plus the added earning power multiplied by the goodwill adjustment factor. For instance, if the net worth of the business is $56,000 and the added earning power is $14,000 a year, and if the business is fairly new but has a medium capital requirement, the price might be $56,000 + ($14,000 \times 4$) = $112,000.

George Douglas, a merger and acquisition specialist, uses another formula to set the asking price of a business:

- 5 times the weighted average pretax profits for the past three years, plus
- 1.5 times the business' net worth (current market value of assets—current value of liabilities)
- Divide the sum by 2
- Add 10% if the business is a retail store with an excellent location; subtract 10% if the business manufactures nonproprietary products (products without a brand name used to manufacture other products). Don't adjust the figure for other types of business.

An asking price is designed to leave some room for negotiation, so it's usually 15–20% above the final price.

Ratios, based on book value or earnings, have also been developed for the sale of various kinds of business. "Book value" is the value of a business calculated purely in accounting terms. It equals the value of the business' assets, using the business' own accounting assumptions, minus the value of its liabilities, using the same assumptions. Accounting, as we will see in Chapter Five, has a subjective aspect, and an accountant has a certain amount of leeway in valuing a piece of equipment, a copyright, or other accounting item. If a business is offered for sale for less than its book value or replacement value (what it would cost you to buy inventory and equipment in a comparable state of dilapidation), either the owner is very naive or s/he knows something you don't. Some business owners keep several sets of books—one to plead poverty to tax collectors and in divorce court, another to demonstrate to prospective buyers that the business is flourishing. It's not a bad idea to have your accountant look at *all* the books, and demand to see the owner's (or corporation's) tax returns to try to reconcile all the figures. It may also be necessary to adjust the book value: that is, to raise or lower it to compensate for changed conditions or unrealistic accounting assumptions.

The normal range for a retail store is 1.2–3 times book value, or 3–5 times net earnings plus the cost of replacing the inventory.

Service businesses usually sell in the range between the adjusted book value (as a minimum) and 4–6 times annual net earnings (as a maximum). If the earnings continue or increase, your investment will be amortized in 4–6 years.

The price of a manufacturing business depends on the business' size, its conditions, and its "sex appeal"—glamorous businesses like cosmetics fetch more than unglamorous, "dirty" ones like sheet-metal fabrication. A business that is losing money may actually sell below book value, or at up to 40% above book value (depending on the likelihood of making it profitable). Small manufacturers usually set at 1.2–3 times book; larger ones for about double the book value. Manufacturers of proprietary products usually sell for the equivalent of 5–10 years' aftertax earnings; nonproprietary manufacturers usually sell at a lower ratio, for example 4–7 years' aftertax earnings. In other words, the investment is amortized after a shorter time period.

For food and beverage businesses, the conventional ratios are:

- Liquor store (including license) = cost owner paid for the existing inventory + gross income for 3–4 months
- Tavern = liquor license + gross income for 5–7 months
- Bar = liquor license + 6 times yearly *profits*—or gross income for 6 months (a hint that your profit is unlikely to exceed 8% of gross income)
- Cocktail lounge = liquor license + gross income for 3–5 months
- Coffee shop = book value + 3–4½ months' gross income
- Hamburger stand = book value + 4–5 months' gross income

A New Location

If you're *really* starting from scratch, the first thing to do is to get construction costs from the architect and contractor—then add 25% for scheduled calamities.

The more usual situation is to rent space in a building that has already been constructed, or is in the process of construction. Factors to consider in choosing a site are:

- Absence of competition
- Presence of noncompeting businesses to attract shoppers
- Availability of room to expand
- Parking facilities
- Closeness to public transportation
- Long lease
- Favorable lease terms (low rent, assignability, permission to alter premises)
- Convenience for receiving and making shipments

If you're renting space in a shopping mall under construction, or a building being renovated, the term "shell" means that the developer just gives you four walls, roof, and a dirt floor. You are responsible for electricity, plumbing, flooring, and interior walls, as well as your fixtures, decoration, and inventory. A "half-shell" has the additional amenities of doors, wallboard, and a concrete floor; a toilet and heat *may* be included. Don't assume this without asking, and without seeing an explicit written provision in the lease. "Key" or "turnkey" means a finished space ready for you to decorate and add fixtures. "Will divide to suit" means that the landlord will make (and pay for) the structural changes needed to provide the space whose dimensions you have chosen (for example, half of a 35′ × 40′ space). You are responsible for painting and decorating the outside and front entrance of your portion of the divided premises.

Other Starting-up Expenses

Whether you buy an existing business or start from scratch, you will have to get a place of business and equip it. Some of the expenses, thank God, occur only once:

- "Preventive medicine" planning advice from your lawyer and accountant
- Actual legal and accounting fees for negotiating contracts, drawing up leases, auditing books, getting licenses, incorporating or forming a partnership, etc.
- License fees
- Security deposit on your rent
- Deposits and installation fees for gas, electricity, telephone
- "Prospecting" trips to examine possible sites
- Cost of materials for renovation
- Labor cost for renovation
- Cost of fixtures (including security system)
- Labor cost for installing fixtures
- Office, packing supplies
- Opening inventory

The cost of renovation can be cut down by choosing a place in decent shape, though this will add to the rent. Renovation costs are paid only once, rent over and over again. If you're paying cash, and if the expense is amortized over a fairly short period of time (five hundred dollars in extra renovation costs versus fifty dollars a month in extra rent), then you might as well pay the money once and have done with it. But if you're borrowing the money at high interest rates, it will probably pay to get a less troublesome, if higher-rent, premise in better shape. Do the calculation with real numbers before you take this advice.

The cost of materials is infinitely variable. At the bottom end, you can slap on some paint (yourself), lay inexpensive self-stick tiles (yourself), and build shelving with lumber from the lumberyard, or even lumber scavenged from buildings being demolished. At this level of expenditure, you will obviously be the only decorator involved in the project. Odds are that this is a small factory, or a business where warmth and funkiness take precedence over chic. At the upper end, you can hire a decorator experienced in creating elegant shops, and have recessed lighting; carpeting on walls, floors, and ceilings; antique furniture; original art; custom-built display units. I suggest you start with the paint first. Any idiot can use latex paint, and it makes an amazing difference. Right now it's fashionable to paint everything white, which has the advantage of looking nice and clean even when it isn't.

Sometimes (especially if you're a decent carpenter with an instinct for simplicity) homemade fixtures are quite good enough. My neighborhood bookstore (now defunct, but for reasons of bad market research rather than bad furnishings) had seven-foot uprights of unpainted two-by-sixes, fastened to the walls and floor with three-inch corner braces. Metal standards were screwed to the inside of the uprights; plywood shelves rested on metal clips fastened to the standards.

This type of shelf is infinitely adjustable, and will hold anything narrow. For wider merchandise, you could try cantaloupe crates (oranges are now shipped in cardboard cartons), chicken coops, or the bolt-together metal shelves. Institutional gray is fashionable now, but the shelves are easy to spray-paint (with a compressor-type paint sprayer—wear a mask—not the extravagant aerosol cans). Wire étagères, from a restaurant supply house rather than a department store, also hold a lot, are easy to adjust, and are currently fashionable. Even after the fashion changes, they'll still be adjustable and hold a lot.

Still, the point is reached where you have to buy conventional store fixtures. Your last resort is to buy new ones from a dealer. Your best bet is a store going out of business (unless you believe the bad karma will cling to the equipment). Early 1981 was a blissful time for those who set up shop in the New York area. The demise of Korvettes put dozens of floors of display, storage, and office equipment up for grabs at very attractive prices. The back pages of the *New York Times* (and, I suspect, other papers) have tiny classified ads giving notice of these sales, and of more modest de-accessioning. The usual rule is cash-and-carry, so bring lots of money and be prepared to rent a truck and recruit your burliest friends to help move the stuff.

The traditional rule of thumb is that the "occupancy cost"—cost of getting ready and opening up—of a retail store should not be more than five percent of the gross sales expected for the first year. But inflation makes seven to ten percent a more realistic goal.

Opening Inventory

Given the premises and the equipment, you'll need parts to fabricate, pots and pans to cook with and food to cook, merchandise to sell, or whatever. As for the amount to buy, there are two general schools of thought. One (the French housewife school) calls for keeping a small inventory. You don't have to tie up a lot of money in inventory; you don't need a lot of storage space; the goods don't get shopworn; and, if the business goes to hell in a handbucket, you have less to dispose of. If you feel this way, you can arrange with your suppliers to hold the merchandise for shipment on command, and you can take advantage of quantity discounts.

The opposite tack is that things inevitably get more expensive as you reorder, that the material won't get any dirtier in your storeroom than in the supplier's warehouse, and that it's worth a little extra trouble and expense to guard against rush orders or running out. Somewhere in between is the theory that normal stock should be low, with frequent reorders—but that the opening inventory should be fifteen percent above the normal level. It sets a bad precedent if shoppers, attracted by your publicity, find that many of the things they want are sold out.

A slightly more scientific approach, if the material is not perishable and you have storage space, is to stockpile based on price. Figure out the lowest price you can count on, and the highest price your suppliers are likely to have the nerve to charge. When the price is below average, stock up; buy only your current requirements at the average price; stop buying when prices are above average, and use your stockpile. Check your contracts with suppliers. Make sure you are guaranteed a firm price for the length of the contract, or at least require the seller to document the cost increases that boost the price you pay.

Here, in a flashback to ninth-grade algebra, is the conventional formula for determining Q, the most economical number of units to buy:

$$Q = \sqrt{2AP/IU}$$

A is your annual usage of the material; *P* the cost of issuing a purchase order; *I* is the cost of carrying inventory, expressed as a percentage of the value of the inventory; *U* is the unit cost of the item.

For example, if you own a restaurant that uses 300 cans of tomato puree each year, it costs you $6.00 to issue a purchase order, inventory cost is 15% of the value of the material, and each can costs $2.00,

$Q = \sqrt{2 \times 300 \times \$6.00 / .15 \times \$2.00}$;

$Q = \sqrt{\$3,600 / \$.30}$; the dollar signs cancel, so

$Q = \sqrt{12,000}$, or approximately 109 cans. Obviously, no distributor will let you buy part of a can of tomato puree (though you might be able to order a quarter of a pound of nails or grommets). In fact, the material you're buying may be sold by the case, with higher prices for broken cases (orders of less than a full case), so you're probably better off getting the closest number of full cases. If the tomato puree is sold in cases of a dozen cans, you can order nine cases (and be one can short of the optimum ordering quantity) or order ten cases and have a reassuring backlog of tomato puree.

Once the business is well under way, you can consult your records for information about *storage costs* (the proportion of your rent, utilities, heating, and taxes, devoted to storage: the floor space used for storage divided by the total floor space, divided by the number of items stored, further divided by the amount of time each item spends in storage) and *ordering costs* (postage, cost of order forms and envelopes, your time, clerical time, perhaps phone calls). In the meantime, you can talk to other people in the same or related businesses. You can also consult the Small Business Administration's profiles on various businesses, or the Bank of America business profiles ($3 each; you can get a free catalog, then order the profile or profiles you want, from Small Business Reporter, Bank of America, PO Box 37000, San Francisco, CA 94137).

Budgeting

Certain expenses recur with dreary regularity, and you'll have to be prepared to meet them for at least a few months before the business breaks even. These expenses include:

- Rent
- Heating bills (if not included in the rent)
- Advertising and promotion
- Telephone
- Taxes
- Insurance
- Everyone else's salary
- Your salary
- Debt service
- New displays
- Window washing, janitorial service (if not done by you or regular employees)
- Deliveries and postage
- One twelfth of your professional fees for the year

The Small Business Administration suggests that you estimate these monthly expenses, and set aside at least three months' worth—and also suggests you set aside four months' taxes (because the IRS can, and will, shut down your business abruptly if you fall behind in your tax payments) and only two months of your own salary, the most dispensable item in the budget. I agree heartily with the tax recommendation and find a three months' reserve a very bare minimum. I think you're better off moonlighting, living on savings, or imposing on a spouse so that you either take nothing out of the business, or take only a nominal amount, for the three years you've allowed to launch the business.

There are budgeting methods based on turnover. For example, a successful bar usually turns over its inventory seven times a year—in other words, a bar that has an average inventory of ten thousand dollars' worth of beer and liquor will buy seventy thousand dollars' worth in the course of a year. Beer turns over faster, call brands (premium brands ordered by name) don't turn over quite as fast.

Bookstores, on the other hand, have less turnover: typically three turns per year on hardbacks, five turns per year on paperbacks. Therefore, since the average hardback inventory is one third of annual sales, and the normal discount is forty percent, the cost of the stock of hardbacks is twenty percent of the sales income expected from hardbacks (one third of sixty percent). So an initial investment of five thousand dollars can be expected, under normal circumstances, to generate twenty-five thousand dollars gross income. If you know the size of your store, and the average sales/square foot of other comparable bookstores (the American Booksellers' Association will know this), you can compute your own sales/square foot and see how they compare to the average. In the planning stage, if you know the average sales of other bookstores and the level of income you expect from your investment, you can decide on the size of the store you want.

Some years back, a typical budget for a bookstore was given as:

	Percent
Cost of books	63
Salaries (including yours)	20
Rent	6
Interest and taxes	1.1
Ads	2
Depreciation, utilities, printing, stationery, insurance, maintenance, miscellaneous	less than 1 each
Profit	2.3

In other words, you need almost fifty dollars of sales to get a dollar of profit (though the picture is a little less grim because your salary was figured into the twenty percent salary expense). Today, postage, taxes, and especially interest would be higher. Rent would probably be higher (by way of comparison, the usual budget for a bar sets rent expenses at ten percent of monthly gross). There's not much fat to trim away in profits. The difference would have to be made up by trimming inventory, having a smaller, faster-moving stock, trying to skimp on rent by selecting inexpensive premises (but these will probably be out of the way, so you'll need more ads) or by economizing on ads (in which case you'd better have a terrific location).

Some businesses have even smaller profit margins—a little over one percent for supermarkets, for example—though high turnover compensates somewhat.

Capitalization

You can also use the same techniques in the other direction—to figure out the amount of money you'll need to start the business by deciding the amount of income you want the business to produce. Modifications will be necessary, either because you won't be able to raise enough capital to start a business with a yield that high, or because you can't, in all honesty, believe your business will produce a gross income that high.

The "owner's income" method uses standard ratios for the industry—how much business an average store does per square foot, average markup, average net profit, and the like. You can get this information from the SBA, the Bank of America profiles, or trade associations.

Start with either the income you want from the business or (less grandiosely) your current income if you stay at your present job and give up the idea of going into business.

Use the net profit percentage for your industry (let's say five percent) to determine the volume you would need to produce this much net income—in this case, twenty times as much as the income figure. If you don't think you can generate that much volume, you'll have to rethink your business plans, the income you expect, or both.

If inventory normally turns over five times a year in the kind of business you own, and you have to do one hundred thousand dollars of business, you'll need twenty thousand dollars in inventory at a time. If the normal margin for similar businesses is thirty percent (that is, if the cost of goods represents thirty percent of the retail price), you'll need six thousand dollars to buy opening inventory (or almost seven thousand dollars, if you overstock by fifteen percent for initial demand).

Add the cost of fixtures and equipment, and the other one-time expenses; add your three-month cash reserve. The total is the amount you'll need to start a business that can reasonably be expected to throw off the income you want.

These calculations are based on average figures. If you can trim costs to the bone and do unusually high volume, you can beat the averages. If, as a result of inexperience, bad luck, or incorrect predictions of public taste, you have slow-moving goods that you bought at high prices, you won't do as well as the average. Don't stack the cards against yourself by including your own salary in the calculations if your first step is based on your desired income. (In a successful business, you can collect a salary *and* a distribution of profits, and the balance between the two will depend on which has the better tax consequences; but at the beginning, you will be lucky to get one or the other. You won't get both, you may get neither.) If you support yourself for a while without income from the business, you can start with correspondingly less volume and less inventory.

The capitalization calculations are a little different if you're opening a factory.

Again, start with the amount of income you want to get from the business. Figure out the gross income you'd need, at your industry's normal rate of profit, to derive that much net income. If you want $30,000 a year, and the normal rate of profit is 10%, you'll need a $300,000 yearly gross. If you produce only one item, you then know how many units you'll have to turn out to generate $300,000—say, 3 million units at $.10 apiece. If you know the product mix you will produce (e.g., 25% sluebings, 50% hemiolas, 25% reciprocating bumble struts), you can compute the number of each that must be produced. If the number seems like more than you'll be able to sell, or more than you can produce in a year with a feasible complement of workers and machinery, your plan will have to be reevaluated.

Again using industry figures, find out the kind, number, and cost of the machines you need to produce these parts (say, one Bewitching machine; new ones run about $25,000, used ones $15,000–$17,000; two Bothering machines, $10,000 each new, $7,200 used; one Bewildering machine, $25,000 new, $20,000 used).

To determine the amount of raw materials you'll need to start, assume that you will produce four "turns" a year—that you will go through the complete production cycle four times. Therefore, you'll need raw materials to produce one fourth the number of parts you decided you'd need to produce.

Add the wages you need to produce one complete turn, and the rent needed for the cycle. (Note that, if you have four turns a year, your budget is equal to the three-month cushion the SBA recommends.) Add the sales and office expenses needed to sell the output of one complete turn. The total machinery, raw material, rent, salary, office, sales, tax, insurance, and debt service expenses equal the capital you need to start a factory producing the income level you expect. You also know the number of items to be produced during the year, so you can schedule production on that basis. (See Chapter Eight for scheduling techniques.)

Capitalization figures can also be used in reverse, if you know the size of the store or the capacity of the factory, and want to figure out the income you will derive from your investment, and if your assumptions about sales/square foot, markup, your potential market, and industrial productivity are correct.

Summary

Plan to deal with four kinds of costs:

- Initial start-up costs (scouting trips, preliminary advice from lawyers and accountants, license fees, cost of incorporating or setting up a partnership)
- Cost of buying an existing business, *or* cost of equipping a shell or converting a location from one kind of business to another
- Cost of additional fixtures and decoration for existing business, *plus* opening inventory for any business
- A "cushion" of at least three months' regular operating expenses, so you can keep going until the business produces income

Given the knowledge of the amount of money you need, the next problem is to start eking out the needed cash.

CHAPTER TWO

Money—How Much Can You Scrape Up?

THERE ARE TWO BASIC sources of start-up money: debt (which is money you have to give back) and equity (which is money you don't have to give back per se, but which gives its contributors a right to share any profits of the enterprise). Failing those, you can start off with an insufficient supply of money and plow all the proceeds back into the business.

Equity capital can come from a sole proprietor's personal resources, can come from general and/or limited partners, or can come from the sale of a corporation's stock.

Any form of business organization (proprietorship, partnership, corporation) can borrow money—that is, if anyone will lend it. You can borrow from friends and relatives, from banks, from the Small Business Administration (SBA) or other government programs, from venture capitalists (but they usually want equity as well), or from any combination thereof. Leasing (discussed in Chapter Ten) is a kind of financing device, because it lets you pay for things in dribbles rather than all at once. Factoring (discussed in Chapter Twelve) is also a financing device. A factor "buys" your accounts receivable, giving you less than one hundred percent of their value in exchange for the right to collect on the accounts. You get less money than if you waited and collected it yourself, but you get the money faster and with more certainty. That's typical of the trade-offs involved in getting money to start or run a business: risk versus possibility of profit versus loss of control versus higher capital versus greater capacity versus timing versus tax considerations . . .

Sole Proprietorship

In a sole proprietorship, one person owns the entire operation, has the legal right to make all the decisions, is legally responsible for the consequences of those decisions, gets to keep all the profits, and is personally responsible for all the debts. One bad season and they can come and take away your collection of Mickey Mouse memorabilia, raid your savings account, and force you to sell the rose-cut diamond tiara that has been in the family for generations.

The advantages of sole proprietorship are complete discretion and unlimited upside potential. The disadvantages are isolation and unlimited downside risk. The risks can be alleviated somewhat by asking for or hiring advice, listening to your employees, buying liability insurance to protect you in case of litigation, and being conservative in your expenditures, especially in borrowing. As they say in New York's Off-Track Betting parlors, don't gamble more than you can afford to lose.

A sole proprietorship ends when you do; if you want the business to survive you, you'll have to make provisions (leaving a will, writing special provisions into your lease and other contracts, training your successor) for continuation.

There are very few formalities connected with sole proprietorship. If you use your own name to do business (Jane Richter, interior decorator), all you have to do is start up the business. If you are using a business name (Quick-Start Auto Service, The Smiling Sheep Sweater Shop), you will have to file a DBA ("doing business as") certificate. You can't use a name already taken by someone else (unless the two businesses are quite different—Acme Hosiery and Acme Orange Juice—and there is no possibility of confusion), so first check the phone books for your area and neighboring cities to see that the name you want hasn't been preempted.

Next, file the certificate. Usually, this is done at the County Clerk's office (look up Montana, State of—or wherever you live—in the phone book). To make sure, call the County Clerk's office, and find out if it *is* the right place to file the DBA certificate, what the hours are, what the fee is, and whether they'll take a personal check; if not, then where to file the certificate. You may be denied the right to use the name you want if it's already on file. You will find, however, that few clerks die of overwork while searching the files.

You'll have to pay cash, or use a personal or certified check to pay the fee, for the simple reason that you won't be able to open a bank account in a business name without a DBA certificate. Open the account as soon as you have the certificate; it takes a while to have checks printed, and, as Chapter One indicates, you'll need lots of checks.

A sole proprietorship must report the business' income on his or her personal tax return, using Schedule C, and must pay Social Security taxes as a self-employed person (Schedule SE). Unless the sole proprietor is having enough tax withheld from a salaried job, s/he must also make quarterly estimated tax payments.

You may also need a license to practice your work, or a permit for your store or for dangerous materials you handle. There are three basic kinds of licenses and permits:

- Professional licenses (e.g., those for doctors, lawyers, architects, engineers, teachers). The official theory is that licensure will protect the public from unqualified practitioners. A competing theory is that the existing members of the profession (who give the exams and control the licensing boards) use the licenses to maintain "professional birth control" and raise fees. In theory, professions call for special education qualifications and are entitled to special status, at the cost of special responsibility.
- "Danger" licenses (e.g., those involving potentially hazardous processes—plumbing, pollution-causing materials, food processing) or "bad" materials—cigarettes or liquor
- Revenue licenses—the state or locality decides to make a few bucks by requiring a license or permit

It would take too much space to detail the various licensing requirements. In 1968, the Council of State Governments found that sixty-seven occupations were licensed somewhere or other—ranging from the understandable (doctor and lawyer) to the surrealistic (feeder pig dealer, milk weigher, cemetery plot salesman).

To find out if your business requires a license, check with your state's licensing authorities or consult Juvenal L. Angel's *Directory of Professional and Occupational Licensing in the United States* (Simon & Schuster, 1970, $25.00). This excellent compendium can be found in major libraries. If you don't bother to get a required license, you won't be able to use the courts to enforce business obligations. If you are practicing a profession without a license, and you get caught, you risk a fine or even imprisonment.

Usually, financing for a start-up begins with the proprietor's savings—and often ends there. If the business is a low-capital, part-time sideline (e.g., typing at home, selling household items or cosmetics through the party plan), your savings should be enough to get the business going, and your regular job will pay the ordinary expenses. If you can't get capital for a more elaborate business, you may have to spend a year or so working double shifts or two jobs to get the money.

If your level of savings is a little higher, you can use that money to fund the business (understanding that it will take several years to break even), consider the business your primary employment, and get a part-time job to pay your rent, food bills, and other tiresome personal necessities. The ideal job for this purpose is somewhat casual (so you can cut back your hours, or quit, if you need more time for your business), fairly lucrative, and compatible with business hours (at night or on weekends if your business runs 9–5; episodic if the business is episodic). Cab driving, waiting on tables where the patrons tip well, and night-shift computer programming, word processing, typesetting, and proofreading fit the bill. The advertising, publishing, legal, and financial communities generate an astonishing volume of verbiage that must be keystroked or printed on tight schedules, so temporary agencies need nocturnal armies.

Taxi driving and waiting on tables pose a real moral hazard: almost all your income derives from tips, so the temptation to underpay income taxes is very great. All I can suggest is that you bear up and pay your share. Theoretically, your employer withholds income tax and Social Security based on your anticipated tips (and, if you own a restaurant, this is what you're supposed to do); in practice, this seldom happens. All these jobs can be boring but can be rationalized as a temporary means to the end of getting your business off the ground.

Apart from your savings accounts, you can mortgage your house (if you have one, and it hasn't got two mortgages already), sell your stocks, bonds, and collection of Chinese porcelains (don't forget the capital gains tax), sell your car, get a roommate, move your family to your in-laws' house (subject to consent all around), encourage your spouse to get a job, or a better job if s/he has one already.

You'll have to decrease your standard of living while depleting your capital—an uncomfortable situation. If you can't face it, you'll have to borrow money, get a partner or partners, or incorporate, either to limit your liability or to sell stock.

General Partnership

A general partnership is something like an agglomeration of sole proprietors: every partner is personally liable (can be made to pay out of his or her personal assets) for the firm's debts and for judgments (court orders to pay a given amount of money) against the partnership, so you may be forced to sell your house because of your partner's imprudence or wrongdoing. The partnership's creditors can collect from *any* partner—not necessarily the one who contracted the debt—and not necessarily in proportion to the amount of money each partner contributed to the partnership. A creditor can collect from one partner and spare the others; it's the creditor's own choice. The shorn partner can turn around and sue the other partners, but it's a lot of trouble, it's expensive, and it causes strained relations at partnership meetings, to say the least. Unless arrangements are made to continue it, the partnership dissolves when any partner dies, retires, becomes bankrupt, or is adjudged insane. This is not to say that the company necessarily goes out of business—only that the deceased (or whatever) partner is off the hook. The other partners can continue without him or her. If the partnership *does* go out of business, the decision to do this, and the process of finalizing accounts, is called winding-up; the actual last gasp is called termination. (Distinctions like these help make the legal profession as beloved as it is.)

A partnership is not considered a separate taxpayer. The partnership files an "information return" (Form 1065) each year with the IRS. An information return contains figures for partnership income and expenses, but you don't send any money with it. Instead, the partners file Schedule E (income from rents, royalties, and partnerships) and Schedule SE (Social Security taxes for the self-employed). They pay taxes on the partnership's profits (whether they receive the profits or plow them back into the business) or use the partnership's losses to offset their other income. (More about this in Chapter Six.) If there is a partnership agreement, and if the agreement covers this point, the partners allocate profits and losses according to the agreement. If there is no agreement, the law of partnership says the partners divide profits and losses equally—not in proportion to the amount of money they brought to the partnership or the number of hours worked.

No formalities are required to start a partnership that uses the partners' own names (Cohen & Gianelli; Harper, Barlow & Richtig). A partnership that uses a business name (Lighting Consultants Forever, Surreptitious Baked Goods) must file a DBA certificate just as a sole proprietor does.

It is a very good idea to have a written partnership agreement spelling out at least these things:

- Who the partners are
- Where they live (It's all right to have partners who live in different states; if this is the case, indicate which state's law will govern the contract.)
- The partnership's name
- Its business address
- Its business purposes (The trick is to express these specifically enough so that, if the agreement becomes the subject of litigation, a court won't toss out the agreement for vagueness, yet also give the business enough flexibility to adjust to changing conditions.)
- How long the partnership is intended to last (e.g., three years; until the play closes; until Ivanov retires)
- Whether the partners will carry on after one partner dies, retires, becomes bankrupt, or is adjudged insane
- Whether the other partners will buy the departed partner's share, and for how much (This is called a buy-sell agreement, and is helpful for the partnership's plans for the future and for each partner's estate plans.)
- Whether the partnership will buy insurance—payable to the partnership—if a partner dies or becomes disabled (key-man insurance)
- How much capital each partner will contribute
  —Whether the contribution will be in cash or in other property
  —When it will be contributed: initial capitalization and later contributions to working capital

—Whether the partners will contribute equally; if not, how their contributions will be divided
- The work each partner will do for the business
  —The amount of time each will give the business (You may want an agreement that each partner will work exclusively for the business, and will not undertake other projects.)
  —Salary
  —Expense account
- How the partners will allocate profits and losses
  —You may want to agree to plow back a given amount of money, or a given percentage of the profits, each year
  —If the partners can take advances from a drawing account (money available so partners can pay their day-to-day bills without waiting for an end-of-the-year tally of the money each has earned as a partner), explain the limitations and conditions on draws
- Decision-making procedures (whether you'll require a unanimous vote, majority vote, give a casting vote to one partner, or let partners be responsible for decisions in their areas of expertise)
- When partnership meetings will be held
- Who is responsible for the books and records; when, how, and by whom they will be audited
- Who is allowed to sign checks
- Limits on the contracts each partner can make, and the extent to which s/he can pledge the partnership's credit
- Rules for adding new partners; you may want different criteria for outsiders and for the children, spouses, or surviving spouses of partners. (If the agreement doesn't deal with this, or if there is no agreement, the general rule of partnership law is that all the partners have to consent to adding a new partner.)
- Procedure for expelling a partner (for example, an embezzler)
- Procedure for going out of business (The partners may agree that if the business loses more than a certain amount of money, or loses money for more than a certain number of years, the partnership will be dissolved, the creditors paid off, the assets sold, and the remaining money divided among the partners.)
- Procedures for changing the agreement

- Procedures for settling disputes (e.g., arbitration; submitting the problem to a mediator named in the agreement)

As you can see, this is quite a long list. I can't urge strongly enough that you have a written partnership agreement. I suggest that you hire a lawyer to write it, or that you write it yourselves and have a lawyer check it out before you sign it. Two cautions: you can have a legal, well-drafted contract and *still* have problems; and lawyers can give stupid advice or draft ridiculous contracts.

Partnership is a difficult way to do business, with inherent tensions. In a sole proprietorship, El Maximo Lider may not know what s/he is doing, but at least the lines of authority are clear. In a partnership, every decision will have to be worked out among the partners. The potential for wrangling is obvious. Some of the most harmonious partnerships have a clear division of labor: an "inside" person (e.g., a designer or a financial genius) and an "outside" person (who is brilliant at client contact). But when the designer enrolls in business school and the accountant suggests that bright colors will make a comeback next season, the problems start up again.

Partnership is an intimate association, and you have to be able to trust not only your partners' honesty but also their good judgment. Suppose you contribute $5,000 and form a partnership to manufacture cosmetics. A few years later, the business is doing well. You devote all your time to getting orders; another partner is in charge of production and advertising; the third partner handles the financial aspects of the business. You return from a trip to discover that the partner in charge of advertising, laboring under the delusion that garlic-flavored toothpaste will be the Next Big Thing, has signed $375,000 worth of contracts for advertising. However, no toothpaste (alliaceous or otherwise) is being produced because the financial partner, busy playing the commodities market (or the ponies) forgot to make a required tax deposit, and the factory has been padlocked by the IRS. You are liable for whatever the creditors can get out of you—no doubt a good deal more than your $5,000.

Or, to cite a somewhat less ghastly case, suppose you have a nosy potential investor who doesn't know anything about computers, catering, magazine publishing, or whatever the business at hand is. You want the money but not the interference. One way for investors to limit their liability and for principals to retain control is to set up a limited partnership.

Limited Partnership

A limited partnership consists of one or more general partners, who are in the same situation as partners in a general partnership (*someone* has to be left holding the bag), and one or more limited partners (who do not have management rights, but who can't lose more money than they invest in the partnership). General partners can sue or be sued for partnership problems; limited partners can only sue the partnership, or be sued by it, for problems that arise out of the limited partnership itself. They can't be sued if the partnership owes money or causes harm to someone.

Creating a limited partnership calls for more formalities than creating a general partnership. Unless the rituals are followed, the would-be limited partnership is treated as a general partnership, and all the partners have to pay up as such. Therefore, good legal advice, which is helpful in setting up a general partnership, is absolutely mandatory in setting up a limited partnership.

The limited partnership *must*, by law, have a certificate, signed and sworn to by each partner (general and limited). The certificate must include at least this much information:

- The name of the partnership
- The character of its business
- Its principal place of business (and, if it will do business in more than one state, its relationship to each state—where offices will be located, who can accept the summons if the partnership is sued, and so forth)
- The names and addresses of each general partner
- The names and addresses of each limited partner
- The length of time the partnership will last
- The amount of money, property, or work each limited partner will contribute when entering the partnership
- Schedule for other contributions of money or property to keep the business in operation
- Whether the limited partners' capital will be returned to them; if so, when
- Rules for distributing profit among limited partners, and whether payments will be made in cash or other property

- Rules for admitting new limited partners
- Whether or not the general partners will continue the business after a general partner dies, retires, becomes bankrupt, or becomes insane

Limited partnerships can have partners who live in different states without running into problems (as long as the partnership agreement makes it clear which state's laws will govern). But there are no settled rules of law about interstate limited partnerships, and lawyers and courts like to transfer their uneasiness to those who appear before them. Limited partnerships that do business in Florida, Hawaii, Idaho, Kansas, Maine, New Hampshire, Oregon, or Texas, and are registered in another state, have to register with those states' Secretary of State—one more formality, and one more chance for things to go wrong.

A limited partnership has the same tax status as a general partnership: the partnership files an information return (Form 1065), and each partner reports his or her share of profits on Schedule E of Form 1040, the individual personal tax return.

The state of a limited partner is an enviable one, and one to which potential investors in your business may well aspire to. In fact, *you* might well aspire to it. To prevent business owners from escaping their debts *that* easily, a person who has management responsibility and can make day-to-day decisions will be treated as a general partner even if s/he claims to be a limited partner. On the other hand, a person can be an employee of the partnership, give advice about business matters, sign loan papers as surety for the partnership, and even cast a vote on extraordinary transactions and changes in the partnership agreement, without being treated as a general partner.

If you can deal with a reasonable amount of formality, and if you have people who are willing to invest in return for a share of future profits, but don't want to manage the business, a limited partnership may be the way to go.

Corporations

According to the general principles of corporation law, corporations are managed by their boards of directors, and not by their stockholders. Therefore, if people buy stock in your corporation, and they don't have enough stock to vote themselves into office (and you don't feel sufficiently grateful to offer them seats on the board), they are guaranteed to stay off your case. You can run the business as you and the other directors see fit. On the other hand, in a very small corporation, all or most of the stock belongs to the directors, so the point is moot.

The conventional wisdom was that you should incorporate your business at once, because a corporation provides limited liability, and because corporations could provide more generous tax-free pension and insurance plans than either proprietorships or partnerships could. However, the Tax Equity and Fiscal Responsibility Act of 1982 eliminated most of the differences between Keogh plans maintained by sole proprietors (or partners) and corporate plans for 1984 and later years.

On the other hand, if you expect to be sued, you can buy liability insurance or clean up your act. No one will lend money to a fledgling corporation without getting the signatures of its officers and making them personally liable. Rich people sometimes enjoy losing money (much as English aristocrats are said to enjoy being flogged), and they prefer to be partners when they lose money, so they can deduct the lost money immediately. (In a corporation you have to wait until you sell stock to take the losses.) To humor rich investors, you can start out as a partnership, lose a gratifying amount of money, then incorporate when the business becomes profitable.

The disadvantages of incorporation include the following:

- It costs money: legal fees, incorporation fees, and annual franchise taxes.
- It limits flexibility: once the business is incorporated in one state, it's hard to move to another state or change the kind of business you do.
- It exposes you to a host of formalities: the corporation has to have Articles of Incorporation, meetings (with written minutes) for directors and stockholders, and written resolutions. There is something melancholy about the spectacle of two people solemnly electing each other to office and seconding reciprocal motions.
- The corporation is considered a person—hence a taxpayer; then whatever leftover money is tranferred to the stockholders (dividends) is taxable income for them. Small corporations

can avoid this double taxation by choosing to be taxed as if they were partnerships. This is called a "Subchapter S" election; more of this in Chapter Six.

Occasionally some drugstore cowboy will suggest that you should incorporate in Delaware to take advantage of its favorable corporation laws. This would have been cogent advice in the nineteenth century when Delaware went out of its way to be agreeable. Since then, the corporate law of other states has become more uniform and more tolerant of the little eccentricities of businesses. The odds are that your business won't do anything particularly unconventional in the legal sense; usually it takes a billion-dollar corporation to really need special provisions of the law. Finally, if you incorporate in Delaware but locate your business somewhere else (Illinois, for the sake of argument), you'll have to register in Illinois as a foreign corporation (you notify the Secretary of State and pay a yearly fee) and appoint a "resident agent for service of process," which means someone in the state who can be notified if you are sued. (You don't have to go out and hire someone; there are service bureaus in every state that will, for a small fee, act as your agent for service of process.) If you want to sue someone in Illinois, the courts will view your corporation with suspicion, as a foreigner.

If you decide to incorporate, and to do this in the state in which your business will be concentrated, you will need:

- Incorporators, or people who will sign their names to the initial papers for the corporation
- Stockholders
- A Board of Directors—the corporate officers—including a President, Vice-President, Secretary, and Treasurer as a minimum, and perhaps including other directors as well. (If you're short-handed, one person can hold more than one office. Most states will permit a one-person corporation, with this industrious person holding all the offices.)
- A corporation kit, including forms for Articles of Incorporation, minutes of meetings, stock certificates, and a corporate seal. Corporation kits are sold at stationery stores catering to lawyers, or through the mail; they cost somewhere between $50–$150, depending on the elaborateness of the binding and the cuteness of the stock certificates. (In some states, you won't be able to use the Articles of Incorporation forms, because you'll need a receipt from the Secretary of State, show-

ing that the articles have been filed, before you'll be allowed to buy the kit.)

The incorporators get the ball rolling by adopting the Articles of Incorporation and holding an initial meeting to adopt the bylaws which govern the corporation and to elect an interim Board of Directors. After the stock has been sold, the stockholders elect the board; the board manages the corporation.

The Articles of Incorporation is a banal document which lists:

- The corporation's name
- Whether it will last an indefinite period or a definite number of years
- The corporation's business purposes, and what it is authorized to do
- The amount of money the corporation needs to raise by selling stock before it starts business
- The number of shares of stock the corporation is allowed to issue, and the par value of the shares (or the fact that the shares are no-par)
- The corporation's main place of business
- If this is different, the corporation's registered office and its registered agent for service of process
- The names and addresses of the incorporators
- The names and addresses of the people who will act as directors until the first stockholders' meeting

By the way, the Articles of Incorporation are called the Charter in Alabama and Tennessee; the Certificate of Incorporation in Connecticut, Delaware, and New York; Form 1 in Maryland; Articles of Organization in Massachusetts; Record of Organization in New Hampshire; and Articles of Association in Vermont. The usual drill is to file with the Secretary of State (check the phone book for your state capital). However, in Arkansas you file with the Commissioner of Commerce. In the District of Columbia, it's the Office of the Superintendent of Corporations; the Director of Regulatory Agencies in Hawaii; the State Department of Assessment and Taxation in Maryland; the Secretary of the Commonwealth in Massachusetts; Michigan's Department of Commerce, Corporation Division; the State Corporation Commission in New Mexico and Virginia; the Corporation Commissioner in Oregon; and the Department of State in Pennsylvania.

Before you fill out the incorporation papers, call or write to the

Secretary of State (or whomever) to find out if the name you want is available. It's like Actors Equity: you can't have two corporations with the same name in a state. You can't choose a name that misleads people (e.g., using the word "bank" or "insurance" if your company is not in fact a properly licensed bank or insurance company; calling a copier company "Xenox" or a beverage manufacturer "Coda-Cola"). Use the same call to find out if you must register with city or county authorities.

When you file the Articles of Incorporation, you'll also have to bring a certified check (Secretaries of State seldom accept personal checks). Some states charge a flat fee. Other states have a sliding scale, depending on the number of shares the corporation is authorized to issue, the par value of shares, or both. (See Appendix A.)

The Articles of Incorporation states the number of shares the corporation is authorized to issue. There is no minimum number of shares that the law compels you to authorize and/or issue. You may need or want more stock later, so it makes sense to authorize more stock than you will sell for initial capitalization. On the other hand, if your incorporation fee is based on authorized shares, you shouldn't go hog-wild.

A stock's par value is supposed to be its normal value, and the issuer is not allowed to sell stock for less than its par value. On the other hand, it's not only allowed, but, in practical terms, inevitable to sell stock above its par value. Most states allow no-par stock, which has no defined minimum value.

The advantage of issuing no-par stock is that it lowers the initial fee and gives more flexibility. The disadvantage is that a corporation's "stated capital" equals the number of shares issued times the par value of each share, and it looks bad if a corporation has no stated capital. A corporation's Board of Directors has a legal obligation to "preserve the stated capital"—that is, to keep it as a sort of nest egg, rather than spending it to further the business. A corporation that needs fifty thousand dollars would be imprudent to issue fifty thousand shares with a one-dollar par and sell them for a dollar apiece. A reasonable compromise might be to authorize twenty thousand shares with a one-dollar par and sell one thousand of them for fifty dollars apiece, keeping the other nineteen thousand shares in reserve. The reserved shares can be sold later to raise more capital, given to employees as compensation, or used to buy other companies.

Corporations have a resource for borrowing unavailable to ordinary human beings: they can sell bonds. A bond is a nicely printed IOU obligating the corporation to pay a certain amount of interest every year, and promising to pay back the face value of the bond at some distant time. People or institutions buy the bonds, in effect lending money to the corporation. They do this not out of the goodness of their hearts but to collect the interest or perhaps make a profit by selling the bond to someone else. In the somewhat un-likely case of your floating a bond issue, consult your investment banker for details.

The law recognizes several different kinds of stock: par and no-par (a corporation can have both kinds); common and pre-ferred (preferred stock gets dividends first; common stock gets whatever dividends are left in the trough); and preferred stock can be convertible or nonconvertible (the stockholder can swap the stock for the corporation's bonds). There are two reasons for restricting your early adventures in stock issuing to one class of common stock:

- Elaboration requires a ravenous horde of lawyers, accoun-tants, and securities advisers.
- If you want the tax advantages of Subchapter S ("partner-ship" taxation for a corporation) and/or §1244 (a provision which allows the stockholders to deduct the corporation's losses from their ordinary income), you're allowed to have only one class of stock. You also need a formal, written resolu-tion from a Board of Directors' meeting before you use either of these helpful tax provisions.

By the way, don't expect to see your name on the stock ticker just because you incorporate. The stocks you see listed in tiny type in the business section of the newspaper are "public corporations." Their stock is available to the general public, who can buy it from stockbrokers or other stockholders, and who can sell it freely. In order to become a public corporation, you have to go through a hideously complicated (I got a D in the course) and expensive (at least a million dollars for each new issue of stock) process regulated by the Securities and Exchange Commission (SEC). After the initial formalities are finished, the public corporation has to make annual and quarterly reports to the SEC.

Even the federal government would not make you spend a mil-lion dollars to raise fifty thousand; so, if an issue of stock is small, not available to the general public, and is bought by people who want to invest in the company rather than resell the stock speculatively, most of the formalities (and costs) can be avoided.

The SEC's Rule 147 allows sales of stock for which all the buyers are citizens of the state in which the corporation is registered.

Rule 240 allows you to sell up to one hundred thousand dollars' worth of stock (that's the amount you get, not the par value) if there are one hundred or fewer stockholders, if you don't advertise the stock, and if you don't pay commissions to anyone who helps sell the stock.

Rule 146 allows you to raise any amount of capital by selling stock—provided that there are no more than thirty-five buyers; these buyers are sophisticated investors who can afford to risk their money; you give them full information about the business; each buyer signs a statement that s/he will not sell the stock without the SEC's permission until the company "goes public"; and you never advertise the availability of the stock. All these rules can be found—if you are an insomniac—in §230 of Volume 17 of the Code of Federal Regulations.

While you're steering toward one of these "safe harbors" (yes, that's what lawyers really call these rules), don't forget to check your own state's Blue Sky Laws. These laws—so called because, in their absence, sharpies would sell the blue sky itself (the rural equivalent of the Brooklyn Bridge)—are the state laws governing the sale of securities. If you're going to get involved in this sort of thing, you really should have a lawyer (preferably one who got an A in Securities Regulation).

If you offer stock under Rule 146, you have to file a simple statement with your local SEC office. Offices are located in New York City, Boston, Atlanta, Cleveland, Kansas City (Kansas), Chicago, Philadelphia, Fort Worth, Houston, Denver, Detroit, Salt Lake City, Los Angeles, Miami, Seattle, San Francisco, and Arlington (Virginia). The central office is at 500 North Capitol Street, NW, Washington, DC 20549; the number for its Office of Public Affairs is (202) 755-4846.

The law may be a ass and a idiot, but it takes at least a minimal level of subterfuge to evade it. Most states will allow a business to be incorporated with only one shareholder (Mississippi requires two shareholders; Nevada, North Dakota, and Oklahoma call for three), but you can't just incorporate and end all your financial worries. The splendidly Freudian term "piercing the corporate veil" means that the organization will not be treated as a corporation if the so-called corporation is a sham, without real existence or business purpose. Like most legal decisions, this is subjective, but factors in the decision of whether the veil can be pierced include:

- Too little capital for the corporation's business
- The corporation's assets are mixed up with the personal assets of its executives and/or shareholders
- There are no regular directors' or shareholders' meetings
- The corporation does not have separate, properly maintained account books and records
- The corporation's officers do not act in good faith

If the veil is pierced, the "corporation" can be treated as a sole proprietorship or partnership—unlimited liability strikes again.

Meetings need not be formal (though, if your state requires a minimum number of meetings per year, you'll have to have at least that many), and minutes of the meeting need not be verbatim. The minutes can be written up later from the notes taken at the meeting. The minutes should contain:

- The name of the corporation
- The date, place, and time of the meeting
- A certified (signed and with an oath that the notice is complete and correct) copy of the notice calling the meeting—or advance waivers, signed by the officers or stockholders, agreeing that they don't have to be notified of future meetings
- A list of the people present (at stockholder's meetings, the number of shares each person at the meeting holds, and the number of shares covered by proxies—a proxy is permission for someone else to cast an absent stockholder's vote)
- The issues on which the corporation has voted to take action, and a tally of the vote

Two peripheral points: attaching the corporate seal (or forgetting to attach it) has no real effect; it's a survivor of the kind of magical thinking that prescribes crucifixes as a vampire preventative. However, if the corporate seal is stamped on a document, it does act as evidence that the document represents an official act of the corporation. Second, you'll need to file Form SS-4 with the Internal Revenue Service to get an Employer's Identification Number (EIN) for the corporation, even if you don't have any employees. You need the number to open a corporate bank account. The EIN, like individual Social Security numbers, helps the IRS track bank accounts to make sure that rendering unto Caesar takes place on schedule.

Whatever your method of initial capitalization, you may not have enough money to start the business, or may need more money for continuing operations; either you'll have to borrow the money (debt financing) or start with too little capital and rely on early sales to keep the business running. Debt financing is practical only if you have reason to believe that you can earn enough with the borrowed money to repay *both* principal and double-digit interest.

Debt: Private Borrowing

Many businesses have been started with the owners' savings, plus loans from friends and family. To avoid hard feelings, write up a loan agreement specifying the amount borrowed, the length of the loan, the interest, schedule of payments, and any collateral (your property used to secure the loan; if you don't pay, the lender can take the collateral, or sell it and keep the money). If the lender is very cooperative and doesn't need the money back immediately, s/he may agree to a demand loan: you agree to pay back the full amount if and when the lender asks for it. Although a demand loan doesn't specify regular payments, honor demands that you repay as much as you can as soon as you can. (For one thing, if you reduce the debt, you won't be struck a fatal blow if need or hostility causes the lender to demand the balance.)

Few of your friends or relatives will have the effrontery to charge you market interest rates (though, if you keep up with the payments, lending money to you is a better investment than six-month certificates or money-market funds; you might make a tactful suggestion along these lines). However, the IRS considers that lending money at below-market interest rates constitutes a gift; the size of the gift is the gap between market and actual rates. If a lot of money is involved, the lender may have to pay a gift tax. (If the lender is that wealthy, no doubt s/he has a tax lawyer and accountant who can give advice.) On the other hand, a *no*-interest demand loan is not considered to be a gift, because the lender can ask for the money at any time. (It's logic like this that keeps tax lawyers in Mercedeses.)

By the way, if you have any rich relatives, you can deliver an impassioned plea for money *now,* while your relative can watch you enjoying it, rather than a bequest, when s/he will not be able to feel benevolent (or anything else, for that matter). This approach will only work if Uncle Mervyn was planning to leave you something in the first place.

Borrowing: Banks

You must be joking. If banks are charging IBM and General Electric what used to be considered Mafia interest rates, you can imagine what they'd charge you for the thirty-five thousand dollars you want to open a chocolate-chip-cookie store.

Banks insist on a solid business record and plenty of collateral— both a trifle hard to come by in a start-up situation. Therefore, business borrowing is covered in Chapter Twelve. Once your business is well under way, you may be able to borrow more operating capital, or the money you need for expansion. As the phrase goes, a banker is a man who will lend you money if you can prove you don't need it.

On the other hand, you will have to undergo the futile and humiliating experience of applying for bank loans if you want to borrow money from the Small Business Administration (SBA). To get a direct loan from the SBA, you'll first have to be turned down by two banks. Getting rejected is easy; getting an *official* rejection you can show to the SBA is hard. Blasé bankers don't even want to read applications or fill out papers. In the old days, a long-term banking relationship might induce a banker to lend you money; now the best you can hope for is that s/he will deign to refuse you officially.

Borrowing: The Government

The best-known government lender is the SBA. Readers of this book should have no problem meeting the SBA's requirement of "smallness": service businesses with annual receipts under $2,000,000, retailers below $2,000,000 in annual sales, wholesalers with yearly sales under $9,500,000, and manufacturers with fewer than 1,500 employees are considered "small." For those of us whose

problems include paying the electric bill each month, these limits
seem ample. Obviously, no business yet unborn has millions of dollars in sales, which highlights a major problem with the SBA: the
limited funds available have to be divided between funds for start-
ups and funds for existing businesses.

The Small Business Administration has a number of programs:

- *Guaranteed Loans*—no, the SBA doesn't guarantee that *you'll*
  get any money. It guarantees that, if a bank lends you money
  and you stiff the bank, the SBA will repay up to 90% of the
  money. The maximum loan involved is $500,000.
- *Direct Loans* (also called 7[a] loans)—the SBA itself lends you
  the money, at below-market though not charitable rates; the
  maximum is $350,000. There is no maximum length of time
  on the loans; the average is 8¾ years. Direct loans are not
  available to investment advisers or those who want the money
  to invest, or to publishers, broadcasters, and others in communications. (The government doesn't want to sponsor anything
  controversial.)
- *Economic Opportunity Loans*—for business owners who come
  from low-income, economically disadvantaged groups. Maximum amount is $100,000, and maximum term is 15 years.
  Again, investment and communications businesses are not eligible. Outright grants of $15,000–$306,250 are available to
  economically/socially disadvantaged entrepreneurs and those
  in high-unemployment areas. These are called "Management
  and Technical Assistance for Disadvantaged Businessman
  Grants," and can be used for planning, research and development, or training (either yours or your employees').
- *Displaced Business Loans*—for businesses pushed out of a location by the federal government, or by a state or local government's use of its power of eminent domain (buying land for
  public purposes—whether or not the owner wants to sell).
  The maximum is $904,000. (I don't know how they come up
  with these figures.) The loans can't be used for speculation, to
  pay the expenses of selling the business, to repay the owners
  their capital contributions, or to pay off unsecured creditors
  (those who have not been given an interest in collateral).
- *Disaster Loans*—for businesses harmed by fire, flood, or other
  natural disaster; the maximum you can borrow is 60% of the

physical loss, plus a maximum of $100,000 to make up for lost business and other economic losses.

- *Consumer Protection Loans*—to help businesses conform to consumer protection regulations; the maximum is $165,000.
- *Energy Loans*—to help potential entrants into energy businesses; no limit.

The SBA also lends money to others, so they in turn can lend it to businesses. There are State and Local Development Company Loans made to the states, or to private development companies that promote economic growth. The SBA also funds private venture capital firms (see page 61).

The SBA's central office is at 1441 L Street NW, Washington, DC 20416. Guaranteed loans, direct loans, and economic opportunity loans are administered through the Office of Financing, (202) 653-6570; energy and consumer protection loans through the Office of Business Loans, (202) 653-6570; displaced business and disaster loans through the Office of Disaster Loans, (202) 653-6664; and management and technical assistance grants through the Assistant Administrator for Financial Assistance, (202) 653-5533.

So, with all these lovely programs, what's the problem? First of all, the SBA doesn't have all that much money (the New York office's funds available for direct loans nosedived from thirteen million dollars to six million dollars from 1980 to 1981); the limited funds must be divided between start-ups and existing businesses; plenty of people want to borrow money; and the SBA is firmly wound in red tape. I dropped into the New York office at 2 P.M. A loan applicant was told that completed loan applications are accepted only between 8:30 and 10:30 A.M. (although, when she telephoned, she was told to come at 2), and the specialist I wanted to see had left for the day. (In fairness, he may have been out in the field.)

If you want to get an SBA loan, start with the Public Information Specialist at the SBA office near you (see Appendix B). To get a loan, you'll have to demonstrate ability to repay; have substantial collateral; have or hire management expertise; and be willing to put up at least twenty-five percent of the capital yourself or with your partners or stockholders.

The SBA also publishes many, many pamphlets (free) and books (inexpensive), available at the local SBA office or from the SBA's central publications office. Most of these publications sound exactly as if they were written by Horatio Alger, and don't even have the campy engraved illustrations to recommend them.

The federal government also has non-SBA programs that make loans and grants:

- Economic Development and Business Development Assistance Loans made to businesses that create or maintain jobs in high-unemployment areas in which other sources of financing are not available. The loans range from $260,000 to $5,200,000. They are administered by:
  Office of Private Investment
  Economic Development Administration
  Department of Commerce
  14th & Constitution, NW
  Washington, DC 20230
  (202) 377-5067

- Loans of $11,000 to $50,000,000 for the development of business and industry in rural areas are administered by:
  Farmers' Home Administration
  U.S. Department of Agriculture
  Washington, DC 20250
  (202) 447-7967

The Department of Housing and Urban Development makes UDAGs (Urban Development Action Grants) to cities and towns which would benefit by private investment. The city either lends the money to entrepreneurs or puts up buildings or equipment that can be leased to businesses.

Once a year, the federal government publishes the Catalog of Federal Domestic Assistance, which describes loan and grant programs. Many large libraries have this book; you can also spring for $20 and order it from the Superintendent of Documents, U.S. Government Printing Office, Washington, DC 20402.

By the way, if you've applied for a loan or grant and the government has lost your papers or otherwise fouled up, you can throw yourself on the mercy of:
Office of the Ombudsman
Department of Commerce
14th & Constitution, NW
Washington, DC 20230
(202) 377-3176

Borrowing and Equity: Venture Capital

One way the SBA makes its money go further is to lend money to privately owned investment companies, who use this money to supplement their own money. Then these companies—called SBICs (Small Business Investment Corporations) and MESBICs (Minority Enterprise Small Business Investment Corporations; also called 301[d] SBICs) lend the money to small businesses, buy equity in small businesses, or do both. SBICs and MESBICs are licensed and regulated by the SBA, but they are private businesses, not part of the government.

SBICs and MESBICs can invest only in small businesses (assets under $9,000,000; net worth under $4,000,000, and average net income after taxes under $400,000 per year). They must diversify their investments: they can't invest more than 20% of their non-SBA capital in any one company. SBICs and MESBICs can have an equity interest in companies they finance, but not a controlling interest. They can't hold more than 49.9% of a company's stock or partnership interests. Most SBIC and MESBIC financing is medium-term—about 5 years—and the money is divided between start-ups and aid to existing businesses. (MESBICs devote more of their money to start-ups than SBICs do.)

There are also private venture capital firms, who do not have any restrictions on the type or structure of deals they can make. However, venture capital firms have very strong preferences. Usually they won't make a straight loan, preferring debt plus equity, or all-equity financing. They want high-profit ventures, and have a bias toward high technology. A biochemist who wants ten million dollars to develop patentable new strains of soybeans through gene-splicing will have a better chance at getting venture capital than an employee of an import-export firm who wants twenty thousand dollars to set up his own store selling Bolivian ceramics. Usually, venture capitalists want to get in and out of a deal fairly quickly (one to five years) rather than becoming part of a permanent management team. When the time is up, they want to sell the stock, which presumably will have ballooned in value. Venture capitalists are attracted by:

- An easy-to-make product or service that will be saleable for many years—not a fad item.
- Projections showing a twenty-five percent annual growth in sales and pretax profits (of course projections can say anything; venture capitalists look for *reasonable* projections).
- An energetic entrepreneur who has business skills and a good management team—and whose own money has been invested lavishly in the business.
- A projected thirty percent annual return on the venture capitalist's investment, and the chance to liquidate the investment in three to five years, getting at least five times the original investment.

Negotiations with venture capitalists require the whole panoply of audited statements, business plans, and projections (see Chapter Twelve)—a requirement that a going business can meet much more easily than a new business can.

It is considered somewhat tactless to approach a venture capital firm directly and ask for money; business etiquette dictates that you work through intermediaries such as lawyers, accountants, and management consultants.

The names, addresses, and phone numbers of venture capitalists can be found in a monthly publication called *Venture Capital Journal;* in *Venture* magazine's annual roundup in its December issue; in *Guide to Venture Capital Sources* (Stanley E. Pratt, editor, Capital Publishing Co., fifth edition, 1981); in *Business Capital Sources* (International Wealth Success Inc., 1980); and in *Small Business Survival Guide* (Joseph R. Mancuso, Prentice-Hall, 1980).

Obviously, then, if you want to bake brownies, sell lingerie, manufacture Christmas-tree ornaments, or launch some other comparably modest venture, and you've piled up your personal assets, what you can borrow from friends or family, or raise from partners or stockholders, and it still isn't enough, you're in a lot of trouble.

One possible—though risky—way to get started is simply to start with inadequate capital, and put all the proceeds back into the business, using the payment for each round of orders to pay the cost of production. If the business catches on immediately, you're a genius; if it doesn't, you're (*a*) an idiot and (*b*) out of business. The margin for error is very small, and the need for creative paraphrases of "your check is in the mail" is very large. This can be exhilarating, and some people enjoy it very much. Others reach the point of insanity even before bankruptcy sets in.

Pyramiding

Even businesses that eventually have stores or factories begin in garages, homes, or a consultant's vest pocket. The permanent address comes with prosperity.

Craftspeople (e.g., potters, metalworkers, weavers) can start out by showing at crafts fairs or shows. Usually, each craftsperson gets an area about ten feet square in which to set up a strong, windproof display that can be folded into a car and yet is light enough for one person to set up. Some craft shows supply tables, chairs, and partitions between displays; others expect the craftspeople to supply these amenities.

A crafts fair provides a captive audience of potential buyers, but is limited in time. A successful crafts fair is one at which the proceeds equal the entry fee, transportation, lunch, insurance, a reserve for theft—and a reasonable profit. It helps to display a number of small, inexpensive items for impulse purchases, in case no one buys the sixteen-hundred-dollar, eight-foot-long pieces.

Craftspeople and clothing designers who do not have their own retail shops can sell their work wholesale or can consign the merchandise. In either case, the proceeds are less than retail, but there are no retailing costs to pay.

When soliciting wholesale orders, it helps to:

- Attach a tag to each sample giving the wholesale price, the available sizes and colors, and the minimum and maximum orders you allow; for large pieces or one-of-a-kind items, use photographs or bring slides to negotiating sessions.
- Make up wholesale and retail price lists—illustrated, if possible.
- Make your sales terms clear at the outset: cash in advance, 2/10/net 30 (see Chapter Five for further explanation), 30-60-90 days, credit references required.

If you do get wholesale orders, you sell your product outright. You know how many units have been sold and how much you get for each. If you consign your product, you let a store display the merchandise. If an object is sold, you get an agreed-upon percentage of the price (usually a good bit more than you would get if you sold wholesale). If the object isn't sold, after an agreed-upon time the retailer (the consignee) can reduce the price or ask you to take the merchandise back. A consignment relationship works best if its terms are discussed in advance and written into a contract; if the consignee handles mostly consignments, not outright sales; if the consigner supplies a variety of items in different price ranges; and if the consigner has the courtesy not to undercut the retail price at crafts fairs.

Many rags-to-riches stories—some of them even true—involve mail-order businesses. A mail-order business can be started at home, with no employees, and on a small investment. Books about mail order tend to say that all you have to do is place a few inexpensive classified ads and watch the money roll in. It's not quite *that* simple, and the ads work only if the product has a high recognition factor (e.g., everyone knows what a sweater is, but not everyone knows what a two-part pipe clamp—or a PLAINTEXT Form—is) and can be described briefly (e.g., the sweater comes in three colors, not twenty-seven).

Mail order can be a distribution method for a product you make yourself (e.g., Grandmother's recipe for cucumber night cream—if you can get it past the food and drug laws). You have all the hassles of manufacturing, but at least by selling mail order you avoid the problems of running a store.

Another aspect of mail-order business is the mail-order seller who sells products made by someone else. A mail-order business of this type requires very little capital: stationery, packing materials, a small initial inventory, and advertisements. The inventory never has to grow very large: most manufacturers will agree to deliver an order in several staggered shipments (one hundred boxes in March, one hundred fifty in April, one hundred in May). The advantage is that the mail-order seller can use the manufacturer as a "warehouse," and need not pay for storage space.

In fact, a mail-order seller who uses drop shipping doesn't need an inventory at all: s/he takes orders, collects payments of the retail price, and forwards the orders and payment at the wholesale rate to the manufacturer, who ships directly to the customer. The advantage to the drop shipper is that s/he doesn't need warehouses, money invested in inventory, or much effort. The disadvantage is that the field is very competitive and the customers always have an incentive to cut out the middleman and deal with the manufacturer directly.

Pricing

Pricing is an important subject for any business—and one of the most important for a business that expects to pull itself up by its bootstraps. There are two basic approaches to pricing: one based on costs, the other based on the competition.

The basic break-even formula (for determining the point at which income equals outgo) is:

$$P = S - (FC + VC)$$

P is profit; S is the income from sales; FC is the fixed cost at zero capacity (i.e., when the business is closed; rent and leasing costs for equipment are fixed costs); and VC is the variable cost (costs that change with sales or production: wages, utility bills, cost of goods to be sold or raw materials for processing). This simple formula can be a little *too* simple, because some costs are semifixed and semivariable. For example, you may have a minimum monthly charge for telephone service whether you make any calls or not; and you may make more phone calls in a bad month (trying to drum up business) than in a good month. However, you will use twice as many ball bearings to produce twelve thousand units as you will to produce six thousand units.

To avoid this simplistic approach, you can use a more sophisticated formula:

$$C = DP (1 + R) + M$$

C is the total cost of the product; DP is the direct cost of labor that can be assigned to the product; R is your overhead for the product (which equals the overhead for your entire operation divided by your direct labor costs for the entire operation) and M is the cost of materials for that particular product.

If you really want to get fancy, you can analyze cost interdependencies as a tool for cutting cost. The cost of manufacturing a product is made up of subcosts: making or buying the components, then putting them together. The total cost (C_T) equals the subcosts, which are easier to work with if you express them as decimals. If a product is made up of four subparts which have to be assembled and then placed in a plastic outer casing,

$$C_T = C_{S1} + C_{S2} + C_{S3} + C_{S4} + C_A + C_C$$

The total cost equals the cost of the four subparts (C_{S1} through C_{S4}), plus the cost of assembly (C_A) and the cost of making or buying the casing and putting the stuff inside (C_C). In this example, let's say:

$$C_T = .08 + .14 + .20 + .08 + .22 + .28$$

Most of the cost goes into putting the parts together, and into the plastic casing. Therefore, since these add most to the cost, you have the most potential for cutting costs there. A ten percent price reduction in a part that accounts for only eight percent of the cost won't do much for you, but a ten percent reduction in the cost of the casing will at least have some impact. (See Chapter Five, page 144, for a discussion of component and labor high-value lists, and related techniques for cost-cutting.) But don't go overboard with this: as Sir Michael Marks of Marks & Spencer says, "We won't spend fivepence to move the safe to get the sixpence that rolled under it."

The most common pricing approach for retailers is to use markup (or gross margin). Markup equals the retail price minus the cost of goods sold; it also equals the expenses of making the sale plus your profits. Since it is both expensive and maddening to figure out the comparative cost of selling chiffon blouses versus Shetland sweaters, retailers usually use a standard markup: the wholesale price plus a given percentage. (If the merchandise is marked with a "suggested retail price," and you know the wholesale price, you also know the conventional markup.) For example, health-food stores usually mark up staples by twenty-five to thirty percent (i.e., charge twenty-five to thirty percent over wholesale price), books by forty percent, vitamins and cosmetics by forty-five percent.

Craftworkers usually use one of two pricing techniques: either the item is priced at three to four times the cost of materials (this is the retail price; wholesalers get a discount), or a formula is used to relate the cost of materials to labor and overhead costs. One formula is:

$$RP = [C_M + C_L + .4(C_M + C_L)] \times 2$$

In other words, the retail price equals the cost of materials plus the cost of labor (either wages you pay, or what you would have to pay someone else to do the work you do) plus an overhead figure (to cover rent, utilities, taxes, and the like; estimated as forty percent of the total for materials and labor). Then you double the total to get the retail price. This formula is more accurate—if more trouble— than the one involving just the cost of materials. Which one you choose is a function of the labor-intensiveness of your product (the extent to which its price depends on the work involved). If you make jewelry by popping simple but expensive semiprecious stones into simple but expensive silver settings, you want to concentrate on the cost of materials. But if you make life-sized portraits out of papier-mâché, labor cost is paramount.

People in the food business have similar formulas: for example, a caterer may price an easy-to-make entrée or dessert at three times the cost of ingredients. Anything involving artistic dabs of butter cream, stuffed snow peas, or other labor-intensive components will be priced at four or more times the cost of ingredients.

The price may also be based on a calculation of the cost of every item in a serving (e.g., a thirty-pound standing rib roast shrinks to twenty-five pounds after cooking. The cost of a four-ounce serving is one percent of the cost of the roast—one fourth of four percent of the cost). If the beef is served with gravy, browned potatoes, and braised spinach, the menu cost should be the cost of each of these items, plus a ten-percent fudge factor, multiplied by three. According to industry figures, the average profit on a meal is eight to ten percent, and food costs range between thirty-three and forty percent of gross sales.

For service businesses, the first principle is to bill all direct costs separately. Direct costs include a photographer's film, a management consultant's trip to the plant, a publicist's cabs and long-distance phone calls. If you bill these items separately, you can distinguish between the cost of your professional services and the cost of doing business. This not only simplifies bookkeeping, it makes it possible for you to keep your fee the same even if the postal rate or the shuttle fare to Boston goes up.

A service business will still have overhead—rent, phone calls that can't be billed to clients, salaries, taxes, mailings to get new clients. To price a job, you can either charge an hourly rate (calculated to cover your overhead and leave a decent income for you) or charge a flat rate per job. Fast workers will prefer the latter, slow workers the former. The first few times you photograph a wedding, decorate an office, or help a client get out an advertising campaign will take much longer than subsequent trips over the same ground; it's not really fair to make the first few clients subsidize your education at hourly rates.

To calculate a flat rate, figure out the number of jobs you expect per year (let's say 24), your annual overhead ($600 a month, or $7,200), and a yearly income that sounds fair to you (say, $18,000).

$$P = O/N + I/N,$$

where P is the price per job, O is your annual overhead, I is your yearly income, and N the number of jobs per year.

$$P = 7,200/24 + 18,000/24 = \$300 + \$750, \text{ or } \$1,050$$

If you think 24 people or institutions per year will pay you $1,050 plus direct costs to do whatever it is you do, your income estimate is reasonable. If you think more of them will, or the traffic will bear more than $1,050, you can expect a higher income. If you can't conceive of getting that much money, you'll have to lower the price and hustle more to get the same income, or accept a lower income.

This brings us to the question of what the competition is doing. Charging more than your competitors do is called "skim pricing" (if not something worse), and can be managed if:

- Your product or service is a novelty, or is unique
- It's hard for others to go into business copying you
- You control the source of materials or license the item or its name (e.g., Vuitton luggage)
- It's a status item (luxury goods such as leather luggage or face cream; a service like management consulting or psychiatry where the service is valued in proportion to its price)

It's against the law to get together with your competitors and decide what the prices will be. However, most of the time prices will be fairly similar if the market is highly competitive (many sellers of similar products). If Toaster A has no real advantages over Toaster B, there's no reason to pay more for it. Even if there are only a few sellers, if the product is exactly the same (matches, charcoal briquettes), it's hard to get a higher price unless you sink a fortune into advertising to create a belief that your product is better.

You can also cut prices (if you're a retailer) or lower your wholesale prices (if you're a manufacturer). Paradoxically, this approach only works if you have lots of capital. If you don't, larger businesses can engage you in a price war, cutting prices below their own costs. You either have to go along or lose sales; they can afford to lose the money and you can't. Discounting and price-cutting work only if the product is expensive (e.g., stereo equipment), so the customers can save a lot of money by shopping around, or if the markup is very high (e.g., cosmetics). However, status goods (cosmetics, "designer" items) are attractive primarily because of packaging and image. A less expensive product—even if it provides the same benefits—is less salable.

Luckily, prices are not cast in stone. Most customers are wearily resigned to price increases and can probably absorb increases without lowering their level of buying. And if you do cut the price, they'll be pleasantly surprised and may even stock up on your products, raising your sales figures. You can adjust the price at any time if your original calculation has a bad effect on sales or profits.

CHAPTER THREE

The Office and Its Alternatives

EVERY BUSINESS HAS RECORDS, and therefore every business has an office of some kind, even if it's only a corner of the kitchen table and a couple of shoeboxes. Communications businesses (publishing, advertising, public relations) and those concerned with image (the main offices of large corporations) can have offices of unparalleled splendor: room after thickly carpeted room in glass-and-steel boxes on the best blocks. The office is a small but necessary part of a factory or restaurant. Offices can be rented, or real estate bought, with professional assistance in furnishing and remodeling. At the other extreme, the office can be part of your home, furnished with Salvation Army furniture and old fruit crates.

No matter how ample or how scanty your resources, you'll need some kind of work space. The factors involved in matching your business needs to available resources include: choosing a suitable space; devising the best layout inside that space; using ergonomics (the study of human measurements) to select and place furniture and equipment within the layout; heating, cooling, and lighting the space effectively. The chapter concludes with suggestions (and condolences) for those working at home.

Choosing Space

If your business is open to the public, a "good" location is one that is easy for your customers to reach, easy for your suppliers to deliver to; one that conveys the status level you have in mind (whether upper-crust elegance, bourgeois solidity, or wild bargains); one located in a shopping area, so there'll be plenty of passers-by, but not too close to direct competition.

If you think that the landlords of apartment buildings take advantage of their tenants, you ain't seen nothin' yet. The feeling is that booting people out of house and home is unsporting, and that reasonably well-behaved residential tenants who pay their rent are entitled to keep renewing the lease at rent increases somewhere short of intolerable. None of these considerations applies to commercial leases. There's no rent control and, when your lease is up, the landlord can hike your rent up to any altitude, or toss you out on a whim even if you agree to pay the higher rent. Due to lack of construction in recent years, you may also face a shortage of space—which inflates rents even higher, and lessens your already feeble bargaining power. Looking at the bright side, however, in some cities the economic situation is so bad that a surplus of office space and plenty of room in ghost-town "industrial parks" exist; the streets are littered with the bleached bones of your defunct competitors. In that case, you have more room to negotiate.

The base rent will be stated in a standard commercial lease, and it's not uncommon to find an "escalator clause" which raises the rent as the owner's costs go up. Some considerations in dealing with an escalator clause:

- Is it clear which situations will trigger an increase, and how much the increase will be?
- If the building is under construction, will you have to pay a higher rent when the tax assessment is raised to cover the value of the completed building? Does the owner agree to protest an excessively high assessed valuation (the taxes on which are passed along to the tenants)? If so, who pays—landlord or tenants?
- Will the rent be *lowered* as a result of the tax cuts in the Economic Recovery Tax Act of 1981? These tax cuts are phased in over several years, so a 1983, 1984, 1985, or 1986 lease could be affected.
- Are you allowed to audit the landlord's books?
- Must you pay a higher rent if any of the landlord's operating expenses increase? Most escalator clauses exempt these expenses:

—Advertising

—Cost of evicting tenants

—Capital improvements to the building

—Repairing damage caused by a casualty for which the landlord did not carry insurance

—Services available to other tenants but not to you

- Will your rent be raised if unrented space in the building
raises the landlord's costs per square foot? Will the rent be
lowered if occupancy increases after you sign the lease?
- Can your rent be raised to pay for improvements that only
benefit the landlord (e.g., automatic elevators that let him fire
all the elevator operators)?

When you compare rents, remember that the services included
may not be equal. One rental may include janitorial service; an office suite can be partially or fully furnished (though the furniture
may be so hideous that you think it decreases the value). Utility bills
are lower in energy-efficient buildings, where natural sunlight and
openable windows provide a measure of climate control. Some
buildings have a central switchboard, a post office, a freight elevator, and loading dock, or other conveniences available. An old
building may have plaster walls with beautiful moldings and cor-
nices; a newly constructed building may have unpainted plaster-
board walls. You may have to pay for painting the space, or for
installing the extra outlets, phone lines, or heating and cooling
equipment you need to keep your computers amiable.

All things being equal, you'll want a long-term lease, so you
won't get kicked out just as prosperity sets in. On the other hand, if
you are forbidden to sublet, and you can't cancel the lease on short
notice by paying a manageable penalty, you'd be in a lot of trouble
if the business went sour. You could also have the opposite problem:
you may need more space later or feel a higher degree of elegance is
justified—but you're stuck with the same damn space. If you think
rents will go up in the future, you may decide to rent extra space for
future expansion—especially if the lease lets you share the space
with another tenant who pays rent to you. But if you expect
cheaper, or better, space to be available later, you would tend toward a small space allotment and/or a short lease (although the
horrors of moving have to be factored into the equation). If you rent
space in a building under construction, make sure that the lease
gives you a rent rebate if the building isn't ready for occupancy on

schedule; if you negotiate hard, you may even get an extra amount for damage to your business.

It would be wonderful if the space you decide to rent were perfect for your purposes. This seldom happens. In a buyer's market, landlords will divide a large space among several tenants, putting up partitions between the areas, even partitions inside the units. In a seller's market, you take whatever is available. The landlord agrees to provide a certain number of running feet of plaster or drywall partitions with accompanying doors; you have to supply any other partitions you want. If the floor is carpeted, you also have to supply the baseboards in a new building.

Traditionally, the landlord pays for painting the walls every three years (usually you have a choice of white or white); sometimes the landlord has the walls washed in the second year of each cycle and has the walls painted in the fourth year. If your negotiating position is good, you may be able to get a lower rent if you do the painting yourself or hire your own painters.

Most leases require you to get the landlord's permission before you make alterations (e.g., knock down or add walls, change the electrical system, brick up windows or add new ones). Usually you pay for the improvements, but you have to use contractors approved by the landlord, who gets to keep the improvements. The landlord also has the right to order you to restore the premises to their original condition before you move out. It follows that, if possible, you should meet your needs with furniture and movable partitions rather than built-ins and permanent walls.

Before you sign a lease, ask your lawyer, or your broker if you have one (if there's only one broker, s/he works for the seller or landlord), what the relevant zoning and building regulations are. If the area is zoned for "business," you'll be allowed to maintain an office but not a factory. A garment factory is permitted in a "light industrial" zone; a coal gasification plant, with its fumes, sludge, and danger of explosion, is not. Zoning laws can also limit the size or prominence of signs you can use, the kind of displays permitted, and the hours at which trucks and cargo unloading will be permitted. Factories must also meet OSHA (Occupational Safety and Health Administration) and local standards for number of exits, stability of ramps, protection from toxic materials, number of fire extinguishers, sprinkler systems, and the like.

The developers of the building, or of the shopping center in which the building is located, may have put "restrictive covenants" in the deed. These are contract provisions that limit activities that are permitted on the property. For example, food service may be forbidden—so your bakery would not be allowed to add five tables and an espresso machine. Your boutique might be forbidden to sell cosmetics to avoid undue competition for the drugstore. One shopping-center tenant was forbidden to sell her trademarked cookies from street pushcarts: the developers felt this populist distribution method detracted from the image they were trying to project.

The standard arrangement is for the landlord to supply heat, air conditioning, and elevator service from 8 A.M. to 6 P.M. on weekdays, 8 A.M. to 1 P.M. on Saturday, and on advance request at other times. If you're a workaholic or observe Saturday as your Sabbath, you'll need more hours and will have to negotiate with the landlord or locate among like-minded people. A tenanted building is safer than a deserted one when you're working late; and, if possible, have the floor-scrubbing and vacuuming done when you're not trying to concentrate.

Also, if possible, try to have the messy work (installing partitions, Sheetrock taping, running electric lines, painting) done before you move in—not always possible if finding space, or getting it fixed up, takes longer than anticipated. Make sure your telephone service can be augmented later on without tearing up the walls. You want as many jacks as possible for extensions and the capacity to add a switchboard, intercoms, connection to computers or teletype, or whatever exotica develops later. You may be able to pick your own telephone number. Make a list of numbers that appeal to you for some reason (222-6666—"Dial a Doctor") and call each one in turn, until you find one that is not in service. A recording will come on the line to inform you of this. Then ask the phone company if you can have that number.

Layout

A small store usually needs 1,500 to 2,000 square feet; in an office, the usual allocation is 100 to 150 square feet per person. A one-person operation can rent a small room in an office building; a larger company can rent a suite or part or all of an office building. The dictates of geometry and status call for at least 11′ × 18′ for a reception area; 20′ × 20′ is the maximum for reasonable needs. An ordinary private office with full walls is about 10′ × 12′, but an executive office is larger—say, 12′ × 15′. In an open-plan office, with shoulder-high partitions, the spaces allotted to each person can be a little smaller. The clear space overhead prevents the inhabitants from feeling caged. A conference room 10′ × 15′ can seat 4 people at a 5′-long rectangular table; a 12′ × 18′ room with a 10′ table can accommodate up to 10; and a 20′ × 20′ room with a 12′ square table can handle 24. Larger meetings take a great deal of skilled organization, or interaction gets lost as people shout down a bowling alley.

One possibility is to have several smaller meetings at different times; another is to use a larger room with several smaller tables. The former solution is more time-consuming for the person who has to go to all the meetings. The latter tends to turn into a series of submeetings, each with its own dynamics. People often pay more attention to their table mates (or the crossword puzzle) than to the alleged reason for the meeting.

The optimum layout for a business is the one best suited to its particular needs, whether selling philodendrons or chain saws or insurance, devising ad campaigns, or baking pumpernickel. The comments below are basic and rather generalized.

STORES

In a small store, the usual division is eighty percent sales and customer service area, twenty percent for storage, work areas, and the office. In a shop selling take-out food, a fifty-fifty division between kitchen and selling space usually works well.

Customers who want to buy a few convenience items from a store and then leave have been observed to turn left—so the left side of the store, near the door, is a good place for convenience and impulse items (e.g., toothpaste, milk, candy bars, daily newspapers). Shoppers—who want a more leisurely view of the merchandise—have been observed to turn to the right. (According to Jessica Mitford, the most expensive coffins in an undertaking establishment are set out in a clockwise spiral, starting at the center.)

Usually, most sales are made from the front of the store. The "4-3-2-1" rule suggests that forty percent of inventory value be put in the front quarter of the store (the section nearest the entrance), thirty percent in the next quarter, twenty percent in the third, and only ten percent in the last quarter. If you have two window displays, one on either side of the door, a location behind the right-hand display is the best location for selling high-ticket merchandise. If you have a showcase in the center of the store, customers will tend to walk all around it and see the merchandise on both sides. A fairly wide aisle is required for traffic—say, four feet—so in a small store, the central showcase can end up consuming all the space. A "figure 8" design with two circular showcases is chancy: the customers tend to walk around the front loop and leave without seeing the merchandise on the second showcase. Impulse items are auspiciously located near the cash register. Honest customers can buy a few extra things, and the person working the cash register can make sure that dishonest customers don't snap up a few unconsidered trifles.

Normally, the dressing room in a clothing store is in back; the adjoining areas are not "hot locations" and therefore can be used for classic, unchanging merchandise like white shirts and navy-blue skirts, rather than for fashion items. But a display of accessories (ties, cuff links, scarves, jewelry) near the dressing room can spark impulse purchases to complete an outfit.

For some deep psychological reason, displays above eye level are associated with cheapness (maybe people won't bother to reach up unless they're getting a bargain). Therefore, high shelves are in order for a discount store, but inappropriate for a luxurious establishment. Large, heavy items should be displayed near the floor, so the display won't look as if it's going to fall over (and, in fact, so it won't fall over). Maybe expensive items have psychological weight; in any case, a waist-level display is effective. In a discount store, waist level is good for loose, unpackaged items; eye level is effective for small packages.

OFFICES

A large, undivided room democratically shared by all is chummy and conducive to accords openly arrived at. You can make decisions quickly and reduce the "paper blitz" by reviewing documents together rather than circulating endless memos with supporting evidence.

If you all like each other, it is conducive to marathon bull sessions and gin games; if you don't like each other, this layout can lead to loud sotto voce remarks, simmering hostility, or billingsgate. Of course in one room it's impossible to make a private phone call (whether business or personal) or close the door to get some privacy.

For reasons of efficiency, most offices install some kind of partitions. An "open office" usually gives each worker an individual desk, with five- to six-foot partitions between desks or surrounding each desk. In a hierarchical organization, a row of closed-in offices is built next to the windows, with an open office arrangement in the center. A more democratic setup consigns everyone to open space, but sets aside private telephone rooms, conference rooms, and "quiet rooms" for unbroken concentration. All the employees can use these rooms as needed. Optimally, desks in an open office should be six feet apart; you can put desks closer together if partitions are high enough to give a feeling of privacy. Small items of office equipment are best located near their users; large items (over four feet high) should be grouped in banks or near the walls, for visual balance and to avoid blocking traffic.

Although, as Robert Townsend pointed out in *Up the Organization,* the best offices should go to those with the worst jobs. Executives get to spend time in other people's posh offices, in expensive restaurants, and on golf courses. Clerical workers spend the whole damn day crouched over a ledger or a keyboard; they would certainly appreciate thick carpeting and a panoramic view. A conference room can be lavishly furnished to impress clients, who can be ushered at once into this mercantile Potemkin village; they won't have to see the bullpen or the comparative squalor of the private offices.

RESTAURANTS

Restaurant design involves a number of trade-offs. At first glance, it seems as though restaurant design focuses on tablecloths and bentwood versus Barcelona chairs in the dining room, but far more thought should be devoted to setting up a kitchen that is easy to clean and operates safely and efficiently. The more you alter the existing design of the premises, the more you have to pay for the changes. But if you keep an inefficient layout, it's harder to run a profitable restaurant. If you cut down on kitchen space, you have more room for tables and perhaps for a bar, but the kitchen becomes crowded and therefore inefficient, and the quality of the food suffers.

Several things must go on in the kitchen at the same time: food must be taken from storage, prepared for cooking, and cooked. Servers have to bring the diners' orders to the cook, collect the food, and bring it to the diner. Dirty dishes have to be returned to the kitchen, washed, and put away.

The cook is metaphorically (and often literally) in the center of all this. A restaurant stove gives off a lot of heat—heat that must be dispersed before it melts the ice cream and wilts the salad. The cook needs to have ingredients, tools, and pots and pans within reach, but s/he also needs elbow room to work without disturbance from servers and dishwashers. In a small restaurant, the dishwasher often helps the cook with preparation; in a very small restaurant, the dishwasher is also the server; in an *extremely* small restaurant, one person may have to handle each of these functions at various times.

The ideal layout starts at the back door, with a receiving station for supplies: a loading ramp, record books, a cash register or checkwriter, and a pantry for storing nonperishable items. The restaurant needs adequate refrigerator and freezer space, and there must be enough partitions to keep pungent foods away from those less strongly perfumed.

The elements of the "work triangle" (sink, stove, and refrigerator) should not be too far apart, unless the chef is to wear roller skates. But, for obvious reasons, you can't install the refrigerator right next to the stove. Shelving or work counters can be installed anywhere, but stoves must be near gas lines, dishwashers and refrigerators must be near electric outlets, sinks and dishwashers near water. One way to handle these conflicting needs is to break up the "triangle": put the stove along a side wall, toward the back of the kitchen, with the refrigerator along the same wall, but closer to the dining room. The center of the room is reserved for counters used for preparation and storage. The wall on the other side holds the dishwashing machine and space for dirty dishes brought in by the servers and clean dishes for storage or use by the cook. If possible, it's better to have enough storage space so dishes can be handled and stored in one layer; stacking makes breakage more likely. However, few restaurants can afford the luxury of large dirty-dish tables or storage racks.

There must be an area (preferably with a steam table, warming lamps, or heating coils embedded in a counter) for the cook to place finished platters of cooked food. The server must be able to reach this area without colliding with the cook. Finally, the closest to the dining area, there must be refrigerated and unrefrigerated storage for items prepared in advance (e.g., coleslaw, marinated mushrooms, banana cream pie). The server picks up these items without interrupting the cook's or dishwasher's work. Obviously care is required to keep the marinated mushrooms from smelling like banana cream pie, and vice versa.

In the quite likely case that the kitchen is too small for an optimum layout, probably the first thing to go will be extensive storage space. In a pinch, dishes can be stacked; basement space may be available for food storage. The trade-off is more breakage and more time spent retrieving supplies. Unless you have money for structural alterations, perfect placement of equipment will have to be sacrificed to the need to use existing lines and outlets. You may have to cut down on preparation space, but the last thing to go should be the actual cooking space. The chef needs room to work without spattering hot fat, dispersing live steam, or spilling soup.

A coffee shop or lunch counter usually has a smaller kitchen area, because much of the food preparation is done on griddles behind the counter. A cafeteria setup eliminates the need for servers, but someone has to collect dirty dishes and bring them to the dishwasher. Usually, restaurants try to minimize the visibility of the kitchen (especially if they don't want the customers to see that frozen pre-prepared dinners are being warmed up in microwave ovens). However, some restaurants deliberately open up the kitchen area and treat the preparation of food as a kind of floor show. An expensive restaurant has to stress elegance and smooth service; a fast-food operation centers on convenience. The kind of kitchen you need depends on the kind of restaurant you want to run.

MANUFACTURING

A factory or warehouse must meet standards for worker safety and safe disposal of wastes. The machinery must be placed where electricity is available (or the electric system of the building must be altered), and heating, cooling, and water must be supplied where necessary. The floor must be strong enough to support the machinery and the workers who use the machinery; the floor must be kept free of scraps and grease.

Picking and loading merchandise can be expedited by locating the pick racks (shelving used for storing and selecting parts and merchandise) at right angles to the loading dock. The fastest-moving merchandise should be closest to the dock; aisles should be four to six feet wide (wider if you expect two-way traffic, if the machinery gives off heat, or if workers have to make U-turns with loaded pallets). Dollies and multilevel racks on wheels are an excellent investment because they keep the merchandise in better condition while they save work for your employees. If pallets or dollies have to be pushed through swinging doors, you can keep the door from getting chewed up by bolting a metal plate to the point of impact.

You'll be able to keep better track of your inventory if you use a clipboard or a card system to note when parts are taken for use in manufacturing or when merchandise is shipped to customers. You'll be able to keep better track of your costs if you identify the price you paid for each item and the date it was ordered. You don't need anything very elaborate—a stick-on label on a shelf or parts bin, saying something like "6/2/82, 200 frammis @ $.27 ea." will remind you of the size and cost of the order—and will be a subtle reminder that this stuff costs money and shouldn't be treated cavalierly.

FLOW CHARTS

After you've rented space, and before you've moved anything into it, a few hours with graph paper and a pencil will pay off handsomely. The graph paper represents the floor plan; you draw in windows, doors (showing which way they open), furniture, machinery, phone jacks, and electric sockets. Architects and designers take care of this for people who have money, but obviously this may not be an option in your case.

The most common scale is to have one inch of floor plan equaling one foot of space. If this is inconvenient, you can use any scale, as long as you keep it consistent, and explain it to other people who use the plan. There are different kinds of graph paper—the little squares can be ¼", ⅕", or ¹⁄₁₀" on a side. You definitely do not want log graph paper, which is used for plotting ratios. If you calculate measurements in feet and inches, ¼" paper is the most convenient; the others are more convenient for metric calculations.

Make a couple of dozen copies of the finished plan, and label each one for a different activity (drink and dinner order, dictation, assembling an amplifier). Take a pen and trace the path a worker would have to follow to perform the activity. In the first case, the path would be: go to table; write down order; go to bar and place drink order; go to kitchen and place dinner order; go to bar and pick up drinks; serve drinks to patrons; go to kitchen and pick up appetizer; serve; and so on. Then measure the overall length of the path (count the little boxes). Analyze the route: does the worker have to retrace steps? Are there any bottlenecks (path to bar is blocked by a table used for holding dirty dishes; water cooler is directly in front of copying machine)? Would it be easier to carry out the activity if the plan was changed? This is an objective decision, not a subjective one: draw another plan and measure. It's easier than moving furniture.

There will never be a perfect plan: as you improve the layout for one purpose, you louse it up for another. Expediting the busboy's job may make the waiter's job harder, or may make dining less pleasant for the customers. When something has to give, favor the most important function. If you dictate letters twice a day, this should proceed more smoothly than the twice-a-year search for something in the dead files. It's almost always a bad idea to block a window or a door, or to plunk a desk or a piece of equipment in front of a pillar. If you are short on electric outlets and phone jacks, make sure that the putative typewriters and telephones can be connected to something.

Ergonomics

The varied shapes and sizes of human beings actually fall into a fairly narrow range. Most adults are somewhere between 5' and 6½' tall. In 1962, the average woman was 5'4" tall, the average man a little under 5'10". (The averages may have gone up a bit since then.) The most comfortable counter for a standing person is either 3" below the elbow or 8" below the elbow (different motions are used in each case). An average female elbow is about 40" off the ground when its owner is standing; a male elbow, some 45" high. Therefore, if a counter will be used by standing people, its height should be in the 37"–42" range, or 32"–37". Standard counters are 36" high; you may want to lengthen the legs or put the counter on a plinth. A counter should be at least 18" wide—people are usually fairly close to 18″ wide—and 5′ is about the maximum a person can reach by standing at the center of the counter and extending both arms. A depth in the 14″–24″ range will be comfortable for most people.

Again using the 1962 figures, the average seated height was 33.4″ for women, 35.6″ for men; the width of a seated person was 18.5″ (female), 20.6″ (male), and the seated lengths (back of rear end to front of shin) were 23.4″ and 25.1″, respectively. Most people can move their arms over a radius of about 15″—so a 30″ × 60″ desk can be used fully by a seated person. A larger desk may provide an impressive bulwark, give you lots of room for piles of long-forgotten papers, or be easy to build by plunking a flush door on two two-drawer file cabinets, but the desk owner will have to get up to reach the stuff at the ends of the desk. Most people are comfortable when typewriters are 28″–30″ from the floor (that's why the typing area on an L-shaped desk is usually lower than the 29″–32″ desktop). However, CRT screens (cathode-ray tubes—those computer terminals that look like TV screens) are aimed upward, so the counter should be a little lower—say 26″—for optimum efficiency.

People not only take up space, they need space around them: a clearance of 24″ is needed to walk past a seated person, 38″ to walk past a standing person, or for two people to pass in a corridor. A desk user needs 3′ of clear space behind the desk; 3½′ to use a file cabinet. (The extra space is needed because the file drawers pull out farther.) Cabinets with doors need clear space equal to the swing of the doors. These are minimal dimensions: expansive personalities or oversized furniture call for more room. Ordinary armless chairs can slide under ordinary tables. If the chairs have arms or a curved back, or if the table has a thick or elaborate apron (the part connecting the tabletop to the legs), you won't be able to push the chair under the table, and you'll need a wider aisle around the table. Every law library I've ever been in ignores this simple rule: massive tables and oversized Windsor and captain's chairs are stuffed into narrow aisles, and you can pass through only by drastically compressing the lawyers.

A restaurant needs space between tables (36″ for servers carrying trays) and in corridors (at least 30″). The tables should be about 28″ high for comfortable dining; the chair seats about 17″ high, about 15″ × 17″. A table 27½″ × 24″ will seat 2; a square table for 4 can be 36″ on a side; a rectangular table of 30″ × 48″ will also seat 4, though without excessive generosity. If your tables for 6 have 2 chairs on each side, 1 on either end, 30″ × 60″ will do; if there are 3 chairs on a side, 30″ × 72″ is more like it.

Restaurants, factories, and some offices store supplies on metal shelving. Stock shelving comes in a variety of widths (36″ is typical), heights (usually 5′, 6′, or 7′), and depths (12″, 18″, and 24″ are standard). The shelving you choose depends on what you're storing. It helps to have a separate place to store each item, and to sort items functionally: that is, put ingredients for curry, or components for subassembly A, near each other. Don't stack items unless their dimensions are identical or unless you like picking things up off the floor. Items that come in corrugated cartons (tomato paste, motor oil) can be handled more easily if you cut off the top of the carton, a diagonal section of the side, and part of the front, before you stack the cartons. The cans will still have some protection, but you can remove cans without unpacking. If the cans are stored only one row deep, you can tilt the shelf a little from back to front, and install a front lip and partitions between rows of cans. Then, when one can is removed, the next one rolls down to take its place.

Make sure you buy genuine, weight-bearing industrial shelving (the extra-heavy reinforced, if necessary) and not the high-tech imitation designed for holding a couple of perfect roses in someone's living room. (I loaded up an étagère like that once, and the side supports buckled, dumping about eighty reams of paper onto my desk—none too stable to begin with—and scattering index cards to the four winds. It was just like in a disaster movie. It was awesome. There was a wrenching of metal and a slow, inevitable crumpling.)

Heating, Cooling, Lighting

Patriotism—or prudence—dictates a winter office temperature of 68°, and for God's sake discourage your landlord from air-conditioning the office in the summer so that it resembles a walk-in freezer. Part of the problem is that many newer buildings have a computerized heating and cooling system. In theory, this promotes splendid efficiency. But if the sensor is located in a particularly warm place (near a stove or a piece of machinery throwing off heat) or a particularly cool place (a delicate computer kept cool at great cost and inconvenience), the furnace will work too hard or not hard enough because the sensor does not get a representative reading. You can try to get the sensor moved, or the system recalibrated, but your landlord may not be too enthusiastic about these prospects.

A 68° office with a relative humidity of 50% feels as comfortable as a 70° office with a relative humidity of 30%. Most offices have a relative humidity of only 20% during the winter, so the temperature has to be raised to provide comfort. On the other hand, a restaurant kitchen or welding shop may have to be air-conditioned all year.

Using a humidifier in the winter (a pan of water on the radiator will do, if your image is not at stake) and a dehumidifier in the summer (a pan of silica gel) will help maintain comfortable conditions. Traditional thermal practices (opening the window, closing the blinds, putting on a sweater, working in shirt sleeves) reinforced by traditional pedagogical methods (screaming and threats of bodily harm) can also be effective. If your office is in one of those glass-box buildings with excessive window area, you can buy a tinted film that sticks to the window and reduces heat loss in the winter and heat gain in the summer. The material is somewhat expensive, easy to apply, and acts something like sunglasses do. Either you appreciate the decrease in glare or resent the reduced light.

Average office work requires 50–80 footcandles of light. A footcandle, reasonably enough, is the amount of light one candle a foot away from you would provide. You can check with a light meter borrowed from a photographer friend. Very detailed work (drafting, embroidery) calls for 100 footcandles.

A restaurant, depending on the image you want to promote, needs 30–75 footcandles. Low-traffic areas in a store (halls, stockroom, bathroom) should be all right with 30 footcandles; merchandise can benefit by 100, 200, even 500 footcandles for emphasis.

The amount of light in an area depends on conditions in the area as well as the number and strength of the light bulbs. Light and shiny surfaces reflect light; dull, dark surfaces absorb it. Mirrors, of course, reflect light and make small rooms look larger. Contrast also makes a difference: eyestrain is likely to result if one object (say, a piece of paper) is more than three times as bright as the adjacent object (the desktop). Since most desk workers spend their time with papers, a light-colored desktop, or at least a light blotter, will be easier on the eyes than a black desktop.

Most office buildings provide the equivalent of 50 footcandles; if you need more light, you'll have to add more overhead lights or add standing or desk lamps. If the office is in an older building with incandescent bulbs, you're more or less stuck with them, though you can buy circular fluorescent lights that screw into light bulb sockets. Dusting the light bulbs occasionally keeps the dust from obscuring the light. A long-life bulb gives less light than a regular bulb of the same wattage and costs more, so long-life bulbs are practical only if the bulb is particularly hard to reach. For inaccessible areas, you can also get a gadget called a "Bulb Miser"; they cost about $2.00 apiece and are screwed into the socket before adding the bulb. The Miser preserves the bulb from the strain caused by the initial surge of electricity when the switch is turned on.

Fluorescent bulbs use less electricity than incandescents: a 30-watt fluorescent gives more light than a 75-watt incandescent bulb, and lasts 20 times longer. Fluorescents also generate less heat, so your air conditioning bill will be less. (Unfortunately, using incandescent bulbs won't cut your winter heating bill much.) Incandescent bulbs are more flattering to the complexion than most fluorescents, but various tints of fluorescent bulb are available: daylight, white, cool white, deluxe cool white, warm white, deluxe warm white. The deluxe cool white is the most flattering to most colors—especially good for foods; the daylight bulb is the most natural; the deluxe warm white the most pleasant to work under. By the way, don't leave fluorescent lights burning just because you think switching them on and off burns out the bulb. That was true of the first generation; modern fluorescents should be turned off to save energy unless you expect to be back within ten minutes or so.

Working at Home

Or, as many would say, Losing Money at Home in Your Spare Time. However, there are several very valid reasons for working at home:

- You can't afford to rent space anywhere else
- You can, but don't want to spend the money until you're sure the business will take off
- You're needed at home to care for a child or an elderly or sick person
- You have a health problem that makes it hard for you to work outside your home

Valid as they are, none of these factors is the stuff of which *Business Week* articles are made. Some home businesses have become highly successful, but be aware that the odds are against you.

The advantages of working at home: no rent to pay, no commuting, no child care expenses. The disadvantages: unless you live alone, there's no privacy; if you do live alone, you face isolation; and people will tend to think of your business as less than professional. (If you have rented office space, and especially if you have employees, potential suppliers, potential customers, and friends and family are more likely to feel you have a "real" business.) Customers may distrust you because you lack the trappings of success; suppliers may refuse credit and may even refuse to deliver. Your personal associates may expect you to drive in the car pool, coordinate the United Fund drive, babysit for a sick child, or other inconvenient tasks they would never ask a person with a regular office job to perform. After all, you're not busy, are you?

When you work at home, there's the ever-present temptation to sleep until noon and watch the soaps all afternoon. If you can square this with your spouse or other companion, it helps to keep the alarm clock in the bathroom. Then you'll have to get out of bed to shut it off; once you've used the bathroom, you'll feel a little more awake. Make the bed before you have a chance to climb back into it.

There's also an orthopedic problem with working at home: deliveries are made to the *sidewalk*. I used to live in a fourth-floor walkup, and I spent a few happy afternoons hauling sixty-pound boxes of printed forms up to my apartment. The truck drivers always said that they'd like to help, but they couldn't lift anything heavy like that. Chivalry is indeed dead. (I bought a house shortly thereafter, and I now live on the first floor, with only five steps at the entrance, though I wouldn't claim a causal connection.)

The first step in working successfully at home is to find an area which can be set aside and used only for work. (The IRS also requires this for a home-office deduction—see page 90.) You'll never get anything done if you have to wait until the dishes are off the table or the kids are finished with their homework for you to get work space. Unless you have a separate work area, you won't be able to work on a project for a while, then leave it to be finished later. On the other hand, if you *don't* have a separate work area, you may be forced into efficiency: if it's hard to set up and clear away your work, you may plan your time more effectively and finish the projects you start without procrastination.

The second step is to stop doing housework intentionally. That is, don't plan to defrost the refrigerator and wash and wax the floor, then prepare those dresses for shipment or finish the comps for that ad campaign. Work expands to fill the time available; and, defying the laws of thermodynamics, it expands further if there's something you don't want to do on the other side. So do the paying work first, and leave the housework for light comic relief. It's amazing how interesting cleaning the bathtub or vacuuming can be when you have a deadline.

If you used to work outside the home, your family will be seeing a lot more of you and this can cause stress. If you used to be a full-time homemaker, your family will be seeing you as much as ever, but you will be less available, with more to worry about, and more time-consuming tasks. Your family will have to start doing more housework, helping you as much as possible with the business, and staying off your case when you're busy. The cries of a husband who believes hand-starched shirts are his divine right, or of a child who wants you to look at her frog *this minute,* can be heartrending. Anyone who says that starting a business does not put stress on a family is hallucinating, or lying. Both the business and the family can survive, and prevail—but only if everyone works hard, and with good grace. Single people face the opposite problem: you can go for days without seeing a living soul. No more of the carefree badinage with officemates; no need to dress up or charge onto the commuter train, with its bracing effect on the adrenal glands.

An obvious home address is not considered chic; if this bothers you, you can get a post office box (though I think a PO box sounds fly-by-night). You can also get a service that lets you use its address to receive mail at; either you have a private lockbox or you collect your mail from the service's employees. Some of these services also have a spare office or a conference room available: when you have a client conference, you sign up for the conference room in advance and pay a small fee to rent it. Before you sign up with such a service, have stationery printed, and let customers know where to send orders; check the service out a few times. Make sure that chaos is kept within reasonable bounds and that mail is promptly and correctly sorted.

Unless you can guarantee that someone will be waiting expectantly near your phone at all times, a home business should have an answering machine, an answering service, or both. One place can combine a function of mail and answering service. But call a few times before you commit your money. Some services employ people who are guaranteed to lose your mail, misfile it, and annoy people who try to leave messages for you ("Wha? You wanna talk to *who?* Waiddaminnit . . ." [puts victim on hold] "Whaddaya want? *Who?* Waiddaminnit . . ." [disconnects victim]).

As a conscientious person, you will, of course, want to get a separate phone line installed in your home at the higher business rates, or inform the phone company that your existing home phone will be used for business, so they can raise the rates. If you don't do this, you can't list your business name in the telephone directory; if you're not listed, no one will be able to look up your number and call you cold. This is not necessarily bad; you won't have to spend a lot of time with people trying to sell you insurance or copies of your company logo made up as blazer buttons. But you won't get business from people who have heard about you, but did not get your business card, your literature, or a direct referral from a customer.

More about answering machines in Chapter Ten. If you get a lot of calls, consider getting a telephone with a hold button and multiple lines; or get call waiting, which beeps when another call is trying to come through. You can put the first call on hold or promise to call back, then attend to the second call. If you move around a lot, you can get call forwarding: you notify the operator that you will be at a particular number from ten until one; calls to your number are then put through to that number.

All the members of your family have to agree to keep the phone clear during business hours, and small children have to be discouraged from picking up the phone and saying adorable things.

ZONING

Most people live in areas zoned "residential," which means that, strictly speaking, it's illegal to run a business in that area. (It's also usually illegal to live in a commercial zone, so you can't avoid the problem by moving the home into the studio.) Sometimes small, quiet, nonpolluting businesses that add convenience to a residential area (groceries, hardware stores, real estate agencies) are allowed in storefronts on certain streets; sometimes businesses are allowed on corners but not in the middle of the block.

Many zoning laws have an exception for permitted "home occupations" which vary from city to city. Usually, doctors are allowed to maintain offices in their homes; less frequently, dentists, lawyers, music teachers, and dressmakers are specified. You will not be surprised to know that running a funeral parlor out of your home is universally disapprobated. Some zoning laws put space restrictions on home businesses (for example, not more than twenty-five percent of the home), or limit the size of the sign you can put up (say, no larger than one foot square). Zoning laws look more favorably on an operation in which the business owner works alone (some zoning laws forbid home businesses to have employees), and which is visited by a limited number of clients—not the large population visiting a store.

If your business does not fall into a recognized "home occupation" category, you can either apply for a zoning variance or go ahead anyway on the (probably correct) assumption that no one will notice. If you do get haled into court by a zoning authority asking for an injunction (a court order that you stop conducting your business at home, or that you take down the six-foot neon sign, or vent the incinerator properly), you can argue that:

- Your business does not produce noise, fumes, or disorder
- It does not increase the need for sewers, parking spaces, or garbage disposal
- Either the business is not open to the public, or the number of clients is small enough to prevent disorder

By the way, the fact that all your neighbors will come to court and swear that they don't mind what you're doing is no defense. If all else fails, you'll have to relocate.

The one area in which you may find opposition is if you try to run a food business (catering, candymaking, baking) from your home. The opposition is not entirely illogical: home kitchen equipment isn't designed for heavy use or for sterile conditions. You may be able to get around this problem while maintaining what is basically a home business by renting space in a professional kitchen in an off-hour. (The kitchen will be more receptive to this idea if you're not a direct competitor.) A restaurant that is open only for dinner may let you bake quiches in the early morning; if you live in a resort area, you may be able to use a summer camp's kitchen during the winter.

THE HOME-OFFICE TAX DEDUCTION

A sole proprietor, partner, or Sub S stockholder is entitled to deduct the expenses of maintaining an office at home if at least one of these is true:

- The office at home is the principal place of business for a trade or business
- Patients, clients, and/or customers come to the office in the ordinary course of business (e.g., doctors, lawyers, and others who consult with the public)
- The office is in a structure belonging to, but separate from, the house itself (e.g., a garage) and is used in connection with the business
- The taxpayer's house is the only fixed location for the business, *and* the home office is used regularly to store business inventory

If your office takes up ten percent of the floor space of your house, you can deduct ten percent of the fuel, utilities, depreciation, and other costs of running the house. (You can't deduct anything for mortgage interest or real estate taxes, because these items are fully deductible whether or not you have a home office.) In this example, the maximum permissible deduction would be your business' gross income minus ten percent of your mortgage interest and taxes. If you have more than one business location, the maximum home-office deduction is the gross income attributable to *that* location, minus the relevant percentage of interest and taxes.

If you have several businesses (e.g., a commercial artist free lances as a typesetter and proofreader), you can have a separate "principal place of business" for each. If your businesses involve partners, each partner can take a home-office deduction for the principal place of business for another business (provided, of course, that the partner's home satisfies one of the tests).

If your business is organized as a corporation and has not elected Sub S treatment, you can collect rent on your home office from the corporation. As long as the rent is reasonable, the corporation gets a deduction for the full amount—even if the rent is higher than the office's proportionate share of the house expenses. The money you receive is ordinary income for you; you report it on

Schedule E (rents, royalties, and partnership income) of your Form 1040.

A home office must be an identifiable area—say, a bookcase, desk, and file cabinet in a studio apartment—though it need not be an entire separate room. If you sometimes use a multipurpose room as an office (for example, you type invoices in the den if the kids aren't watching television), you can't claim it as a deduction.

For a fuller explanation, you can get free IRS Publication 587, *Business Use of Your Home.* Make sure you get the most recent edition; the home-office rules get tinkered with frequently. If you want to do some independent research, the rules can be found in §280A of the Internal Revenue Code.

LAST RESORTS

If you find you can't get any work done at home, either because piles of undone laundry haunt you or because you decide to call just one more friend at your old office and gloat, you could exchange your house for someone else's home office. (If you have small children, you either bring them with you or exchange child care as well.) Find an entrepreneur in a similar fix, and exchange keys. Put on a nice suit or dress (it's hard to feel like a titan of commerce in jogging shorts and bunny slippers). Promptly at nine, or whatever hour you agree on, report to the reciprocal home; work for as long as seems necessary. If the phone rings while you're there, answer it, "Ms. Sidon's office . . . no, I'm sorry, she's not here right now. May I take a message?" When you get home, you return your own calls. This system may be more effective than just staying home and picking up the phone when it rings. People in business tend to distrust those Jacobin—or destitute—enough to answer their own phones.

If you don't need equipment or extensive files for your work, and you don't live in a major city (where library tables are always taken), you can set up a temporary "office" in the local public library. If you're reasonably quiet and well behaved, and the chair would otherwise be empty, no one will mind if you plan a publicity campaign, write a computer program, or balance February's books. And, if you need only an occasional haven, you can get a most elegant retreat for only a few dollars a year by going to the best bank in town, the one with the marble walls and coffered ceilings, and renting the smallest safe-deposit box. When you need an hour or two of elegant solitude, produce your key and ask to see your box. The guard will hand you your safe-deposit box and show you into a private cubicle. Stay as long as you like (after all, you could be re-writing your will or restructuring your investment portfolio). When you're finished meditating or working, surrender the box and leave.

But who will be holding the fort while you're out? No one, if you're sole employee as well as sole stockholder. When you no longer can do everything by yourself, you need some combination of independent contractors, service bureaus, temporary employees, part-timers, time-sharers, and full-time permanent employees. Choosing, compensating, pensioning, and coping with these people is the subject of the next chapter.

CHAPTER FOUR

Employees and Their Alternatives

PROBABLY, BEFORE YOUR INCARNATION as a business owner, you served some time as an employee. Now, with the prospect of becoming an employer, a full range of revenge fantasies opens up before you. You'll be able to see people squirm as you sneer at their qualifications during job interviews! You'll be able to see employees cringe when you throw a tantrum because yet another unreasonable deadline has not been met! However, unless you are a constitutional sadist, this will not be as much fun in actuality as in prospect.

The employment process begins with hiring, as does this chapter. The chapter then moves on to the legal definition of who is an employee and also discusses some alternative ways of getting work done (temporary workers, part-timers, independent contractors, job-sharers).

Employees bring with them a host of practical as well as morale problems: compliance with minimum wage laws, tax withholding, payment of tax by the employer, pension plans, and other employee benefits.

Hiring

Never hire anyone, in any capacity, who does not know how to type. (If you don't know how yourself, learn.) There are three reasons behind this dictum: in a small operation, crises come up often

93

enough so that everyone has to help with the paperwork. At especially busy times, anyone may have to process invoices or retype an
important, much edited proposal or report. Anyway, as is explained
later on, the easiest way for president, salesperson, or consultant to
handle correspondence is for the person who gets the mail to open
it and sent out replies right away. Secondly, if the much heralded
electronic office does come about, executives will have to apply
their manicured fingers to the keyboard. Finally, the average office
today has a caste system: those who know how to type are the un-
touchables. You won't be able to make any money if you typecast
your employees this way. If the business is to survive at all, it will
be by recognizing talent, wherever it is, and developing the potential of everyone within reach.

A high salary, of course, is one of the things that distinguishes a
good job (from the employee's point of view) from a lousy job. Just
as obviously, you won't be able to offer high salaries, so you'll have
to provide other motivating factors: responsibility, interesting
work, variety, feedback, the chance to develop new skills, the
chance to do a piece of work from beginning to end (not fragments
of a job), opportunity for promotion. In a new business, there's nowhere to go but up. The fact that staffing is too thin for rigid job
roles is an advantage: people have a chance to learn new things and
exercise judgment.

As for the mechanics of hiring, the easiest thing to do is to take a
box-number ad ("Send resume and writing sample to Box RM 6").
That way, people don't telephone, drop in, send up resumes in the
form of giant chocolate bars, or exhibit other prodigies of demented
ingenuity required by economic distress. If you do run the ad under
your name and address, ask that potential employees refrain from
calling. Some of them will anyway, but at least you can stem the
flow.

When you place a help-wanted ad, you undertake certain moral
obligations: to deal with the applications with reasonable prompt-
ness, to send some kind of notice to everyone, and to rise above
two-bit sadism during the interviews.

Sort through the heap every day; many resumes will be Impos-
sibles, and the rest can be sorted into Maybes, Probables, and
Must-Sees. After the mail has tapered off, you can reclassify the
probabilities.

Applying for a job is a matter of at least some concern, and the process of sending out endless resumes which apparently sink into a bottomless pit is discouraging. You should have the decency to send out a form letter—or even a printed postcard—saying something like "Thank you for your interest. We do not have a job for you now, but we will keep your resume on file." If you set up your reply as a memo rather than a personal letter, you can type up a bunch of envelopes or mailing labels from the discard pile, stuff the envelopes, and file the resumes. (Yeah, really file them; you never know when you will need to hire someone in a hurry, and what's one more file in the back room?)

There are such things as employment agencies, but, since they have to be paid, the salary you can afford to pay will decline from low to laughable. There is also the "hidden job market": hiring people you met at the squash club or your women's network; relatives and friends of friends; the kid on your block who's just finished secretarial school; or the chemist you met at a professional organization's convention. You can post the job on school bulletin boards, mention it to a school placement office, or advertise in a professional or trade journal rather than in a daily newspaper. All of these methods can work, but it's really the luck of the draw whether the employees you end up with will do a good job and—if they do—if they'll stay on rather than head for greener pastures.

The interview is a wonderful—and usually missed—opportunity to discuss what your business does and what the new employee's responsibilities and activities will be from day to day. What usually happens is a mating display (interviewer and interviewee strive to impress each other), or Old Home Week ("After Binky and Mimsy got a divorce, he went with U.S. Steel and she's with Exxon . . ."), or an elaborate display of cool (two hours of talking about anything, except the job or money).

Large corporations pretend that they have to woo applicants, but, really, the interviewees are trying desperately to land the job. You may really have to do a selling job. The applicants probably have never heard of you; and they are entitled to their doubts as to whether you'll be around by next payday.

The attempt to sell oneself is inherently embarrassing, but you don't have to make it outright humiliating for the person you are interviewing. You should avoid these favorite tactics, devised by interviewers (who must pull the wings off flies between interviews):

- "What is your biggest weakness?" (The standard Uriah Heep answer is "I'm a workaholic. I never relax," or "I'm too devoted to my employer's success.")
- "What are your salary requirements?" (Tell people what the goddamned job pays; if there's anything to negotiate, negotiate. But don't ask stupid questions for the express purpose of eliminating those who fail to guess the Secret Woid and win $200.)
- "Where do you see yourself in five years?" (You won't get an honest answer. The de rigueur reply if you are being interviewed is to place your future nose to whatever grindstone the company assigns you. It's too threatening to say, "In your job, stupid"; too smarmy to say, "Wherever I can help humanity"; too honest to say, "I don't really care, as long as the salary is decent and the work isn't too nauseating.")

Your objective is (I hope) to find skilled, talented, imaginative people who will perform a variety of functions well and enjoy performing them. If your hiring criteria are expertise in toadying and a well-articulated contempt for anyone stupid enough to fall for the tired lines above, you deserve what you get.

Salesmanship, however, is very important if you are hiring salespeople, so a certain amount of razzle-dazzle is appropriate. You are more likely to have manufacturers' reps—who work for several noncompeting companies—than full-time salespeople, because a new company is unlikely to generate enough business to support a salesperson. Manufacturers' reps usually get somewhere between ten to thirty percent of the wholesale price of the item as a commission; it depends on the price of the item and the parties' negotiating skills. You can get a free booklet, "How to Succeed with Manufacturers' Reps," from the United Association of Manufacturers' Reps, 808 Broadway, Kansas City, MO 64105.

The process of selecting professional advisers or consultants is a little different; for one thing, they won't be hanging around the office all day, every day. Things to look for include:

- Education (including continuing professional education)
- Professional certification and honors (e.g., Chartered Life Underwriter, Certified Public Accountant, American Society of Interior Designers)
- Length of time the firm has been in business

- Its financial status
- Names and addresses of past clients you can contact
- How much repeat business does the firm have?
- Who will *really* handle your account? (Although a Wasp was prominent in every Wasp, Wasp & Token contract negotiation, the actual work was done by obscure helots like me.)
- What is this going to cost? Is anything (hourly rate, number of hours, deadline, expenses, payment schedule) negotiable?

Sometimes, an employment or professional relationship just doesn't work out. If you have a contract, it should include provisions for termination. If you don't have a contract with a professional firm, send them a letter terminating their services, pay any accrued but unpaid fees, and get back your plans, drawings, files, etc., so you can deal with any problems yourself or hire someone else. (It's much easier to get your files and other information if you're paid up.)

When "dehiring" or "outplacing" an employee (no, I'm not making it up—those are real words), state firmly and clearly that the employee has been fired. This is not negotiable. (I once dissuaded an employer from firing me because she couldn't bring herself to say that fatal word; I turned it into a chat about the possibilities of promotion.) Explain what you'll do to help (severance pay, a few weeks on the payroll to finish projects and make phone calls to possible new employers). If you can say anything to soothe the wounded ego, say it—but without getting into a fight, or finding some rationalization for hiring him or her all over again. And for God's sake don't maunder on about what a blessing in disguise it is and all the wonderful opportunities s/he now has. You're firing the employee for the business' own good, not the employee's.

Employees

For legal purposes, an employee is a person whose employer has the power to decide what work will be done, on what schedule, and how the work will be done. What counts is the power; mere laxity won't turn an employee into an independent contractor. If the employer provides tools, materials, and a place to work, this is evidence that the worker is an employee, not an independent con-

tractor. It doesn't matter whether the worker receives compensation called wages, salary, commission, or anything else; an
employee is always taxed as an employee.

An independent contractor, on the other hand, is an entrepreneur whose services are offered to the public and retained by individual clients. The distinction is not just hairsplitting: employees
are protected by minimum wage laws; you will probably have to
withhold income and Social Security taxes from their wages, and
you may have to pay for workers' compensation and unemployment
insurance. Eligible employees must be covered by your pension and
benefit plans.

Whether a person is an employee or an independent contractor
depends on function and working conditions, not job title or income. The chairman of the board of Exxon is an employee, but a
college student who types other people's term papers is an independent contractor.

The accountant you hire once a year to do your taxes in his or
her office is an independent contractor; an accountant who works
full-time for you, in your office, is an employee. These are clear
cases; the gray areas occur when the workers are part-time or
casual, subject to some direction but less than full supervision. A
salesperson is an independent contractor if s/he gets paid commissions only, generates his/her own leads, and sets up his/her own
schedule. On the other hand, a salesperson who gets a salary or a
guaranteed minimum income for working specified hours following
up leads compiled by the employer is an employee. Manufacturers'
reps, who are more independent of the companies whose goods they
sell, are more likely to be independent contractors. The IRS has decided that home demonstrators (e.g., Avon ladies and Fuller Brush
men) are independent contractors.

Also according to the IRS, a part-time bookkeeper, who sets her
own schedule, works without supervision, and is paid by the hour
with no minimum or guaranteed wage, is an independent contractor. A typist or tailor who works at home for hourly rates (again,
with no guarantee) is an independent contractor when it comes to
income tax withholding—but is treated as an employee for FICA
(Social Security tax) purposes. But craftworkers who use company-
provided equipment in their homes are independent contractors if
they do not have a contractual obligation to sell the finished product to the company.

These distinctions are rather Talmudic; so, if you're really confused, you can ask your lawyer (if you have one) or file Form SS-8 with the IRS. On this form, you describe the situation, and the IRS characterizes the people involved as either employees or independent contractors. As you can imagine, the IRS tends to resolve close calls in its own favor.

The Alternatives

It's been estimated that a full-time employee's tax, bookkeeping, and fringe benefit costs are almost forty percent over and above his or her salary. Therefore, if you pay an independent contractor the same amount as an employee, or even one third more, to do the same thing, you'll have lower tax and bookkeeping costs. On the other hand, an independent contractor, as a person with an unsteady income, is likely to charge more than a nine-to-fiver would; and you have less control over the finished product.

It's almost impossible to characterize a factory worker, keypunch operator, or receptionist as an independent contractor. People who do jobs like this are fairly obviously employees—but they don't have to be yours. If your needs are fluctuating, you can hire people from temporary agencies (e.g., Manpower, Office Temporaries, Kelly). Temps work as long as you need them; if you don't like a particular worker, or don't think s/he is doing a good job, you can get rid of him/her and get a replacement fast. You pay the agency rather than the worker; the agency takes care of all the bookkeeping, withholding, and tax remitting.

Naturally, there are drawbacks: you have to pay the equivalent of the worker's salary, plus the taxes, plus the temporary agency's cost of record-keeping, plus a little something for their trouble. Figure on paying from seven to fifteen dollars an hour; more for professional workers (you can get accountants by the hour) or those with technical skills like word processing or computer programming. A disadvantage is that the temporary employee will have to be shown where everything is and introduced to little individualities of procedure. Another disadvantage, if you like a particular worker, is that s/he may not be available when requested. If you don't have any regular employees, and don't need to have someone covering the phone or factory full-time, temporary workers can justify their extra cost by saving the money and *tsuris* of record-keeping. If you already have regular employees, though, the cost of keeping track of one more won't be too great, and it may be cheaper to have at least one full-time person (who knows the ropes and provides continuity), rather than temporary workers or independent contractors.

If you can't do the laundry yourself, so to speak, you can hire a laundress to come in, or send the clothes out. In corporate terms, you can have your direct mail done by a letter shop; your typing done by a typing service; your payroll, accounts receivable, and accounts payable handled by a computer time-sharing service; your collections handled by a collection agency.

The advantages are convenience for you and the specialized expertise developed by the agency. Some service bureaus are superb; others abominable. In a crunch, they may give the best service to the largest accounts. Therefore, a newer agency for whom you are a leading client may be better for you than a well-established operation for whom you represent petty cash. And for God's sake don't expect strict adherence to deadlines; and don't devise tight schedules dependent on getting things back from a service bureau on time.

Maybe you need employees, but not full-timers: you could have a student come in after class and handle the phone, the typing, and shipments. Maybe you need a commercial artist one day a week to prepare your newspaper ads. Part-time employees subject you to tax withholding and Social Security payments, but they're seldom covered by pension plans. Part-time workers often have a compelling reason for avoiding full-time work (they're full-time students, aspiring actors who need mornings free for auditions, parents of small children). To be crass about it, these needs for flexibility and time off depress part-time wages. Part-timers are almost as productive (sometimes as productive) as full-time workers. Under Parkinson's law, there is less time for the work to expand into; part-timers have less need to accumulate brownie points by staying late or shuffling papers in order to look busy.

Until recently, part-time work was usually restricted to low-status jobs that did not involve much creativity or authority. Now, under the name of "job-sharing," part-time work by professionals and executives has gained a certain vogue. Either the job-sharers split the day (McGowan in the morning, Pelerini in the afternoon) or the week (Kaplan on Monday, Tuesday, Thursday; Diaz on Wednesday and Friday). If you can swing it, it's better to have them share the day, so the morning person can tell the afternoon person the latest disasters and so they can collaborate for at least an hour or two a day. The following organizations can give you more information about job-sharing:

- Flexible Careers
  37 South Wabash Avenue
  Chicago, IL 60603
- Flexible Careers Project
  PO Box 6701
  Santa Barbara, CA 93111
- Flexible Ways to Work
  c/o YWCA
  111 SW 10th Street
  Portland, OR 97205
- Job Sharers Inc.
  PO Box 1542
  Arlington, VA 22210
- New Ways to Work/Job Sharing Project
  149 Ninth Street
  San Francisco, CA 94103
- Work Time Alternatives
  PO Box 7514
  Albuquerque, NM 87194
- WORKSHARE
  311 East 50th Street
  New York, NY 10022

Under most circumstances, job-sharers are part-time employees and therefore need not be included in pension and benefit plans for full-time employees. However, job-sharers may have enough power to be included under the plan as a matter of individual negotiation. You'll have to straighten out with the job-sharers the way benefits will be divided: a middle-aged job-sharer may prefer to get pension coverage, a job-sharer with a growing family may prefer health insurance.

One point to remember: you'll have to pay more Social Security tax for two moderate job-sharing salaries (say, $17,000 apiece) than for one person making $34,000. This is because there comes a point in the high-middle-income bracket ($32,400 in 1982) when Social Security tax is no longer required. Of course, if $17,000 is the net worth of your business, this isn't much of an issue; instead, the problem may be how little you can pay without dire mutterings about indentured servitude.

There's a fairly simply mathematical technique for comparing the relative effectiveness of low-wage, low-skilled workers and more skilled, better-paid workers. Like all mathematical tools, it works only if your assumptions turn out to be correct.

Let's say that the lower-paid workers' wages and benefits total $5/hour; the more skilled get $10/hour. Let's also say that the job involved is the provision of a service, or the production of a piece of merchandise, whose price is $3,000. The first thing we have to know is the profit potential: the $3,000 income from the job, minus the cost of labor. (We won't worry about the cost of materials or overhead at this stage.) We need to know the profit potential for three possibilities: the job will take 200 hours, 150 hours, or 100 hours.

Hours	Profit Potential		
	200	150	100
$5/hr	$2,000	$2,250	$2,500
$10/hr	$1,000	$1,500	$2,000

Remember, the profit potential is $3,000 minus the labor cost (number of hours times hourly rate).

The next step is to weight these figures by multiplying each by the probability that it will occur. The probability that one of the three profit potentials will occur is one, or one hundred percent; to make the arithmetic easier, express the probabilities as decimals adding up to one. Probably, the less skilled workers will need more time to finish the job:

$5/hr	*200 hrs*		*150 hrs*		*100 hrs*		
Profit Potential	$2,000		$2,250		$2,500		
× Probability	.8		.1		.1		
	$1,600	+	$225	+	$250	=	$2,075

$10/hr	*200 hrs*		*150 hrs*		*100 hrs*		
Profit Potential	$1,000		$1,500		$2,000		
× Probability	.05		.20		.75		
	$50	+	$300	+	$1,500	=	$1,850

In this case, the profit potential is better with the lower-paid workers, even though the job will take more time to complete. If there's a lot of time pressure, the higher-paid workers might be a better choice.

This analysis assumes that skilled workers produce more units per hour (and thus need less time to finish a job) than unskilled workers. Sometimes production is the same, or almost the same, but skilled workers do a better job. You'll have to decide whether less skilled workers can produce material of adequate quality; if not, maybe you can train them on the job. They'll probably want higher wages, but the increase may be below the wage level for skilled workers.

This analysis also assumes that both sets of workers use the same equipment. Sometimes the higher-paid workers are more productive because they have both greater skills and better equipment. To assess the impact of wages and better equipment on productivity, you'll need discounted cash flow analysis (to determine the impact of spending $X now on immediate costs measured against forgone opportunities), and a bit of calculus; since I'm not too good with either of those, I drop the subject here.

Minimum Wage

The federal minimum wage for 1981 and subsequent years is $3.35/hour. Ordinary employees must receive time-and-a-half if they work more than forty hours in a given week. "Exempt" employees—professional and managerial employees—don't get overtime pay. The determination of who is an exempt employee is somewhat imprecise. The vice-president of a major corporation is obviously exempt, a janitor obviously entitled to overtime. The gray areas, so to speak, have white collars. Secretaries are often considered exempt employees, though it seems to me that, since secretaries get precious little respect, they should at least get extra money for extra work.

A sole proprietor's spouse, and children under twenty-one, working in the proprietor's business, are exempt from minimum wage laws. The Department of Labor can issue a special certificate exempting employers of handicapped workers or full-time students or students in work-study programs from the minimum wage requirements.

Tax Withholding

Once you have employees, you need never feel lonely or bored: you have a never-ending parade of officials to contend with and forms to fill out.

You have to withhold income taxes from the employees' wages, and send the money to the IRS. You have to withhold and then deposit and pay the employees' Social Security taxes. You have to pay Social Security taxes on the employees' salaries; you also have to pay federal unemployment insurance (FUTA), state unemployment insurance, and workmen's compensation. (As for the taxes you pay on your own income and business profits, consult Chapter Six.)

THEORY

Starting with the easiest, workmen's compensation is an insurance program administered by the individual states. The office is usually called the State Accident Insurance Fund. Call up and find out the insurance rate for your industry and how to make the payments. The minimum rate is a little less than half of one percent of the employee's salary. This rate would apply to a low-risk occupation (e.g., office work), where the employer has maintained a good safety record. The highest rate is fifty-one percent (yes, over half) of the wages for a very dangerous industry (e.g., skyscraper construction) or a hazardous job where the employer has a bad safety record.

You have to pay FUTA (federal unemployment tax) if, in *any* quarter of this year or last year, you paid over $1,500 in total wages, *or* if there were 20 weeks in the past year in which you had at least one employee, no matter how ill-paid. The basic FUTA rate is 3.5% of the first $7,000 you pay each employee. However, you can subtract 90% of the state unemployment tax from your FUTA payment, so the FUTA rate can go as low as 0.8%. In 1985 the FUTA rate will go up to 6.2% of the first $7,000 pay; you can subtract up to 5.4% of state unemployment taxes (if they meet federal standards) so the federal amount could stay at 0.8%.

If you hire your father or mother, you don't have to pay FUTA, but you do have to withhold income tax and pay FICA (Social Security). If you hire your spouse, or an offspring under twenty-one, you have to withhold income tax but not pay FICA or FUTA. If you participate in a work-study program and hire a full-time student, you have to pay FICA and withhold tax, but not pay FUTA. (Someone must stay up nights dreaming up these rules.)

Moving right along: for FICA, you have to withhold a certain percentage of the employee's income and pay the same percentage of the employee's income yourself. For 1982–1984 the percentage each of you pays is 6.70%; in 1985, it's 7.05%; in 1986–1989, 7.15%; and from 1990 onward (provided the republic and the Social Security system are still standing) it will be 7.65% apiece.

FICA is not a progressive tax (i.e., one with higher rates for higher incomes). In fact, you only have to withhold and pay FICA tax up to an income limit (e.g., the first $32,400 in 1982). However, I don't think you'll have $1,000-per-week employees, so this is the least of your problems.

You have to withhold income tax on each employee's "income." What constitutes "income" is a subtle question of tax law but the best rule is, if it moves, withhold on it.

There are two basic methods: the wage bracket and the percentage methods of withholding. In either case, you get the most current table from the local IRS office or a stationery store. The table tells you how much to withhold for a given income and number of withholding exemptions. You can also use any other method that gives about the same results. The table runs out at about $20,000 income for a single taxpayer, $30,000 for a married taxpayer. After that, you stop withholding, and the employee has to pay estimated tax.

You also have to withhold state income tax (provided the state you do business in has such a thing). Contact the nearest IRS office to find out if your state is part of the "piggyback" system, under which employers withhold state income tax and submit it to the IRS with the withheld federal tax. The IRS forwards the money to the states.

PRACTICE

If you have, or plan to have, employees, you need an EIN (Employer's Identification Number). This is true whether or not your business is incorporated. You get an EIN by filing Form SS-4 with the nearest IRS district office.

After you shake hands with a new employee, hand him or her a W-4 form. The IRS will give you as many as you want for free, or you can buy them in stationery stores. After the employee fills out the form, you will have the employee's address, Social Security number, and number of withholding exemptions (one for him/herself, an optional extra to prevent overwithholding, one for a spouse, one per child, and one each if the employee is over 65 or blind). Additional exemptions are available for two-income married couples, workers with IRAs, workers entitled to a deduction for moving expenses, and those who anticipate business losses. The amount you withhold is based on the number of exemptions the employee claims. If the employee deliberately claims too many exemptions though, s/he will have to pay a stiff penalty for underwithholding. To avoid this, some people claim fewer exemptions than they're entitled to (which is perfectly legal). In effect, they're making a no-interest loan to the government. Patriotism is all well and good, but that's excessive. If the employee's W-4 indicates that s/he had no income tax liability last year and expects none this year (for example, a student who works part-time only during summer vacation), you don't withhold taxes.

By January 31 of each year, you have to give each employee two copies of the W-2 form for the preceding year. (If the employee has to pay city as well as federal and state tax, it's a nice gesture to provide three copies.) The W-2 form gives the employer's name, address, and EIN, the employee's name, address, and Social Security number, total wages, and the amount withheld. You send one copy to the IRS, one to the Social Security Administration by February 28.

For each independent contractor that you pay $600 or more to, you have to send a Form 1099 NEC (nonemployee compensation) to the contractor and to the IRS. A 1099 NEC is an "information return": that is, you owe the IRS facts but not money. You send copies of the 1099 NEC, plus any of its relatives you have to file (rent payments, interest on corporate bonds, unemployment compensation), plus a Form 1096 (a summary of information returns) to the IRS on April 15 or whenever you file your taxes for the year.

I can hear your sigh of relief—that wasn't so bad—but it is premature. We still have the FICA and FUTA to worry about. If the amounts involved are small, you have to file returns and make periodic payments. If the amounts involved are larger, you'll have to send in the money at closer intervals; you'll also have to deposit the tax money on specified dates.

Required deposits must be made to a bank, savings & loan, or credit union authorized by the IRS (ask before you open an account). You need a Form 501 for each deposit. Usually the IRS sends these forms to you when you get your EIN; if not, you can get them from the district office. The IRS doesn't require you to keep a special separate account for tax money. However, keeping a separate account is well worth the bank charges. Once you withhold money or incur the obligation to pay FUTA or FICA, it's not your money anymore. If you mix this money with *your* money, the temptation to pay bills with it is very great.

You have to pay FUTA and FICA taxes at least once a year, by February 10, by filing Form 940 (FUTA) and Form 941E (if you don't owe any FICA amounts) or 941 (if you do).

Every month, figure out the amount of withheld taxes, FICA, and FUTA you'll eventually have to pay. If the total, minus the amount already deposited in the bank, is more than $500, you have 15 days to deposit the rest. If the amount owed but not deposited at the end of a quarter is less than $500, you can deposit the money, or hold onto it and pay the full amount you owe when you file your quarterly return (one month after the quarter ends). You don't have to make FUTA deposits if you have to pay less than $100 a quarter (which is probably true if you have only 1 or 2 employees). You have to make a deposit within a month of the end of the quarter if your liability is over $100 a month.

If a *lot* of money is involved (if there will ever come a time when you owe $3,000 more than you've deposited), you have to figure out the amount owed eight times a month (on the 3rd, 7th, 11th, 15th, 19th, 22nd, 25th, and last day of the month). If the amount owed on any of those days, minus the amount already deposited, hits $3,000, you have 3 banking days to make the deposit.

There are some very unpleasant penalties (fines, even imprisonment) for failing to make a required deposit, file the right forms, pay the correct amount of taxes on time, or follow an IRS order that you collect or pay taxes or establish a trust account for the money. You're in less trouble if you have a reasonable excuse; in much more trouble if your disobedience is willful or fraudulent. Therefore, before you hire your first employee, either make arrangements with a reliable bookkeeper, accountant, or service bureau to prepare your payroll, or make sure you have an efficient procedure which has been approved by a tax lawyer or tax accountant.

TIPS

The subject of withholding on tip income provides a glimpse of your government in action. In 1982, faced with the need to raise billions of tax dollars to balance the budget, the House of Representatives decided to limit the deduction for business meals. The plan was to limit the deduction to 50% of the cost of the meal, unless it occurred away from the business person's home city as part of a business trip.

A funny thing happened on the way to the statute books. Congress found the real cause of the fiscal crisis: unreported tips. Therefore, the business-meal deduction was left intact, and the IRS will pursue those villains who fail to pay every cent of tax due on the tips they receive.

If you're a restaurant owner, you have to file information returns with the IRS, showing your gross receipts from meals consumed on the premises (not take-out orders), the amount charged on credit cards, the tips shown on the charge slips, and the tips your waiters and waitresses report to you. If the tips the employees report are less than 8% of your gross receipts, you have to assign the "missing" amounts to various employees. You can either sign a contract with your employees specifying how you will make this allocation, or you can follow the IRS regulation on the subject.

These rules apply to "large food and beverage establishments," which are not those serving large food but those with more than ten employees (all employees, not just those who get tips), and that are not fast-food or carry-out establishments. The test is whether tipping is customary. You can avoid the whole allocation routine if you include a mandatory service charge of 10% or more in every check.

The allocation rules take effect March 31, 1983. In addition to this folderol, you also have to withhold and pay FICA and FUTA taxes. FICA and FUTA are based on the tips your employees report, not the 8% figure.

Productivity and Quality Control

A commonplace jeremiad is the declining productivity of the American worker. Part of the problem is outdated manufacturing equipment—since Europe and Japan had their obsolete equipment bombed to hell and gone, they have nice new equipment, much better than ours. Part of it is the fact that growth cannot continue to increase forever. Partly it is the shift from the primary sector of the economy (farming, mining), past the secondary (manufacturing), and into the tertiary (retailing, information, recreation) in the United States. You can see if a worker is schlepping hods or sitting down smoking a cigarette, and you can count the number of relocated hods at the end of the day. How do you measure the productivity of someone who gives out telephone numbers at Information? They can't start telephoning each other to keep busy. A word-processor operator can type fast, but can't create documents to process out of thin air.

But even in a tertiary economy, certain principles can be relied on: that any job can be done either well or badly; that, within limits, people will get better at their jobs with practice; and that the people who do the job often have insight into ways to improve working conditions and output.

In order for free human beings (not slaves or prison inmates) to continue doing a job, they have to find something interesting about it. The best case is one in which the job is inherently enjoyable because of its creativity, its challenge, or pleasant working conditions. The next best is a situation in which the workers are proud of their craftsmanship and productivity, and are satisfied because their wages or psychic satisfaction increase with output. If there's nothing interesting about the work itself, but the atmosphere is pleasant, a great deal of energy will go into setting up lunch dates, baby showers, and round-robin tennis tournaments. In an atmosphere of suspicion and intramural competition, workers will amuse themselves with sniping, making each other look bad, slowing down production so everyone has plenty of opportunities for relaxation, and beating your homegrown Gestapo by kiting expense accounts and stealing stamps.

The vaunted "quality circles" in Japanese factories are groups of workers who meet with their managers to talk about production problems and how they can be solved. One reason this works in Japan is that Japanese workers take great pride in their hard work and skill. Another reason is that the workers are in a position to see what happens on the assembly line. If managers really do listen, they can get useful information. If they only seem to listen, at least the workers have a comforting (if inaccurate) sense of being heard. In a very small operation, it isn't necessary to have formal meetings. It is necessary to pay attention and listen to suggestions.

The most effective form of monitoring is self-monitoring: employees analyzing their own work and its quality. Exaggerating for benefit of the supervisor is common human behavior, but you have to be pretty far gone to bullshit yourself.

For example, you can provide employees with charts to measure production:

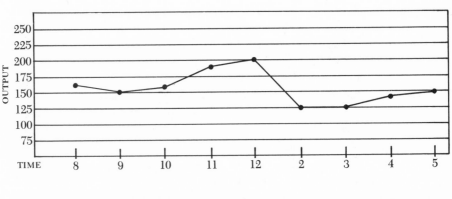

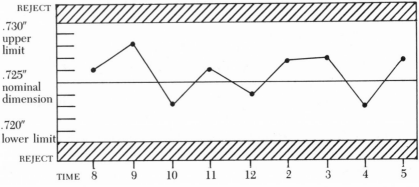

In either case, the chart shows one inspection per hour, not including the one hour for lunch. The first chart shows output per hour—you can tell that the employee is a morning person. The second one shows variation from the standard size of a manufactured item. The heavy horizontal line shows the nominal dimensions of the item (in this case, only the diameter, nominally .725″, is significant). Acceptable items can be .05″ larger or smaller, so there is a reject zone for parts .730″ or larger, and another one for parts .720″ or smaller. At each inspection, the dimensions of a sample item are checked and plotted in the graph: this worker has managed to keep all of the parts in the acceptable range.

Another way to check quality is with a tally card. In this example, the specifications are the same, and each X represents five parts made during a given hour:

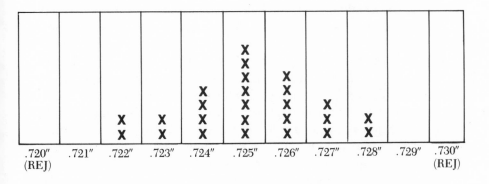

Again, the worker has managed to keep everything out of the reject pile. S/he has a tendency to make parts slightly larger than usual, so the check sheet can be used as a reminder to cut the part a little closer.

The charts work best as part of a serious, though periodic, drive to improve output and quality. Obviously you can't devote one hour a day to manufacturing and seven to filling out charts. If workers fill out the charts themselves, and are neither rewarded for lying nor punished for honesty, you'll get better accuracy and less hostility than if you have a supervisor compile the chart while breathing down the worker's neck.

The charts have to be interpreted in light of the fact that productivity also depends on experience. Most factory work has an 80%

learning curve—that is, time to do the job decreases for every time the number of actions is doubled (5 hours to do 100 units; 8 hours to do the next 200; 13 hours to do the next 400).

According to the Administrative Management Society, you can get 4,000 sheets of paper into a file drawer, and a file clerk can handle 60 drawers. The Society expects a secretary to be able to type 70 words per minute, to take 120 wpm shorthand, and to transcribe shorthand at 45 wpm. One misfile for every 10,000 cards, or every 333 letters filed, is considered acceptable. The Society says you should be tolerant of ½% errors in card punching (counting only errors that the operators miss, not the ones they spot and correct), but under ½% errors in invoices and bills. Be especially vigilant about bills: you will certainly hear from the customer who is charged $279.50 for $79.50 worth of goods, but you won't hear from the happy recipient of a $479.50 bill for $749.50 in merchandise.

As you would expect, the federal government—those wonderful folks who gave you Elizabeth Ray—have more lenient clerical standards.

The General Services Administration (GSA), in its *Records Management Handbook,* suggests that a secretary can be expected to type 3 pages per hour (though it defines a page as 30–40 lines, and a standard double-spaced page has 25 lines). The GSA allots 25 minutes for transcribing a page of shorthand, so you can expect 2 letters per hour from steno notes. The GSA figures you should expect 42 wpm typing of straight copy, 30 wpm working with a dictating machine, and 15 wpm transcribing shorthand; form letters should be produced at the rate of 20 per hour.

If this is true—and it may be, if your clerical workers are inexperienced or haven't worked recently, or if you're trying to read some scrawl you perpetrated in a subway three weeks ago, or if the secretary is also the receptionist/shipping clerk/copywriter/outside salesperson—there's a lot to be said for typing your own letters and sending out form letters to a word-processing service.

If you spend two hours on an assembly line, you will make about twice as many items than you would if you spent one hour (productivity falls off if you're tired or militantly bored). But if you make two sales calls instead of one, you will not necessarily make two sales, or double the amount ordered. A manager who increases the number of reports to be prepared by subordinates is not improving business efficiency unless the information in the reports is accurate, and unless someone will read the finished reports and use the information. It is not possible to become twice as good a composer as Mozart by dint of living twice as long.

If work depends on creativity, inspiration, or other people's decisions, there is no dependable correlation between hours and results. It is especially unproductive to reward people in judgment jobs merely for working long hours—or to punish them for working reasonable hours.

Otherwise, people start drifting in around nine-thirty or ten in the morning, read the newspapers, review last night's football game, look through the mail, then go out for a two-hour lunch. Serious work begins about four, and continues (with a break for dinner, of course) into the evening, and you can't expect an employee who works until 11 P.M. to show up at nine the next morning, can you? Apart from anything else, this sort of one-upmanship increases your electric bill, as the employees struggle to be the last one out at night.

No matter what the job, people will do more and better work if they enjoy the job and feel that the business' success is in their own best interests. These days only Republicans claim that a rising tide lifts all the boats; however, in a sinking boat, the crew members usually drown before the captain does.

Surviving Bosshood

In a group of IBM, Exxon, Merck, or other large-company executives, some will have grander titles, higher salaries, or posher offices than the others. Still, by dint of talent, persistence, or back-stabbing, everyone has the same (i.e., fat) chance of reaching the very top.

On the other hand, at Borowitz Brothers Fine Furs, Richmond & Spencer, or any small, closely held business, the Borowitzes et al. are visible every day, and work with the employees, but the employees know damn well there is no way *they* will ever become owners of this business. The potential for resentment is obvious. You can combat it by developing your employees' talents, listening to their ideas, not stealing credit for other people's ideas, and by judicious raises and/or profit sharing if and when the business becomes viable.

You can have a successful business in which decision-making is democratic: everyone discusses the issue, and each person has one vote. You can adapt this system to permit free discussion, with a casting vote given to the most knowledgeable (the marketing expert on marketing issues, the first-line supervisor on questions of shop procedure). Or, like the Arabic *majlis,* all the subjects can appeal to the ruler for justice. *Any* kind of decision-making procedure can be effective and relatively conflict-free, provided that:

- Everyone knows the procedure in advance
- It's clear who has power to make decisions
- The decision-maker(s) has (have) accurate information and good judgment

The lines of authority must be clear. Many times, at Wasp, Wasp & Token, we would finish a project and get the approval of the person we thought was in charge, only to find a furious Wasp demanding extensive changes. Sometimes, after the changes were made, the original supervisor would demand that the project be restored to its original state. Once the work got out to the clients, there were endless opportunities for misunderstanding: O'Reilly wants the commas taken out, Harris wants them back in, Morgan wants the whole thing turned ninety degrees and painted blue . . . Before you do any work for a client, you have to establish reporting procedures and find out who has veto power. If everybody does, consider whether you really need the money that badly. And before you even begin to look for clients, establish your own procedures.

I don't think you can get anything done if you require consensus. To get everyone to agree, you have to dilute all ideas to inoffensiveness (and probable ineffectiveness), or you have to browbeat the dissidents into line. If you put too high a premium on agreement, the originators of an idea will devote a few preliminary weeks to lobbying. They could have used the time to implement the idea, or to think of a better one. You may even fire good people (or they may feel impelled to quit) because they "don't fit in with the team." Unless you happen to be part of the NFL, team-playing is irrelevant. What does matter is the ability to listen to other people, and to cooperate with the decision finally arrived at.

Either you have to trust a person's discretion or give explicit orders. Only a masochist enjoys working for someone who reveals the rules of the game after the last hand has been played. Everyone enjoys praise, and praise can be nonspecific. ("Your work this month has been really terrific." "You're the best chef this restaurant ever had.")

Criticism, on the other hand, should be extremely specific and should focus on the work done, why it is inadequate, and how to improve it—not on characteristics of the worker. In other words, "Don't press the lever so hard," or "Section Three is unclear, because . . . and cut four pages from Section Four or the text won't fit into thirty-two printed pages," *not* "My God, why do I have to work with idiots?"

If you do explain to people, in advance, what you want and what you plan to do, the results will be better than if you require them to guess. (Some of the guesses will be marvelously creative, but there are easier ways to encourage the imagination.) If you explain why you are satisfied or dissatisfied with the result, you are more likely to get better compliance next time. You may also get an argument which convinces you to change your mind. It's hard to get over the feeling that, as the owner of the business, you should have all the intelligent ideas. Hard as it is, sometimes people of lower professional status have good ideas. Even harder to face is the fact that people who are usually stupid, uncooperative, or politically antipathetic to you can have good ideas—if only by chance.

It's nice if the people involved in your business have similar backgrounds and interests, and if they enjoy each other's company. However, it's not necessary. As long as they are willing to cooperate in the strictly limited confines of the job, it doesn't matter if they all loathe each other. A boring Christmas party at a third-rate country club isn't a benefit, it's a penance; never inflict compulsory socializing. As long as everyone shares the objective of producing the best possible product in the most profitable way, personal conflicts should be manageable. If they don't have to spend hours on busywork, then they can go home at a reasonable hour and regale their spouses with a running account of the idiocies going on at the next desk. They won't have to stay in the office until midnight, with nothing to do except glower and carry on feuds, and they'll be able to relieve their overstrained emotions at home.

Make your demands reasonable. Suicide missions are seldom productive. At times an adequately challenged employee will work wonders; but you can't blame a salesman for selling less charcuterie in Tel Aviv than someone else did in Paris.

Finally, you can drum up only so much loyalty by having everyone sing the company song after calisthenics. Employees will feel that their interests are similar to the company's interests if better performance results in visible gains for the employees: desk lamps, a new dental plan. At first, it will be easy to provide dramatic increases in salary and benefits, as the income statement moves toward the black. Later on, the gains will be more subtle.

Pensions

ERISA (the Employee Retirement Income Security Act) is one of the most complex pieces of legislation ever devised by perverse ingenuity. It—and the regulations devised to explain and supplement it—also get amended frequently, so a profound understanding of pension law implies the ability to hit a moving target. Broadly speaking, ERISA regulates the pension and employee benefit plans of corporations; plans for proprietorships and partnerships are covered in other laws.

Not unnaturally, business owners and high-salaried executives want the eventual payouts of pension money to go to them, not to the wage-slaves. ERISA is designed to keep the high earners from getting *all* the marbles, while still permitting them to derive much of the benefit from pension plans. (After all, a vice-president in a large corporation earns much more than a typist, and probably keeps the job a lot longer.) Occasionally someone will come up with a really clever way of shoving the lower-echelon employees away from the trough, and ERISA will have to be amended to narrow this loophole, and so it goes.

Having an ERISA-type pension plan is difficult (since you have to comply with the law as it was when the plan was adopted and change the plan to conform to changes in the law) and expensive (the legal, accounting, and record-keeping costs are over and above the cost of funding the pensions of the future). If you want to have a pension plan conforming to ERISA, you need experienced professional advice in setting up and administering the plan.

ERISA Requirements

This discussion is necessarily greatly simplified: for more information, burrow into a law library and read a reference book or a loose-leaf service (a treatment of a particular legal topic, constantly updated by adding new pages). The books and articles for laymen are, by and large, written for the employees who want to understand their pensions, not for employers trying to figure out what to do.

A plan providing retirement income can be a pension plan, which obligates the employer to make payments every year, or a profit-sharing plan, for which payments have to be made only in years in which there is a profit. Another distinction is between defined-contribution plans, to which the employer contributes an amount equal to a certain percentage of the employee's salary each year, and defined-benefit plans, where the employer's contribution is large enough to provide $X a month when the employee retires. A defined-contribution plan is easier; you don't need an actuary to recalculate the contributions to deal with economic conditions, and it's easier to budget the known amount in advance.

ERISA deals with issues such as:

- *Coverage:* the plan must cover more than seventy percent of the employees, or eighty percent of the eligible employees, or must have a classification system that does not discriminate in favor of owners, stockholders, or highly paid employees.
- *Eligibility:* either employees can join the plan (more pertinently, the employer will start making contributions for them) when they reach the age of twenty-five or have "one year of service" (one thousand hours of work in a one-year period) or they must be able to join after three years of service (if they are at least twenty-five) and be fully vested right away. Therefore, some part-time workers—those who work at least twenty hours a week for fifty weeks—will have to be covered by the plan.
- *Vesting:* this means the extent to which the benefits will not be forfeitable once the employee reaches normal retirement age. ERISA specifies the vesting schedules employers are allowed to use; otherwise, employers could arrange it so that only the owners and top executives would collect pensions and other workers would forfeit them. (Even so, a worker who changes jobs often can end up with no pension.)
- *Funding:* how much the employer contributes, and how the money is invested.
- *Portability:* the extent to which vested benefits can be trans-

ferred to another pension plan when the employee changes jobs.

Reporting: the Department of Labor, which administers ERISA, requires certain annual and quarterly reports to be made to it and to the plan participants. The department can waive these requirements for small businesses (e.g., plans with fewer than one hundred participants).

It's very difficult to draft a plan that meets ERISA requirements; to help out a bit, the IRS provides "model" and "sample" plans, checklists, and guidelines for plan drafters. You can get these documents from the Freedom of Information Act Reading Room, Internal Revenue Service, 111 Constitution Avenue NW, Room 1567, Washington, DC 20224. Write first for a list of titles and prices— and don't put the plan into operation until you have professional advice.

Other Plans

Any taxpayer—and, for our purposes, a sole proprietor or partner—can establish an Individual Requirement Account for him/herself. The business owner can contribute up to $2,000 to the IRA (the Individual Retirement Account, I hasten to say—not the fellows with the machine guns in Belfast) and deduct the contribution from taxable income. This is true no matter what his or her taxable income is. A sole proprietor who has a nonworking spouse can set up a "spousal IRA" for him or her. A spousal IRA can be a separate account or a sub-account in the business owner's IRA, but joint accounts are not allowed. The maximum contribution for both IRAs is $2,250, or all of the business owner's taxable income, whichever is less. The contributions assigned to each spouse do not have to be equal, but the maximum that can be contributed to one spouse's account is $2,000. If both spouses work, each can contribute $2,000 to an IRA.

IRA accounts can be opened at banks, brokerage houses, or other investment operations. There are many possibilities for investment, but insurance policies and collectibles are not allowed. Interest on the IRA accumulates tax-free; the taxes come due when the taxpayer starts drawing retirement income. Payments must be delayed at least until the taxpayer is 59½ years old and must start by the time s/he reaches 70½.

If you, as the business owner, open an IRA for yourself, you don't have to contribute to IRAs for your employees. If you want, you can open IRAs for selected employees, or discriminate as much as you want. However, if you have a Keogh plan or SEP (two other kinds of retirement plans available to proprietors and partners), you may have to provide benefits for employees. The more employees you have, the more expensive the plan becomes.

A Keogh plan (also called an HR-10 plan) allows a self-employed person to contribute either a defined amount or an amount large enough to fund a defined benefit to the Keogh account each year. The amount contributed is not considered taxable income. Investment options are the same as for IRA accounts; so are the distribution rules. TEFRA sets up intricate new rules for Keogh plans—talk to your accountant, banker, or broker. If you are self-employed and have no employees, a Keogh plan is a better choice than an IRA, because you can shelter more of your income from tax. (You can contribute as *little* as you want during lean years, so it's better to have the flexibility.)

TEFRA makes drastic changes in the treatment of Keogh plans. Starting December 31, 1983, Keogh plans can be used to accumulate as much retirement income for a business's top executives as a corporation's plan could squirrel away: $30,000 is the maximum defined contribution per year, and $90,000 is the maximum defined benefit per year. (Doesn't sound a lot like your business, does it?) There's a freeze on cost-of-living increases in pensions until 1986; even then, the increase will be based only on post-1984 inflation. Now the rules for minimum and maximum contributions are just as complicated as the rules for corporation plans.

TEFRA allows a Keogh plan to be integrated with FICA, so contributions for lower-paid employees can be cut back. But if the plan fits the IRS's definition of a "top-heavy" plan (one that provides 60% or more of its benefits to owners, officers, and other key employees), there are special rules that must be followed. For example, vesting must be faster than in a more egalitarian plan.

In other words, the TEFRA changes take Keogh plans out of the do-it-yourself category. Talk to a lawyer, accountant, or banker with significant experience in pensions and employee benefits—and make sure s/he understands the new law and how to apply it for *your* benefit.

If you are hysterically frugal, you can have *both* an IRA and a Keogh plan covering the money you earn from your business. If you have a salaried job and also own a business, you can open an IRA with part or all of your salary and a Keogh plan and/or an IRA with income from the business.

A Simplified Employee Plan (or SEP) is a streamlined pension plan available to corporations as well as to proprietorships and partnerships. It is a hybrid between a conventional employer-sponsored pension plan and an IRA initiated by an employee. Each employee who is at least twenty-five years old, and who has worked for the employer in the current year and in at least three out of the past five years, sets up an IRA for him or herself. The employer contributes to these IRAs; the contributions are not taxable income for the employees. The employee can also set up an IRA with his or her own money.

A SEP must be officially nondiscriminatory (the employer must contribute the same percentage of every employee's income); but it *can* be integrated with FICA unless the employer has another pension plan that is integrated. An employer can't set up a SEP if s/he or it already has a defined-benefit Keogh plan or a defined-benefit plan that covers shareholders in a Subchapter S corporation.

If you have no employees, a bank or brokerage house can help you set up an IRA or Keogh account. (Even if you have employees, banks and brokerage houses can be extremely useful in setting up plans; but you'll need legal and accounting advice as well.) The IRS' FOIA Reading Room can supply model Plan G (Retirement Plan for Self-Employed Individuals and their Employees) and Plan H (Retirement Plan for the Self-Employed).

Other Employee Benefits

I used to have a job working for a loose-leaf service on pensions and employee benefits. Part of my job was figuring out what ERISA was up to. Part of it was finding newer and more diabolically ingenious ways for large corporations to "motivate" their top executives by giving them tax-free benefits; these employees were so blasé that more money would only drive them deeper into tax shelters, not into harder work. It always seemed to me that an executive should do a conscientious job in return for his or her salary. If s/he insists on spending the whole day swilling martinis and ogling the office staff, the rascal should be thrown out, not "motivated." If your employees are good enough to keep, you can reward them with incentive compensation and/or other benefits.

INCENTIVE COMPENSATION

Within limits, people will feel better if you give them more money, either straight out or as incentive compensation. Incentive compensation for industrial workers is fairly simple and exists in several permutations:

- *Piecework rates:* the employee gets an hourly wage, plus a certain amount for every acceptable item produced.
- *Taylor differential rate system:* one piecework rate for production up to a set standard, a higher piecework rate for higher productivity.
- *Merrick multiple piece rate:* one piece rate is set for new employees, another higher one for average experienced workers, and the highest rate for unusually productive workers.
- *Measured daywork:* a standard of acceptable production is set, and each employee's production is monitored for a period of one to three months. The worker's efficiency (the percent of the standard s/he achieves) times the standard rate becomes his or her guaranteed base rate. S/he earns a piecework bonus for exceeding this personal standard.
- *Inverse bonus:* the employee is assigned a theoretical bonus which is reduced if s/he wastes material or fails to meet production quotas.

Incentive payments work only when your employees are reasonably honest and have the business' best interests more or less in mind. It doesn't help if they rush like hell to produce heaps of unsalable rubbish. Incentive payments make less sense in nonproduction jobs. The relation between hard work and assembly-line productivity is clear; not so the relation between hard work by writers, artists, marketing experts, or sales personnel and the annual sales or profits. Concentrating too much on this year's figures keeps people from cleaning up traditional messes or undertaking short-term expenses that promise long-term payoffs.

OTHER BENEFITS

ERISA defines an "employee welfare benefit plan" as any benefit plan paid for by the employer (or the employer and employees jointly). If the plan fits ERISA's criteria, the employees get benefits, but do not have to pay income tax on the value of the benefits; the employer can deduct the cost of providing the benefits from its own taxable income. In theory, benefits can be provided for a group more efficiently and at lower cost than the individuals could provide these benefits for themselves. Medical insurance, supplemental unemployment insurance, and prepaid legal services plans are all employee welfare benefit plans. The requirements for reports to the Department of Labor and to plan participants are the same for pension and benefit plans.

A benefit plan is much easier to set up than a pension plan. Most of the plans (e.g., health, group life, dental, disability) involve insurance. All you have to do is find out which insurance companies write the kind of policies you want, then compare the premiums and benefits. If you belong to a trade association, you may be able to get a good deal on coverage for yourself and your employees.

Because of the hideous cost of medical treatment, you and your employees will probably want a medical insurance plan as soon as possible. Blue Cross/Blue Shield, the dominant insurer, will write a group policy for a group as small as three people. Group rates are significantly lower than individual rates.

A new employee benefit—made possible by the Economic Recovery Tax Act of 1981—may be attractive if you and/or your employees have small children. The employer sets up a written plan that is equally available to all employees. The plan pays for day care (either at the workplace or somewhere else) for the employees' children, but the value of day care is not taxable income for the employees. Self-employed people and partners are allowed to take advantage of the plan.

In a new business, the best employee benefit is a higher salary. When the business is better established, benefits like health insurance become more important. As the owners and employees get older, retirement benefits become more attractive. As incomes, and tax brackets, rise, tax-free employee benefits are more appealing than greater income. The appropriate balance is an individual judgment for each business.

CHAPTER FIVE

Keeping Track

SOME BRILLIANT INDIAN—probably an underpaid civil servant—invented the zero. An Italian monk, in one of the less aesthetic impulses of the Renaissance, developed double-entry bookkeeping. Without these two scoring devices, it would be impossible to balance a checkbook or prepare a profit and loss statement. (For this reason alone, a movement to abolish both might be of public benefit.)

Some records are required (properly maintained books and records for tax purposes; annual reports for public corporations); more are convenient (a check register, so your checks won't bounce; ratios so you can compare your performance to that of similar businesses). Record-keeping has many levels: from standardized bookkeeping, which tolerates only a minimum of discretion, to the wildest fringes of "creative accounting," that blend of fiction and metaphysics.

This book does not penetrate those farther reaches, secondarily for reasons of space, primarily because I don't understand them. However, it's unlikely that a small business will ever face these delicate situations, calling for the highest-priced legal and accounting talent. Your problems are more likely to be the straightforward crises that result from a lack of money, not the problems of categorizing or pigeonholing your millions.

This chapter therefore covers bookkeeping (one-and-a-half entry and conventional double-entry), basic accounting decisions, preparation of statements and reports, ratio analysis, inventory accounting, budgeting, credit and collections, security and insurance. Tax accounting is discussed in Chapter Six, under the rubric of taxes; cost-benefit analysis and a discussion of leasing vs. buying appears with Equipment in Chapter Ten.

Bookkeeping: One-and-a-Half Entry

This is the method I use, because it seems to me both complete and straightforward. It's an adaptation of conventional single-entry bookkeeping, ably described by Bernard Kamoroff in *Small Time Operator* (Bell Springs Press, 1979).

My "one" entry is made on a twelve-column analysis pad (the kind made for bookkeeping; the twelve columns are ruled for cents and up to $9,999,999—rather more than the amounts I deal with). The "half" entry is made in my cash book, a hardbound book from the five-and-ten.

I have eleven categories for expenses: office supplies; printing and typesetting; independent contractors; advertising; answering service and long-distance calls; postage; photocopies; travel and entertainment; books, publications and organization dues; deductible taxes; and miscellaneous. The twelfth column is for the total. Each category gets several pages in my cash book. Whenever I spend money, I make one entry on the pad (in pencil) and one on the corresponding page in the cash book (in pen). In both entries, I give the date, the reason for the expense (more detailed in the cash book), and the check number. For cash purchases, I make a check mark in this column, which I suppose is illogical, but there it is. I glue an envelope to the inside front cover of the cash book. After I make the entries, the receipt goes into the envelope. If I don't have one, I mark the entry "NR" for "no receipt"; that way, I don't spend time searching for it. When a traffic jam develops, I staple the receipts to sheets of paper and file them.

The cash book gives me a chronological record of spending in each category; the analysis pad gives me a breakdown of each month's spending (or merely gives me a breakdown). The pad also gives me a monthly expense total, which can be compared to the monthly sales, nearly always to the detriment of the latter. I also

CASH BOOK

Independent Contractors

DATE		CHECK#	
4/3	Marcia Baker – pasteup	307	$150 00
5/9	Robert Waters – ad design	325	$100 00
6/11	Stuart Golden – publicist – 6 mos. service	349	$600 00

ANALYSIS PAD

APRIL

	DATE			1 OFFICE SUPPLIES	2 PRINTING/ TYPESETTING	3 INDEPENDENT CONTRACTORS	12 TOTAL
1	4/2	Ace Printing	306		250 00		250 00
2	4/3	Marcia Baker	307			150 00	150 00
3	4/7	Speedy Office Mart ✓		14 63			14 63
4							
5							

use the analysis pad to record the number of orders each day, the total nontaxable amount ordered, the total taxable order, sales taxes for each state for which I collect sales tax, postage and handling, and the total. When sales tax is due, I read the sales tax to be remitted from the column, find the amount of sales by multiplying by the reciprocal of the percentage (i.e., by twenty-five for a four-percent sales tax), and send off the check to the sales tax authorities. I track the postage and handling to see when I need to raise postage and handling charges for orders.

Here are sample (and fictitious) pages from the cash book and analysis pad. Only the first three columns and the total column (12) from the analysis pad are shown here—for reasons of space.

I don't have any employees, so I don't have to deal with FICA, FUTA, and income tax withholding—three very important entries for employers. Office supplies are a more significant item for a typing service than for a steel mill; a restaurant might want to track meat, produce, and dairy items separately. An office with a petty cash box needs a column to record this item.

Bookkeeping is easy enough, if boring, but it must be kept up with. First of all, the IRS requires contemporary records (going so far as to deny travel deductions to one salesman who recorded a whole day's expenses that evening). The IRS position is that you should record expenses the moment money changes hands. Second of all, you will probably forget that you spent money, or forget where it went, unless you update the books daily, or at the very least every few days.

Bookkeeping: Double Entry

I like the one-and-a-half entry system because it provides adequate detail, it's very easy to use, and it's hard to make a mistake (unless you leave out an entry entirely). Still, it's pretty bush league. Double-entry bookkeeping is standard. Your employees, creditors, accountant, and the IRS will be familiar with it.

The basic theory behind double-entry bookkeeping is that every entry you make must be balanced by a corresonding entry: every credit must be balanced by a debit. I have intellectual difficulties with this, because in real life the accounts almost never balance.

Either you're ahead of the game or you're losing money. Sometimes the balance makes intuitive sense: when you sell merchandise for cash, you have less inventory but more money. When you sell merchandise on credit, you have less merchandise but the right to receive money from someone else (an account receivable). But sometimes it doesn't make sense: when you pay taxes, you don't have anything except a continuing right to stay out of jail for fraud.

The contention is advanced that double-entry bookkeeping is more accurate than single-entry bookkeeping, because the second entry acts as a check on the first. If the wrong number is entered, the accounts won't balance. I think this is silly, because doubling the number of entries doubles the number of opportunities to screw up. Even if the accounts don't balance, it's as much fun to find the error as it is to retrieve a lost ring from the sink trap. And if the debit entry is copied from the credit entry (or vice versa) and not from the original document, the accounts will balance but will be incorrect.

Now that my spleen is vented, a basic set of double-entry books includes five journals and a ledger. The sales journal (SJ) is the record of sales of merchandise, the purchase journal (PJ) records purchases of merchandise. The cash disbursements journal (CDJ) shows cash payments, the cash receipts journal (CRJ) shows incoming cash, and the general journal covers everything else. If necessary, other special journals can be opened: notes receivable and payable, returns and allowances, or whatever your business needs.

The basic ledger has a separate account (one or more pages) for cash, merchandise inventory, merchandise sales, merchandise purchases, expenses, proprietor's investment, notes receivable, notes payable, or whatever accounts are appropriate for a particular business. There's also a page for each customer and each creditor. Some small businesses have only one general ledger; others have one called a general ledger and subsidiary ledgers for accounts receivable and accounts payable.

First the bookkeeper records transactions in the journal; then s/he posts them to the ledger. Every month, each account is added up; the overall record is called a trial balance because it is, indeed, supposed to balance. The end-of-the-year figures are used to compute the income statement, profit and loss, and balance sheet (see page 137).

Now we get to the tricky part. Each journal has columns for both debits and credits; the ledger is divided into a debit side and a

credit side. Each entry has to be for the right amount, in the right
journal, posted to the right account—and put in the correct column. This last is more difficult than one might assume. When you
get paid cash, you have more money, and you credit the cash account, right? Wrong. You *debit* cash when you receive cash, you
credit cash when you pay cash. In fact, it's more helpful to think of
debits as "the stuff on the left" and credits as "the stuff on the right"
than it is to try to figure out whether the transaction leaves you
richer or poorer. In the following list, "merchandise" means the
material you sell to your customers. If an entry is called the same
thing in both journal and ledger, there is only *one* item in the list. If
the entry has *two* names, the one in capital letters is the journal
entry, while the other one is the ledger entry.

SITUATION	DEBIT HERE	CREDIT HERE
Selling merchandise for cash	CASH	SALES
Buying merchandise for cash	PURCHASES	CASH
Buying anything you will not resell (office supplies)	GENERAL JOURNAL Specific account in ledger	CASH
Paying an expense	GENERAL JOURNAL Expenses	CASH
Getting income that is not from the sale of merchandise	CASH	GENERAL JOURNAL Interest, or other appropriate account
Selling merchandise on credit	GENERAL JOURNAL Individual customer's account	SALES
Customer pays for merchandise bought on credit	CASH	GENERAL JOURNAL Individual customer's account
You buy merchandise on credit	PURCHASES	GENERAL JOURNAL Individual creditor's account

SITUATION	DEBIT HERE	CREDIT HERE
Item sold for cash is returned	GENERAL JOURNAL Sales returns	CASH
Item sold on credit is returned	GENERAL JOURNAL Sales returns	GENERAL JOURNAL Individual customer's account
Someone borrows from you and gives you a note	GENERAL JOURNAL Notes receivable	GENERAL JOURNAL Individual customer's account
The borrower pays you	CASH	GENERAL JOURNAL Notes receivable
You borrow, and give the creditor a note	GENERAL JOURNAL Individual creditor's account	GENERAL JOURNAL Notes payable
You pay on the note	GENERAL JOURNAL Notes Payable	CASH

To keep track of all this, usual practice is to cross-reference each page. Account books and analysis pads give you a column to note the ledger page (or the ledger, if you have more than one). In the ledger, list the journal and the page the entry comes from (CD16 = page 16 of the Cash Disbursements Journal). That way, if your books don't balance, you can find the corresponding entry without tearing the books apart. Standard operating procedure is to check the ledger against the journal, and to start with the debits.

The simplest, cheapest (under one hundred dollars to set up) system is a manual one: entries are written in books, by hand. For a few hundred dollars more, you can get a "one-write" system which uses specially arranged cards with carbon strips. When you write on the card, you create a journal and a ledger entry at the same time. (One-write checkbooks are also available.) For five hundred to one thousand dollars a month, you can rent keypunch equipment to do your bookkeeping automatically, or use a computer service bureau. But unless you have many employees or an active business that generates a huge number of entries, the latter two expedients probably won't be necessary. If you consult an accountant before you start your business (an excellent idea), get the accountant's advice on setting up a bookkeeping system. This saves a great deal of time when you go back to the accountant to have your tax returns prepared. Your accounts will be in proper order and properly documented; the accountant won't have to dig through a shoebox of assorted receipts and other documents.

Mechanical and computer systems identify the individual accounts by number, not by name. You may want to do this even if you have a manual system—especially if you do the bookkeeping once a week or once a month, or if you hire a part-time bookkeeper occasionally. You can file receipts, sales slips, and other documents by account number, then prepare the journals and ledgers from the files. Group the accounts together in "families" with similar numbers. (For example, 100–199 for assets, 200–299 for liabilities, 300–399 for expenses—or you may prefer to use 300–399 for operating expenses, 400–499 for cost of sale expenses, because they are treated differently for tax purposes, then reserve 500–599 for income.) When you assign numbers, leave plenty available for later entries. For example:

100 CASH

120 INVENTORY

130 ACCOUNTS RECEIVABLE
    130.1 Jones & Solomon, Inc.
    130.2 Mitchell Services
    130.3 Fast-Freez

150 NOTES RECEIVABLE
    150.1 Bernard Hansen

160 PREPAID EXPENSES

170 BUSINESS EQUIPMENT

180 LAND AND BUILDINGS

185 SHORT-TERM INVESTMENTS

190 LONG-TERM INVESTMENTS

Or, you could assign 100 numbers to a category (accounts receivable) and assign an individual number to each account (167 = Miller Industries). It depends on the number of accounts you have, the number of entries in each, and how carefully you track them. In a retail store where most of the business is for cash or involves credit cards, the accounting considerations are different than they would be for a service business with 20 major and 55 minor clients, all of whom must be billed. Although the process of debiting one account and crediting another is constant, you can choose account descriptions and tracking procedures to suit your particular business. You may need to know the effect of a small price change of one component out of 137 used; you may not need to know anything except the amount of sales tax to remit and the amount you can draw without bouncing the rent check.

Accounting: In General

Bookkeeping is the process of writing down figures in an orderly way. Accounting is the science and art of interpreting them. The exchange of $14.95 for a shirt is straightforward enough—but how should the shirt factory's advertising budget be allocated? Should it be divided by the number of shirts produced, and lessen the taxable profit on each shirt? Should it be allocated to the shirts sold (though some were produced in an earlier year), or deducted each year? What if the bill arrives in March, covering a year's service, and is paid in August? How long will the button-making machine last? If some of the shirts are sewn with thread costing $.08 a spool and some with thread costing $.0933 a spool, how much does it cost to make a shirt?

Some of these questions have simple answers. The money you spend on advertising can simply be deducted in the year you pay it (if you're on the cash basis) or the year you have the obligation to pay it (if you're on the accrual basis). You don't have to divide it by the number of shirts. The IRS requires all businesses that have inventory (in other words, most businesses) to use the accrual basis. Money that people are obliged to pay you in 1983—whether they pay it in 1983, or at some other time, or never, is 1983 income. (If they never pay it, you get a bad-debt deduction in the year it becomes clear that they won't.) This is a somewhat subjective determination. You might consider that the debt is uncollectible in a profitable year when deductions come in especially handy. If the deadbeat ever pays up, you report the amount paid as income in the

year of the payment (for cash-basis taxpayers) or the year in which a
credible commitment to pay is made (for accrual-basis taxpayers).
Any deductible item you become obligated to pay in 1983 is a 1983
deduction. The good news is that you can get deductions for bills
you haven't paid; the bad news is that you pay taxes on income you
haven't received.

As for the button-making machine, the question of the length of
time you can use it has three varying answers. In practical terms, its
life-span depends on its condition when you bought it, how often
and how hard you use it, and how well you treat it. For accounting
purposes, the value of the machine must be reduced each year (depreciated) to cope with the fact that eventually a replacement will
be needed, and you must maintain a reserve for depreciation as an
accounting entry. The depreciation method must conform to generally accepted accounting principles. For tax purposes, the Accelerated Cost Recovery System (ACRS) assigns equipment like this a
useful life of five years, and sets the percentage of the machine's
cost you can use as a tax deduction each year. If it is an inexpensive
machine, you may even be able to "expense" it—that is, treat its
entire cost as a tax deduction. (More of this in Chapter Six.)

If you decide that the shirts were sewed with the cheaper thread
until the supply ran out, then the newer, more expensive thread was
used, you have a FIFO (first-in, first-out) accounting system. If you
assume that the newer thread was used, with the old thread remaining on the shelf, you use LIFO (last-in, first-out) accounting.
(FILO is only used in Greek restaurants.) Reasons for choosing one
or the other are discussed on page 166. Once you make the decision,
your taxes will be computed based on that decision—and not on the
actual vintage of the thread in the shirts.

In other words, accounting is a world view, or a related series of
world views, more like metaphysics than like chemistry. Your freedom to make decisions is not absolute, but limited by tax laws, the
common law of fraud, and GAAP (generally accepted accounting
principles). There is nevertheless a great deal of leeway, and questions such as "Am I making any money?" can have more than one
answer. It depends on the depreciation method and useful life chosen, how the inventory is valued, what kind of reserves are set aside
for bad debts and other misfortunes, how your accounts receivable
and payable are treated, and on many other questions.

As befits a world view, accounting has a vocabulary of its own.

The difficulty is that many of the terms used have other everyday meanings.

ACCOUNTS RECEIVABLE are amounts owed to you for merchandise sold on credit.

ACCOUNTS PAYABLE are amounts you owe for merchandise bought on credit; trade credit as well as charge cards is included.

ASSETS are things of benefit to the business. Assets are current if they are in cash, or can easily be converted into cash (e.g., Treasury bills). A fixed asset is used in the business for over one year, not converted into cash. Other assets, such as research and development, copyrights, and goodwill, don't fit into either category.

LIABILITY is an item the business will have to pay (e.g., a mortgage, an account payable). A current liability is due within one year; an accrued liability has not been billed yet; a contingent liability (for example, the amount you'll have to pay if you lose a lawsuit) may never have to be paid. Liabilities are fixed costs. They must be paid whether or not you produce or sell anything or perform any billable services.

EXPENSE (e.g., salaries, typing paper) is a variable cost—you can lay off the workers or stop typing if there's no business activity.

EXPENSE, used as a verb, means to charge an item against current income in this year only.

CAPITALIZE is the alternative to expensing. It is spreading the cost over the life of the object. Because people have a tendency to opt for immediate gratification, the IRS requires you to capitalize damn near anything that can be kept alive for more than a year. (More details in Chapter Six.)

DEPRECIATION is the accounting response to the fact that golden trucks and hammers must, like chimney sweepers, come to dust. The IRS will not let you deduct the price of the equipment in the year you bought it (even if you paid cash). You must apportion the cost among the years the item will be used. If you buy it in May, you get only 7/12 of a year's depreciation in the year you buy it. On the books, depreciation is balanced by an account called reserve for depreciation. This account can be purely fictitious; you don't have to squirrel the money away.

AMORTIZATION is the equivalent of depreciation for intangibles such as patents, copyrights, licenses, and goodwill. These things do not "wear out" in the same way equipment does, but they do become less valuable over time.

CASH FLOW CHART:
Where the Money Goes

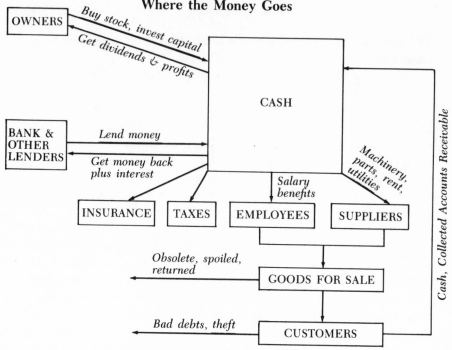

FOLLOWING THE MONEY:
Bookkeeping and Accounting Sequence

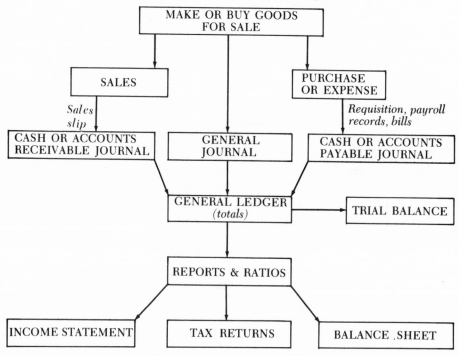

PAID-IN CAPITAL is the amount put into the business by the stockholders, minus the par value of the stock.

WORKING CAPITAL is the business' current assets minus its current liabilities.

Your journals and ledgers alone give you enough information to fill out tax returns. If all you want to do is stay out of jail, you won't need any other records (well, keep the supporting documents in case you get audited). But if you want to analyze your financial performance, cut costs, make projections, budget realistically, or convince a potential lender, stockholder, or buyer that your business is sound, you'll need financial statements and reports.

Money flows both to and from owners and lenders. Employees and suppliers get money, but this money is used to make salable goods so more money comes into the system. There are some "leaks"—insurance (except in case of calamity), taxes, unsalable goods, bad debts, and stolen goods don't bring money into the system. Bookkeeping and accounting keep track of the cash flow; security plugs the leaks.

Statements and Reports

When you start your business, it will be some time before you need statements and reports, simply because it will be some time before you have figures to analyze. Usually, a lender requires income statements and balance sheets as part of a loan application. Many books about business start-ups advise you to prepare projected statements, showing the money you expect to make and the amounts you expect to spend. (These are called "pro forma" reports.) To me, this seems about as realistic as figuring out what you're going to serve Robert Redford for breakfast in bed. I don't think bankers are any more impressed by these fantasies. If you manage a public corporation (highly unlikely if you're reading this book), you are obliged to render an annual report to your stockholders. The Briarpatch, a group of countercultural entrepreneurs (most of them are in California) suggests open records—open to anyone who wants to see them—as a hallmark of honest business. I can't imagine anyone wanting to see the books, so you might as well be a sport.

The two most common financial reports are the income statement (also called the P & L, for profit and loss, although you have only one at a time), and the balance sheet.

The income statement is simply:

NET SALES
− COST OF SALES
GROSS PROFIT (aka GROSS TRADING PROFIT)

GROSS PROFIT
− OPERATING EXPENSES
OPERATING PROFIT

OPERATING PROFIT
+ OTHER INCOME
− OTHER EXPENSES
NET PROFIT (NET LOSS)—figures in parentheses are negative

NET PROFIT
− INCOME TAXES
AFTERTAX NET PROFIT (AFTERTAX NET LOSS)

There, wasn't that simple? Of course, there are a few complications. "Expenses" are things like rent, salaries, and depreciation—costs of doing business other than the costs of buying and handling merchandise for resale. The cost of sales is computed indirectly rather than by trying to allocate wages, stamps, and the cost of new fixtures to each item sold. For income statement purposes:

YOUR OPENING INVENTORY
+ GOODS YOU BUY TO RESELL
− GOODS YOU BUY TO RESELL, BUT RETURN
− DISCOUNT YOU RECEIVE
+ FREIGHT CHARGES YOU PAY
− ENDING INVENTORY
COST OF SALES

The opening inventory is the amount you had on hand before the period for which the income statement is computed; the ending inventory is the stuff left at the end. Note, therefore, that an income statement covers a period of time (a month, a year), but a balance sheet is an analysis of the situation that exists at a particular moment.

Accounting was developed at a time when most businesses were manufacturers or retailers. In today's service-dominated economy, some of the concepts seem a little haywire. A service business' P & L is skeletal: the gross receipts, minus costs of doing business (rent, salaries, equipment, utilities, debt service).

In the balance sheet, assets (written on the left) equal liabilities plus proprietorship (also called capital), which are written on the right. When you draw up a balance sheet, your inventory does NOT include: supplies and merchandise not intended for resale; merchandise you accept on consignment; materials you have ordered but will get later, and to which you do not yet have title; and goods already sold to a customer who has title to them.

Proprietorship is the amount left over, after the bills are paid, for the sole proprietor or partners; capital is the amount of stock outstanding, plus the retained earnings plowed back into the business. It seems a little peculiar to consider the profits as a liability, but this oddity stems from the need to make both sides come out even.

A balance sheet is usually drawn up with a line between the left and the right sides:

ASSETS	LIABILITIES
Cash ....$	Accounts Payable.................$
Accounts Receivable.............$	Notes Payable ....$
Inventory ....$	Accruals ....$
• Raw Materials ....$	
• Finished Goods ....$	TOTAL LIABILITIES ....$
Prepaid Expenses ....$	
Net Fixed Assets.................$	CAPITAL
• Fixed Assets...............$	Common Stock ....$
—• Depreciation ....$	Retained Earnings ....$
	• Net Aftertax Profit ....$
TOTAL ASSETS ....$	—• Dividends ....$
	TOTAL CAPITAL OR PROPRIETORSHIP ....$

Note that a balance sheet doesn't tell you everything. It doesn't include the cost of items paid for in cash, or bills already paid (because they've been shifted out of accounts receivable). A business that buys a lot of poorly chosen inventory or useless machinery will have lots of assets, because the stuff will sit on the shelf and the equipment will never need replacement (because it will never be used). A business like this will have a great balance sheet—all the way to bankruptcy court.

Accounting theory differentiates among three kinds of accounts:

- Real accounts (debts and assets)
- Nominal accounts (which track activities such as sales)
- Proprietorship (or capital)

The nominal accounts (a funny way to look at it, but there you are) appear only on the income statement; the real and proprietorship accounts appear on the balance sheet.

You can get a lot of information about a business—your own, or one you plan to buy or invest in—by reading the balance sheet in conjunction with the income statement. You can get more information by comparing documents from year to year. For example, the balance sheet shows the amount available to the owners—not whether they took the money or reinvested it in the business. If cash goes down from one year to the next, they probably took the money; if cash or other assets go up, they probably reinvested it. But should they have reinvested more or less? Is production being hampered by outmoded equipment? Is the business more profitable because borrowed money increased production and sales, or are interest payments outpacing the increased income? Questions like these are answered by using figures from the income statement and balance sheet to compute and analyze ratios, and to compare this year's ratios to past years' ratios.

Ratio Analysis

The income statement gives you the business' net sales and aftertax profit for a particular time period. The balance sheet yields the total current assets, the accounts receivable, inventory, total fixed assets (tangible things like machinery), current liabilities, total liabilities, and net worth. Working capital is defined as current assets minus current liabilities.

The "current ratio" is current assets divided by current liabilities. Twice as many assets as liabilities is considered an acceptable proportion. The "acid-test" ratio is current assets other than inventory divided by current liabilities. Inventories are excluded because they may have to be marked down.

Liquidity is measured by dividing the value (after depreciation) of the fixed assets by the company's tangible net worth. The two figures should be about equal; if the proportion of fixed assets is much higher, the business may not have enough cash to pay its debts.

To see if the business is head over heels in debt, divide the total debt by the company's net worth. If debt is over seventy-five percent of net worth (probably, over sixty percent in these days of high interest) repayment problems are likely.

You can find out how fast you turn over your inventory (the number of "turns") each year by dividing net sales by the inventory on hand at the time of calculation, and you can see how much of your capital is tied up in inventory by dividing inventory by net working capital. To see how your operation compares with your competitors', check trade publications, or consult your trade association; many of them conduct a survey every year and publish average figures and ratios. (Not everyone is completely candid in these surveys, but anonymity lessens the temptation to show off, and exaggeration is curbed by the need to plead poverty around April 15 and when price increases are due. Things more or less balance out.) Dun & Bradstreet publishes *Key Business Ratios* annually.

Dividing earnings by sales gives your pretax profit as a percentage of sales—ten percent is an acceptable figure, but more is better.

If your ratios deviate from the industry average, your troubles could be caused by a slow start, by inefficiency, or by unusually *high* efficiency. A discount store usually has a lower rent, decorating, and salary budget than a conventional retailer of the same kind of merchandise; it often has a higher advertising budget and a smaller selection of merchandise, with a much faster turnover of inventory. To compare the profitability of two businesses, or the profit potential of two business possibilities, you can use the Profitability Index:

$$P = A \times B / C \times D$$

P is profitability; A is the volume (number of units); B is the price at which one unit is sold, minus the cost of that unit; C is the investment in the project; D is the time (measured as a fraction of a year) devoted to that project.

If the discount store devotes four months to marketing lipsticks, at an investment of $60,000, and sells 100,000 of them at $1.50 each, and if they pay 50¢ each for them, $P = 100,000 \times (\$1.50 - \$.50) / \$60,000 \times \frac{1}{3} = \$100,000/\$20,000 = 5$.

If the regular retail store spends a year at the same task, sells 10,000 lipsticks at $4.00, buying them at $1.00 apiece and investing $15,000 overall, $P = 10,000 \times (\$4.00 - \$1.00) / 15,000 \times 1 = \$30,000/\$15,000 = 2$.

Therefore, the discount operation is more profitable, although the retail store has a lower investment and a higher markup. If the retail store sold its lipsticks faster or marked them up higher, its profitability picture might improve; but it could also lose sales.

If this index is used as a forecasting tool, time is not used as a measure of inventory turnover but of hours, weeks, and months spent on one project and diverted from another.

Another way to analyze the business is to look at return on investment (ROI). Return on equity, one form of ROI, is the net aftertax profit divided by the owner's equity (the "proprietorship" figure on the balance sheet). In public corporations, this figure averages twelve percent. Why not give up on corporations and plunk everything into a money market fund? For one thing, the ship sinks if everyone rushes to starboard. For another thing, investment in a corporation implies the possibility of capital growth: as the company becomes more prosperous and accumulates more assets, a part-share in the company, or shares of stock, becomes more valuable.

Return on invested capital (averaging about nine percent) is the net aftertax profit plus interest on long-term debt, divided by the owner's equity plus long-term debt. This is an ambiguous measure because it combines good news (higher profit) and bad news (higher debt). With interest rates (even long-term rates) at unprecedented highs, this measure is especially important because it demonstrates whether or not the borrowed money is effective in generating profit.

Inventory Accounting

At the very start of a business, you can't be too scientific about inventory levels, because you have no experience to go on. (You can consult inventory ratios, helpful colleagues, or management consultants, but their figures will only approximate your situation.) After a while, you'll have a profile of your own sales and sales trends, though you'll need at least a year to understand the effect of seasonal buying. Financial writer Albert J. Lowry says that the cost of keeping $100 of merchandise in inventory for a year ranges between $15–$25 when you factor in the cost of storage space, handling, interest on loans to buy the stuff, deterioration, and obsolescence. You can lower these figures significantly, if you buy for cash or on trade credit, and if the storage space is your aunt's garage in Secaucus. Still and all, it *is* money. On the other hand, if you're out of an item, unless you can talk the customer into substituting another item, you've lost that sale and perhaps the goodwill built up with that customer.

A statistical tool called the Gaussian curve can be used to predict sales of a given item if you know the average monthly sales. If you sell an average of 10 alpaca sweaters a month, the odds of selling fewer than 5 or more than 15 in a given month are only 5%. (Of course, there was the tragic case of the statistician who drowned in a pond with an average depth of only three feet; and Christmas ornaments don't follow the same pattern of sales as, say, pillowcases.) You should have adequate stock 95% of the time by keeping a reserve equaling 1.6 times the square root of expected sales. If you expect to sell 25 units/month, you should stock 33 units: 25, plus a safety margin of 8 (1.6 × 5).

Another approach is to use an OTB (Open to Buy) formula. For example, if you sell 7,500 jars of imported marmalade a year, turn over your inventory 5 times a year, and expect to sell 1,000 jars next month (December, with heavy entertaining and gift-giving); and if you have 800 jars on hand and open (unfilled) orders for 50 jars, your OTB, or desired inventory level, is:

(Total sales/turnover) + anticipated sales for coming month − (inventory on hand + open orders), or (7,500/5) + 1,000 − (800 + 50) = 1,500 + 1,000 − 850 = 1,650.

You should have 1,650 jars on hand to meet the December demand without depleting your stock; since you have 850 jars on hand or ordered, you need to order 800 more.

This degree of sophistication is only worth bothering with if the material involved is fairly expensive and is significant to your business as a whole. A boutique needs to keep better control over its supply of dresses than over its supply of paper clips. Errors in the former cases are both more significant and more costly than in the latter case.

You can also set an automatic ordering level (600 boxes of transistors a month), and review the order sheets each month. You can increase, decrease, or omit an order if stockpiles are particularly high or low. If an item has a long lead time for orders (imports, crafts ordered from a craftsman who has a backlog), make sure your order is large enough to last a full order cycle. If you sell 15 pottery bowls a month, and orders take 4 months to fill, reorder 60 at a time when your inventory dips to 60.

Inventory accounting also covers inventory valuation. The two accepted systems are FIFO (first in, first out) and LIFO (last in, first out). I use FIFO because it's easier, and because I really do use the first items first. However, choosing between FIFO and LIFO is purely an accounting decision; the IRS doesn't send an agent into your stockroom to measure the thickness of the dust on your inventory.

In a stable economy, there would be little difference between the two, because prices wouldn't change much. In an inflationary or deflationary economy—and especially when prices fluctuate—the choice makes a great deal of difference.

If your opening inventory of an item is 100 units, which you bought for a dollar apiece, you buy 200 during the year for $1.50 each, and sell 150 at $3.00, and if you use FIFO, your cost of sales is $175. You are deemed to have sold the 100 old ones ($100) and 50 new ones ($75). Therefore, your pretax income is $275 minus overhead ($3.00 × 150 − $175); your aftertax income depends on your bracket.

If you use LIFO, you sell 150 of the new items, which cost you $1.50 each; your pretax income is $450 − $225, or $225 less overhead.

If you use FIFO, your income is plumper—but your taxes are higher. LIFO makes your earnings per share look anemic (a real concern if you're trying to sell stock, or your business); but your available cash is greater because the taxes are lower, because nominal income is lower. If prices go down and you use LIFO, you won't have an accurate picture of the cost of goods sold, because you'll be using more expensive, older inventory but deducting only the later, lower cost. For example, if you pay $1.00 a unit in January, and $.50 a unit in June, the deduction is limited to $.50 a unit until the number of units sold equals the number of units purchased in June.

During inflation, FIFO overstates paper profits; cash takes a beating when items have to be replaced.

Cash Control, Forecasting, Budgeting

During the first year, or the first few years, entrepreneurs spend most of their time dealing with crises as they arise. After a while, sales figures and expense figures are available. Once it seems likely that the business will survive, that survival can be made more likely by planning and budgeting, and by making optimum use of cash. "Cash" in a business is not necessarily synonymous with "money." A shop full of shiny, new equipment improves the balance sheet and provides trouble-free operations, but it won't pay the electric bill. A seasonal business can be quite prosperous when the yearly figures are computed, but desperately strapped for cash before the high-earnings period. Usually, it's worth taking advantage of a trade discount for prompt payment; but not if you have to borrow at high interest rates to pay the invoice. You can also control cash by:

- Sending out your invoices faster
- Speeding up your collection process
- Using night deposit boxes to get your money into the bank faster
- Paying late in the day, and on Friday or the end of the month, to take advantage of the float
- Keeping your checking balance low and parking spare funds in an interest-paying account: even better, invested in T-bills, Ginnie Maes, or money market funds

Compare every year's figures with the budget for that year. If you managed to bring anything in under budget, how did you do it? When you went over budget, was the budget unrealistic, or was the business run wastefully or inefficiently? Were there factors you should have taken into account, but didn't? Analyze sales trends by item: often a company's improved profit picture masks the fact that some items are profitable and others are losers.

In cost analysis, price is defined as the direct cost of materials, plus the direct cost of labor, plus the cost of running the operation, plus profit. In turn, direct material cost equals the cost of subcontracted items plus raw materials plus purchased parts. Because it's very hard to determine general and administrative costs directly, these costs are usually estimated as a percentage of the total of material, labor, and factory costs. The Small Business Administration or your trade association can provide average figures and percentages.

In order to see where your budget deviates from reality, and to see if your problem lies in bad purchasing or inefficient production, compare the budgeted cost of raw materials per unit to the actual cost, and find out your scheduled purchases and the number of units you actually bought. The "budget cost" is the hypothetical quantity times the hypothetical price. The "actual cost" is the real cost times the number of units you really did buy. The purchasing department (or you, in your capacity as buyer) is responsible for the price variation (actual price minus budgeted price) times the real quantity; production is responsible for the variation in quantity (budgeted quantity minus quantity bought, or vice versa) times the budgeted price.

If the budget calls for 150 pounds of an industrial chemical at $.49 a pound, the budget cost is $73.50. If you only use 143 pounds at $.52, the actual cost is $74.36. The variation in cost is −$.86— that is, $.86 over budget. But the responsibility for going over belongs to purchasing: at $.02 a pound overrun × 143 pounds, purchasing is responsible for −$2.86. Production, saving 7 pounds at $.52 a pound, saved $3.64. Production more than achieved its goal, but purchasing fell short. Next year, either the budget will have to be raised and price increases anticipated better, or purchasing must become more efficient by making better use of discounts or doing better comparison shopping.

If you deal with thousands of components or ingredients a year, and monitor each one closely, you won't have time to do anything else. It makes more sense to concentrate on the most important items. "ABC budgeting" is a simple way to do this: a small change in the price, or your use, of an A item has a large impact on your profit (e.g., ground beef in a luncheonette). A B item has a moderate impact; a C item a slight impact. You might give 60% of planning time to A items, 25% to Bs, 15% to Cs.

A slightly more elaborate way to do this is to establish a high-value list. For materials, you list everything involved in a product—including nuts, bolts, and pencils—the unit price, and the amount of each item. (If prices change, use that same accounting assumption—LIFO or FIFO—you use for tax purposes.) Then compute the total cost (unit cost × usage) for each item, and arrange them in descending order. The items at the top of the list are A items; and they're not always the ones you would expect. You can also make up a labor high-value list by computing the number of hours used times the wage rate for each operation, and adding overhead costs. Again, the items at the top of the list deserve more attention than those at the bottom.

Once the past has been analyzed, it's time to make plans for the future. At the simplest level, you can get a weighted average figure for estimated profit (or estimated costs, sales, or anything else) by determining the worst-case figure, the most probable figure, and the most optimistic estimate. P (for pessimistic) is the worst case, M the most probable, O the most optimistic. The weighted average is:

$$O + 4M + P / 6.$$

One level of complexity up is the formula for determining the priority of a project:

$$V = AR - OC / IC$$

V is the value of the project; AR is its annual return, OC is its ongoing cost (cost per year once the project is well established); IC is the initial cost. You'll get a fairer picture if you take the average return and cost over several years, because a new product or process takes time to win adherents. If V is less than 1 (a dollar of return for a dollar of investment), the project is not worthwhile unless substantial return can be expected later, or unless there are other benefits (publicity, research and development).

The figures for costs and return are projected (less kindly, they're guesses), so the less accurate your projections are, the less useful the final figure will be.

With the same caveat, you can use a decision tree to choose between or among alternatives. You set out the alternatives, give the probability of each, and assign a numerical value to each outcome. Usually, the value of 10 is assigned to the worst result, 20 to a moderate result, 30 to the best (or 10, 20, 30, 40 if the tree has four branches). But you can go a little crazy once the tree goes beyond three choices; more elaborate exercises should be left to a computer. Most of the time, the worst that can happen is a disappointing sales figure; but if the outcome is really terrible (e.g., the plant blows up, all your products are declared illegal), you can assign a negative figure and reduce the other benefits of the course of conduct.

The probability figures have to add up to 100%, because something has to happen. To make the arithmetic easier, the percentages are usually expressed as decimals adding up to 1.

More specifically, let's say you have to decide whether to boost your sales by advertising more, cutting prices, or both. You think there's a 20% chance (.2) that advertising will help; a 40% chance (.4) that price-cutting will help; and a 40% chance (.4) that both will help. You aren't too optimistic about doing both, because you're afraid the ads, which focus on your quality goods and personal service, may conflict with the price-cutting drive.

The tree looks like this:

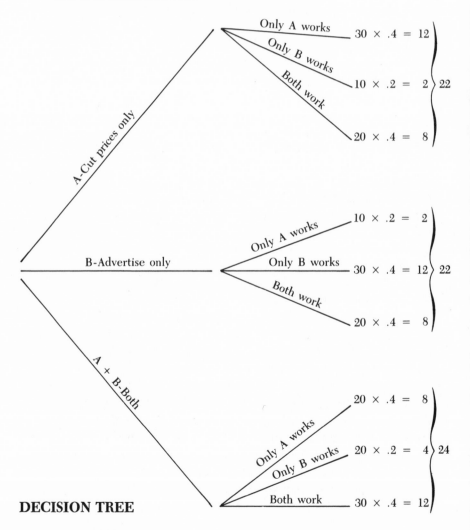

DECISION TREE

If only A works and you do B, this is a worst-case (10) situation; if only A works and you do A, you're home free (30). If both work and you only did A, this is a medium (20) result, because you didn't take full advantage of the opportunities.

As you can see, the decision-tree procedure favors using both of the alternatives (since you don't get a negative response; both alternatives work). However, if you do both, you'll spend more money. You can extend the decision tree by dividing the final "point scores" (in this case, 22, 22, and 24) by the cost of the alternative. If it costs $10,000 for a stepped-up advertising campaign and $45,000 for storewide price reductions, the "cost per point" of advertising is much lower; the "cost per point" of doing both is even higher. So, if you want to play the percentages, do both; if you want the most bang for your buck, choose the advertising campaign only.

You can also use a two-branched decision tree if your alternatives are mutually exclusive (you can't open one new plant simultaneously in California and Ohio; if you sell to Israel, you can forget about selling to Libya).

Once you're forcasting the future, you might as well budget. You can do this by listing each item (wages, taxes, rent, each item or each class of raw materials) and figuring out how much you intend to spend next year. If you worked out your unit cost of production, you can adjust that figure for inflation, then multiply by the number of units you expect to produce. You can take the old budget and simply index every item for inflation; or you can decide which items need to be increased (more advertising, a new piece of equipment) and which can be cut back (overtime when business is slow, production of items that don't sell well), then adjust these figures for inflation. Or, you can figure out the amount of money you expect to have available, then figure out the percentage each item deserves. You'll probably have to do this several times, since the first budget will be at least 357% of available funds.

Zero-base budgeting got a flurry of attention when Jimmy Carter was President and sank back into obscurity when he left the Oval Office; but it's a tool with potential usefulness for Republicans and Democrats alike.

Zero-base budgeting assumes that all spending has to be justified each year. There are no automatic allocations and certainly no automatic increases.

Every activity is described in a "decision package" giving the alternatives, what each one costs, the benefits of each, and what would happen if the activity were discontinued altogether. Alternatives are structured as 1 of X—the bare-bones minimum; 2 of X—a slightly higher level of operations; 3 of X, and so on, with running totals. For a package of office renovation, there might be four levels:

1 of 4: replace broken venetian blinds, paint
over stains, replace broken swivel chair.   Cost: $200

2 of 4: also buy 2 new desks, plants, repaint
reception area.   Added cost: $300
Cumulative cost: $500

3 of 4: buy modular sofa for reception area,
repaint rest of office, buy refrigerator,
replace venetian blinds with
energy-saving blinds.   Added cost: $1,000
Cumulative cost: $1,500

4 of 4: new desks for everyone, rug for President's
office, new lamps for desks, 3 new light fixtures.
Added cost: $2,500
Cumulative cost: $4,000

These packages assume a greater acquaintance with the Salvation Army than with first-line office furniture showrooms. A less financially strapped business would assign higher figures to these packages.

The budgeter compiles the budget by arranging the decision packages in approximate order of importance (approximate, because it doesn't pay to worry whether Office Supplies is number 27 or 29, as long as it comes well below Salaries, Raw Materials, and Rent). Given a projected figure for the total funds available, the budgeter uses the benefits described in each package to decide the level of funding. If new equipment seems likely to improve productivity, the budgeter may decide to go to level 4 of 5; Office Refreshments may be lucky to get 2 of 8 (no Perrier this year, either). Again, it's easy to decide that funds far in excess of those available are absolutely necessary. If you can't get the money somehow, the budget will have to be revised downward. And once again, a scientifically worked-out budget based on unrealistic figures is useful only as a piece of speculative fiction.

Credit and Collections

Unquestionably the easiest, safest credit policy is to demand cash on the barrelhead. It's easy, you never get stiffed (unless you accept checks, and someone gives you a bad one), you don't have the trouble and expense of billing, you don't have to disclose anything, and it's nondiscriminatory. In a period of rapid inflation, the money you get back after a lag of several months is worth less than the money you could have gotten earlier. If the inflation rate is 15%, $25,000 due January 1 and paid February 1 has a real value of $24,688; $24,375 if paid on March 1, and only $23,125 if paid on September 1. If you had gotten the money when it was due, you could have paid your own bills, expanded your plant, or invested the money. Therefore, you lose twice. In fact, when interest rates are high and bank loans hard to get, many businesses finance their inventory, or even expansion, by stocking up and paying bills very, very slowly rather than by taking out a loan and paying cash.

On the other hand, granting credit has obvious advantages. Business customers are used to having at least a month to pay; they expect it and may refuse to deal with a supplier who demands cash. Willing or not, seasonal businesses don't *have* cash in the off-season.

The human brain has an interesting psychological mechanism which doesn't identify credit purchases as costing real money. People therefore buy more on credit and are more tolerant of price increases. If you do grant credit, trade credit has quite different procedures and pitfalls from consumer credit. The two paths come together when you have collection problems, and when collection becomes impossible and you're faced with bad debts.

When you grant trade credit (sell to other businesses on credit), you face two major decisions: whether a particular business is entitled to credit at all, and how much. The proverb is that credit depends on the 5Cs: character (whether the business is run by scrupulous people who intend to pay their debts), capacity (number of years the business has operated at a profit), capital (its debt-equity ratio), collateral, and condition (whether your customer's industry is expanding or contracting).

You can get credit information on larger, older businesses from

Dun & Bradstreet, The Lyon Red Book, or specialized industry sources like the *Fruit and Produce Credit Book* or the *Red Book* for jewelers. Dun & Bradstreet analyzes a potential debtor's size, from 5A (multibillion-dollar corporation) to GG (very, very small), and its credit rating from 1 (excellent) to 4 (bad news). Some large libraries subscribe to D & B. If you have a strong relationship with a bank (often a euphemism for owing them a lot of money), you can ask the vice-president servicing your account to tell the clerk who files the D & B reports to let you look at them.

You can also participate in the Credit Interchange Bureaus run by the National Association of Credit Management, 1104 Arcade Building, St. Louis, MO 63101. The interchange gathers information on the transactions between a particular buyer and a particular seller: how long an account has been open, terms of sale, amount owed, amount past due, and prior payment history. Not all large businesses pay their bills promptly; they may be overextended or may feel their business is valuable enough to make suppliers forgive their slow payment. Most small business owners are as honest as you are (though this is not necessarily saying anything) and mere lack of size or years in business is not always evidence of business instability or bad credit risk.

The most common trade credit terms are 2/10 net 30: 2% discount if the bill is paid within 10 days, with full payment expected in 30 days. EOM means end of the month, so net 10 EOM on something shipped in December is supposed to be paid by January 10. A customer who makes a lot of small purchases scattered throughout the month may be granted MOM treatment—anything bought before the middle of the month is treated as if it had been bought on the 15th; purchases after the 15th are treated as if they were made the first of the following month.

Sometimes large orders get 30/60/90 treatment: one third of the price is due 30 days after shipment, one third 60 days after shipment, the rest 90 days, with no discounts for earlier payment. It's very common for customers to take discounts they're not entitled to, if and when they get around to paying. Your reaction depends on the value of that customer's account. It may be worthwhile to shrug and let them get away with it, bill them for the difference, or notify them that you'll have to stop selling to them unless they start paying on your terms. It is not customary to charge interest on late payments, but there's no reason why you can't if the interest rate is below the state's usury threshold and the interest provision is clearly spelled out in your contract with the customer. But your customer may prefer a more gentlemanly supplier who is prepared to be magnanimous about late payments.

The other dimension of trade credit is the amount of credit to extend. You can't tie up too much of your own capital in credit sales—particularly not in credit sales to one company. And, while you may sympathize with the problems of an overextended company, you don't want to share them. One approach is to ask potential credit customers for balance sheets or to use D & B or other published information. In the clothing business, most suppliers won't make a credit sale that exceeds five percent of the customer's net worth; in other industries, the conventional limit is ten percent of net worth, or twenty percent of working capital. Normally, sales growth is to be applauded, and large orders are cause for celebration. However, when credit is involved, you should be cautious when orders from a particular customer increase suddenly—especially if the orders were unsolicited. It may be a recognition of your superb product line; but it may be an attempt by a poverty-stricken business to find new suppliers who don't have a pile of unpaid bills.

Although there are other forms of consumer credit, the three you are most likely to encounter are:

- Letting customers run a tab, billing them once a month
- Taking credit cards (e.g., MasterCard, Visa, American Express, Diners Club)
- Selling merchandise in return for installment payments—the popular name is "selling on time"; the technical term is "closed-end credit"

Customers who can run a tab feel benevolent toward your establishment, and are more likely to buy a round of drinks (or the equivalent product) for their friends than are customers who must produce spot cash. Usually, no interest is charged, and customers are expected to be polite enough to pay promptly. For the system to work at all, you need good records. Make sure that customers sign for every transaction, and that each transaction is explained and the price stated. Bill promptly and regularly. The easiest way to do this is to send a copy of the tab, refreshing the customer's recollection and verifying that s/he really signed for the stuff. (I do all my photocopying at a shop that lets me run a tab. It took six months for them to send me a bill, and now they're three months behind in billing me. I pay my bills promptly, but I'm not a telepath. Their cash flow must be atrocious. The situation isn't ideal for me either: it's nice to take advantage of the float, but the size of the eventual bill is daunting.)

Accepting credit cards has two disadvantages: it does cost money (a percentage of the amount billed, and in some cases a fee for entering the system) and you have to wait for the credit card company to send you your share of the take. But customers buy more, you have less cash in the till (less temptation for robbers), and you don't have to trust anyone except the credit card company. The card company provides you with sales slips and a cute little machine to use them with. You send the slips to the card company; they take out their cut and send you the rest of the money. They, not you, face the trouble and risks of collection; in that sense, it works like factoring.

If people want to pay by check, you can set aside a certain amount as a reserve, or get insurance. If you deal with large sums, it could be worthwhile to subscribe to a service like Check Telecredit (1901 Avenue of the Stars, Los Angeles, CA 90067). You pay a fee (in late 1981, $5 a month and $.75 per check or 4% of the face value, whichever is higher) for the right to call their toll-free number ([800] 421–0839) and give a potential check customer's name and driver's license number. Check Telecredit lets you know if it has any adverse information; if not, it approves the check. If the check bounces, Check Telecredit will reimburse you up to $600.

If you grant closed-end credit, you will have to comply with the Federal Truth-in-Lending Law and with Regulation Z, which is the Federal Reserve Board's amplification of Truth-in-Lending. Your state may have its own demands for candor.

A closed-end credit sale is one in which the buyer buys one or more objects at a time, for personal or family (not business) purposes, and agrees to pay for the merchandise in four or more installments, to pay interest, or both. (The law also applies to the provision of services, but the installment sale of merchandise is much more common.) Both the seller and the buyer know at the beginning how much merchandise is involved, and what the price is. The seller also knows the other costs of the sale and is compelled by Federal law to tell the buyer. Selling a refrigerator for $100 down and $100 a month is closed-end credit; giving someone a revolving charge account is not. (The revolving charge account is a form of open-end credit—a subject which, to the eternal gratitude of both writer and reader, will not be covered here.)

The "agreement" is important. If you allow someone to pay in installments—if the initiative comes from you—you have to go through the whole song and dance described in Regulation Z. But if someone owes you $300, you try to collect it, and the debtor strings you along by paying you off a little at a time, you can't be penalized for failing to disclose.

This is a complex and technical area of the law, but in broad outline, you have to disclose:

- The amount financed, which is more or less the purchase price plus certain fees
- The finance charge, which is the interest plus certain other fees
- The annual percentage rate, which is approximately the same as the interest rate
- The total of payments, which equals the amount financed plus the finance charge
- The number of payments, their due dates, and the amount of each payment
- Security provisions (if and when you can repossess the merchandise, or other property the buyer puts up as collateral)
- An explanation of any charges you assess for late payments
- An explanation of any restrictions or penalties on prepayment

All these disclosures have to be typed or printed together, and they have to be separated from other information in the contract or security agreement they appear in. If the buyer takes out credit insurance (which pays the unpaid balance when the buyer dies or becomes disabled), there are additional, complicated disclosure requirements. In addition, the Equal Credit Opportunity Act forbids discrimination in credit sales based on a person's race, nationality, or sex; you must give married women equal access to credit that you would give a single woman, or a married or single male; and you can't ask a woman about her family plans or contraceptive practices as a condition of granting credit. The Fair Credit Billing Act lets consumers have access to their credit files and lets them challenge statements they feel are incorrect; it also requires credit-card issuers to let customers challenge their bills without penalty.

In short, this stuff is nothing to fool around with. The Federal Reserve Board publishes standard formats for Truth-in-Lending documents. You don't have to use these, but you can't be accused of a Truth-in-Lending violation if you do.

If you do business in Connecticut, Hawaii, Maine, Minnesota, New Jersey, or New York, the sales documents (like all documents involved in consumer transactions) must be in plain English. Plain English is a metaphysical concept not subject to easy definition, and the laws vary somewhat. But, in essence, your documents must:

- Explain technical terms in layman's language
- Be divided into sections
- Have captions for each section
- Use everyday words—short words and short sentences, if possible
- Be printed in type large enough to be read easily

If all goes well, your customers—whether businesses or consumers—will pay promptly. However, this is not the usual case: some will pay slowly, some not at all. Nobody will pay without being billed, so you should give billing a high priority. Then you can keep track by maintaining an aging schedule for large accounts: chart which accounts are paid on time, which are 30 days behind in payment, which are 60 to 90 days behind. Then you can concentrate on the largest overdue bills, those with the most mold on them, or some hybrid rating system. Update the aging schedule each month.

Your average collection period is computed by dividing your average accounts receivable by your annual sales, and mutiplying the result by 365 (or 360, to make the arithmetic easier). You should calculate this figure several times a year. A shorter collection period is good; but if the collection period lengthens, you should step up your collection efforts. Otherwise, you can develop a shortage of working capital as your own bills have to be paid.

The conventional strategy is to send out a series of collection letters ranging in tone from whining to bullying. The advantage of collection letters is that they don't cost very much to send. The disadvantage is that a clerk in your customer's Accounts Payable department is unlikely to be overcome by tears reading of your pathetic plight and is just as unlikely to feel threatened by your dark hints of "legal action" or "pursuing further remedies."

Usually consumers don't pay on time for one of two reasons: they want to beat you out of the money or they would pay you if they could scrape up the money somehow. (If it's any consolation, the collection industry estimates that only three percent of the population consists of real deadbeats; the other ninety-seven percent will cough up eventually.)

What I would suggest is that you send out *one* form letter asking what the problem is and courteously asking for payment. Sometimes the buyer is withholding payment because there is a legitimate dispute. Sometimes the buyer is fabricating a dispute to put off payment. Make note of the more creative excuses you are given; they'll come in handy when you owe money.

Try to get a definite commitment as to how much will be sent when, and establish a "paper trail" showing the nature of the transaction and how much is involved. Make it very clear that, if you accept smaller amounts, the amount is a partial payment and *not* a settlement under which you agree to forget about the rest of the money. If the customer is a consumer rather than a business, and if you agree to accept repayment in four or more installments, you have to comply with the Truth-in-Lending disclosure requirements.

If you are gifted with a fair amount of effrontery, and the customer is physically within range, you can say, "Don't bother to mail the check—I'll come right over to pick it up." If you don't believe the check has been mailed, and you have even greater effrontery, you can ask the customer to stop payment on that check (offer to pay the bank fees) and drop by to pick up another check. If you *really* want to collect a bill from a business customer, you can find out where the business keeps its bank account, then have your bank draw a draft against that account. If your debtor protests, it's a confession that the business is not paying its bills. That business will never, never order from you again—but you don't want to develop a large clientele by virtue of giving your merchandise or services away. "We cannot ship your latest order until your account has been settled in full," wrote the creditor. "Cancel our order," the indignant debtor fired back, "we cannot wait that long for the merchandise."

After you send the letter and fail to get the check, my advice is that you stop screwing around and sue. This costs money—the Commercial Law League of America recommends that collections attorneys and agencies charge 15% of the first $750 at stake, 10% of the balance, with a minimum of $15—but you may be able to find a struggling young attorney who will accept a retainer (a yearly fee in exchange for handling all your collections work). The lawyer can accumulate cases, then group them all together to make efficient use of office and court time. Just make sure that the lawyer (or lawyer's secretary) is an efficient sort, so that none of the files get lost and no case is dismissed because the statute of limitations has run out.

No matter what you do, though, some accounts will simply be uncollectible. Bad debts can be deducted from ordinary income in the year they become uncollectible (a somewhat subjective judgment). You can either deduct the specific amount that must be written off each year, or set up a bad debt reserve. If you issue audited statements, you must use the reserve method. The reserve can be a purely formal one; you don't need a shoebox or a special bank account for it.

After a few years in business, you can estimate bad debts by figuring out the percentage of credit sales or of receivables that could not be collected. You can also assign percentages to your aging schedule; the older a debt is, the less likely it is to be collected.

Security

Bad debts are one category of events that will cost you money. Others are shoplifting, burglary, bad checks, cheating by your suppliers, and embezzlement. As long as larceny is in the human heart, these problems will not be eliminated, but at least you can minimize them.

You can lay out your store so that the salesperson at the counter, perhaps aided by mirrors, can see all the shoppers. You can have a pressure mat at the door, which rings when someone steps on it, so you can monitor the comings and goings of customers. For high-ticket items, you can use a reverse pressure mat, which rings when the merchandise on it is lifted. You can lock a flexible cable through the shelf and the handle of lightweight appliances. You can display only one of each item, with the rest in a locked stockroom; you can keep everything in a locked showcase, which minimizes theft but increases your need for sales personnel. Clothing stores can keep tabs on items going into the dressing room, making sure that the same number of items—and the same items—emerge as went in.

Not all the checks you get will clear. If you ask for phone numbers on all checks you accept, you can contact reasonably honest customers whose checks bounce as a result of sloppy bookkeeping or bank errors. If the check is described as having "insufficient funds," tell the customer you will wait a few days, then redeposit the check—and you expect it to clear this time. If payment has been stopped, either there's a legitimate dispute you'll have to resolve, or the customer is playing a little game with you. If the check is marked "account closed," the customer had better have a damned good excuse; otherwise, the inference of fraud is irresistible. If the check is large, it may be worth the bank fee to "put the check in for collection." To do this, you submit the check to your bank. Your bank submits the check to the customer's bank, which pays the check as soon as money appears in the account. If all else fails, you'll have to put the check in the "bad check" file.

Burglary is a significantly more dramatic form of theft. If all the other merchants in your area have heavy steel window gates, this should give you a clue. Make sure that all your doors are well locked, and are either double-keyed or out of reach of smashable windows. Windows and skylights must be protected, but in a way that won't block escape in case of fire or other emergency. Burglar alarms aren't free, and they must be very reliable. After a few false alarms, the police will stop coming, and the neighbors will react to the ear-splitting howl with unmixed disgust.

Some store owners leave the cash registers open at night, with a few dollars in each. The theory is that at least the registers won't have to be replaced since the burglar won't have to smash them open.

Don't post your home phone number in the store; it gives crooks the chance to rob *you* once you arrive to check the store. Before you respond to a "burglary" call, a "gas leak," "fire," or whatever, tell someone where you're going and why. Ask him or her to call the police if you're not back by a specified time. Lock up your home securely, in case the burglars send the junior varsity to rifle the premises. When you respond to an "emergency" call, check with the utility, police, or fire department first. If you don't see the appropriate trucks or vans when you get to your business place, don't go in.

The vast majority of suppliers are honest, but that leaves the rest of them. Truck drivers have been known to help themselves, and so have warehouse personnel. Therefore, when you get a delivery, have someone you know you can trust check the order to make sure that everything was delivered, that boxes contain what they purport to contain, and that the material is put away where it belongs (not where an employee can lift it on the way home) and is entered into inventory records. When truck drivers arrive to pick up your merchandise, have it waiting on the loading dock; don't let them wander through your warehouse.

To remove temptation from the path of employees who work cash registers:

- Keep the keys yourself
- Assign each clerk to a specific register, so shortfalls can be attributed to a particular person
- Give the clerks prenumbered sales tickets in duplicate or triplicate, and make sure all tickets are accounted for
- Balance the sales tickets against the register tapes
- Remove cash and sales slips from the registers twice a day

(The sales slips have other uses: you can use them to plot sales trends and find out your best- and worst-selling items.)

If you open the mail yourself, employees won't be able to remove cash or checks from incoming orders. If you require two signatures—one of them yours—on all checks, it's hard for employees to write checks to themselves (unless you spend a lot of time on automatic pilot and don't read the stuff you're supposed to sign). Watch out if a "supplier" you can't remember ordering from gets paid right away—not ten or thirty days after the "bill" arrives. Confirm your suspicions by looking for the invoice or packing slip. These documents *could* be lost or misfiled (though your efficient filing system will prevent this, n'est-ce pas?) but the odds are that an embezzler is at work. Make sure that your bookkeeper takes a nice long vacation every year—at least two consecutive weeks. If the bookkeeper is uneasy at the prospect, it may be due to workaholicism (in which case s/he should certainly learn to relax and unbend), but it may also be an attempt to keep a criminal scheme from fraying.

Your employees' "exposure index" is the amount they could steal by trying very hard. The exposure index equals: 5% of goods on hand + 20% of (current assets − goods on hand) + 10% of annual gross sales (or annual gross income). The exposure index is used to determine the amount of fidelity insurance you need.

Insurance

If the exposure index is under $25,000, you should have at least $15,000 fidelity insurance (insurance which pays if you can prove an employee stole from the business). For an exposure index of $25,000–$125,000, at least $25,000 coverage is recommended, and $50,000 is not excessive.

If you don't have any employees, fidelity insurance is obviously beside the point; but if you have an office, factory, or warehouse, fire and general property insurance (which covers you for damage caused by fire, wind, hail, or vandalism) is a strong priority. Expanses of show window imply plate-glass insurance. A store or restaurant open to the public needs public liability insurance (which defends you if a member of the public gets hurt in your business establishment and reimburses you for any judgments you may have to pay). Manufacturers often find product liability insurance (glass in the stewed tomatoes, exploding kerosene heaters) a necessary expense. Consequential loss insurance pays the extra expenses you incur when a catastrophe closes your business (overtime, substitute quarters) and also reimburses you for lost earnings. Coverage is also available for fraud (including counterfeit money and bad checks passed to you), damage to and caused by boilers, and workmen's compensation (discussed in Chapter Four). "Key-man" insurance pays the company if the president or other key employee dies or becomes disabled.

"Self-insurance" means either that you can't afford insurance and therefore must take all the risks yourself or that you've decided to budget money as a loss reserve rather than for insurance premiums. The best economic candidates for self-insurance can spread the risk among many people and locations; so small businesses are, once again, at a disadvantage. Self-insurance works best for contingencies that are very unlikely (damage caused by falling parts of airplanes) or very likely (burglary in a high-crime area). In the former case, you're very, very unlikely to collect; in the latter, the premiums will be about as high as the loss you suffer—and your premiums will go up, or your insurance will be canceled, after you make a claim. Insurance premiums are set by deciding the amount of potential claims, the likelihood that they will happen, brewing the two together and adding something for the insurance company's profits. You make a similar determination, without allowing for the insurer's profits, when you decide whether you can do better buying an insurance policy or setting aside and investing a sum equal to the premiums.

You can also steer a middle course between self-insurance and conventional insurance coverage: you can decide the largest loss you could absorb without going bankrupt, then buy an excess-loss policy (also called blanket or umbrella coverage) for the rest.

An insurance broker sells policies issued by several companies. An agent represents only one company. Therefore, a broker permits a certain amount of comparison shopping. Those who sell insurance develop a good deal of expertise about the value of property and the levels of risk. Since they get paid more if they sell more insurance, however, their judgments on the amount of insurance required cannot be entirely objective.

If your policy contains a coinsurance clause (most do), you will have to maintain insurance in an amount equal to a stated percentage of the insured premises' or object's value (usually 80%) to collect the full covered value of your loss. If you have less coverage, you will receive only part of the covered value. If a building is worth $100,000 and the coinsurance percentage is 80%, you have only $60,000 worth of coverage, and if the building is damaged $20,000 worth by a peril covered by the policy, you will only collect $15,000: $60,000/$80,000, or ¾, times $20,000. Whether you meet the coinsurance percentage is determined at the time of the loss, not at the time you buy the policy. You're responsible for increasing your coverage as property values go up.

Accurate records are needed for making business judgments, paying bills, and reporting to the stockholders—but, above all, for calculating and paying taxes. With some basic accounting principles under the collective belt, we can now consider taxes.

CHAPTER SIX

Survival and Taxes

IF THE WORLD OF accounting is indeed a separate world—self-contained and a little odd—when it comes to taxation we enter the world of the truly bizarre. Not only can't most taxpayers understand the Internal Revenue Code, most lawyers can't either. In this exotic realm, losing money is a good thing (but only if you're rich) and corporations could pretend to sell equipment that would never be moved, so that they could pretend to lease it back from the new "owners" in 1982 and 1983, but not 1984.

There are several reasons why taxation is so cryptic. First of all, the tax system is patched together. The last comprehensive revision of the federal Internal Revenue Code was done in 1954; Presidents, Congress, the IRS, and the courts have been fiddling with it ever since. And neither the 1954 revision nor the subsequent fiddles took simplicity or clarity as a goal.

Second of all, the federal income tax system has many objectives, and some of these aims are contradictory. The tax system raises money so the government can beat plowshares into swords and pruning hooks into spears, and so forth. The tax rates are cut to encourage people to work harder and invest more. Nominally, tax rates are progressive (those with high incomes pay a higher rate of tax), so income and estate taxes act to redistribute income from the rich to the poor. Then again, tax deductions and low rates on capital gains redistribute income from the poor to the rich. (The less hostile term for this is "encouraging investment.") Oil companies are cosseted with special provisions and slapped with windfall profits taxes. By raising or lowering taxes, assorted Presidents have hoped to stimulate productivity while cooling down an overheated economy, to fight inflation while increasing buying power.

Third, legislators seldom think through the consequences of changes in the law. A change in income tax laws can interact with pension, bankruptcy, or contract law about as harmoniously as anchovies and ice cream. A sloppily written provision intended to increase taxes can provide a bonanza for clever accountants and tax lawyers, and perhaps for their clients. Discovery of the inconsistency prompts another round of legislation. The Economic Recovery Tax Act of 1981 (ERTA) used accelerated depreciation and tax credits as business incentives; the Tax Equity and Fiscal Responsibility Act of 1982 (TEFRA) limited those incentives.

Fourth, the tax laws involve money and therefore engage the passions. What is a loophole to one is tax justice to another. No legislator wants to acquire a reputation for raising his constituents' taxes (or, for that matter, diminishing the federally funded benefits available to them).

Imagine that a senator from a cucumber-growing state gets a bill passed that permits a ten-cent tax deduction for every cucumber in the taxpayer's possession. That seems simple enough. But is a pickle a cucumber or only a former cucumber? What about pickle relish? Bread-and-butter pickles? Cucumber face cream? Can two taxpayers divide the deduction if one sells the cucumbers to the other on December 30th? On March 9th? Each of these profound questions must be settled somehow. Perhaps Congress will pass a bill; maybe the IRS will issue official Regulations or a semiofficial Revenue Ruling or unofficial Letter Ruling; it could be that the Tax Court will decide the case.

All this is an explanation of why the subject of taxation can't be treated very thoroughly in a book of this size. The topic defies comprehension, and just as it seems you understand the rules for a particular situation, they change the rules on you. Therefore, in this chapter I try to explain basic tax concepts rather than give specific advice, which in any case should be personal rather than directed at the entire world.

In this necessarily oversimplified treatment, I'll deal with the commonest situations facing small business. For example, in the discussion of capital gains on page 174, I talk about the sale of assets. There are further refinements if capital assets are exchanged for other assets, or if the transaction is part sale, part exchange. If that's your situation, consult a full-scale reference book on taxation (Sidney Kess and J. K. Lasser are recognized authorities) or get professional advice. IRS Publication 334, "Tax Guide for Small Business," is reasonably lucid and has the advantage of being free.

Who Is a Taxpayer?

A taxpayer (or TP, in IRS and legal jargon) is, reasonably enough, anyone who has to pay tax. A sole proprietor is a TP, but a sole proprietorship is not. A corporation is a TP; so are its stockholders. But a Subchapter S corporation (a small business corporation that chooses to be taxed like a partnership) is not; neither is a partnership. The Sub S corporation's stockholders and the partners report their proportionate share of the corporation or partnership's gain or losses on their own individual tax returns. This is true even if their share is purely hypothetical, and the money is plowed back into the business.

The temptation to avoid this obligation is enormous, so partnerships and Sub S corporations must file information returns (Form 1065) showing their income and deductions. The IRS can (and does) match information returns against partners' and stockholders' individual returns.

The Tax Flow

It is hubris to attempt to reduce the splashing torrents of federal taxation to one simple stream. However, certain currents can be detected.

There's a basic distinction between *capital* and *ordinary* transactions. In broad outline, an ordinary transaction is one that comes up in the normal course of business: for example, a sale from your inventory or the provision of the services your business was organized to provide. A capital transaction is an unusual one. If your business is selling men's suits, income from selling suits is ordinary income, but the sale of your pipe racks and mirrors would be a capital transaction, and any gains would be capital gain. The gain would be long-term if you owned the items for more than a year,

short-term otherwise. But if your business is selling store furnishings, the sale of racks and mirrors would be an ordinary transaction,
yielding ordinary income or loss.

To compute your taxable income, start with your gross income
from ordinary transactions and the gross proceeds of capital transactions. The stream diverges at this point.

From the ordinary income, you subtract the cost of goods sold.
"Cost of goods sold" has a special tax meaning; see page 168. Then
adjust the result to get "adjusted gross income" (AGI). A corporation can take deductions that pertain to property that is rented to
other people. An individual can deduct these same amounts, plus
IRA or Keogh contributions, certain business expenses, expenses of
moving to a new business location, and some nonbusiness deductions.

Then, from adjusted gross income you subtract other deductions:
interest you pay, depreciation, amortization, among others. The distinction between an AGI deduction and an itemized deduction is
meaningful for sole proprietors, partners, and Sub S shareholders
because it affects their estimated taxes and Social Security taxes.

Finally, you figure out the amount of tax due on your taxable
income, which equals gross income minus all legal deductions. If
you have made deposits of withholding tax, made estimated tax
payments, or overpaid the year before, subtract these amounts from
the tax that is due. If you are entitled to an investment credit, a tar-
geted jobs credit (for employing members of minority or disadvantaged groups), or a business energy credit, you can subtract the
amount of credit you are entitled to from the amount of tax you
owe. Therefore, a credit, which reduces the amount of tax you pay,
is better than a deduction, which reduces your taxable income and
potential tax. The lower your income—and therefore your tax
bracket—the more useful a credit is.

If the bottom line is negative, it is unfortunately impossible to
demand that the IRS send you money to make up for it. You have a
net operating loss, and you cope with it for tax purposes by adjust-
ing your tax returns for the preceding three and the following fifteen years. You (or more sensibly, your accountant) refile a return
for the year before the net operating loss, asking for a refund. If the
loss is too large to be absorbed by the prior year's return, you move
back two more years; if there's still some loss to be absorbed, you
use it every year after the loss until the entire loss is absorbed. If
you have a net operating loss in several years, there are further rules

about parceling out the losses. Thus my suggestion that you turn to an accountant for help.

As for capital transactions during a tax year, you classify them into four categories: long-term transactions yielding a gain, long-term capital losses, short-term gains, short-term losses. Then you follow the rules on page 174 to amalgamate them again. Whether you have a gain or a loss depends on your basis. A capital gain is the amount received minus your adjusted basis; a capital loss equals your adjusted basis minus the amount received.

Remember that an interest in a partnership is a capital asset. Its basis starts with the partner's original capital contribution and is adjusted as necessary (e.g., increased by further capital contributions, decreased by depreciation).

Your basis is the tax value of the capital asset you sold; basis is not necessarily market value. If you bought the asset (i.e., it was not a gift or an inheritance), your basis starts out as the price you paid. If part of the price was paid in cash and you got a loan or mortgage for the rest, the basis includes the borrowed amount as well as your cash down payment.

Your basis changes over time. Basis goes up if you make capital improvements to the property (e.g., building a sidewalk cafe for a restaurant building you own). Your basis goes down if you are entitled to a depreciation or amortization deduction (even if you don't *take* the deduction). If you took a casualty or theft deduction because the property was damaged or lost, the deduction lowers the basis. If a corporation gives money or property to its stockholders, and this distribution does not come from the corporation's earnings and profits—in other words, if the distribution reduces the corporation's capital—the stockholders must subtract the distribution from the basis of their stock.

All this hugger-mugger is necessary because the higher the basis, the lower the potentially taxable gain. If your adjusted basis is twelve thousand dollars for an asset you sell for fifteen thousand dollars, your gain is three thousand dollars; if the basis were eighteen thousand dollars, you would have a loss of six thousand dollars. Or, in Orwellian terms, high basis good, low basis bad.

Note that the basis is a purely formal tax concept and has nothing at all to do with whether the transaction really was profitable. Also note that you don't pay tax on the increased value of your property until you dispose of the property. Even then, you may not have to pay tax if you exchange business equipment (not inventory) for similar property, or if you dispose of the property as part of a reorganization or liquidation (see Chapter Eleven).

Choices

When you set up your business, you make some elementary tax choices: how your business will be organized, whether a corporation will be taxed as if it were a partnership, whether a corporation wants §1244 treatment (capital gain but ordinary loss) for its stockholders who sell their stock.

You must also decide whether, for tax purposes, your business' year is a calendar year (January 1–December 31) or a fiscal year (starting on any other date and ending 364 or 365 days later). A calendar year is simpler. A partnership must be able to demonstrate a good reason if its tax year is different from that of *any* partner who has more than a five-percent interest. (If all the partners have different tax years, that's a pretty good reason.)

You must pick an accounting method: cash, accrual, or a combination of the two. A service business has a free choice. A business (either retail or wholesale) that has inventory must use the accrual method or a combination. For example, the buying and selling of inventory could be computed with the accrual method, with other expenses handled by the cash method. A combination method, to be acceptable to the IRS, must be a clear reflection of your actual cash flow; and you must use the same method to compute your gross income and your business expenses.

If your business has inventory, you must decide whether to value it at cost, cost or market price (whichever is lower), or some other system. If you pick another system, you have to explain on your tax form what you did and why.

INVENTORY VALUATION

For connoisseurs of subtlety, the subject of inventory valuation will be a treat; to anyone else, it will be a headache.

If you don't say anything, the IRS assumes that you use FIFO: first in, first out. That is, if you start out with 100 items, each costing you $1.00, buy 200 more for $1.25 each during the year, and sell 150 units for $2.00 each, for tax purposes you sold the cheaper units first, then 50 of the more expensive ones.

If you prefer, you can use LIFO: Last In, First Out. Under LIFO, you would assume that you sold 150 of the newer, more expensive units. Since the cost of the units is higher than under FIFO, you have less taxable income; and if you switch from FIFO to LIFO when prices are rising (and when are they not?) the change has the same effect as a one-time "deduction" of the price increase. The IRS is quite aware of this, and therefore puts limitations on LIFO:

- You can only use it if you value your inventory at cost
- You must notify the IRS if you adopt LIFO (though you don't need permission) by filing two copies of Form 970 with your tax return for the year of the change
- If you adopt LIFO, then change to another valuation method, you have to wait ten years to switch back

The mathematics of changing to LIFO after a considerable time of another method can be difficult; the Bureau of Labor Statistics publishes indexes of retail costs as an aid to retailers who switch to LIFO. You're allowed to use these indexes to adjust your records.

LIFO and FIFO are not the only accounting methods; the IRS will let you use various methods of segregating your inventory by class and averaging the cost of the items in each class. Averaging is allowed if you use it for all classes of inventory, if you don't distort or misrepresent your income, and if averaging conforms to trade or industry practice. If your annual receipts have been less than two million dollars for the past three years (no problem if this is your first year in business), you can also treat your entire inventory as a single pool, and average costs within that pool. To make any change in inventory method except a change to LIFO, you need IRS permission. You ask for permission by filing Form 3115 within six months of the end of the tax year of the change. If the IRS refuses to grant permission, you have to redo the tax return. A powerful argument can be made that you should avoid doing *anything* which makes the IRS look especially closely at your tax returns. I suggest that you use LIFO or FIFO unless a competent professional demonstrates that an averaging method is better for your particular business.

Cost of Goods Sold

The IRS requires you to take inventory at least once a year to determine your closing inventory. If you are a calendar-year taxpayer and you don't have a date on New Year's Eve, taking inventory is a superlative way to feel *really* sorry for yourself.

There are eight steps in computing the cost of goods sold. You perform these steps on Schedule C-1 of Schedule C (for proprietors), Schedule A of Form 1065 (for partnerships), or Schedule A of Form 1120 (for corporations).

The first step is to note down your inventory at the beginning of the year. Normally it will equal your closing inventory for the year before; if it doesn't, you have to attach an explanation (e.g., a delivery on New Year's Day) to your tax return.

Next, you compute the amount of inventory you purchased during the year (e.g., the dresses and blouses bought by a clothing retailer; the furniture bought by a furniture store), and subtract the cost of items you used personally (your spring wardrobe and the sofa installed in your living room). The result is your "net purchases."

The third step is to compute the cost of labor directly involved in producing inventory items. This figure does not include your own salary, or wages paid to employees who did not work directly to produce inventory items.

Fourth, compute the cost of materials and supplies directly involved in inventory production and handling. Don't include office or general business supplies; they're deductible, but not on this Schedule.

Fifth, make a list of other inventory-related costs, and compute the total.

Next, you add the opening inventory for the year, net purchases, labor costs, material and supply costs, and other costs. Then you subtract the closing inventory for the tax year. The result of the subtraction is your cost of goods sold.

Business Deductions

For tax purposes, your ordinary income from business operations is reduced by all of your "ordinary and necessary business expenses."

An ordinary and necessary business expense is, indeed, any expense that is related to making money and is appropriate for your business. A multimillion-dollar business can justify a higher level of expenditure than a mom-and-pop operation can. As was said in Latin, "Quod licet Jovi, non licet bovi": what is permitted to Jupiter is not permitted to a cow.

Schedule C for sole proprietors lists twenty-four separate deductions:

- Advertising
- Amortization (for intangible assets)
- Business bad debts
- Bank charges
- Car and truck expenses
- Commissions (e.g., to salespeople)
- Depletion
- Depreciation (see page 172)
- Dues for business organizations (e.g., Lingerie Manufacturer's Benevolent Association); cost of business-related books and publications (*Heavy-Metal Trade Outlook Quarterly*)
- Employee benefit programs (e.g., health insurance, tuition reimbursement for employees)
- Freight for your products (unless freight costs were included in the cost of goods sold)
- Insurance
- Interest on business borrowing
- Laundry and dry cleaning
- Legal and professional fees
- Office supplies and postage
- Pension and profit-sharing plans
- Rent
- Repairs

- Supplies (other than office supplies, and not included in the cost of goods sold)
- Taxes
- Travel and entertainment
- Utilities and telephone bills
- Wages and salaries

There's a twenty-fifth catchall category for other expenses—for example, a private carting service for trash removal, heating oil for a business furnishing its own heat.

Partnership and corporation returns provide fewer lines for a detailed breakdown of business costs; you have to provide your own lists to attach to your tax form.

If you use a car or truck in business, you can either keep detailed records of expenses or keep mileage records and deduct the IRS standard per-mile allowance. If the vehicle is used for both business and personal trips, only the business trips affect your business taxable income. You will usually get a larger deduction if you record actual expenses, but it's a lot easier to take the mileage allowance. Many of the business diaries sold in stationery stores include mileage and expense records.

If collective awards were given, America's travel and expense deductions would probably win the Pulitzer Prize for fiction and poetry each year. Few areas are so susceptible to chiseling. Many meals and travel expenses are paid in cash, and anyone can be identified as a "supplier" or "potential customer." If you've ever wondered why stationery stores have a sale on last year's diaries every April, the sale is an aid to this particular form of imaginative literature.

Travel expenses (air fare, hotel/motel, meals, etc.) are deductible if they are ordinary and necessary. If a trip is part business and part vacation, only the business part is deductible. As you can imagine, trips to Hawaii receive more IRS scrutiny than trips to Secaucus.

President Kennedy inveighed against the "martini lunch" deduction; President Carter directed similar (and similarly futile) invective against the "three-martini lunch." Evidently inflation was at work. A quiet business meal, at whatever proof, is deductible if you keep detailed contemporaneous records showing the date, time, and place of entertainment, who was entertained, that person's (or those people's) business relationship to you, what was discussed, and the cost of the entertainment. You don't have to document the outcome of the discussion. If business entertainment takes place in a setting that is not conducive to business discussion (a hockey game, a disco) you must be able to show that a business discussion occurred during quiet intervals. To substantiate cash expenditures, you'll need your diary plus the receipt. If you pay by check, your canceled check is evidence. For those who use both belt and suspenders, paying by credit card gives you a diary entry, a credit card voucher, a credit card bill, and a canceled check as evidence. Paying by credit card has another advantage: it takes time for the transition to be posted, and the bill prepared; you have a few weeks to pay before interest charges are imposed. If you are just as broke in the succeeding month as in the month of the expenditure, this advantage is nullified.

Capital Punishment

Whether an item is an ordinary asset (providing ordinary income or loss) or a capital asset (providing capital gain or loss) depends more on the owner than on the item. In a bar, the booze is inventory (ordinary income) but the piano is a capital asset. In a Steinway showroom, a piano is inventory. Corporate stocks and bonds are capital assets to investors, but inventory to licensed securities dealers. (I say *licensed* because every once in a while some sharpie tries to reduce ordinary income by claiming that s/he is really a broker, and the unfortunate stocks were really inventory.)

For an individual, partner, or Sub S stockholder, a long-term capital gain (a gain on an asset held more than one year) gets very favorable tax treatment, so the distinction between capital and ordinary income is very meaningful. For corporations, the difference is less meaningful. The net long-term capital gain equals the total long-term capital gain minus the *short*-term loss. It's grace notes like this that make tax law so much fun.

After buying an asset and before getting rid of it, the asset must be dealt with somehow. The Economic Recovery Tax Act of 1981 (ERTA) lets you expense (take as a deduction) a certain amount of the cost of capital assets. In tax year 1983, you can expense up to $5,000 worth; in 1984 and 1985, up to $7,500 a year; in 1986 and afterward, $10,000 per year. In other words, you can get an immediate write-off up to the limit. But if you do expense an item (let's say, a new dictation system) you can't take an investment credit on the property; and when you sell expensed property, you have ordinary income.

For property over the limit, or if you decide not to expense items, you must depreciate them (if the assets are tangible) or amortize them (if they are intangible). Copyrights, patents, and contracts are intangible assets; forklifts and panel trucks are tangible assets.

DEPRECIATION: ACRS

Nothing lasts forever, and equipment has to be replaced sooner or later. For accounting purposes, you "write down" the value of depreciable items each year they are in service; you probably maintain an accounting reserve for depreciation. Before ERTA, the tax treatment of depreciation was fairly similar to the accounting treatment. You decided the useful life of the stuff, subtracted its salvage value from the original price, and allowed a certain amount of depreciation, deducted from gross income, per year of useful life. To stem the flow of creativity, the IRS instituted a system of classes of useful life; if you see a reference to CLADR in a book, that's what it referred to.

ERTA changes the system completely by introducing ACRS (Accelerated Cost Recovery System). Under ACRS, you can depreciate the full cost of an item, without worrying about salvage value. You don't even have to worry about the real useful life of the item. Cars, light trucks, and equipment used in research and development, plus certain special tools, are depreciated over three years. Just about everything else you are likely to use in business is depreciated over five years. (There are special rules for real estate, which I won't go into here, because very few small businesses own real estate.)

In fact, ACRS even eliminates most of the arithmetic involved in computing depreciation. ERTA provides official tables giving the percentage of the original cost to be deducted each year: For three-year property, it's 25% the first year, 38% the second, and 37% the third. For five-year property, the percentages are 15%, 22%, 21%, 21%, and 21%.

If, for some sound reason, you want to avoid ACRS, you can use straight-line depreciation (price minus salvage value, divided by 4 or 6, depending on the kind of property involved). Property that would be depreciated in 3 years under ACRS must be depreciated 25% per year in each of 4 years; 5-year property under ACRS is depreciated 16⅔% a year over 6 years.

AMORTIZATION

ACRS applies only to tangible property. For intangibles, you determine the real useful life (for example, a contract's useful life is the duration of the contract) and divide the full cost by the useful life. Intangibles don't have salvage value, either.

You can make life much easier by maintaining one schedule for depreciation and another for amortization. Use the analysis pad described in Chapter Five, or whatever record book you use instead. Use one column for the description of the asset; another for its price; another for its ACRS class or useful life. Assign a column to each year the property is in use, and enter the appropriate deductible amount. Then, each year you can read down the column to find out the amount of depreciation and amortization that can be deducted.

INVESTMENT CREDIT

The investment credit is the federal government's version of cherry-flavored castor oil. It's good for you (in this case, capital investment) but you won't swallow it (costs too much) unless we make it taste good (lower your tax bill). The investment credit lowers your taxes, not just your taxable income, so it is more valuable than a plain, common or garden-variety deduction.

If you buy new or used property for service in your business, you get a credit of 10% of the purchase price (if the property is 5-year property under ACRS) or 6% of the purchase price (for 3-year property). You get the credit in the year you put the property in service (cash basis) or the year you accrue the obligation to pay for it (accrual basis). The maximum investment credit is $25,000 plus 85% of whatever your tax bill would be over $25,000, but somehow I suspect that's the least of your problems right now. What you will have to decide, when you buy investment property, is whether to take a smaller credit (8% instead of 10%, or 4% instead of 6%) right away, or whether the basis of the property will be decreased by half the amount of the credit when the property is sold or exchanged: in other words, Do you want to cut your tax bill now, knowing that this year's cuts mean a higher tax bill later? If you take a business energy credit or a credit for rehabilitating a certified historic structure, the credit will also be recaptured when you sell the property, because your basis will be lowered by half the credit. But you don't get a choice between basis reduction and a lower credit; your basis will be reduced, period.

CAPITAL GAINS TAX

You start by segregating your capital transactions (sale of capital assets) into two classes: short-term (property you owned under one year before the sale) and long-term. Remember, gain equals sales price minus your adjusted basis; loss equals your adjusted basis minus the sales price. Your basis is lowered (adjusted) by the amount of depreciation you have taken. Next, you combine all the transactions in each class to see if you have a net long-term gain or loss and/or a net short-term gain or loss.

For example, if you are a proprietor, partner, or Sub S stockholder, and you have 3 short-term transactions (gain of $200, loss of $800, gain of $1,200), you have a net short-term gain of $600. You add the 2 gains, and subtract $800 from the $1,400 sum. If you have 2 long-term transactions (gain of $3,000 and $1,500, say) your net long-term gain is $4,500. In this fortunate situation, your $600 net short-term gain is taxed as ordinary income. However, net short-term losses don't reduce your ordinary income; you subtract them from your long-term capital gains. You subtract the net short-term losses (if any) from the net long-term gains (if any) and ignore 60% of the result. You pay ordinary income rates on the other 40%. In this example, you pay your regular rates on 40% of $4,500—that is, on $1,800. (You may have heard that the maximum capital gains tax rate is 20%; it is, because the highest tax rate on personal income is 50%, and 40% of *that* equals 20%. Before ERTA, the maximum rate was 40% of 70%, or 28%.)

Corporations must pay their usual income tax rate on the full amount of the net long-term capital gain; they can't take the 60% deduction into account. However, they can use an alternative capital gains tax rate of 28%. Since a corporation has to have $50,000 of taxable income to be in a bracket higher than 28%, small corporations don't spend much time trying to get capital gains instead of ordinary income. Noncorporate taxpayers and Sub S shareholders, who would face a 50% rather than 20% tax, are more enthusiastic about capital gains.

Not all capital transactions produce a gain, and not every year has a net gain. If you have a net long-term gain and a net short-term loss, you use the short-term loss to reduce the long-term gain. However, if your only capital transactions are long-term, and you have a net loss, only half of the loss is deductible. If you have a net short-term loss *and* a net long-term loss, you can deduct the entire short-term loss plus half of the long-term loss. However, you may not be able to take all the deductions in the year of the loss. The Internal Revenue Code limits the amount of capital loss that can be deducted. For sole proprietors and partners, the maximum capital loss deduction is the *smallest* of:

- $3,000
- The taxpayer's taxable income for the year
- Net long-term loss minus net short-term gain divided by 2

For corporate taxpayers, capital losses can only be deducted up to the amount of capital gains.

However, "leftover" capital losses can be used eventually to reduce the taxpayer's overall tax liability, in the form of "carrybacks" and "carryovers." In a carryback, tax returns for earlier years are recomputed with an additional deduction because of the later capital loss. In a carryover or "carryforward," a later tax return takes the earlier capital loss into account. Ask your accountant; if you have capital loss carryovers and carrybacks, you need an accountant. Subchapter S corporations have especially stringent limitations on capital loss carryovers; if you expect substantial capital losses, Sub S may not be a good choice for you.

Two tax breaks are available: Internal Revenue Code Sections 1231, 1245, and 1250 allow gains on business property and real estate that was owned for more than a year before the sale to be treated as long-term capital gains. Losses are treated as ordinary losses, not capital losses. And if your corporation elected §1244 treatment (see page 166), the stockholders can treat any loss from selling stock in your corporation as an ordinary loss. This is a tax break for the stockholders, not the corporation itself.

Special Situations

Some commonly encountered tax problems are:

START-UP EXPENSES

You are entitled to a deduction for ordinary and necessary business expenses—that is, the expenses of a going business. The expenses of setting up a business (scouting trips, lunches with the owners of a business you might buy) can't be deducted. However, they can be amortized over a period of at least five years. If the business' expected useful life is less than five years (e.g., a corporation organized to produce campaign buttons for the 1984 election), the expenses can be amortized over the life of the business.

The basic distinction is one between expenses that a fully functioning business would encounter and those only a starting business would have to pay. The fee you pay a lawyer on whether or not to incorporate is a start-up expense. The fee you pay a lawyer to sue a supplier over defective merchandise is a business expense. This is true even if it's the same lawyer, and both fees are paid or accrued in the same year.

If you prefer, you can capitalize start-up expenses: that is, add them to your basis for your share of the business. You can also capitalize the interest on loans used to buy business equipment and state and local sales and use taxes. Whether this is a good idea is an accounting decision.

HOBBY LOSSES

The IRS will cheerfully accept taxes on income earned in any way whatever, but a sole proprietor, partner, or Sub S stockholder is not allowed to deduct losses from activities that were "not engaged in for profit." If you go to the trouble of incorporating, the IRS will take it on faith that your activities are engaged in for profit. The test of whether an activity performed by an individual is for profit is whether the activity showed a profit in any two of the preceding five years. Therefore, you can lose money for three years with impunity (after all, you *could* turn a profit in the next two

years, so you'd meet the test by the time there were five years to
scrutinize). By the fourth year without taxable income, you face a
possible disallowance of your "business expense" deductions. In
other words, if you are audited, the IRS could increase your taxable
income by the amount of those deductions, and demand more
money.

You can stave this off by filing Form 5213, which keeps the IRS
from checking on you until you've been in business for five years.
However, if you file Form 5213 and go through the five years without two consecutive profitable years, the IRS can haul out your old
tax returns and increase your tax liability.

CASUALTY AND THEFT LOSSES

You are entitled to a deduction for the value of business property stolen from you and for business property damaged or
destroyed by a casualty. A casualty is something sudden and unex-
pected (i.e., fire or flood). You get a depreciation deduction to account for ordinary wear and tear, so you don't get a casualty loss for
the same process. Your casualty loss deduction equals the property's
adjusted basis at the time of the incident minus the property's salvage value and any insurance you collect. If the property is only
damaged, not destroyed, your deduction equals the decrease in
value caused by the casualty. However, the deduction can't be
greater than the precasualty adjusted basis. The deduction for a
theft loss (embezzlement and robbery as well as good old-fashioned
burglary and shoplifting count) is the pretheft adjusted basis of the
property minus any insurance recovery.

Often, businesses have a real dilemma after a casualty or theft.
If an insurance claim is made, insurance could become unavailable
or prohibitively expensive later on. The IRS' original position was
that the deduction would have to be reduced by the amount of insurance that *would* have been paid if a claim had been filed. The
Tax Court has decided several cases for the beleaguered taxpayer,
so the IRS may change its stand.

EMPLOYEE BENEFITS

Some benefits for employees, paid for by employers, are deductible for the employer:

- Certain pension plans (see Chapter Four)
- Free meals for employees (the rules change often, so ask your lawyer or the nearest IRS district office)
- Term life insurance bought as a group
- Group health insurance
- Prepaid legal services
- Child care for employees' children
- Workmen's compensation
- Supplemental unemployment insurance (a private plan mandated by a union or other contract with employees)

Only a fairly solvent business can afford these benefits, so I mention them only in passing. Insurance companies, banks, and plan administrators will be happy to give you free advice, and business publications usually inform their readers of new developments.

BAD DEBTS

You can either deduct the actual amount of bad debts in the year they become worthless, or deduct the amount you maintain as a bad debt reserve. The bad debt reserve must be a reasonable one, grounded on your own or industry experience. You choose one of the methods in the first year you have bad debts, and you can't change methods without IRS approval.

REHABILITATION CREDIT

If you own a building, or if you are an exceptionally ambitious tenant, you can get a tax credit for substantial rehabilitation of a mature building. "Substantial" means that, in the 2 years before you claim the credit, you spent at least $5,000 *or* the building's adjusted basis as of the start of rehab work. The credit equals 15% of your expenditure (if the building is 30–40 years old), 20% (if it is over 40 years old—the dangerous age, so to speak), and 25% if the building is a certified historic structure (which depends on its age and particularly on its location). You can take the credit for rehabilitating a certified historic structure that is residential or part residence, part business property; but the other credits are available only for business property. The building's adjusted basis decreases by half the amount of credit, so the potential taxable gain is higher when the building is sold. (But I must warn you that I live in a certified historic structure in Jersey City, and I no longer believe in rehabilitation of older buildings. I now advocate the death penalty.)

PERSONAL HOLDING COMPANIES, COLLAPSIBLE CORPORATIONS

The IRS permits a fairly wide scope for tax planning, but it hates to be played for a sucker. Therefore, substantial tax penalties attach to these two tax devices. A "personal holding company" is sometimes referred to by the eloquent title of "incorporated pocketbook." It's a corporation that receives the bulk of its income from interest and investments, not business activities. Its raison d'être is to transfer income from a high-bracket individual to a corporation taxed at lower rates. Since you are unlikely to have that much income or that many investments, you are unlikely to fall afoul of the IRS on this one.

A "collapsible corporation" is one created to change ordinary income from business activities into capital gains on the sale of the corporation's stock. The corporation gets contracts to sell goods, or perform services, then "collapses" (is reorganized) before the contracts can be carried out. The stockholders of the original corporation get money for their stock, taxed at capital gains rates; the buyer performs the contracts and collects the proceeds. Unfortunately, if the IRS decides a corporation is collapsible, the stockholders lose capital gains treatment. To avoid this unpleasant possibility, make sure that, if you sell your business, the sale documents demonstrate that the sale served business motives, not just tax avoidance.

Through the Tax Return with Gun and Camera

Part of the fun of being a taxpayer is the quarterly or annual obligation to cover pieces of paper with figures and attach money. The principal piece of paper are:

ESTIMATED TAX

The federal government isn't going to sit around and wait a year for your tax money. The requirements for withholding and depositing taxes on your employees' wages are described in Chapter Four. If your business is incorporated, and if you are an employee of the corporation as well as a stockholder, these requirements apply to your salary as well.

If you are a sole proprietor or partner, you will have to make quarterly estimated tax payments on your own income (unless you have a salaried job somewhere else that withholds enough tax to satisfy your tax liability). The estimated tax payment includes your Social Security self-employment tax. You must make estimated income tax payments if you expect your gross income to be over $5,000 (if you are married but file singly), $10,000 (if you file a joint return with a spouse who is employed), or $20,000 (any other taxpayer). But you don't get off that easily; you must also file an estimated tax return if you have over $500 income that does not come from wages (not necessarily business income; it could be interest, dividends, or rent from the other half of your two-family house) and if your estimated tax minus the amount withheld is more than $300 (for 1983), $400 (1984), or $500 (in 1985 and later years).

The self-employment tax is based on your net earnings from self-employment, not your gross income. Net earnings from self-employment mean your gross business income plus your share of gain or loss from any partnership, minus your allowable business deductions. You have to pay self-employment tax if your net earnings are over $400. Once you reach the Social Security maximum, you don't have to pay self-employment tax on the excess.

Both sorts of estimated tax are filed and paid with Form 1040ES; you get a package of four forms, four envelopes, worksheets, and instructions once a year. The term "quarterly" might delude you into believing that you pay once every three months, but that only demonstrates your lack of appreciation of subtlety. Quarterly returns and payments are due on the fifteenth day of the fourth, sixth, and ninth months of your tax year, and the first month of the next year. For calendar-year taxpayers, this means April 15th, June 15th, September 15th, and January 15th.

You can skip the January 15th payment if you complete your 1040 (long-form tax return for the year) and mail it, with whatever sum you owe, by January 31. This is a better strategy if you're entitled to a refund than if you owe a lot of money. But there are some practical difficulties with early filing. Very few people or institutions will be efficient enough to send you the information *you* need that early (e.g., W-2 forms on your own wages from a part-time job, bank statements of interest you earned). It is also unlikely that the IRS will have the blank forms you need by January 31. Of course, by late March the IRS has run out of forms. There must be some point of exquisite balance—say, February 25—at which forms are freely available.

Again for calendar-year taxpayers, on or before April 15th you must file a tax return for the entire preceding year and estimate what that year's income will be. There is no real way to do this. Once your business is established, you can get some guidance from earlier figures; in the first years, it's pure guesswork.

If you overestimate, you're making a no-interest loan to the government. On the other hand, you can use the overpayment as your first estimated tax payment for the next year; it hardly hurts at all that way. This is a good technique if you're undisciplined about money.

If you underestimate, and you pay less than 80% of the real tax due, you are subject to large financial penalties unless you have a good explanation for the shortfall. (File Form 2210 with the IRS to convey your good explanation.) Fortunately, you can amend any subsequent quarterly estimated tax declaration, and raise or cut back your payments if your income exceeds or fails to meet your prediction.

Corporations have to make quarterly estimated tax payments if the corporate income tax for that quarter is higher than $40. Estimated tax payments are due on Form 1120W on the fifteenth day of the fourth, sixth, ninth, and twelfth months of the corporation's tax year. (Presumably the IRS doesn't worry about ruining a corporation's Christmas.)

SOLE PROPRIETORS

If you're a sole proprietor, you file a Form 1040, complete with furniture and accessories, by April 15th or the fifteenth day of the fourth month after your fiscal year ends. The 1040 itself is a summary of income and deductions. Schedule A is for personal itemized deductions; Schedule B for interest and dividends you receive. Schedule C is for income or loss from business operations.

Schedule C calls for:

- Basic information identifying your business
- Your gross receipts minus returns and allowances and cost of goods sold, plus other income

- Your deductions (copy the information from your ledgers or analysis pad)
- Cost of goods sold
- A depreciation schedule (life is much easier if you maintain a depreciation schedule among your books and records)
- Expense account information

If you sold or exchanged depreciable business property during the year, you'll also need Form 4797. (Partnerships and corporations also use Form 4797 for this purpose.)

Sometimes you may have a choice whether to take a deduction on Schedule A or Schedule C; if you do, deduct the item on Schedule C, because that way your liability for self-employment tax will be lower.

You figure out self-employment tax, reasonably enough, on Schedule SE.

When you attain new and higher levels of poverty, it may be worthwhile to use income averaging. Income averaging, which is done on Schedule G, allows you to pay tax on one year's income, significantly higher than past years' income, as if the high income were earned in equal increments through the years. Lower income is taxed at lower rates, so income averaging can save money. It's only worth the trouble if income in one year is much higher than in earlier years.

A potential pitfall for sole proprietors: Schedule C includes a question about whether or not you claim deductions for an office in your home. There's some evidence that saying "yes" dramatically increases your chances of a tax audit. Unless you're sure that your tax returns are strictly kosher, it may be worth bypassing a small deduction for a home office. On the other hand, if your home-office expenses are substantial, it's worth spending the money for professional advice so that your return *will* be clean.

As a sole proprietor, you don't have the right to deduct your own salary as a business expense. In fact, your taxable income is based on the business' income—even if every penny of surplus is sitting in the business' bank account and you haven't touched a cent. It is quite legal (though extremely imprudent) to "comingle" business and personal funds: that is, to pay personal bills with business funds, or vice versa.

PARTNERSHIPS

The partnership must file an information return, Form 1065, by the fifteenth day of the fourth month after the end of its tax year. The front of the first page of Form 1065 calls for general information about income, deductions, and the cost of goods sold (Schedule A). Form 1065 doesn't have a Schedule B or C; Schedule D summarizes capital gains and losses, Schedule H the income the partnership receives for renting its property. Schedule I is a bad-debt schedule.

The real meat comes in Schedule K, which analyzes the total income, credits, and deductions available to all the partners. The 1065 must also include a Schedule K-1 for each partner, showing that particular partner's share of the goodies. Remember that a partner's share of income, deductions, or expenses doesn't have to be the same as his or her share of the work or the total contributions to capital. However, if the partnership has losses rather than gain, a partner's loss deduction can't be bigger than his or her adjusted basis or the amount "at risk" (the amount the partner is personally liable for and can be forced to pay).

Schedule L is a comparison of the partnership's balance sheets at the beginning and end of the tax year; Schedule M shows changes in the partners' capital accounts, and Schedule N gives information about the makeup of the partnership.

Partnerships don't exactly get a tax deduction for salaries paid to partners, but they do get a deduction for "guaranteed payments," either in return for services or in exchange for the use of their capital. The partners report their guaranteed payments and their share of the partnership's gain or loss on Schedule E attached to their Form 1040. Guaranteed payments based on services to the partnership are self-employment income to be reported on Schedule SE (Form 1040).

Before TEFRA, if the IRS felt that a partnership was handling its tax affairs improperly, it would go after the individual partners. As a result of TEFRA, the IRS will take up any quarrels it has with the partnership in one proceeding, and partners must treat all tax items consistently—in other words, if there are six partners, each one can't take 25% of an allowable credit. However, if there are ten or fewer partners (a husband and wife count as one partner—a charming little nineteenth-century touch) and if all the partnership allocations are made the same way—that is, if a 10% partner invests 10% of the capital, gets 10% of the profits, 10% of the investment credit, and is liable for 10% of the partnership's liabilities—the partnership can choose to be examined by the IRS at the individual level, not the partnership level. Talk to your tax adviser about whether this is a good idea for you, and how to do it if it is.

SUB S CORPORATIONS

A Sub S corporation is not a taxpayer; it files an information return by the fifteenth day of the third month after the end of its tax year, using Form 1120S. Form 1120S looks a lot like a 1065. The first page covers gross income, deductions, and a tax computation. Page two has Schedule A (cost of goods sold), Schedule E (officers' salaries and stock ownership), and some information about the corporation's business affiliations. Page three holds Schedule K, summarizing the Sub S corporation's taxable income and distributions to its stockholders. A Schedule K-1 showing income and tax deductions must be completed for each stockholder. Page four of the 1120S calls for beginning and ending balance sheets for the corporation (Schedule L) and Schedules M-1 and M-2 are used to compare the corporation's books and its tax return.

The stockholders, in turn, report their share of the Sub S corporation's property, income, and undistributed taxable income on their own tax returns. A Sub S corporation is still a corporation, so these payments are treated as dividends.

If the Sub S corporation has a loss, the stockholders do get a loss deduction, but the deduction can't be larger than the stockholder's own adjusted basis for the stock plus any money the corporation owes to the stockholder. The stockholders don't get to deduct pro rata shares of the corporation's net operating loss, so a particularly dreadful year may yield losses that reduce the corporation's coffers without diminishing anyone's tax bill.

OTHER CORPORATIONS

A corporation is a taxpayer and so are its stockholders. The corporation pays taxes on its taxable income (gross income minus allowable deductions). Taxable income is more or less equal to "earnings and profits," an accounting term used to distinguish between a corporation's current income and invasion of its capital.

The distinction is meaningful because corporations make distributions to their stockholders. The distributions are dividends (and the stockholders who get them pay ordinary income tax rates on them), if they come out of earnings and profits. The corporation must file a Form 1099-DIV with the IRS for each stockholder who gets more than $10 in dividends in any tax year; all the 1099-DIVs are bundled together with a Form 1096 and are sent to the IRS after the last dividend payment of the year and before the last day of February of the next year.

If the distribution comes out of capital, the stockholders don't pay tax right away, but they must reduce the basis of their stock by the amount of the distribution, increasing their taxable income when they sell the stock. However, corporations have a duty to preserve their capital structure, and corporate officers who start handing out capital to avoid taxes face the wrath of dissenting stockholders and state corporation regulators as well as the IRS. Distributions of this type are considered so exceptional that no ordinary 1099-DIV will do. You must file Form 5452 with the Director, Corporation Tax Division, T:C:C:3:E & P, IRS, Washington, DC 20224 by March 1 after the year of the distribution.

The normal impulse, then, would be for the corporation to hoard its earnings and profits, thus sparing the stockholders the burden of paying taxes (though depriving them of the opportunity to spend the aftertax income). However, the Internal Revenue Code anticipates this by putting a surtax of 27½% to 38½%, over and above normal corporate income tax, on corporate earnings that are accumulated for tax avoidance rather than for the corporation's real economic needs. A corporation in a service business can accumulate up to $150,000 a year; a retail or manufacturing corporation can accumulate up to $250,000 a year. When your earnings after taxes reach that point, you'll simply *have* to start paying dividends.

The corporation pays taxes on its income, then distributes much or all of the aftertax income as dividends. Then the stockholders pay tax on the dividends, which becomes part of their personal taxable income. This is "double taxation," and it's a disadvantage of the corporate form of doing business. If you worry about it a lot, consider a Sub S election. However, ERTA lowered corporate income tax rates; the first $25,000 of taxable income is taxed at 15% (1983 on), the next $25,000 at 18%. But a corporation's taxable income is a lot less than its gross income, and tax brackets work incrementally. That is, the higher bracket applies only to income over the maximum for the lower bracket. Therefore, a corporation's (or, for that matter, an individual's) average tax rate is lower than the highest bracket at which s/he or it pays taxes.

Well, you'll still have to pay something if you have taxable income. Form 1120, the corporation income tax return, is due on the fifteenth day of the third month after the corporation's tax year ends. Page one of the 1120 summarizes the corporation's gross income, deductions, and tax due. Page two contains Schedule A (cost of goods sold), Schedule C (dividends received by the corporation on stock it owns), Schedule E (salaries of the corporation's officers), and Schedule F (bad debts). Page three calls for information about the corporation's business affiliations and includes Schedule J for computing the tax due. Page four contains Schedule L (balance sheets for the beginning and end of the year), and Schedule M-1 and M-2 (used to reconcile the corporation's accounting and tax treatments of income and expenses).

Corporations, too, have to make quarterly payments of estimated tax. TEFRA tightens up the requirements for accuracy in estimating. Before, corporations had to pay at least 80% of the final amount of tax via the estimated payments, or there would be a hefty penalty assessed. TEFRA makes the penalty higher, and requires that 90% of the actual sum be paid in the form of estimated tax. But if the estimated tax paid is somewhere between 80%–90%, only three quarters of the penalty will be charged. Don't you feel better?

TEFRA also includes some new and highly technical rules for treatment of income that is not stable from month to month. After all, the worst pitfall for estimating taxes is income that has spectacular peaks and valleys. Once again, your tax lawyer or accountant should know this stuff.

A corporation is entitled to deduct salaries paid to its officers, even if the officers are major stockholders, provided that the salaries are not unreasonable and represent ordinary and necessary business expenses. A corporation can't justify paying a large salary to a stockholder/officer who merely drops by the office occasionally on the way to the track. On the other hand, a large salary can be justified for a full-time chief executive of a flourishing business. If either the time commitment or income is missing and the return is audited, the IRS is likely to disallow the deduction and treat part or all of the payment to the stockholder/officer as a dividend. For the recipient, it's six of one, half a dozen of the other, since salary and dividends are both taxed as ordinary income. But for the corporation, a tax-deductible salary is better than a nondeductible dividend.

Amendments, Extensions, and Pleas

If you find out that your estimate of your tax liability is wrong, you can simply raise or lower the subsequent estimated tax payments for the year. You don't need permission, and you don't have to file any special forms.

If you discover that a return for one of the past three years should be corrected (either because you made a mistake or because losses have been carried back), you can file an amended return: 1040X for individuals, 1120X for corporations. If you're entitled to a refund, you can expedite it by attaching a Form 1045 to a 1040X, an 1139 to an 1120X. The IRS will process the form and send you the refund within ninety days.

Understandably, some people have trouble coping with tax returns, particularly if they wait until the last minute and discover that important records are cryptic or unavailable (e.g., you have a bunch of envelopes with scrawls on them and a pile of illegible canceled checks). Individuals can file Form 4868 on or before the due date of the 1040 or 1120S, and get an automatic two-month extension for filing said 1040 or 1120S. Corporations can get an automatic three-month extension by filing Form 7004. Before the three months expire, the corporation can file Form 7005, demonstrating a damned good reason for the delay, and get IRS approval for another three-month extension.

The problem is that the extension applies only to the amount of time you get to *file* your return, not the amount of time you get to *pay*. Therefore, it doesn't help very much to get an extension unless you send in a chunk of money hoping it will be sufficient, or unless you know that you will get a yet undetermined refund.

If your problem is paying rather than filing on time, what you need is Form 1127 (request for more time to pay) backed up by a statement of financial and other information. The IRS has the discretion to either grant or refuse your request.

Tax Planning

Sometimes there is a fine line between illegal tax evasion and permissible tax avoidance. If you plan the sale of your business so that it conforms to the Internal Revenue Code's definition of a tax-free reorganization (see Chapter Eleven), this is tax avoidance. If your salary as president of a one-person corporation is rather higher than the prosperity of the corporation would justify, it's a borderline case. A CPA fee paid to your cat and deducted by your business is tax evasion.

There are many recognized and legitimate tax planning devices, many of them inspired by the kind of thinking that gives Jesuits a bad name. The strategies discussed here are somewhat simpler. Whether or not a particular device is worthwhile for you depends on:

- Its complexity (you don't want to disrupt your business and personal life for a measly hundred dollars)
- Its cost (you don't want to spend $500 in professional fees)
- Other practical consequences (it's worth adding a few dollars to your tax bill to cement or save a good relationship with a customer or supplier)
- Its effect on your cash flow
- The result in aftertax dollars (a highly taxed but highly profitable deal is usually better than one with no tax but precious little yield to you)

CHOICE OF FORM

If you expect lots of deductible losses, a limited partnership is a good choice of organization. If you want to be able to offer very large pension benefits, you must incorporate to take full advantage of the tax laws. A sole proprietor who plows all the business' income back in pays personal income tax on money s/he never sees. Whether or not to incorporate, whether a corporation should select Sub S or not are individual decisions, but tax considerations are very important factors in the decision.

DEFERRAL

The human psyche is such that an obligation to pay tax later is less painful than an obligation to pay tax now. After all, the Last Judgment may intervene before the tax bill falls due. There are several legitimate ways of deferring tax. The trade-off is that you also defer income: that is, you agree to wait to receive money you have a legal right to receive currently.

- Tax shelters—usually, investors in tax shelters have heavy paper losses at the beginning of the tax shelter project. They deduct the losses, reducing their tax bill, then later achieve profits and concomitant tax liability.
- Installment sales—a business that sells an asset and gets at least one payment after the year of the transaction is entitled to special tax treatment (see page 319).
- Deferred compensation for employees and officers—for example, a corporation president accepts a pension plan instead of a salary increase, so that s/he will have income after retirement when s/he will probably have a lower income and therefore be in a lower tax bracket.
- Capitalization of expenses—start-up expenses can either be amortized over a period of at least five years or added to the basis for the business interest; state and local taxes can either be deducted or capitalized. If these amounts are capitalized, they increase the basis of the business interest. The taxpayer has to wait until the business interest is sold, but s/he or it realizes less taxable income from the sale than if the expenses had been amortized or deducted, and if the business interest had a lower basis.
- Tax-free reorganization (see Chapter Eleven)—in the short run, a tax-free reorganization means that you can sell your business with no immediate tax bite. In the long run, you will probably pay tax—when you sell the stock of the corporation that bought your business.

There are two problems with deferred income. If you had the money now, you could invest it. Then again, a deferred payment may never materialize. The present value of a bird in the hand is equal to the present value of approximately 1.7864 birds in the bush.

CAPITAL VS. ORDINARY INCOME

As we've seen, this is no big deal for a small corporation. However, a wealthy person has good reason to prefer long-term capital gain taxed at twenty percent to salary income, taxed at fifty percent. Good advance planning would allow this individual to sell stock in a corporation instead of receiving dividends from the same corporation, or distributions from a successful proprietorship or partnership. However, a bad stock market can make the stock less valuable, even if the underlying business is sound.

DEDUCTIBLE EXPENSES VS. CAPITALIZED ITEMS

If your business leases its equipment or borrows money, the lease payments and interest are deductible expenses. If, instead, the business buys equipment for cash or issues stock, the equipment must be capitalized for accounting purposes and depreciated (usually under ACRS) for tax purposes. When a corporation issues shares of stock, this is not a taxable event for the corporation; but the corporation does not get a deduction for the dividends it pays to the owners of these shares of stock.

INCOME SPLITTING

Theoretically, people with higher income pay tax at higher rates. Therefore, if income can be "moved" from a higher-bracket person to a lower-bracket person, the overall tax bill is less. Family businesses are famous (or notorious) for income splitting. For example, a retail business can justify hiring a stock clerk, and deduct his/her wages as an ordinary and necessary business expense—even if the stock clerk is the teenaged offspring of the owner. However, if the salary is forty thousand dollars and/or the business is in Wisconsin while the scion is in Hawaii, the deduction is improper.

Family income splitting requires expert planning, or it can backfire. For example, you lose the dependency deduction if you hire a family member and then require him or her to pay room and board out of the salary you pay.

In accounting, the bottom line shows whether a business has achieved profits or losses. In tax planning, the bottom line is the amount left over after all allowable adjustments, deductions, and credits have been taken, and after all required taxes have been paid. The best tax planning scheme is not necessarily the one that yields the largest deductions or the smallest taxable income; it's the scheme that leaves the most money in your pocket after all bills have been paid.

State and Local Taxes

In one of Donne's greatest works, the poet begs God to forgive various enumerated sins. After each sin, the refrain is "I still have more." When you have computed and paid your federal income tax, you also still have more.

Most states have an income tax; so do some cities. Generally, quarterly estimated payments will be required for your own income (if you are a proprietor or partner) and you'll have to withhold income tax from each paycheck for each employee.

When you compute your own year-end tax return, you stand a better chance of retaining your sanity if you do your federal income tax return first. The state tax returns often call for figures taken from the federal return. The computation process is similar, but not identical, for federal and state forms. ERTA lowered tax rates and changed the treatment of business assets for federal tax purposes, but the states did not follow suit.

States and localities also charge a host of business taxes other than income taxes. To find out which of these you are subject to, ask your lawyer, the local taxing authorities, or call City Hall (obviously a more practical strategy in a small city than in a large one). The best time to find out is before you start doing business. But don't worry, returns for some of the more obscure taxes will be mailed to you, because the taxing authorities will find *you*. If you find out about a particular tax some time after you should have made the first payment, you can file back returns as soon as you find out. If there is a penalty for late filing, it will probably be a percentage of the tax due. Five percent of $13.04 probably won't put you out of business.

You may have to pay some or all of these taxes (plus a few even I've never heard of):

- Unincorporated business tax (a percentage of your business' net income)

- Annual license tax
- Franchise tax (for the privilege of doing business in a particular state as a corporation. Usually foreign corporations pay more than domestic corporations.)
- Commercial occupancy tax (on the amount of rent you pay)
- Real estate taxes (if you own your business premises)
- Chain store tax (on each store in a chain—e.g., your six Decoglo Paint Stores)
- Use taxes (if you bought something out of state and thus didn't have to pay your state's sales tax)

There are also taxes you may have to collect from customers and remit to local taxing authorities: sales tax and excise tax on gas, cigarettes, alcoholic beverages, and other legalized vices.

If you have a little extra money and very good records, you can have an accountant fill out your tax returns. Not only will this make your life easier, you'll be able to discuss tax planning for future years.

Lacking one or both of these essentials, you'll have to do the returns yourself. This is peculiarly discouraging, because if you have a small income you feel like a failure, and if you have a large income you have to pay lots of money. If you feel that your return does not deserve especially close scrutiny, send it in close to April 15 (or whenever it's due): the busier the IRS is, the less attention they'll lavish on your own masterwork. The IRS does not give Neat Taxpayer Awards for particularly spiffy examples of the genre. However, if you wait until the last minute, you may find that critical information is missing. The best strategy is to do the computations early—say, February 15—then sign and date the return about April 10 (calendar-year taxpayers), make out the check, and mail it.

If your bookkeeping is good (as it should be, if you read Chapter Five), preparing tax returns will be merely unpleasant, not traumatic. To prepare your books and records, and to find past years' receipts and tax returns, you'll need a good system for filing and retrieving paperwork—which you should have, if you read Chapter Seven and take it to heart.

CHAPTER SEVEN

Paperwork—Is This Form Really Necessary?

MOST AMERICAN WORKERS are not gandy dancers or hashslingers, but paper shufflers. An army of female fingers dances over the typewriter keys and through the file drawers. Sexually integrated battalions squint over CRTs and push pencils across a snowy plain of papers. Status inheres in either the stacked desk or the clear marble shelf with nothing on it but a gold pen. The first implies a never-ending flow of responsibilities; the second, inhuman efficiency and a corps of underlings.

Once again, the shoestring entrepreneur, bereft of an audience and very nearly bereft of money, will have to do without this cellulosic security blanket. Established businesses usually have a few sacred forms that must be regularly completed and ritually filed, although no one remembers their purpose. The file system has a few glitches, but it's too damned much trouble to move everything. So a starting business has a once-in-a-lifetime opportunity to set up an efficient paperwork system—one in which information is collected only if it's really necessary, and can be retrieved easily.

According to Olsten, the temporary office-personnel firm, sixty-five cents out of every record-keeping dollar is wasted, and eighty-five percent of documents filed are never looked at again. Isn't that inspiring?

The "electronic office" is the much-heralded cure. But it implies a vast, universal capital expenditure (at a time when loans are high-priced even for major corporations, and very nearly unavailable to anyone else.) Anyone who's ever gotten a utility bill will understand the gallows humor behind the claim of improved efficiency. A secretary's job, which is hardly nirvana, at least involves human contact with varied tasks; the brave new electronics sweatshop's female employees bash away at a keboard all day, afraid to look up from their flickering screens in case the supervisor sees a drop in their hourly keystrokes. And, of course, in case of an interruption in electric service, or the long-plotted revenge of a disgruntled employee, all of a company's files can be wiped out in a few seconds. For all these reasons, I recommend that you stick with paper, in discreet amounts.

The discussion of paperwork breaks down neatly into substantive and procedural—the paper (actual sheets to be manipulated) and the work (what you do with them).

Business Stationery

To a certain extent, you will be judged by this, so be sure that you get the fullest measure of class for your dollar.

Peg Bracken (of *The I Hate to Cookbook* fame) said that there are three variables: ease, elegance, and economy. You can have any two at once, but never all three. It is very easy to have elegant stationery merely by sending your butler over to Tiffany's to have it engraved. Ease and economy can be combined by dispensing with stationery and sending your letters out written in pencil on yellow lined paper. Less dramatically, you can have stationery in a standard color, with a standard type style, thermographed by a discount printer or a mail-order stationer. (Thermography is fake engraving: raised black letters without a corresponding depression on the back of the page.)

I think the gain in class is worth the extra money spent on heavy watermarked paper with some rag content: 20-lb and 25% should do it. You can get damn near any color you want for a small price increase. My preference is white stationery. Conservative white is always acceptable, but the main reason for my recommendation is that you can always get white correction strips and correction fluid, and they always match. Your custom-blend Tahitian Tangerine supplies always cost a lot more but don't always match. If you can, save work by starting your heading where you plan to type the left margin of your letters (usually 1″–1½″ from the edge of the paper), and have a small black dot printed at the left margin of the last line on the page. Thus, the person typing the letter (generally, you) will produce a nicely lined-up letter with minimal effort.

I recommend ordinary 8½" x 11" letterhead. Monarch-size stationery is also available; evidently it was named by a Jacobin, since it's quite a bit smaller than ordinary stationery. I think it's sleazy-looking, but it does have the advantage of using less paper, and short notes or informal bills seem less out-of-proportion.

If you want a fancier letterhead, or one with your logo or some other picture, the easiest and cheapest way to go is to make a mechanical for the stationery on the kind of art board that has nonreproducing blue lines ruled at ¼" intervals. You use the blue lines to align transfer type, hand-drawn letters, pictures, line drawings, set type, tapes from a KroyType machine, or indeed anything else. Then you have the mechanical offset-printed on good quality paper. Working with transfer type is one of the tortures of the damned in the inferno, so get lots of art board and lots of whiteout and be prepared to spend all day at the task.

You will also need #10 business envelopes; my recommendation is for envelopes at least of the same quality as the letterhead, with your address imprinted in the upper left-hand corner. You can have the address printed on the flap, but you might as well let the recipient know who you are right away. If a piece of mail has to be returned to you (for example, if the addressee has moved, or if the nonadhesive stamp has fallen off), the Post Office probably won't notice the address on the flap; your letter winds up in the Dead Letter Office, and you won't be able to correct your mailing list.

I use my stationery and plain #10 envelopes for all correspondence, because it's classy and convenient, and the letters are anonymous enough to be at least opened rather than tossed out immediately as junk mail. But if you want to save time, and elegance is not your primary concern, you can get "speed letters" imprinted with your name and address. The letters are made up as carbon sets. You type or print the recipient's address and your message; you file one copy, and the recipient writes a reply directly on the speed letter. S/he files one copy and sends one back to you. Speed letters are designed so that the address appears in the opening of a window envelope. I think window envelopes are the last word in tackiness, but if you disagree, you can order window envelopes imprinted with your address, and set up your outgoing letters and bills so that the address shows through.

The standard sizes for correspondence envelopes are:

$6\frac{1}{4} = 3\frac{1}{2}'' \times 6''$	$9 = 3\frac{7}{8}'' \times 8\frac{7}{8}''$
$6\frac{3}{4} = 3\frac{5}{8}'' \times 6\frac{1}{2}''$	$10 = 4\frac{1}{8}'' \times 9\frac{1}{2}''$
$7 = 3\frac{3}{4}'' \times 6\frac{3}{4}''$	$11 = 4\frac{1}{2}'' \times 10\frac{3}{8}''$
$7\frac{3}{4} = 3\frac{7}{8}'' \times 7\frac{1}{2}''$	$12 = 4\frac{3}{4}'' \times 11''$
(Monarch)	
$8\frac{5}{8} = 3\frac{5}{8}'' \times 8\frac{5}{8}''$	$14 = 5'' \times 11\frac{1}{2}''$
(check)	

As you can see, they were named by the same fellow who named the two-by-four. Monarch envelopes are, of course, required if you have Monarch stationery. Check envelopes are good for mailing checks, and make excellent business-reply envelopes if you require advance payment. It's no fun trying to accordion-pleat a check into an envelope that's just a little too small, and it doesn't do the check much good either.

Many mail-order firms include an envelope printed with their address in every solicitation, so customers don't have to exert themselves unduly. Usually they use a $6\frac{1}{4}$ or $6\frac{3}{4}$ envelope. If you do this, be sure the envelope is opaque enough to hide the checks or money enclosed.

If you really want to save work for your customers, you can stamp the envelope (which often impels them to keep the stamp and toss the envelope) or get a permit for business-reply envelopes and have them printed to order. You pay postage only on those envelopes actually mailed to you; but the Post Office charges you a nickel apiece over the regular third-class postage rate. Particularly hostile consumers have been known to attach bricks to the envelope before mailing it back. My advice is that, unless you're selling something expensive enough to survive these postal contretemps, force the buyers to provide their own envelopes and stamps for their orders.

Shipping Materials

If you mail large things (e.g., manuscripts) or irregularly shaped things (e.g., nuts and bolts), you will need heavy mailing envelopes, which are normally available in white, manila, or a greenish gray. Stock sizes for open-end envelopes are:

1 coin = 2½″ x 3½″	5 coin = 2⅞″ x 5¼″
3 coin = 2½″ x 4¼″	5½ coin = 3⅛″ x 5½″
4 coin = 3″ x 4½″	6 coin = 3⅜″ x 5½″
4½ coin = 3″ x 4⅞″	7 coin = 3½″ x 6½″

plus these nameless sizes:

5½″ x 8¼″	9″ x 12″
6″ x 9″	9½″ x 12½″
6½″ x 9½″	10″ x 13″
7″ x 10″	11½″ x 14½″
7½″ x 10½″	

The stock sizes for booklet envelopes (the ones with the flap opening along the side) are:

2½ = 4½″ x 5⅞″	7 = 6¼″ x 9⅝″
3 = 4¾″ x 6½″	7½ = 7½″ x 10½″
5 = 5½″ x 8⅛″	9 = 8¾″ x 11½″
6 = 5¾″ x 8⅞″	9½ = 9″ x 12″
6½ = 6″ x 9″	10 = 9½″ x 12⅝″

Mail-order stationers or local printers can imprint your name and address on the envelope. If you're really short on money, and prestige is not your first consideration, you can have a rubber stamp made up with your name and address (or the name and address of a frequent correspondent) and use that for the address and/or return address.

I favor mailing labels with your name, address, and the space to type the recipient's address. These labels can be used for envelopes, packages, and miscellaneous labeling jobs (identifying the contents of a liquor carton used to store low-priority files after you clean out the file cabinet). All the mail-order stationers sell pressure-sensitive labels in strips or in rolls. The strips are more compact, but the rolls are easier to use in a typewriter. For the same price, or a small surcharge, you can buy labels identified as first class mail, third class mail, or with a series of boxes to check for the class of mail you want to send. In the alternative, you can add this information to the finished package with a rubber stamp, or get a separate stick-on label saying "First Class," or whatever. If you need several copies of the label (for example, if you file them as evidence of shipment), you can buy labels in carbon sets. One typing produces several labels, but you'll have to wet and stick the original label to the package.

If you are both dexterous and anxious, you can use ungummed

labels and stick them on with clear, pressure-sensitive tape. The tape keeps the label clean and dry, but it sticks to itself like mad.

Mail-order stationers also sell forms for packing lists and other shipping documents, plus tough, waterproof squares of plastic emblazoned "Packing List Enclosed," or whatever. The list is sealed to the outside of the package, so that the buyer can examine the list before opening the package. The plastic square protects the list against rain and shipping damage.

You'll also need paper without your letterhead, for typing the second sheets of letters, reports, proposals, and the like. Carbon sets are a great convenience, but expensive. Use a thinner paper (13–16-lb) or even an onionskin (5–8-lb) for making multiple copies; a paper that matches the letterhead for second sheets; a decent-looking paper (20-lb or, if you can afford it, 24-lb) for documents sent to others; a 20-lb duplicating (no rag) paper for plain paper copiers; and use outdated letterhead, the back of junk mail, or the cheapest paper you can find for single carbons and first drafts. I use robin's-egg blue photocopying paper for carbons and drafts. It has three advantages: it's pretty, it costs $1.99 a ream, and I never send out a carbon or first draft by mistake, because the blue is so distinctive.

Business Cards

You'll also need business cards as much as a Victorian lady needed visiting cards. Usually the minimum order is five hundred, which for most people is a lifetime supply. If you change your address, the backs of old business cards are very good for your scheduling board (see Chapter Eight) or for taking notes. My preference is for normal-sized, white business cards on heavy stock, with the business name in the middle and your name in the corner. Business cards are also available in colors, on parchment, with stock logos (inexpensive and hideous), with custom logos (expensive and aesthetically variable, it depends on your taste), and in unusual shapes. Flamboyance is more acceptable in a record producer than in an insurance broker. One innovation of which I approve is the practice of cutting the bottom of the card so it will fit into a Rolodex or similar card index. (The term "circular file" has a different connotation.)

If you go to a public relations firm for a "corporate identity program," they will pick your best-looking item of stationery and tell you to conform the other items to it in type style, proportions, and color. Personally, I don't think anybody gives a good goddamn whether your business cards match your invoices, but if you disagree, you can save the PR firm's fee by standardizing these items at the outset.

Checks and Recordkeeping

As soon as you have a company name and address and have filed your DBA certificate ("doing business as"; official registration of your business), you can get business checks printed up. Do this as soon as possible; as you will find out quickly, spending money is more or less a full-time job for an entrepreneur. Besides, a real business check looks infinitely more professional than a starter check or a personal check.

If you have a choice of styles among the conventional checks available from your bank, opt for the largest possible check stub—preferably one that leaves room for a cogent explanation of what the check was for. If you have a numerical coding system, or if you keep conventional double-entry books, be sure to put the coded entry on the check stub (e.g., 40733 or GJ16). If you use window envelopes, see if you can have the checks printed with lines for the payee's address, in the right place for your envelope.

Once you have an account, and the corresponding account numbers (the magnetically coded numbers at the bottom of the check), you can get various kinds of unconventional checks. Multiple-voucher checks are printed as carbon sets. The top copy, on safety paper, is the check you write or type; it goes to the payee. You file one of the carbons by check number, instead of keeping a check register. You attach the second carbon to the invoice you're paying, and file the invoice alphabetically. The file of paid invoices is your substitute for a cash disbursement journal. You can also have single-voucher checks printed, with boxes on the check itself for filling in invoice number, withheld taxes, or other information; the voucher is perforated and can be removed from the check before sending it out.

For those willing to sacrifice some elegance and economy in return for ease, various "one-write" check systems are available. You send in a sample check, and the stationer puts the same magnetic code on the one-write checks, which also have your company name and address. The one-write checks are bound in overlapping rows; each check has a strip of carbon paper on the back that transfers information such as the check's date, payee, and amount to a combination check register and bookkeeping journal below. You can order one-write checks set up for paying bills (with space for dates, numbers, and amounts for the invoices you are paying), payroll (with space for hours worked and withheld taxes), or a hybrid. One-write checks are ugly, and the carbon strip on the back makes them damn near impossible to endorse, but they do save time and effort for a one-person business that is not highly concerned with image.

Accountant's Computer Service, Inc. (443 East Westfield Avenue, Roselle Park, NJ 07204) and McBee have taken the one-write idea a step further. McBee's Folding Bookkeeper Accounting Systems are one-write checkbooks available in payroll, receivables, payables, or disbursements configurations—and as part of Op Chek, a computerized system. Op Chek assigns each check a voucher with numbered boxes to be filled in. Each box corresponds to an accounting entry (e.g., travel & entertainment). The user sends the vouchers and the journals prepared with the carbon strip to a bank participating in Op Chek. The bank uses its computer system to print out daily balances, balance the checkbook, print out a general journal and a general ledger, and prepare balance sheets, operating statements, and financial ratio analysis reports. Business owners who have computers or use service bureaus can do the same thing on a more modest scale by assigning code numbers (e.g., A40 = depreciation, C15 = utility bills, E92 = long-distance telephone calls), and inputting this information into the computer. In fact, entrepreneurs without computers can handwrite the code number on the check (somewhere that it won't be mistaken for the amount) and make sure the postings are current when they balance the checkbook each month.

Selling: Forms for Your Customers

If you have a retail store where cash on the barrelhead is the rule, the only document you'll need will be the cash register tape. However, for various reasons (inventory control, your customers' request) it may be a good idea to have sales slips, with your name and address printed or rubber-stamped on the top, and with lines for filling in what was purchased, the amount, and the tax. At a minimum, you'll need an original (for the customer) and a carbon (for your records). It may be worthwhile to have several carbons: one filed by date, one by type of purchase, one by salesperson (especially if they get a commission on sales). Most of these sales slips are prenumbered. If yours are, and if a sales slip is ruined, mark it "void" and leave it in the sales book. Otherwise you can go crazy figuring out why number 4703 is missing.

Consignment is an intermediate step between a loan and a sale. The consignor (often an artist or craftsperson) allows a retail merchant to display the goods in a shop. If someone buys the merchandise, the shopkeeper gets a commission (less than the normal retail markup), while the artist or craftsperson gets the rest. A consignment is more trouble for all concerned than an outright sale, but it allows the consignee (the store owner) to test new items and new suppliers without money risk. It pays the consignor more than an outright sale. Whether you are consigning your pottery to a housewares store or displaying hand-knitted sweaters in your boutique, you should have the protection of a formal, written consignment memorandum giving at least this much information:

- Name and address of both consignor and consignee
- Date of consignment
- Description of items consigned
- Quantity of each item
- Retail price of the item
- Amount to be retained by the consignee; amount to be paid to the consignor
- The consignor's right to inspect the merchandise (usually allowed at any time during normal business hours)
- Consignee's responsibility to make reports (usually once a month, giving a description and price for each item sold, and including a check)
- Status of items lost, stolen, or damaged (they're usually considered sold; the consignee has the responsibility for protecting the items)
- Consignor's right to retrieve the items, and consignee's right to return them (usually unlimited)

- Insurance provisions
- Legal provisions required by the Uniform Commercial Code, or by local law (ask your lawyer, and get a lawyer for this purpose if you don't have one)
- Signatures of both consignor and consignee

INVOICES

The next level of complexity comes when you ship items for later payment. The usual document for demanding payment is the invoice.

Preprinted invoices are available from job printers, in stationery stores, or from mail-order stationers. If you often use standard legal language ("boilerplate") that does not appear on the printed form, you can have these provisions custom-printed on the form, or have pressure-sensitive stickers printed and attach them to the forms.

Usually, invoices are prenumbered, 8½" x 11" or 8½" x 5½", and come in carbon sets or carbonless reproducing sets of two, three, or four copies. You write out or type the invoice, and send the original to the customer. The second and third copies can be filed in the customer's file, under the date of the order or the date of shipment (particularly useful if you give trade credit terms such as 2/10 net 30), in numerical order, or in an "unpaid" file, with the invoice shifted to the "paid" file when you get the money. A four-part set usually has a "blind" copy with the prices blocked out. This goes to the customer; the customer sends this packing slip to its accounting department, which checks the invoice and authorizes payment.

The invoice includes:

- Your name, address, and phone number
- The buyer's name and address (perhaps placed so that you can mail the invoice in a window envelope), and the shipping address if it is different from the buyer's address
- Date the invoice is issued
- Invoice number
- The customer's order number, if there is one
- What was sold
- Price per unit
- Number of units
- Price

- Insurance charges
- Shipping charges
- Sales tax
- Total
- Payment terms (COD, due immediately, 2% discount if paid within 10 days, full balance due in 30 days, or whatever; if the buyer has already paid and the invoice is just for the record, it's called a "pro forma" invoice)
- Date of shipment
- Shipment method
- Whether freight is prepaid or collect
- FOB point (the point at which the buyer becomes the legal owner of the goods. The seller pays shipping costs to the FOB point and is responsible only for damage that occurs before the merchandise reaches the FOB point.)
- Any limitation on damage claims (for example, claims must be made within 10 days of delivery)

With any luck at all, your invoices will be paid promptly, and you can stamp them "paid" and move them to a paid or chronological file. If they aren't, the statement will serve as a gentle reminder.

STATEMENTS

A statement is a monthly summary of a customer's transactions. Purchases and payments are listed by invoice number. It's not an official request for payment, but it may remind your customers that money is due. If your business is a rather informal one, you can do without statements altogether. However, if you feel you need them, or if your customers insist, and if you have individual ledger cards for each account and a copying machine, you can superimpose the ledger card on a printed statement form, copy the two of them on one sheet of paper, and send the result out in lieu of a typed statement. One reason for bothering with statements is that, when you sue to collect unpaid bills, you want to establish a paper trail demonstrating repeated requests for payment—and the absence of complaints on the customer's part. The legal term for this is an "account stated": both parties agree on the amount involved, and the buyer has lost the chance to complain about the quality or quantity of goods delivered. (If you are the tardy payer, of course, you can't complain either if you have received the goods without complaint.)

BACK-ORDER CARDS

If you have more orders than you can handle or face shipping delays, it's a convenience for your customer if you have back-order cards printed. They can be ordinary postcards, addressed by hand or typewriter, with a message printed on the back advising the customer that you're sorry, but the item ordered (leave room to describe it) is out of stock, that you have reordered and the order will be filled in about (fill in the blank) days. The number of days you stipulate must be large enough so that you can meet the new deadline, and avoid infuriating your customers at that time; but small enough to avoid infuriating them immediately.

Buying: Forms for Your Suppliers

If you do all your buying from retail stores or mail-order catalogs, all you have to do is fork over the money and fill out the order form. However, if you have (or want to establish) a continuing relationship with one or more sellers, you may want to have purchase orders and/or request-for-quotation forms printed.

Purchase orders are usually 8½" x 11", made up in four-part sets; the top copy is on bond paper, the other three on tissue paper. The seller gets the top copy and one tissue copy. You file one of your tissue copies alphabetically by seller, and one numerically by order number or chronologically by date of order. Purchase orders include this information:

- Number of the purchase order
- Date it's issued
- Seller's name and address (this can be positioned for a window envelope)
- Your name and address
- Shipping address, if it's not the same
- Catalog item numbers, or price quotation references
- Number of the vendor's bill of lading
- Quantity of each item ordered
- Unit price

- Total price for each item
- The discount you were quoted
- FOB point
- Whether freight is collect or billed
- Amount of freight charges
- Amount of insurance charges
- Total
- Method of shipment (say "best way" if you have no preference)
- Your budget code
- An authorized signature

If you're not paying in advance, include financial references—at least the name of your bank, although it's not too likely that any reader of this book will be in Dun & Bradstreet.

If you have a lot of trouble with late orders, it may be worthwhile to have double postcards printed up. Half of the postcard gives your name and address and boxes for you to check off: Have you shipped order #_____? When? When will you ship it? Can you make a partial shipment? Leave lines for fill-ins so you can deal with other problems as they arise. This half is addressed to the seller. The other half, addressed to you, gives them room to explain what has happened to your shipment, and when it can be expected to arrive.

If you will be making major purchases, you can probably do a little better than the catalog prices; you can also check *Thomas' Register,* which lists manufacturers, to find manufacturers who don't issue catalogs. The way to keep track of various prices, specifications, and shipping dates is to use a uniform request-for-quotation (RFQ) form. Usually RFQ forms are prenumbered, 8½" x 11", and made up in sets of five. You mail four copies to each potential bidder, and file one; they keep two copies and return two copies with their bid. Xerox Data Systems does it a little differently. It uses a 7-part carbon set: two copies for each of three bidders, and a work copy with all three names and addresses. That way, the number of forms to be typed is reduced by two thirds. The bidders' copies have patterned or blocked-out carbons or patterns printed on the forms so the other bidders' names are not visible. The RFQ form includes:

- Your name and address
- Supplier's name and address (Maybe you can reduce the

work, sacrificing a little style, by positioning the address for
use in a window envelope.)

- Description of the material for which you want bids
- The quantity you need; whether this is firm or estimated; if
  you will accept overruns or less than the amount needed
- When you need the material
- How the items will be supplied (by the dozen, in gallon jugs)
- FOB point—preferably your address
- Form of quote you will accept (letter, phone call, form)
- Last date bids will be accepted (give them at least two weeks)
- If you supply blueprints, ask for them back, and indicate that
  they are confidential
- Indicate the quality tests you will use
- Specify whether you will supply materials for the order, or
  whether you expect the bidder to provide them
- Ask for alternative proposals that will lower the price, im-
  prove the quality of the material, or both

Make sure the RFQ form states firmly and in large letters that it is
not an order and that you will not reimburse the bidder for any expenses involved in giving you a quote. Some vendors won't bother
to reply—an index of how much they value your patronage. The
quotes you do receive will have the same format, so they will be
easy to compare. If you don't want to go to quite that much trouble,
you can type up a letter on your stationery explaining what you
want and asking for quotes. Make as many photocopies as you have
potential suppliers, type in the addresses individually, and type an
envelope for each letter.

Internal Paperwork

So much for the forms you send winging out into the world.
Other forms will stay within the four walls (or twenty-two partitions, if it's an open plan) of your office.

If yours is a service business (e.g., photography, auto repair) or if
you manufacture to order, you will need job tickets. The job ticket
can be a separate piece of paper (if you're going to attach it to
something bulky like a car), or can be written directly on the file
folder or 9" x 12" envelope (if your merchandise can be kept in

either). The front of the job ticket gives the job number, customer's name and address, customer's order number, specs of the order, shipping information, and the scheduled delivery date. Leave room for notes. The back of the job ticket is used for a running record of the cost of completing the job: time spent, materials used, delivery costs. Receipts, correspondence, and other papers pertaining to the job can be stuffed into the envelope or file. When the job is finished, loose job sheets are filed numerically in a loose-leaf book; files or envelopes are filed in the filing cabinet or a transfer file, again by job number.

If you pay workers by the hour, you will need either a system of sign-in sheets or a time clock. If you bill your customers by the hour, you will need time sheets. Time sheets include the date, the client's name, what was done, the amount of time used (maybe the start and finish times as well), the rate per hour or per unit, and the total amount owed. If you have a computer or use a computer service bureau, you'll need a code number for each client, and a place on the sheet for the code number. If the time sheet is not sent directly to the client, it saves bookkeeping time to include columns for the date billed and the date you get paid.

It saves a lot of various kinds of trouble to keep a phone log. The easiest way to do this is to take a plain piece of paper and type out a heading giving date, time, person called, number called (or person who called you and his/her number), and (if you don't run a solo operation) the person making the call. On the body of the paper, type out at nice long intervals: Point #1, Response, Point #2, Response, and so on. Have 500 copies made on 3-hole paper, and give each of your employees a loose-leaf binder with about 100 sheets. Before you make a phone call, you can jot down what you want to say, then record responses, and your responses to your caller's statements. Log all long-distance calls, without exception, and all significant local calls (sending out for sandwiches doesn't rate). You'll have a way of checking your phone bill and also a reference for later arguments ("... But on November 3 Mr. Bertocci said that you would credit my account with $679.08 because all 3,000 of the bushing flanges were defective ...")

You may want to keep a separate register, or a similar register using different colored paper, for phone orders: record the date, your order number, the items ordered, quantity ordered, and price; then update this register to give the invoice number, invoice date, your check number, and the date you paid for the merchandise. The register acts as a check if a phantom invoice appears and no one can remember ordering the stuff.

If you buy a lot of merchandise or components and have a number of suppliers, it can be efficient to maintain a suppliers' file—anything from a shoebox full of 3″ x 5″ cards to a Rolodex to 8½″ x 11″ sheets in a file folder or a notebook to magnetic tape in a computer. The vendor file includes:

- Vendor's name, address
- File number (for cross-references)
- Phone number
- Contact person
- Local representative
- Items you might order
- Terms
- FOB point
- Lead time for delivery
- Past orders—date, quantity, price
- Notes on performance ("Whole shipment of sweaters water-damaged, very hard to get refund")

If you sell to a relatively small number of clients (for example, if you're a caterer, photographer, harpsichord maker) rather than to an anonymous public, you can make it easier to get repeat business by keeping a customer card file or set of files. One file is alphabetical by name, one chronological (by date of last contact or date when you can expect a reorder), one by product type (so you can set up a mailing list when you introduce new products or have a special sale). The customer file includes:

- Customer's name, address, phone number
- Contact person and his/her telephone extension
- Buying history
- Payment history
- Special requirements
- Size of customer's business (you can't get blood out of a turnip)
- Your major competitors for their business
- Strategies for overcoming competition

If you do a few large jobs every year (e.g., if you're an architect, photographer, publicist) write a resume for each job as soon as it's finished. Number each resume and index it by number and by name.

That way, if you ever need to write a proposal, need copy for a brochure, or just want a demonstration of how great you are, you can pull the relevant resumes quickly and arrange them (or modify them) to prove your point. For the same reason, keep a current resume of all your employees, consultants, and anyone who might be dragged into a project. Update each resume to include newly earned degrees, publications, or professional honors.

Watch out for opportunities to recycle. Not just papers—although you can sell used uncoated paper and data-processing punch cards—but also images and information can be "melted down" and resold. Photographers file their negatives carefully in glassine to prevent scratches, and they index and cross-index the negatives by client and subject. They do this not only out of respect for the hard work that produced the image, but because clients may order more prints later; and unsold images can be sold to another client or to a stock photo service.

Sketches rejected by one design client may be accepted by another or can be used in a sales brochure. Articles can be rewritten for another audience ("The Elephant in Song and Story" leads to "Socio-Linguistic Aspects of the Elephant," which leads to "The Elephant and Your Dyslexic Child," "Integrating the Elephant into the Second-Grade Curriculum," and so on eternally.) Whitney Wasp III is a past master of this technique. Versions of a few, prototypical articles—which were ghost-written anyway—have been appearing under his name for years. Publication enhances his resume, and makes Wasp, Wasp & Token a stronger bidder for government contracts.

Designing Your Own Forms

Sometimes, despite the best efforts of printers and stationers, stock forms won't be enough, and you'll have to design a form to your own specifications. A good form is easy to use—for your customers, but especially for you. Aesthetic considerations can be thrown overboard with impunity. I've seen teensy, tiny coupons printed in full-page ads graced with generous white space: lovely to look at, but the coupon can only be filled out by people who can engrave the Lord's Prayer on the head of a pin. It can't be any treat to process the minuscule coupon, either. So always make coupons as large as you can (without buying a ruinously expensive ad), make them square or rectangular so the typist can handle them, and leave adequate vertical and horizontal room for filling in information. Order forms should include a place for you to fill in the shipping date when the order is processed—and the date should not be hypothetical.

There are two basic approaches to amateur forms design. First, and easier, is to lay the forms out on a typewriter, hand-rule any lines needed, and have the forms photocopied or photo-offset. The more elaborate approach is to do a layout on graph paper (make sure the blue lines won't reproduce when you print the form) or art board, using transfer type, pressure graphics, and/or set type, and then have the result offset-printed. You can also design the form and have the type set by cold composition or in metal, then printed by photo-offset or on a rotary press. The advantage of rotary printing is that both sides are printed at once, so it's easy and cheap to put instructions on the back of the form. The disadvantage is that people are likely to fill out the form (wrong) before they read the instructions. (If the forms are printed by photo-offset, the back has to be printed separately, which costs more.)

The cheapest way to go is to print all your forms in black on white paper. The most convenient way is to print each form in a different ink color, or on a different color of paper; or to use a half-tone screen to highlight part of a form, or to distinguish the copy used for a particular purpose (e.g., the lab copy). If you have a few major customers, it saves time and temper to conform your forms to theirs as much as you can.

The kind of paper you need depends on the way the forms will be used. Sulphite papers (with no rag content) are graded from 1 (top quality) to 5 (the pits). Grade 4 or 5 papers won't stand up to much handling. If the records have to be kept for more than 3 years, choose paper with at least 25% rag content. Choose 50% rag paper if the forms must be kept for more than 6 years. If the forms have to last more than 10 years, you'd better use 100% rag paper or say to hell with it and microfilm anything that must be kept for the ages.

For an ordinary, single-sheet form, 16-lb paper is usually good enough. A form printed on both sides gets more handling, so 20-lb paper is a better choice. If the form will be made up into a carbon set, the first and last pages should be 16-lb paper, but the other sheets can be 12-lb. To make the set easier to use, make the carbon sheets a little shorter than the sheets to be copied, and make the sheet that will be removed first at least ¼″ longer than the other sheets.

The normal margin for an 8½″ x 11″ form is ⅜″ all around, but you'll need at least ⅝″ (more is better) if the form will be punched to fit a 3-hole binder. If you expect the form to be filled out on a typewriter, and if you type or handwrite the mechanical, leave ⅓″ for each vertical line. In other words, you can get 22 lines on a page (8½″ minus ¾″). Allow ⅕″ horizontally for each letter to be filled in, and allow 3″ for writing or signing a name. If you can, leave extra "headroom" over a signature; most people sign their name with at least a bit of a flourish.

Usually, the captions or instructions for a line go in the upper left of that line—convenient for forms filled out by hand, less so for typed forms—typing can't be made "shorter" to fit under the caption. If there are many long captions, consider running them in vertical columns, or at a 45°–60° angle:

People are used to seeing a check box before a question such as— ( ) Yes ( ) No   Are you a registered voter?—so you might as well do it that way, even though in the abstract it makes more sense to ask the question and then provide the space for answering it.

The perfect form, though no one will ever design it, is lovely to look at, cheap to produce, easy to fill out and absolutely idiotproof, and easy to process and absolutely idiotproof. Beauty is sacrificed first; absolute cheapness goes next, convenience only last. Your mail will be filled with strange and wonderful documents in any event, so try to minimize the difficulties by giving clear instructions and using an unambiguous layout. Some things always slip through the net: one federal bureaucracy requested a list of em-

ployees, by grade level, broken down by sex. One administrator re-
plied, "None—we find our real problem is alcohol."

Coping with Correspondence

In a one-person operation, naturally you will read the mail. In a
larger operation, I suggest that you do it anyway. First of all, it
gives you an intimate overview of the business, unexpurgated by
secretary or assistant. Second of all, if you do have employees, it's
harder for them to embezzle if you open the mail.

For those who are even more paranoiac, or who want to see the
mail immediately (at the price of several daily trips to the Post Office), customers can be directed to send their checks to a Post Office
Box (or several of them, for several types of orders). If you have
reason to suspect that you have a light-fingered employee, send
yourself a cash payment occasionally to see what happens. Ads in
different publications, or different kinds of orders, can be coded
("Write to Department A4"); and you can sort out the orders without even opening the envelopes.

The normal human tendency is to open mail, then distribute it
into various shuffle-stacks, to be dealt with at some hypothetical future time. A few months later, most of the problems will have
sorted themselves out anyway; it's a kind of passive triage.

The only time to answer the mail is immediately. I suggest that
you open all the mail and sort it: junk mail for immediate disposal;
junk mail for filing (e.g., catalogs); orders (don't throw out the envelope until you make sure that the letter or order form has a complete and intelligible address); requests for information; bills; letters
requiring an answer; letters not requiring an answer. Discard anything that can be discarded—perhaps the most satisfying part of the
procedure. Enter the orders in your journal or order log. Separate
out the checks and cash. Make up deposit tickets. Since the financial apparatus is engaged anyway, pay the bills, or at least file them
on the date you expect to pay them.

Now we reach the radical part of the proposal. I suggest that
you turn on your typewriter, place a sheet of letterhead, one of carbon paper, and one of scratch paper in the machine, and answer the
first letter on the heap. Do not call in your secretary (even if you
have one), or switch on the dictating machine; figure out what

you're going to say and say it. Letters typed by a secretary have to be proofread and signed (unless they bear the rather contemptuous notation, "Dictated but not read"). Dictating involves a cumbersome routine of spelling things out and a Distant Early Warning System for punctuation.

But don't open the mail until you plan to cope with it. If you open it, sort it, and ignore it for a couple of days or hours while you do other things, you'll have to read everything all over again. If you need information to deal with a particular letter, it's easier to get the information right away and send out your reply. The ideal situation is to look at each piece of paper only once. If you put it aside for later consideration, later may never come.

Next, file the letter by date, or in the customer's file, or, if your volume of correspondence is low, in this month's incoming correspondence file. The carbon goes in a date file, or in this month's outgoing correspondence file, or is clipped to the letter it answers and filed by date. If you expect a reply you can attach a paper clip to the carbon to be removed when it comes in. This way, you can also see which replies are overdue. An alternative method is to keep a "suspense file" by date: file the carbon on the date you expect an answer, then check each day to see if that day's pending matters have been cleared up.

Of course, for those not easily shocked, there is a third alternative: send an informal written note, DON'T MAKE A COPY OF IT, and file the original letter you got. Most of the time, neither you nor your correspondent will ever refer to the file copy again. If this makes you nervous, you can draft your answer on the back of the original incoming letter and handwrite a note to your correspondent.

This strategy only works with people of reasonable honesty and efficiency, and when the relationship is reasonably civilized. If your vis-à-vis constantly loses things, fabricates disputes to avoid paying you, or if you wind up in court, you will need complete texts of correspondence.

Under more harmonious circumstances, you're better off with neat, uncluttered files. Some documents explain themselves: a two-part check with an explanation on the counterfoil, an invoice. You don't need a cover letter saying "this is a check" or "this is an invoice" when you have your checkbook, ledger, and invoice file to back you up in case of a dispute.

If you're still determined to send formal, typed letters, the Administrative Management Society has worked out a new letter format. The Society says this format will save 10% of the time needed to type a 96-word letter. Everything starts at the left margin, without indentation. The salutation and complimentary close are left out, and a subject heading is added. The letter looks like this:

```
Date

Address

Subject

Paragraph 1

Paragraph 2, etc.

Your Name
Your Title
Signature
```

Sometimes you can do without a typed reply, even if you must write back. If the message came in on a speed letter, you can handwrite on its other side and send it back out. You can use speed letters for your own outgoing correspondence. You can handwrite a reply on the letter itself, perhaps with a stamp saying something like "We use this informal method to increase efficiency and reply faster." Some people prefer to get a splendidly typed letter on your opulent stationery, but still others will prefer to get what is obviously a personal letter written by an actual human being. (No doubt someone is working on a computer that scrawls things in the margins.) In any case, your correspondents will certainly prefer a prompt response to one that has to wait long enough for you to produce a masterpiece.

When a letter has to be circulated in your own office, you can pass the original around with routing notes. ("Show it to Mike after you're finished, Ann.") Or you can use initials on a letter or memo to be circulated: JT, PB, LO'C. JT passes it on to PB, who sends it to LO'C. But a circled initial (JT, PB, LO'C) means that PB should keep this copy; JT and LO'C have also been given personal copies.

If you have a lot of routine correspondence and no word-processing equipment, you can have the stuff tended to by a service bureau, or you can type out the text of the most common letters used, leaving plenty of room for date and address, and have a few hundred copies offset or photocopied. To send each one out, type in a date and address and sign your name—using a colored felt-tip pen gives a note of jaunty personalization—type the envelope or label, and off it goes.

If your routine correspondence calls for rearranging stock elements, with fill-ins ("We're sorry your *Model 3211* was not delivered due to a *trucking strike;* however, it will be delivered on *Tuesday, May 6.* Thank you for your patience."), you can type up a selection of standard paragraphs, number each one, and keep the anthology in a loose-leaf binder near your desk. If you hire a temporary or part-time typist or typing service, you can issue each typist a formbook and a list of instructions ("Goldberg Brothers, 2209 Varick Street, paragraphs 3, 17, 19, 20; terms 2/10 net 30, 10 gross #A3274"). After all, a computer or word processor just arranges and rearranges discrete units of information; a human being can do the same thing at less capital cost, if less conveniently. You can also use plain postcards, or postcards printed with your address and a standard message, to send short messages. ("Send information about your Bright Star equipment line.")

If you maintain a mailing list, your two biggest challenges are updating the list and selecting from it. You may decide that only firms over a certain size get Catalog A; others get Catalog B. For a small list, I recommend that you use ordinary 3″ x 5″ index cards, one per name, filed alphabetically. Type the envelopes or labels by flipping through the cards. The next level of sophistication is to color code the cards (blue for customers who ordered up to $10,000 last year; green for up to $20,000; or red for hard-to-collect accounts, white for accounts with an established credit history, yellow for new accounts in the process of establishing credit) or write notes on the cards. Another step is to use McBee, KeySort, or UniSort cards: these have a border around the text area of the card, with numbered circles or dashes printed in the border. You set up a code system (1 = retail store, 2 = auto repair shop, 3 = manufacturer, 34 = payment due 10/15/83, 35 = 11/15/83, or whatever). You punch the appropriate holes, then use a device that looks like a shish kebab skewer to find the cards punched at that hole. However, it takes a juggler (or a Cossack) to maneuver the skewers without dropping and disarranging the cards.

Another approach, if you mail to the same list over and over again, is to use copier labels. Each package of labels comes with specially ruled paper. You type the addresses inside the cells on the paper, load a plain paper copier with the labels, and copy the list onto the labels. Then you peel off the labels and put them on envelopes, or directly on your catalog.

Every mailing list must be updated to reflect deaths, changes in address, or simple lack of desire to receive your materials. If you buy mailing lists, or combine several lists, you'll also have to eliminate duplicate names. A card system makes this very easy: you pull out duplicate cards (making sure that Katy Johnson is really the same as Mrs. Kathryn T. Johnson) and toss them away. When you use copier labels, the process is a little more difficult. I strongly suggest that you use a separate page (or pages) for each letter, even though you'll waste some labels. Attempts to keep the list in strict alphabetical order will lead to madness. Instead, add new names to the end of the list for the appropriate letter, skimming through the rest of the names to make sure the new name is not a duplicate. However, if you have a bulk mail permit, you must presort your mail by zip code; so you'll have to file according to zip codes, perhaps alphabetizing within the zip code categories.

When the process becomes overwhelming, it's time to use a service bureau which will whirl your mailing list through a word processor or computer. When the service bureau bills fly thick and fast, it's time to consult Chapter Ten and start shopping for equipment.

Sometimes you can finesse writing a letter entirely. A phone call gets you instant response, often well worth the price of a long-distance call. Be sure to enter the call in your telephone log, send a confirming memo, or both.

Coping with Files

A good file system has the irreducible minimum of ambiguity. If possible, there is only *one* place something could be filed; at most, two or three places.

File folders can be used at least four times, if you turn the folder inside out, then reverse it twice more, adding new labels each time. After that, it may be time to retire it. Plastic file folders, in various cheery colors, are available and nearly perpetual.

Some of the possible filing systems are:

- Alphabetical (best for a small volume)
- Subject (make sure only one person classifies the files, have plenty of cross-references, and keep a separate box of alphabetized file cards, listing the subjects)
- Numerical (give each file a code number; again you'll need cross-reference cards)
- Geographical
- Chronological
- Customer (put documents inside, keep a record of transactions and payments on the front of the file folder)

If you have several people in your organization, put a stack of "out" cards on top of the file cabinet, and instill in everyone the necessity of filling out an "out" card and inserting it in place of each file taken. Also mention the fact that a file, if not used promptly, will probably languish on someone's desk for the ages. That way, you have a fighting chance of locating your files.

You can buy suspension files if you plan to pull the drawers in and out frequently or militantly; you can get frames for any file cabinet that allows you to use Pendaflex folders (hanging files). The advantage is that files don't slip to the bottom of the drawer and get crushed; the disadvantage is that the temptation to toss things into the Pendaflex folder, rather than a file folder, is irresistible, and everything ends up crushed on the bottom of the folder.

Filing is a boring activity, which for some reason is repugnant (like dishwashing). Like dishwashing, you have to keep up with it. I limit the amount of filing to be done by reserving one desk drawer each for incoming letters, outgoing letters, orders, and inquiries (requests for information). After I do the correspondence, I dump the mail into the appropriate drawer. At the end of the month, I put the letters into incoming and outgoing file folders, and file them behind last month's. Orders and inquiries go into labeled 9″ x 12″ envelopes (recycled from incoming brochures), and go into the bottom drawer of the filing cabinet. If you have fewer desk drawers than I, it helps to get things off your desk and into the filing cabinet quickly.

I must confess that I don't follow my own advice about prompt filing. Newspaper clippings, rate cards, session laws, or anything else that has to be filed gets tossed into an old dish drainer on top of my desk. Eventually, when the drainer is full or I particularly want to avoid doing something else, I file everything in the drainer.

My most cherished and least crumpled file is the "repro" file—that's where I keep the original, or a good copy, of press releases, promotional material, order forms, phone log pages, form letters, or anything else that may have to be copied at short notice. The repro file ends that feeling of stupidity that comes when you realize that you've just mailed out the last copy of a layout with four hard-to-type tables, and you need two hundred more copies by next week.

I also keep a file for every source of free-lance income; on the front of the file, I write the date and amount of each payment. At tax time, it's easy to find the total. (This is special to photographers, commercial artists, free-lance writers.)

Items other than papers have to be filed too: professional journals, catalogs, phone books. Your five-and-ten or a mail-order house can provide cardboard files that are sold flat; you fold them into shape. The files are about three inches wide, so they take only that much desk or shelf space, and have ample room for labeling the file and changing your mind a few times. Try to keep catalogs in alphabetical order, and throw out the old catalog when the new one arrives.

The same cardboard files can be used to hold file folders, packed in upright, at your desk, so you don't have to keep filing and retrieving your most-used folders. You can also get plastic self-adhesive wall pockets, metal or plastic sorters, or plastic modular dividers called "Add-a-Files" for the desktop. Try to resist the temptation to park all the files on your desk.

Don't pack file drawers too full; after all, you may want to look at some of that stuff again. When a file gets thicker than ½", break it down into subfiles. While you're poking around in the file, throw out duplicates and extraneous material (television listings from three months ago and the sandwich order from some long-forgotten meeting).

Anything that could be considered a legal document (a contract, a lease, your written Equal Employment Opportunity policy) should be kept in perpetuum, though not necessarily in your office. So should past tax returns. Supporting tax documents (receipts, canceled checks) should be kept for at least seven years; other financial records, at least five. This is not to say that all this rubbish must be hoarded next to your desk. After each year's taxes and balance sheets are prepared, the supporting records can be moved from the filing cabinet to cardboard transfer files (or in cardboard cartons from the grocery or liquor store for that matter—but not too big, paper is heavy), and placed in your basement, Uncle Henry's attic, or rented space in a mini-warehouse. Label every transfer file in great detail, and keep a running list of what's in each box. Otherwise, you may be subjected to a nostalgic week of plunging through musty cartons. The sorting-out process will be much easier if you decide how long things will be kept in the current files (one week, one year, five years), then use color-coded file folders or file labels. At the end of June, say, you can yank all the purple folders, and put the contents in transfer files or the wastebasket, as the case may be. You have to do it to know how satisfying it can be to transform an overstuffed file cabinet into a half-empty cabinet, three transfer files, and five bulging lawn-and-leaf bags.

Inventory Control

The secret of inventory control is what one might call the KKK technique: segregation, segregation now, and segregation forever. (Not, I hasten to add, of employees, but of inventory items.) The IRS forces you to take inventory once a year, and in any event you'll want to know where the money goes. The process is much easier if you, and everyone who works for the business, make an inflexible rule of never opening a new package until the old one is used up, and if you store similar packages together and away from other packages. If you have one area where material is kept for immediate use and another area for long-term storage, arrange the two areas in the same way. Label everything with as much information as can be crammed onto the label. To simplify accounting, you may also want to include the date you bought the material, and how much you paid for it.

Whenever any employee takes parts or merchandise, s/he notes the date and amount taken on the box or bin, on the clipboard attached to the shelf, or in a special notebook or card file set up by item.

Life will be much easier at inventory time if you mark the halfway and quarter-way level on parts bins with colored tape; and if you weigh a full box or bin and an empty one so you'll know how much a full load of cotter pins (or whatever) weighs. To take inventory, count the number of full boxes, then estimate by eye or determine by weight the number of components in the other boxes.

So you won't run out of supplies, you should set an inventory level for everything you buy for resale or use in manufacturing. Indicate this level on the storage unit, or on the notebook page. Reorder more or less promptly when you reach this level. Your inventory record system should include, for each item, what the item is, your supplier(s), the size or specifications, amount on hand, amount ordered, and price paid. The last item is hellishly depressing, but it appeases the suspicions of taxmen.

Retailers need a second inventory control system: one which records sales as they are made. John De Young's inventory control system is especially helpful if a certain amount of bargaining is allowed. Choose a phrase that has at least ten different letters, and assign a number to each:

G.   Bernard   Shaw
1   23456 7   89 0

Then tag each piece of merchandise with its inventory number, size, the retail price, and the code letters for the wholesale price—say, RBNW for $42.50. The wholesale price shows the amount of leeway you have in bargaining, and the amount of profit on the final transaction. When an item is bought, put the tag code on the sales check; then use the sales checks to make up a monthly tally sheet, which will show the amount taken in minus the cost of goods sold.

Bookstores, card stores, sellers of art prints, and other sellers of high-volume goods that can't be tagged and are not one-of-a-kind, do it a little differently. They use notebook pages (one per title or item) or cards (the front of the card gives a monthly breakdown of copies on hand, copies received, copies sold; the back gives ordering information). Sometimes the cards are punched to fit a multiple-ring notebook, and arranged so only the top line shows. That way, it's easy to flip through the book and find the item you want.

When a sale is made, the person making the sale can keep a record, or file a duplicate sales check. Some bookstores put a "Looreen" card giving the author, title, publisher, and price in each copy, or use a McBee, Keysort, Unisort, or IBM card. The clerk collects the cards, which are processed later to determine reorders. Coded adhesive labels on books, pieces of pottery, or framed pictures can be used the same way. The "greeting-card system," used for duplicate items sold on racks (books, small toys, household items), is utilized to establish a reorder level. An inventory card is placed on the rack so that it shows when the reorder level has been reached (e.g., when twenty out of thirty items have been sold). When you see the card, you reorder; write the amount ordered on the card.

The best inventory system for a particular business is the one that produces the greatest amount of useful information, at the lowest cost in money and trouble, and with the least damage to the merchandise—scrawling "$1,750.79" in Magic Marker across a canvas is counterproductive.

Interoffice Communications

In a one-person business, interoffice communication is simplicity itself. However, even though you can usually get an appointment with yourself, memory fades over time—so be sure to save your desk diary to substantiate your tax deductions.

In a small operation, *some* memos may be necessary, but try to keep them short, direct them only to the attention of people who care about the information in them, file one copy by date so you'll have a complete record, and make as few copies as you can get away with. Doing your own typing and photocopying will do wonders along these lines.

If the memo is of general interest, post one copy on a central bulletin board and file one copy for future reference. Train everyone to read the bulletin board (try posting it near the coffee machine) and appoint someone to clear off the board as memos become obsolete. If a memo is of interest to several people, don't make a copy for each one. Make *one* copy, and have each one pass it along after reading it. Surely grownups can be trained to read a one-hundred-word memo in less than two weeks.

People who have nothing better to do can generate splendid gothic structures of memos, involving multiple drafts and hours of secretarial time. People who do have better things to do can limit the time spent on paperwork by using efficient procedures and well-designed forms, and by dealing with things immediately, when memory is still fresh and ideas still sparkling.

CHAPTER EIGHT

Time's Winged Chariot

One of the saddest things is that the only thing a man can do for eight hours a day is work. You can't eat eight hours a day, nor drink eight hours a day, nor make love eight hours a day—all you can do is work.—WILLIAM FAULKNER

TO A CERTAIN EXTENT, cruelly long hours, a perpetually heaped desk, and regularly scheduled crises are status symbols. The intrepid executive must cope with calamity as the phone shrills and the filing cabinets bulge. At Wasp, Wasp & Token one of these war-room scenarios literally continued for forty straight hours (and one of my colleagues and I had to buy lunch for sixteen people, because no one had had the sense to keep some petty cash for this purpose).

However, the owner of a small business also has a small audience (or none at all) to applaud these feats. Therefore, s/he might as well anticipate the crises, clear the desk, and go home after getting things more or less taken care of. (I was about to say, after everything is done; but this is impossible. There is always something else that *could* be done. The trick is to figure out when the law of diminishing returns sets in, and it's time to go home to a hot bath and a bad book.)

There are at least two basic approaches to time planning. One of them calls for you to keep current, handling each small task as it comes up, so you never have a vast pile of work. The other, or Augean stables, approach lets you let things slide until you have a dramatic pile of related work to do. Then you wade in and dispatch it. Intellectually, I favor the first approach; temperamentally, I lean toward the second. Certain pusillanimous compromises are possible: you can group together a related group of tasks, moderate in number, arising from the past few days. This partakes of the assembly-line process. If you have a real assembly line, you will need methods of scheduling the ordering of materials, deployment of workers, and use of machines. Finally, your long-range plans call for modifications of short-term planning techniques.

Time Planning for Office Work

First of all, you have to decide which tasks are the most important (perhaps by characterizing things as Drastic, Important, and Trivial, or by making A, B, and C lists). However, there are two cautions to relying too heavily on this approach. First of all, it's easy to get wrapped up in analysis, testing, and networking (aka schmoozing) to the exclusion of locating actual potential customers, making sales, and producing your product or service. Second of all, reality will warp your neatest "To Do" list. Many of the most important tasks are also the most unpleasant. If you had perfect self-discipline, you would get these tasks out of the way. If I had perfect self-discipline, I would weigh a hundred and twenty pounds and would have finished this book eight months earlier.

It's also possible for something to be urgent but not important—if you drop live cigarette ashes into a well-filled wastebasket, the ensuing wastebasket fire will effectually take your mind off everything else. A particularly whiney customer, a catatonic bank teller, or a balky car can all do the same. So don't make schedules that depend on split-second coordination, and leave room for contingencies.

Not all of your time planning is under your control. You may get your best ideas at three in the morning, but unless you are a corporate despot like Charles Revson, or share your bed with an understanding person who cares about your business, you will have no one to discuss them with. You can only go to the Post Office when it's open. The workers on the graveyard shift won't be available at noon. It is generally a waste of time to return phone messages at seven in the morning their time (although, if the recipient has twenty-four-hour staffing or an answering machine, it's a fine form of one-upmanship).

Unless you believe that poverty, cold showers, and wind sprints are good for your soul, remember to take your own rhythms into account. There *is* some time of day at which you are your most effective—and another at which you are at your sappiest. Reserve the most menial tasks (filing, typing lists, stuffing envelopes) for your vegetable state. Make decisions when you feel most alert. However, if you know that you're putting off the decision, or some particularly unattractive piece of work, until some hypothetical moment of paranormal alertness, do it right away.

Those who work at home have an additional advantage: compared to being browbeaten by an encyclopedia salesman, or cleaning the pulpy rotted leaves out of the leaders and gutters, any workaday task looks pretty damn good.

The conventional advice is that you must, every Friday, prepare a list of objectives for the following week, rating each objective by priority, and assigning it a day to be performed and an allotment of hours for its completion. Then, each day, you set up a schedule of appointments and a parallel list of tasks, each task described, assigned a priority, and given a chunk of time for its completion. You check off tasks as you complete them, transferring undone tasks to tomorrow's or next week's list. Again, if this helps you, well and good, but from my own experience and the work of ergonomists, you can spend an hour a day looking for, updating, and otherwise playing with these lists.

Just as I have a one-and-a-half-entry bookkeeping system, I also have a one-and-a-half-entry time-planning system. I have a large corkboard hung over my telephone. The board is divided into eight vertical columns: Monday–Friday, Weekend, Next Week, and Later. I keep a pen and a supply of outdated business cards near the phone. Whenever I make an appointment, I write it on the back of one of the cards, then tack the card to the board under the appropriate day. I also make up a card for callbacks ("Call Dr. Joanna Loeffle [404] 602-1972, after 3 and before 5"), and reminders ("Check UCC 2-608"). When I finish doing something, I get the satisfaction of removing the card, tearing it up, and throwing it away. At the end of the week, "Next Week" becomes this week, and the cards are transferred to the appropriate days. You can do the same thing by marking a large stretch of the wall with tape and using 3M Post-It Notes; or use cork and thumbtacks, or a blackboard and an eraser. The important factors are ease of reshuffling and proximity to the telephone—that way, you can check the board and make appointments without fumbling for your desk calendar or promising to be in two places at once.

I don't bother with a desk calendar, but I am utterly dependent on my appointment book. I have a largish book (about 5″ x 7″), with half a page per day and ruled lines for appointments every hour from 8 to 5; there are also five lines for notes. (Naturally, all my appointments are on the half hour.) I transfer all appointments to this book—first of all, so I don't get lost on the way to someone's office; second of all, as a permanent record for unnatural disasters, such as litigation and IRS audits. I also transfer reminders that have to be handled outside the office (topics for library research, calls to be made in transit) but I don't bother with things like "Proofread Chapter 6 footnotes." My biographers will just have to get this information somewhere else.

I bought my book at Lamston's—I think it cost about three dollars—but appointment books are available on a steeply ascending scale of elegance. It may be worth the extra money if you spend a lot of time in the company of people who are easily impressed. The itsy-bitsy morocco leather books with the blue pages are very elegant, but give you precious little room for writing six addresses for sales calls and a few hot leads. The large, floppy books with one line for every fifteen minutes are great for psychiatrists, tax lawyers, and others whose clients come to them and need only be identified by name, but not so great for people who travel to appointments, or who need copious notes on visitors. ("Tonarelli, Yale grad, bought 16 cases #0943 last year, 19 cases this year to date, wants custom stamping at additional price 12¢/unit.")

Once you have set up an agenda for the day, you can get to work. I suggest setting up a routine that conforms to your own rhythms. If you're a morning person, spend a few productive hours (say, 7–10 A.M.) on policy-making, budgeting, and important unfinished projects (e.g., the annual report, a sales presentation, your tax returns). Schedule important meetings for the late morning, if you have the clout to do this. Best is for the person you are meeting with to buy you an excellent lunch. Since you're already finished with all your judgment work for the day, you can afford to get half-bagged or pig out. Finally, you can waddle back to the office and handle some challenging task like going to the Post Office, reordering mailing labels, or answering routine correspondence.

On the other hand, if you can't cope with mornings, but must appear at an office during normal business hours, start off with routine tasks and build toward a big finish. (If you're a writer, freelance artist, or inventor, of course, most of the time you can sleep all morning and work when you damn please.)

I do, however, suggest that laissez-faire be tempered by the principle of keeping up to date, or at least reasonably current. I always expect some glorious surprise in the mail (and am always disappointed), so I recommend opening the mail right away. If you feel differently, or if you get more than one mail delivery a day, I suggest grouping all the mail and dealing with it at a time when you're not quite a world beater but not quite comatose either. The sorting process is described in the preceding chapter. If you write the responses and make the calls right away, at least you'll remember what you're talking about. If you keep shuffling the letters from heap to heap, you may need considerable detective work to find the answer to a question, or what your cryptic marginal notes mean.

When the mail has been dealt with, two approaches present themselves: since you're already at your desk, if you have any routine typing to do, you can warm up with that. Perhaps you have the final version of an ad going to the typesetter; then you can try something more challenging, like a business proposal. Or, particularly if yours is a mail-order business with a gratifying fistful of checks in each mail delivery, you can update the books, prepare the bank deposit, make out payroll checks, pay bills, do some budgeting, make a few phone calls to check figures, and deal with your phone messages.

People differ in their attitudes toward distraction. Some people prefer uninterrupted blocks of time so they can start and finish a job. Others prefer to work on a task for a short time, set it aside, do something else, and parcel out the work on each project over a period of time. (This chapter is being written at a quarter to one in the morning, on the border between Sunday and Monday. Today I reshuffled some file cabinets, ate breakfast, did some research, went shopping, watched a movie on television, did the correspondence, wrote a sales letter for a business deal I'm trying to get started, got the *Times,* read the news and did the crossword puzzle, ate dinner, called some friends, and finally sat down at the clipboard with my index cards. This may indicate my belief in the smorgasbord method of time planning.)

If you hate being distracted and work in an office with other people, you can discourage the formation of a salon by getting rid of your guest chairs, turning your desk so your back is to the door, posting a clock in a conspicuous location, or trying to hold conversations in settings that are less than comfortable. A drafty or stifling hallway is ideal. However, these tactics can backfire if you have to move the furniture to present an inviting atmosphere for the clients. If you have a door, you can close it. If this doesn't work, try the time-honored preppie expedient of draping a tie over the doorknob. This will indicate your unavailability, though probably not for the traditional reason. One man who works in an open-plan office puts on a red baseball cap when he doesn't want to be disturbed. Finally, at some point you will have to tell your co-workers that you don't want to be disturbed unless an authentic crisis is erupting. Either you have a cooperative team of thoughtful people, or you have your techniques of despotism down pat. It's no use owning a business anywhere in between.

The telephone, of course, is the all-time champion distracter. You should answer your own phone if this is at all possible. But when you're very busy or very frazzled, you can have someone screen your calls, forwarding only those that meet a prearranged test of importance. You can also flip on your answering machine, if you have one. Some companies schedule "quiet hours" during which phone calls are not taken. You can tell your most frequent callers that you prefer not to take calls at certain hours. If that doesn't work, you can come into work early and beat the rush, or you can stay late in the evening, or go to a nice quiet place and let the office phone ring. If you have an answering machine with two cassettes, you can have one of them announce your quiet hour.

Finally, when you've parceled out your time, you may have to record it. Lawyers, publicists, writers, and others who charge by the hour need time sheets of some kind. It's very hard to decipher random bits of paper, or to remember how long a job took eight months ago. Time sheets must be filled out at least once a day—it's better if you can update the time sheet each time you finish a billable operation.

The basic time sheet has the client's name, just what it was you did, and how long it took—though it usually suffices to say "2¼ hours" without mentioning that 10 minutes of this time was spent between 9:23 and 9:33, 16 minutes from 11:08 to 11:24, and so on. If the time sheets are, or might later be, computerized, both the clients and the tasks should be identified by numbers (30284 is Mintz Associates; A227 is research). The problem with this system is that you are unlikely to bill Florine Vespucci for Huang Tse-Yao's work (at least not by mistake), but you may confuse account 67204 with account 67024. For those who like machines, Dantronics, Inc. (St. Paul, MN) makes a desk accessory called Timelogger 201. As you work, you note the time spent on each of up to 10 accounts. You can press a button and get a readout of your nonbillable time and your total billable time per account.

Then again, you can charge a flat fee for each job. I much prefer this system. Looking out the window, having sexual fantasies, going to the water cooler, and answering the phone are integral parts of life. It's hard to decide when to stop the chess clock and parcel out your consciousness among accounts. Sometimes the solution to a problem will force its way into your consciousness on someone else's time. (The traditional lawyer's solution is to bill both of them; and lawyers, like taxis, charge for waiting time.)

If it makes you feel any better, the American Management Association suggests you worry 38% of the time about today's problems, 40% a week ahead, 15% a month ahead, 5% 3–6 months ahead, and the remaining 2% a year ahead. There's no suggestion about problems held over from yesterday's "To Do" list—or last week's.

Scheduling Other Workers

At the beginning of any work operation, or each time you start a new project (if you hire workers by the day or by the job), you'll have to decide how many workers you need. This is a fairly simple matter to determine—if all your workers are trained to handle all aspects of the production process and you have a fairly accurate idea of their productivity. This highlights an important factor in time planning: the closer your estimates are to pure fantasy, the less accurate your final decision will be. This is a special case of the general law: Garbage In, Garbage Out.

If you produce three products (a reciprocating bumble strut, a two-part furbish, and an O'Connor truff), and the productivity and order figures are as follows:

	RBS	*TPF*	*O'CT*
# of Employees	10	2	1
Daily production	50	10	3
# ordered	1,000	250	60

you need to reduce all three to the common denominator of mandays. To produce 1,000 reciprocating bumble struts you need 200

man-days (because each employee produces five per day). To produce 250 two-part furbishes, you need 50 man-days (because each
employee produces 10 per day); you need 20 man-days for the 60
O'Connor truffs. The total is 270 man-days.

You can use this figure several ways. If you have 9 workers, it
will take at least 30 workdays; accounting for weekends, holidays,
and a fudge factor you've derived from experience, you know it will
take at least a month and a half.

On the other hand, if you need the stuff in 10 days, you'll need
27 workers. If your machinery and plant can only accommodate 9
workers, you'll have to go on triple shifts, or keep the production
process going 7 days a week.

Not every business is on a Monday-to-Friday schedule. Some
businesses have to be open off-hours (e.g., 24-hour day care centers);
others have a business advantage because they're open late (e.g.,
convenience stores); others figure they might as well amortize the
rent by staying open as late as possible. (Sometimes utility rates are
cheaper at off-peak hours—a factor if you use a lot of power.) It
may be easy to attract some workers—students and moonlighters—
but offering unusual shifts can also turn away other workers. You
may also have to pay extra for weekend work and overtime.

Setting up the shifts is a pencil-and-paper job. For example, if
there are three employees, two of whom work each day, you can set
up a repeating cycle that lasts six weeks. Each worker has a four-
day "week" and two days off. Everyone gets one normal weekend,
one Saturday and one Sunday off in each six-week cycle.

Then the cycle starts again; Week Seven is like Week One. If
you have nine workers and need six on at a time, you assign two to
each shift pattern. If you need other shift patterns, you can figure
them out on graph paper with colored pencils.

Production Scheduling

Sometimes you know how many workers are available, and
when they'll be working, but you don't know how long a given job
will take or how to deploy the work force to advantage. A cynical
mathematical rule of thumb is that the average time something will
take equals $(A + 4M + B)/6$, if A is your most optimistic time prediction, B your most pessimistic, and M your most likely estimate.

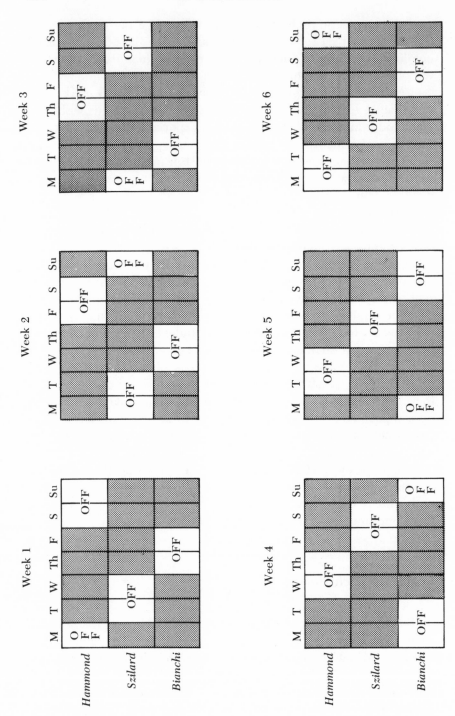

So, if you hope a report will take 10 days to write, but you're afraid it will take 20, and you assume you can probably knock it off in 12, budget: $(10 + 48 + 20)/6 = 78/6 = 13$ days. These are workdays, of course; unless you work a seven-day week, it will take almost three weeks to write the report.

Government proposals or those solicited by large corporations usually include a simple "step-forward" chart showing the alleged completion schedule for the project. If you do get the contract, save the chart. It's not merely useful for impressing procurement officers; it's actually helpful in doing the work.

Let's say you have been hired to do a six-month pilot study of your teaching machine, "IVAN," which you claim will teach sixth-graders to speak Russian. The chart will look something like the one on page 232.

This simple chart highlights a number of issues. First of all, some tasks depend on the completion of other earlier tasks. (If there are no teaching machines, no one can use them.) Some tasks can overlap (teacher orientation can start before all the machines are ready). These points will come up again in the discussion of PERT on page 239.

Second of all, the comfortingly abstract numbers can bump up alarmingly against reality. For example, if you start the pilot test in May, there will be a dearth of sixth-graders. You will either have to corral all the subjects into summer school, or allow for downtime during the summer. Furthermore, the sixth-graders will be seventh-graders by then, won't even be in the same school, and your contract requires sixth-graders anyway. So, to finish the study during the year, you must start in September, October, November, December, or January.

You must be able to order efficiently to assemble all the components. In order to avoid downtime on the machines, you can use the GANTT technique, which is a "packing" process for making optimum use of machinery. If you do get the contract, you'll have to know how long it will take to produce one hundred machines from the prototype. If you know the time it takes to order materials, process them, and assemble them, you can figure out the date when the project will end. If you know the capacity of your machinery and the time each operation requires, you can use the machinery to its fullest. If you know how long the various steps take and the required finish date, you can use production charting and PERT to figure out the start date. All these techniques are like a simple

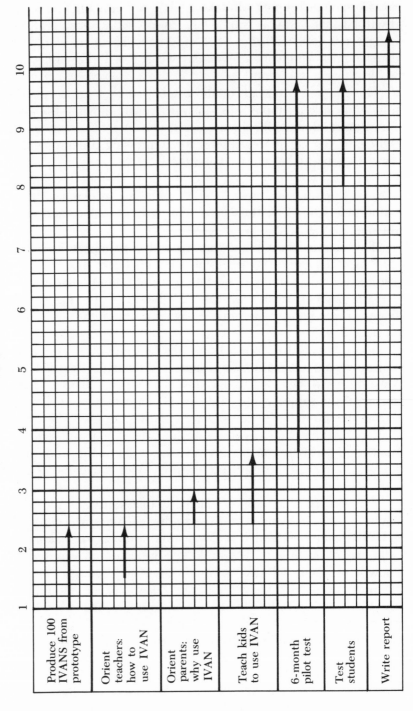

MONTHS AFTER AWARD

	1	2	3	4	5	6	7	8	9	10
Produce 100 IVANS from prototype										
Orient teachers: how to use IVAN										
Orient parents: why use IVAN										
Teach kids to use IVAN										
6-month pilot test										
Test students										
Write report										

equation, $A + B = C$. If you know any two of the numbers, you can get the third fairly easily.

Materials Resource Planning

Materials Resource Planning (MRP) is a fancy way of deciding when to order materials. You set a date by which all materials must be on hand. Unless your faith in human nature is boundless, this had better be a week or two earlier than the date you start assembling the IVANs. The figures for time required for ordering come from your own experience, the experience of others in the same business, or (very cautiously) the shipper's promises.

If an IVAN has eight parts, assume that the lead time (in days) is as follows:

ITEM	DAYS
Reciprocating bumble strut	on hand (produced in-house)
Two-part furbish	on hand (produced in-house)
O'Connor truff	on hand (produced in-house)
Hemiola	2
Grivvenes	5
Puggix	6
Concave mudge	7
Sluebing	9

Again, if these days are business days, you'll have to add extra time for weekends and holidays. It's also worthwhile to keep the names of some alternative suppliers who can fill emergency orders, even if their prices are higher. When you have the order times, you can make up an MRP graph (page 234).

The first three items are already on hand and need not be ordered. For the others, count back from the assembly date to find out the date the parts must be ordered. You can make up a card for each order (e.g., order 2 gross Puggix from Cincinnati Puggix Co., $67.50 + $2.94 shipping) and put the card on your corkboard, then take care of the order as part of the day's correspondence.

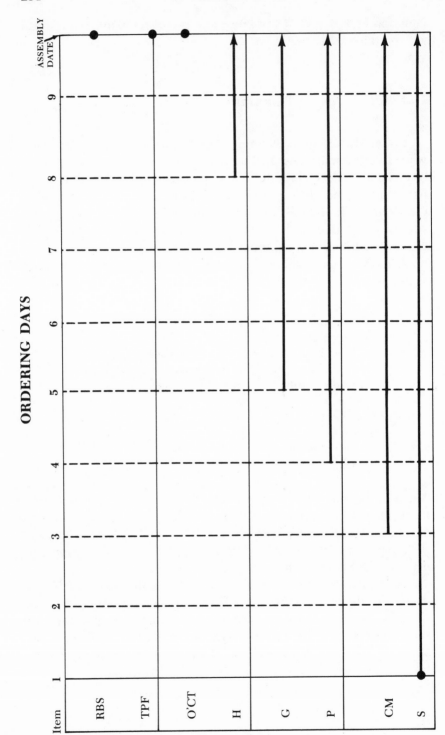

Step-Back Scheduling

Given all this useful information, and with all the parts on hand, how do you make up the production schedule? If you have the date the work must be finished, and if you know how long it takes to work with each component, you can set up a production schedule.

If IVAN is built by assembling the eight components, and if all of them except the grivvenes have to be processed in your plant, you can construct a simple bar graph showing the start and finish dates. (You can set up the same graph with arrows, like the charts on pages 230 and 232; you can also use a PERT chart, but we haven't gotten to that yet.)

Assume that the completed IVAN must be assembled by December 22 (to avoid the Christmas holidays and to be ready to start the project in January), and the tasks take this long:

Assembly	3 days	G	no work
RBS	2 days	P	3 days
TPF	4 days	CM	2 days
O'CT	1 day	S	1 day
H	2 days		

Just to make things easier, let's assume that December 22 is a Friday. If only one job can be done at a time, the entire process will take 18 working days. This means 4 5-day weeks: 11/27–12/1; 12/4–12/8; 12/11–12/15; 12/18–12/22. The production schedule looks like the chart on page 236.

If nothing goes wrong, you can schedule the sluebings for November 29, the O'Connor truffs for the 30th, the concave mudges for the 1st and 4th of December, and so on. You might also want to change the order and do the longest, not the shortest, tasks first in case there's a delay of some kind.

GANTT

The step-back scheduling technique just described will work when there is only one worker or team of workers. (It also works only when your estimates are accurate, but that's a limitation on all

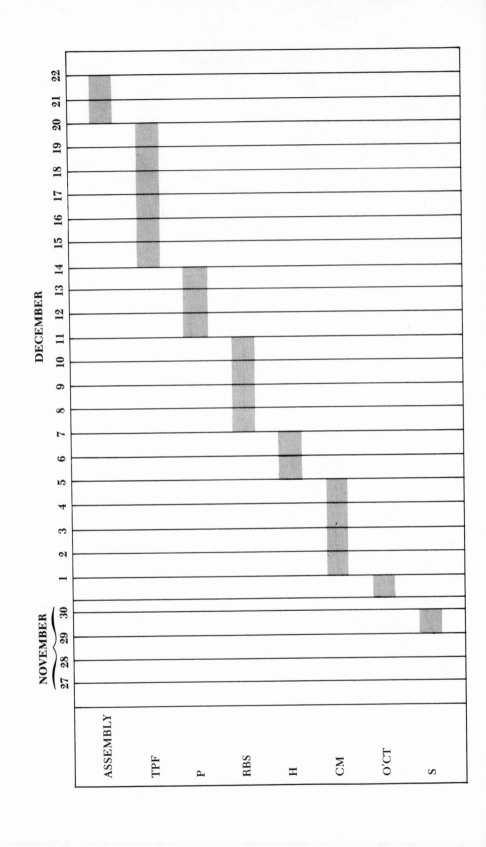

scheduling systems.) If you have several workers or teams and lots of machinery, a scheduling process like that requires a great deal of downtime, with workers and machinery standing idle. If each part must go through several processes, you have another layer of complexity in the scheduling process.

GANTT charts deal with this. (GANTT is not an acronym; it's the name of the engineer who developed the technique.)

Assuming the same miserable IVANs (yes, I know; there'll be another example in the next section), and assuming that all the parts except the grivvenes have to be put on three separate machines to be Bewitched, Bothered, and Bewildered, and if each process takes this much time:

	TPF	P	RBS	CM	H	O'CT	S
Days	4 × 7	3 × 7	2 × 7	2 × 7	2 × 7	1 × 7	1 × 7
Bewitched	15	6	5	3	6	3	2
Bothered	9	7	4	8	2	1	4
Bewildered	3	2	5	2	2	3	1

The first line is the number of days it takes to process each part; this number is multiplied by seven working hours a day to compute the number of days it would take to process this part. If it takes more than 7 hours to process a part, it must be called 2 days; more than 14 hours must be called 3 days, and so on. The Bewitched machine would be used for a total of 40 hours (6 days); the Bothered would be used for 35 hours (5 days); and the Bewildered machine used for 18 hours (3 days).

Get out the graph paper and colored pencils to draw up a GANTT chart. Start out by assigning weekdays, but not dates, to the columns (page 238).

Start with the two-part furbish: it goes on the Bewitched machine for 15 hours—all day Monday and Tuesday, 1 hour on Wednesday. Then it goes on the Bothered machine for 9 hours—6 hours on Wednesday, 3 hours on Thursday—and then to Bewildered for 3 hours on Thursday.

Meanwhile, the Bewitched machine can be used for 6 hours on Wednesday. The puggix needs 6 hours, so it fills up Wednesday. Then the puggix has to wait until late Thursday morning, until the two-part furbish is off the Bothered machine. Six hours are available on the Bothered machine; the seventh hour is on Friday morning.

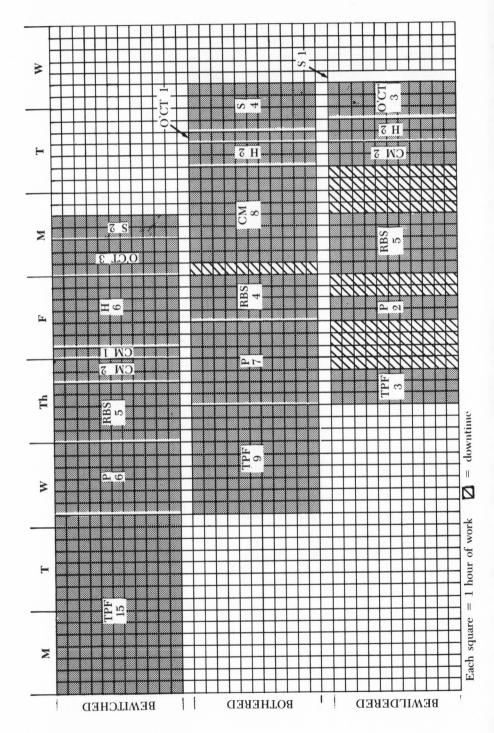

Each square = 1 hour of work   ▨ = downtime

Then the puggix goes to the Bewildered machine for 2 hours on Friday.

The reciprocating bumble strut gets Bewitched for 5 hours on Thursday. The Bothered isn't available right away, but the reciprocating bumble strut can get its 4 hours on Friday afternoon. You can split the Bewildered between 1 hour on Friday and 4 the next Monday, but it seems more realistic to shut down a little early on Friday and start again on Monday. Continue the process with the other components. As you can see from the chart, the last component (sluebing) will be finished on Wednesday of the second week. If assembly takes 3 days, the project will be completed in 11 working days from start to finish.

This schedule is an efficient use of the equipment. There's no downtime on the Bewitched machine; Bothered and Bewildered don't start until a part is Bewitched, so there's a little bit of downtime on these machines. It might be possible to arrange operations to eliminate the downtime. If the production time has to be shortened even further, it may be possible to change the production technique—for example, to allow a part to be Bewildered before it is Bothered.

You can use a finished GANTT chart in several ways:

- To decide when a project can be completed if it is started on a given date
- To find the start date for a project that must be finished at a specific time
- To set up a daily schedule for each machine
- To set up detailed production goals for each part
- To integrate various projects. For example, if building the IVANs is your highest-priority project, you know that Bothered and Bewildered capacity is available at the beginning of the cycle for lower-priority work. Using these machines on the first Monday or Tuesday won't interfere with building the IVANs.

PERT

And now, to everyone's relief, we can move to a new technique, and a new example.

PERT is an acronym: it stands for Program Evaluation and Re-

view Technique. PERT (also called CPM, for Critical Path Method-
ology) is used when a number of subtasks comprise a finished
project.

For example, if the overall task is to prepare a series of magazine ads for a client, the simplified subtasks might be:

- Plan campaign
- Write copy
- Design visual aspects of ads
- Run ads in magazines
- Do market research on the effectiveness of the ads
- Report to the client on the success of the campaign

Those are the overall steps toward the goal; those steps must be
broken down further. One sequence of subtasks is:

A. Plan campaign (estimated time, including both work time
   and lead time = 10 days)
B. Write draft ad copy (10 days)
C. Have head of agency review draft (4)
D. Have client review draft (10)
E. Sketch visual "look" of ad (10)
F. Have head of agency approve sketches (4)
G. Have client approve sketches (10)
H. Hire photographer, models (6)
I. Buy or rent props (6)
J. Choose magazines where ad will run (3)
K. Have photographs taken (6)
L. Select best photographs (2)
M. Have copy set in type (5)
N. Combine photographs and copy in final ad (5)
O. Run ads in the magazines already selected (3)
P. Market research: survey consumers (21)
Q. Prepare report to client (14)
R. Present report

Some of these steps are preparations for other steps, but some
are completely independent operations that can go on at the same
time. To draw a PERT chart, you draw a circle for the beginning of
the process and one for the end; label the circles with the appropriate letters. You arrange the circles for the other subtasks between
the start and finish. Each chain of events is horizontal (in other
words, if B precedes C and D, draw circle C to the right of B, and D

to the right of C). Activities that go on at the same time are arranged vertically. Draw a line between each pair of circles; write the number of days each activity takes on the line. (If an activity includes waiting or lead time—say, if 3 days of work are spread out over 14 days—use the larger number.) The completed chart for the ad campaign looks like this:

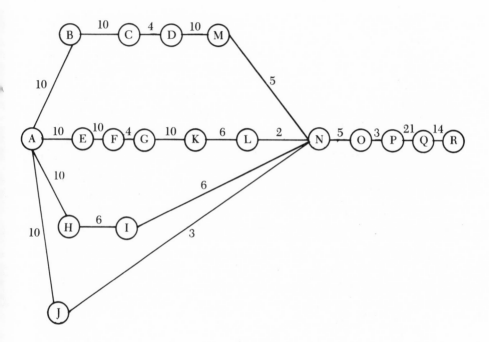

Or, rather, *one* completed chart looks like this. I'm assuming that the art department is responsible for shooting the photographs and choosing the best ones from the contact sheets. If the people who handled tasks H and I had this responsibility, the chart would look different: K and L would be on the same path as H and I, and the path from A to N would be shorter.

The work chain that takes the longest (in this case, A-E-F-G-K-L-N) is called the "critical path." The market research depends on consumers' reactions to the ads; the ads can't be placed until they are designed, written, set in type, and mechanicals are prepared. The whole campaign will take at least 85 days (the 42 days of the critical path, plus time to place the ads, do market research, write the report, and present it to the client).

If you know the starting date, you can set the earliest feasible end date; if you know the completion date, you can schedule the other activities.

You can also use PERT to integrate various projects. For example, you could construct a PERT chart for each month:

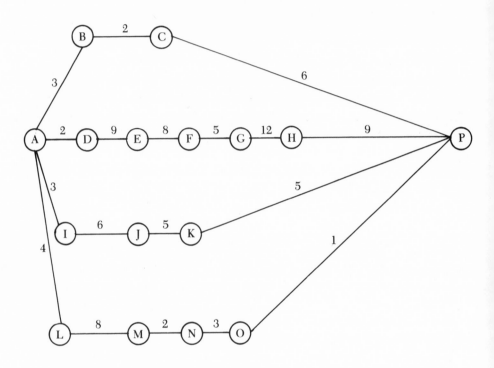

A and P are the beginning and end of the month, and A-B-C-P, A-D-E-F-G-H-P, A-I-J-K-P, and A-L-M-N-O-P are the paths for the four projects you're working on. As you can see, project A-D-E-F-G-H-P is not going to get finished during the month. If there are 22 working days in the month, work will have to stop between F and G. In fact, one of the most useful things you can do with PERT is demonstrate that a schedule is impossible or indicate that a proposed new project would overcrowd your schedule and keep you from meeting other deadlines. The cost of overtime, long-distance calls and telegrams, messengers and Air Express on a rush job can lower or eliminate the profit on the job. This was commonplace at Wasp, Wasp & Token, where the peons would slave away on one job, unaware that it wasn't due for three months, while another job, due the following week, hadn't been started. Once someone woke up to the fact that the Consolidated Amalgamations project was late, the cycle of late nights and Express Mail packages began again. The problem could have been solved if a Wasp had been delegated to maintain a complete and current PERT chart, with a copy posted for everyone's reference.

A PERT chart can also be used to plan daily schedules. Using the PERT chart just given, if P is the 30th of the month, task C must be finished on or before the 24th; if A is the first of the month, on the first and second you'll be working on tasks B, D, I and L; D must be finished on the second. On the third, you're scheduled to finish tasks B and I.

You can use the same technique to sketch out a year's projects; be sure to include market research, sales, and publicity.

Long-range Planning Techniques

These techniques can be extended to make long-range plans. For example, an MRP chart can be drawn up every three months and used to plan ordering for the quarter. A GANTT chart can be drawn for a piece of equipment you're thinking of buying—will you use it enough to justify the cost or will there be long periods of expensive downtime? You can also make GANTT charts with employees rather than machines on the vertical axis—will employees be too busy to take on new projects? Is there enough work to add an employee?

PERT charts can be used to plot out the subprocesses in one job, or to see the relationship among projects planned a few weeks, months, or a year ahead.

Just remember that a chart, even a multicolored chart of jewel-like beauty, is valuable only to the extent that it reflects, or at least can be reconciled with, reality. A strike, a report that molders on someone's desk, a shipping delay, a broken machine can all destroy a carefully carpentered schedule. Therefore, try to build in some extra time for slippage; a jigsaw puzzle that depends on pinpoint accuracy is a precursor of disaster. The further a plan is made in advance of the event, the more likely reality is to deliver a swift kick in the planning genius' pants. Remember electric power from nuclear energy, "too cheap to meter"? None of this is an argument against long-term planning or for short-term planning, for that matter, but both must constantly be adjusted to conform to events. This is very sad, because plans are inevitably shapelier and more rational than reality. But, as my eleventh-grade American Studies teacher used to say, "That's the way the matzoh ball sinks."

CHAPTER NINE

Smile When You Say That: Advertising and Public Relations

ADVERTISING, for purposes of this book, is defined as giving people accurate information they don't already have. I know that this is not the usual definition. Indeed, in October of 1981, James Miller III, Chairman of the FTC, said that he saw no reason for the FTC to protect consumers from inaccurate advertisements. But I don't expect the readers of this book to live down to Reaganite standards of business ethics any more than I expect them to live down to Caligulan sexual mores, so I reiterate that advertising should be truthful and should contain only statements which can be substantiated.

If a toothpaste contains fluoride, it's perfectly honest to *say* it contains fluoride, and to present whatever scientific evidence there is that fluoride is helpful. It's morally suspect, to say the least, to imply that fluoridated toothpaste provides unlimited sexual access, success in the Little League, or both.

As for the second part of my statement, I don't see why it's necessary to tell people that Coke® is the "Real Thing," or that Kellogg's cereals produce the effects usually associated with a combination of extreme affluence and youth. Since soft drinks and breakfast cereals are freely available everywhere in the United States (and, I suspect, in Tibet), the rising generations have every opportunity to decide for themselves if they want to consume. But people don't know necessarily that a new store has opened, that a new product has been introduced, or that all sport jackets are twenty percent cheaper until next Thursday, unless someone tells them.

245

That's why people read ad-filled newspapers with pleasure. Unlike television and radio ads, which are usually considered a nuisance, newspapers aren't noisy, and you can read them on your own schedule, not the sponsor's. In addition, the ads convey new, useful information (the price of a leg of lamb; a sale on garden tools), not stale commonplaces. Wednesdays are high-circulation days because of the supermarket ads.

Another way to let people know what you want to tell them is through publicity. Newspaper articles, radio talk shows, and television interviews are all publicity. You don't pay directly for publicity (though you do pay for press releases and follow-up calls, and may have to hire a publicist). You don't control the content or timing of the publicity. On the other hand, a good publicity campaign can produce the same results as a much more expensive ad campaign. People may believe publicity, which is at least somewhat objective, more than they believe advertising. Sometimes they get the two mixed up: many's the time my business has been written up in some publication, and people will write in, "I saw your ad in . . ."

You probably can't afford television ads, full-page ads anyplace except the high school yearbook, four-color printing, or the services of an expensive publicist. You can also forget about advertising agencies: the normal compensation for an ad agency is the 15% discount the agencies get for placing ads in commercial media. Since 15% of $236.50 wouldn't keep an adman in martinis for two lunches, you're on your own.

Therefore, this chapter deals with the writing of classified ads, small display ads and flyers, and the design of ads, flyers, and catalogs. Because direct-mail sales depend so heavily on advertising, special consideration is given to writing and designing mailing pieces. This in turn brings up the subject of writing press releases and levitating them out of the editor's wastebasket. There are also hybrid forms of promotion between advertising and publicity (fashion shows, dog and pony shows, go-sees), discussed with particular reference to the strategies service businesses can use to get clients.

Copywriting

I believe in the hard sell, I really do. Shipping the whole crew out to Aspen to shoot some gorgeous scenery is all very well—nice work if you can get it—but on your kind of ad budget all you can do is tell people what you want them to buy and why they should buy it.

U.S.P., in ad parlance, means not United States Pharmacopeia but Unique Selling Proposition. The Unique Selling Proposition is what sets your product or service apart from the competition. Your shoes are the most fashionable, the most classical, the best made. If there's no difference between your product, or your store, or the service you provide, and any one of a dozen others, why in hell are you doing it? If you just want to make a living, get a job.

If you're going to bombard audiences with your advertisements, four times an hour, it is a corporal work of mercy to make your ads beautiful, charming, or memorable in some way (though even the best joke palls after a while; and the fondly remembered Alka-Seltzer ads were a notorious failure at selling Alka-Seltzer). If you have to raid the cookie jar to place any ads at all, get to the point quickly.

Start with an arresting headline. I have a regrettable weakness for puns, especially elaborate, terrible ones; but there's nothing wrong with a headline like, "July 4 Swimsuit Sale." Advertisements have to be personal. You have to promise a benefit to the reader; it's not enough to make general statements. Even "public service" messages are a none-too-subtle plea that the Megalithic Corporation, or whatever, be considered a bunch of all-around good guys.

After creating the desire to buy your product or service, you must provide a means for satisfying the desire. If all you can afford is a tiny ad, all you can do is drop a few tantalizing hints and indicate how to get further information. In a larger ad, specify the choices available (sizes 4–14, in teal blue, forest green, or apricot; all kinds of masonry work, fireplaces our specialty; speech training for actors, academics, and executives). Provide a complete address, with store hours and directions, for a store; provide complete ordering information (price, shipping and handling or freight, whether credit cards are acceptable, sales tax) for mail order. If you are advertising a product, it helps to be as specific as possible. Services are usually expensive, and tradition-bound, enough so that negotiations are best done in person, so your ad may contain less detail.

Ad Design

Six magic words for advertisers with inadequate budgets are: ALL BLACK AND WHITE LINE WORK. Either your ads will be all type, or they will have some sort of illustration that has no half-tones or shading. No colors. No photographs. No mezzotints. Line work is cheaper to produce—in fact, you'll probably design and paste up the ads yourself—and cheaper to run. Newspapers and magazines usually charge extra for ads that have to be screened (photographed through a screen to produce a pattern of tiny dots). Line work only goes through the press once, so there's only one chance to screw up. Halftones or color work go through several times, multiplying the possibilities for disaster as well as the cost of producing an ad and running it in periodicals.

If all you can afford are classified ads, you have no design problems. You send in the copy and your check. They set the copy in tiny, hard-to-read, smeary type. No problem.

A display ad is any ad that isn't a classified. The newspaper or magazine gives you a certain amount of space (e.g., 3″ x 5″; ¼ page) for you to fill as you wish (within reason). You can have all type; all type using several kinds of type; type plus a border; type with an illustration; type between two, or among several, illustrations. If the ad includes a coupon, you'll probably want a border or some kind of distinguishing device around the coupon. Sometimes the rate card (more about this later) will indicate that, for an additional fee, you can send in your copy and a rough sketch; they'll set the type and take care of everything for you. This can be a lifesaver.

Whatever your aesthetic convictions are, remember that a cheap ad should lean more toward Bauhaus than Art Nouveau. Either your ad is one of many small ads on a big page, or the publication is—how shall we say it—not of large circulation. (When a poor man gets to eat a whole chicken, one of them is sick.) So your ad must be a beacon of clarity, impelling the eye to your message.

These are the steps in designing a display ad. The order of the steps can be varied a little; after all, some musical comedy teams write the lyrics first and others start with the music.

- Write the copy.
- Decide if the ad will have some kind of artwork in addition to the type.
- Make a rough sketch showing the relative size and position of the elements (headline, body copy, artwork). This is called a croquis—pronounced croakie—which is French for rough sketch. You don't have to letter in the body copy; just draw pencil lines to indicate each line of type.
- Find out if the copy will fit into the allotted space. The process is called copy-fitting, and I'll get to it in a moment.
- If it can't, rewrite to fit, or change the design.
- If the ad will be hand-lettered, do the lettering; if typed, type a perfect copy. If you're using transfer lettering, do the lettering. If you'll be having type set, type out a perfect copy and spec it (q.v.).
- Do the artwork, or have someone else do it; or use a clip book, clip service, or mat service.
- When you have all the elements in hand, paste up the ad.
- Get lots of veloxes. (A velox is a particular kind of photostat; it's black on a white background and slightly shiny. Typesetters and large copy stores make veloxes.)
- Send veloxes—not originals—to the publications carrying your ads.
- Save the originals (the mechanicals) in a well-protected file, and the spare veloxes in another. You may want to run the ad again, or make some changes, and you don't want to go through the whole process again.

Since it's easier to work from a 6″ x 9″ than a 2″ x 3″ ad, even if all you can afford is the latter, you can make up the original ad in the larger size, then have it photostated in the smaller size ("statted down"). You can even make up an all-purpose "generic ad." Check the rate cards of the publications you plan to advertise in; usually the ad sizes will be fairly similar. Design the generic ad so that it can be squeezed or stretched a little to fit: leave some white space that can be trimmed or augmented, or put a border around the edges that can be removed in a tight space or surrounded with white in a large one. If this surgery doesn't work, stat the ad to the size you need.

ARTWORK

Remember, for lower ad rates and less trouble, stick to line work. You can make your own drawings or designs. Sometimes this works, sometimes it doesn't. You can use a logo. (When your logo is designed, get—and file—lots of veloxes of it in many different sizes.) You can go to a local college or art school that offers advertising courses. Students need a portfolio of samples to get a job after graduation, so you should be able to find a talented person who will work for a small fee, or just for the experience. You can probably find a copywriter in the same way, but you are more likely to have an ego involvement in your own deathless prose than in your artwork.

You can also use published artwork. This is not to say that you can slice up any magazine that strikes your fancy; that stuff is copyrighted. But you can use clip books, which are compilations of noncopyrighted artwork (either old or recently done by hired artists) that you are allowed to use freely. A clip art service charges you a fee for one-time use of its material, or gives you nonexclusive rights (or rights limited to a specific area or industry) to use the material as many times as you want. Nonexclusive rights mean the same artwork can turn up in many other ads. It's like two women in identical dresses at a party: it's supposed to be a big problem, but I don't see why. Some clip art is line work, easy to use in pasteups; some of it is screened, which is very convenient for newspapers, inconvenient for magazines. If you do a lot of newspaper ads involving stock artwork, consider subscribing to a mat service. The service sends you mats—cardboard coated with rubber "carved" into the shape of your copy and artwork; newspapers can print directly from the mats.

TYPE SPECKING AND COPY-FITTING

The first type consisted of individual letters carved out of wood or cast in metal; the letters were placed together, with blank bits between words. To increase the space between lines, one or two pieces of lead were put between the lines. Material with widely spaced lines is still called "leaded" (the e is short). You can still find typesetters who use metal type; because they're somewhat marginal businesses, you may be offered attractively low rates.

Today, photocomposition is the more common method. Instead of juxtaposing pieces of metal, the photocompositor uses a camera to photograph the outlines of letters displayed around the edges of a series of disks.

Photocomposition ("cold comp") is more flexible than metal ("hot type," so called because the shop has a machine to melt down old blocks of type to make new letters). In hot type, if you decide to change a word or increase spacing, a piece of metal consisting of several lines has to be broken up and reassembled. In cold comp, your original instructions are embodied on a paper tape or magnetic disk; the operator just has to change the instructions, and the machine redoes the job, repeating the unchanged material and modifying according to the new instructions. Metal type is limited by the fact that each letter takes up a certain amount of space, and has a certain amount of metal around it; letters and lines can't be compressed beyond a certain point. The photographic lens can make an image of any size. You can even have "minus leading," with lines closer together than metal type could be placed.

But both systems use the same, traditional system of measurements and specifications (specs). The size of type and the dimensions of typesetting jobs are measured in picas (a pica is ⅙″) and points (a point is 1/72″, or 1/12 of a pica). Type is described as "8 point," "12 point," "36 point," or whatever. The point size is the height of the letter—but the height is measured from the baseline of one line of type to the baseline of the one above it, or from the bottom of the descender (the long stroke on the p and q) to the top of the ascender (the long stroke on the t, f, b, and d). (This is the origin of "mind your p's and q's." In the early days of printing, the apprentice had to take apart the letters after a job was printed, and put each letter in the appropriate little compartment in the type case. When they're upside down and backward, it's easy to confuse a p and a q.) Different type styles have different proportions. Some are, you might say, long-legged; others are stocky. So two different typefaces in the same point size can look very different, and one can look much larger. "X-height" is the height of the main part of the character (not the ascender or descender). A typeface with a large x-height will look larger than a typeface with a smaller x-height and the same point size.

Typefaces can be classified as serif (with small lines perpendicular to the main strokes of the letter) or sans serif (without these strokes). This book is set in a serif typeface. Roman type is straight up and down; italic is slanted. Boldface is darker than ordinary type.

Typefaces come in families. A given face will be available in different sizes and in roman and italic versions. It may also be available in condensed (narrower, elongated) and expanded (shorter, broader) versions.

Although the number of existing typefaces is frightening, any given typesetter has only a certain number available. The typesetter will give you a brochure or a sample page; you choose the face you think is best for your purposes. If the name starts with "ITC," the typeface is copyrighted, and an extra fee is charged. This is one instance in which a brand name identifies a genuinely superior product.

Type design is a complex subject, and my own views are strong and slightly eccentric, so I suggest you read a standard reference like James Craig's *Phototypesetting: A Design Manual* (Watson-Guptill Publication, 1978) or Ben Rosen's *Type and Typography* (Van Nostrand Reinhold, 1976). Rosen's book has samples of various typefaces, each in different sizes and with different amounts of leading, set in 3″ x 2″ chunks, so you can see how the type will look in action.

Specking ("type specification") gives the typesetter instructions. Type the copy neatly, leaving a wide left margin. If you can, get it perfect. You can mark corrections in the left margin, but the less work the typographer has to do, the less likely s/he is to make mistakes. You have to indicate the typeface(s) you want, the size and leading for each, where the use of each typeface begins, and any special letterspacing or wordspacing (changing the normal space between letters or words). If you don't know what you're doing, stick with normal spacing. If you want your headline to be two inches wide, set in 16 point Bodoni Bold, write "Set 16 pt Bodoni Bold x 12 pi," because an inch equals six picas. If you want all capital letters, type it that way. If you forget, or change your mind, underline the heading three times—the signal for setting material in capitals. Underlining something once will get you italics; twice will get you small capitals; twice with initial letters underlined three times gets you capital initials with small caps in between.

For the text of the ad, you'll have to indicate the typeface, the point size, and the width. If your typeface is 9 point Century, and you don't want extra leading between lines ("set solid"), and the ad is still two inches wide, the instructions are "Set 9/9 Century x 12 pi." For one point of extra leading, say "Set 9/10 Century x 12 pi."

After the typesetter has had his way with your copy, you'll get a proof, which shows how the set type looks. Check it to see if there are any mistakes. If the mistake is your fault (you spelled something wrong, and they copied you) or if you changed your mind in the interim, you have to indicate in the margin that this is an AA, or author's alteration; you pay extra for this. If the typesetter screwed up, this is a PE, or printer's error (because, in the old days, the printer set type himself). There are about three dozen standard proofreading marks. Using them is easy to do but cumbersome to explain, so I refer you once again to Craig or Rosen.

You send the corrected proofs back to the typesetter, and then you get back repros (reproduction proofs). If the copy isn't right this time, try another typesetter the next time.

Never make the mistake of going to an "advertising typographer" just because you want the type for ads. Advertising typographers usually work for Madison Avenue folk who are willing to pay through all orifices for perfection. You don't need that degree of perfection and you don't have that kind of money. You can also save money by getting as much type set at one time as you can; it's the small jobs that kill you. Beyond your immediate needs, you can get a few pages of useful headlines like "20% Off," "Washington's Birthday Sale," a clever pun on your business name, or other tidbits that will come in handy sooner or later.

If you're very lucky, or have good instincts, the type you order will be just the right size for the ad. If it isn't, you have the type statted up or down—or resolve to copy-fit it next time.

There are elaborate and exact methods of copy-fitting, but I don't think you'll need more than a rough-and-ready method. First, figure out the area in the ad occupied by the copy (not the headline, artwork, borders, or margins). For the sake of the argument, say it's two inches wide and an inch and a half deep—three square inches. This chart gives the approximate number of words that can be stuffed into a square inch of type. Type set solid packs in more words than leaded type, because there are more of the closely packed lines. An average word has five letters, so if your ad deals with organic compounds or Germanic literary terms, expect to pay for more space.

Size in Points	Set Solid	Leaded 1 Pt	Leaded 2 Pts
6	50	45	36
7	36	32	29
8	28	24	23
9	23	20	19
10	18	17	16

You probably won't want to use type less than 6 point (too hard to read) or larger than 10 point (it looks like a first-grade reader, and the ad rates get out of hand). If the ad is three square inches of 9/9 Century, you should be able to fit in about 69 words. If the ad copy runs 120 words, you'll need some combination of blue pencil, smaller type, and larger ad. (The arithmetic is based on the size and type style of the finished ad. If you're simplifying your life by pasting up an oversized ad and statting it down, do your figuring using the larger dimensions: e.g., 12 square inches of 14-point type.)

PASTEUP

A mechanical is a copy of your ad that is set up to be photographed and then printed on an offset press or made into a mat (rubberized cardboard) for newspaper reproduction. The camera photographs anything that it interprets as black—black ink, typing, green felt-tip pen, greasy fingerprints, or cigarette ashes. The background is anything the camera interprets as white—white, and a particular shade of light blue. You can write on a mechanical with a "photo-blue" pencil or pen, and the writing won't show up on the printed copy. Just to be on the safe side—if the pen is the wrong shade—put the instructions in the margin or on a separate piece of paper. The separate sheet is neater, but susceptible to loss. Then again, you can cut a piece of tracing paper the same width as the mechanical and a little longer, and write the instructions on the part of the tissue that corresponds to the mechanical beneath. Finally, use the extra margin to tape the tissue in place. The tracing paper protects as well as explains corrections to be made on the mechanical.

Usually, the type and artwork are pasted up on a kind of thin cardboard called illustration board. You can also get illustration board with a grid of photo-blue squares. This is a godsend for getting things lined up properly. If you're designing a mailing piece or a large ad, you can get 8½" x 11" illustration board printed with little squares, and with a decorative black border.

To make a mechanical, you attach the individual elements to the board. Rule a box the size of your ad on the illustration board, using photo-blue. Extend the lines a little beyond the corners, so you have a right angle outside each of the four corners. Go over these angles a few more times so they stand out.

Now arrange the elements inside the box; move them around until you're satisfied with the placement. Get a large piece of white paper, some rubber cement, a small paintbrush, a sharp knife (X-Acto Brand is standard) or a razor blade, a T-square, and a metal straightedge. Cut the elements down to size—but leave as much white border as you can, because it's hard to paste a very small bit of type. Use the knife and straightedge to cut.

Take one of the elements, turn it upside down on the white paper. (Don't succumb to the temptation to use an old newspaper: rubber cement dissolves newsprint into gray grunge). Use the paintbrush to apply a thin, even coat of rubber cement to the back of the piece. A paintbrush is larger and better made than the brush in the rubber cement jar, so it gives you more control. Make sure that you cover the part of the paper you're holding; get the glue all the way to the edges.

Turn the piece right side up, position it over the mechanical about where you want it, and ease it down. You'll be able to move the piece around until the rubber cement dries. Use the printed squares, or a line you've drawn, to align the piece; use the T-square to make sure the type isn't running uphill. Smooth the piece down and tap the edges to make sure they adhere. Rubber cement will ooze out, but this is no problem. After it dries, it will roll right off the mechanical; use your finger or a ball of hardened rubber cement to lift it off. It also rolls right off your hands, though not necessarily off your clothing.

The camera can "see" shadows, so if the edges of the pasted pieces cast shadows, dab some opaquing fluid (Liquid Paper, White-Out, or the like) around the edges. Also use the fluid to cover smudges and fingerprints.

If your finances won't allow for typesetting, handwrite or type the copy; handwrite the headline, or use transfer type. Transfer type is printed on the back of a sheet of clear plastic. One version requires you to cut out the letters you need and stick them down;

the other version involves rubbing the top of the sheet, so the letter slides onto the paper below. Both of them are diabolical. The letters slide, break, and fall out of alignment. Never put transfer type directly on the mechanical: one mistake with the damn transfer type, and you've loused up the mechanical. Instead, transfer the type onto white pressure-sensitive mailing labels. Expect to ruin a few letters before you get a complete headline. The bottom of the label is a nice straight line for aligning the lettering. Then lift the mailing label (first trim it, if it won't fit onto the mechanical) and put it in place. This is a little harder than using rubber cement: you can't reposition the label, and you have to make sure it doesn't wrinkle.

Transfer type comprises more than lettering; you can also get ornaments and borders, which are equally hard to work with. You can also get tapes with borders and ornaments (some like printed Scotch tape, some like ultra-narrow adhesive tape) to embellish your ad.

Given this gorgeous ad, what do you do with it?

Where to Advertise

On a small budget, you can be a moderate-sized fish in a small pond, or a minnow in a larger one. If your message is a short one ("The Smiling Sheep. Fine Pure Wool Sweaters. 702 Ailanthus Lane. Open Mon–Sat 12–8") and your appeal widespread, small ads in large-circulation periodicals could be your best strategy. If you need more space to explain, if your clientele is purely local, or if you appeal to a specialized interest (collectors of barbed wire or Victorian mourning brooches; people in wheelchairs), you would probably do better with larger ads in publications of smaller circulation.

There is a correlation, although not a perfect one, between a periodical's circulation and its ad rates. Mass-circulation periodicals are never cheap; small-circulation periodicals can be quite expensive.

The expense is worthwhile if the periodical appeals to the buyers you are trying to reach. SpeciaList, 134 Manchester Road, Baldwin, MO 63011, publishes an annual *Directory of Magazines*

With Classified Ads, so you can locate these specialty outlets and find out their rates.

If you're interested in a publication, you can write to the address on the masthead and ask for a rate card. (Once you start sending out press releases, you'll get a flood of rate cards whether you want them or not.) "Card" is something of a misnomer; the range is between both sides of a sheet of paper and a small booklet. The rate card contains a lot of information you don't have to deal with (discounts for running thirty-six ads in the next three years, or in ten related publications; charges for bleed pages, which are color photographs with color running all the way to the binding). The information you have to worry about:

- The rate per word or per line for classified ads, minimum charges and maximum size
- Size of the page, number of columns in a page, number of lines in a column
- Minimum size for display ads (usually fourteen lines)
- Requirements for preparing ads ("mechanical requirements")
- Minimum space or frequency required to get a discount
- Close date for each issue (date by which copy must be received)
- Cancellation date (last date to cancel or change an ad)
- The periodical's circulation

If you don't have the rate card you need, check *Standard Rate and Data Service,* a set found in most library reference sections.

Usually rates are quoted by the line. Classified ads are often set in agate type (very small; 14 lines are only an inch deep). Lines (a measure of depth) multiplied by the number of columns give the measure of the space you pay for. For example, an ad 3″ deep and 2 columns wide is an 84-line ad (3 x 14 x 2).

Usually, a very deep ad (say, 270 out of the 300 lines on a page) will cost as much as a full page (because a newspaper or magazine will be hard-pressed to find something to fit underneath the ad). However, if you fill 7 out of 8 columns, your ad will look a lot like a full-page ad, but you'll be charged only for the space you use. After all, they can run a short article, or the continuation of an article, in the leftover space. If the rates are not quoted by the line, they'll be quoted by the column-inch (one inch of depth by the width of one column). The 84-line ad would be 6 column-inches.

A periodical's open rate (aka basic rate or one-time rate) is its highest charge, the charge to one-time advertisers. Volume and frequency discounts are measured from the open rate.

ROP means run-of-paper: the person designing the periodical's advertising layout puts your ad anywhere it fits. You may be buried among ads for corn removers and mail-order wonder drugs. Even worse, your ad may abut your major competitor's much larger and more professional ad. You pay extra for full position (at the top of a column near the front of the periodical) or for preferred position (you decide where the ad goes). More people read the front of a newspaper or magazine than the back. On the other hand, people who might buy food processors read the recipes, and people who might buy cross-country skis read the sports page.

If you advertise in a newspaper that also has a morning or evening edition, you may be able to get a lower combination rate if you advertise in both. This is not automatically a good idea: the demographics of the two editions are different. Commuters read the morning edition en route to work; families read the evening paper. If your product appeals to both groups, the combination rate can be worthwhile; otherwise, concentrate on one or the other.

Some publishers have a special ad section for mail-order businesses; they may also give a 10%–40% discount from the open rate to mail-order advertisers. You may be able to trade merchandise or services for ad space, or get per-inquiry ads. You don't pay for the space if you have a per-inquiry ad; instead, you pay a certain amount for every person who responds to the ad. As a service to readers, some periodicals include a single business-reply card for all the advertisers in the issue. The reader circles a code number for each advertiser s/he wants more information about. The publisher sorts them out and informs you; you then send out catalogs.

Book publishers and other manufacturers sometimes have co-op ad programs. They pay for part of the cost of an ad, featuring their product, advertising your store. ("Fall Fashion Winners: Princess Magda of Detroit Sweaters at The Smiling Sheep.") The amount of co-op money can be set at a percentage (say 10%) of your yearly purchases, or a percentage of the cost of the ad. The manufacturer may require you to put up at least ⅓ of the cost of the ad, even if you haven't reached your percentage ceiling. If you buy $4,000 worth of sweaters from the Princess, a 10% co-op allocation would be $400; but you may not be allowed to sink it all into one

$400 ad. If you put $100 each into two $300 ads, the Princess might pick up the rest of the tab.

A twice-a-year periodical—the Yellow Pages—can be a very effective advertising medium. Almost everyone uses the Yellow Pages—almost once a week, on the average. The phone book is an important source of referrals for service businesses, because people who need a plumber or a publicist are apt to start looking in the phone book. You have an advantage if your business name begins with one of the earlier letters of the alphabet; people tend to run out of patience before they reach "Walter's Rapid Answering Service." You can have your name listed in the Yellow Pages just by maintaining a phone at business rates. If you pay a little more, you can have your name in boldface type. If you pay a lot more, you can have a display ad. A ⅛-page ad, with good copy and artwork, can be an excellent investment.

Ad Budgeting

Obviously, it depends: on how much money you have, whether you're just starting out or can expect repeat customers, the extent to which you can count on referrals or walk-in business. If it's any help, the advertising and promotion budget for consumer package goods usually ranges between 6%–12% of sales (or projected sales of a new product). For high-priced consumer items (e.g., refrigerators), more money is spent but it represents a smaller percentage of sales: usually 4%–8%: Service businesses catering to consumers usually spend in the range of 5%–8% of sales on advertising and promotion. Manufacturers of industrial equipment spend less (2%–4% of sales), presumably because those who need forklifts know it and don't need some celebrity to tell them.

Usually, isolated ads fall as noiselessly as a tree in the uninhabited forest. You need ads in several well-chosen periodicals, and you need repeat ads in each. Because you can't go on throwing money down the drain indefinitely, you have to assess the effectiveness of your ads.

The basic measures are cost per reply (the cost of the ad divided by the number of people responding to it), the cost per sale (ad cost divided by the number of sales), and the income ratio (income produced by the ad divided by its cost). It's simpler to count only the cost of running the ad, not the cost of producing it. If you spend a lot of money for type or artwork, amortize this amount (divide the cost among all periodicals in which you run the finished ad).

It's easy to get information on how effective your advertising is if you key each ad (the one in the March 4 issue of the *Washington Post* asks customers to write to Department WP ¾); include a line in your order form ("How did you find out about us?"); or ask customers and clients. The first method is the most scientific; the second and third can give you valuable information about all sources of referral, not just ads. ("My sister ate here last week and said the Chicken Kiev was very good"; "I passed by on the way home from work and the display looked nice"; "You had that book on mid-Byzantine grammar, so I thought you might have a good political science department.")

At any rate, once you have the information, you make a chart to analyze it:

Periodical	Key	Cost of ad	# of Inquiries	Cost/ Inquiries	# of Orders	Cost/ Order	Income	Ratio
Modern Archaeologist	MA1	$60	12	$5	4	$15	$137	2.28
Digs!	D1	$75	200	$.375	28	$2.67	$280	3.73

If your purpose is to get a lot of people interested, familiarizing them with your name and your products or services, *Digs!* obviously does a better job than the *Modern Archaeologist.* On the other hand, one third of those who responded to the *Archaeologist* ad bought something; only about a seventh of those who responded to the *Digs!* ad did. Therefore, *Digs!* is cost effective if you want to distribute a lot of promotional material to interested people, or make a larger number of sales. These are usually, but not always, your objectives. If you spend a lot on an elaborate, full-color catalog that's heavy and therefore expensive to mail, if you send out salespeople to follow up leads, or if your packing and shipping costs are high but your overhead is low, you may prefer a more limited "carriage trade" business. In that case, your strategy is to attract fewer inquiries, but to translate a higher percentage of them into high-ticket sales. After all, it takes time and costs money to send out the damned catalogs. You have to weigh the value of building identification for later sales against the nuisance of doing things that don't produce immediate sales.

If you run the same ad in all publications, you'll have a basis for comparing the relative effectiveness of each, and you can amortize the cost of producing the ad over several uses. On the other hand, if you tailor the ads to the readership of each periodical, the results will probably be better. And don't blame either the ad or the periodical for the normal cycles of business.

Mail-order sales almost always lag in the summer and pick up again in January, February, October, and November (for Christmas gifts). (Those who sell bathing suits have a different cycle from those who sell snowshoes, and from those who sell costume jewelry or porcelain figurines.)

To get maximum effectiveness from your budget, you can stagger your advertising. If you plan to advertise in eight different periodicals, try running an ad in each of them in January, February, September, October, and November; then run an ad in four of them in March, May, and July, and in the other four in April, June, and August. Or, you can simply run ads in four periodicals in January, and in alternate months after that; advertise in the other four in February, April, and so on.

Catalogs

If you have only one store, product, or service, you can do without a catalog. If your ads and publicity get people into the store, or buying the peach preserves or personalized exercise plans, you're home free.

But if you have many products and you want to remind purchasers of one item that all sorts of other wonderful items are available, you need a catalog.

At one extreme, there's the multipage, full-color catalog; at the other extreme, the mimeographed price list. This discussion stays closer to the latter.

You can fit a lot of information, and even some drawings, onto both sides of one 8½" x 11" sheet. You can save money by typing the copy; if there's a lot of it, you can have the typescript statted down and then make a mechanical. Make sure that the folder includes complete ordering information; it's easy to do this by way of a coupon at the bottom of the back of the sheet.

You can even turn one page into a "six-page" catalog by turning the paper sideways and dividing each side into three panels:

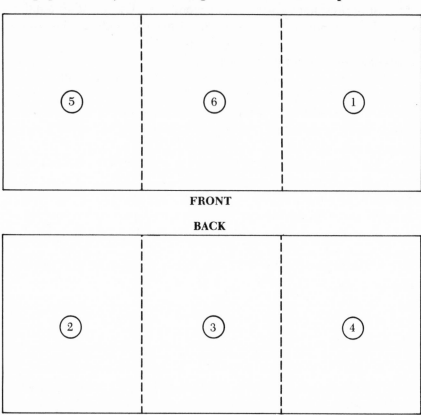

FRONT

BACK

Use Panel 1 for identification (your logo, if you have one) and general information about your business and your products. Use Panel 2 for an order blank; 3, 4, 5, and 6 describe your products or services.

The reason for this particular layout is that you can fold the brochure like a letter; it fits into a #10 envelope. When people write in for information, or when you buy or assemble a mailing list, you just have to address the envelope, stuff in the brochure, and you're finished.

You can also leave Panel 1 blank except for your return address. then staple the folder closed, address Panel 1, and mail it without an envelope. This is called a "self-mailer," and works out best in "cover stock," which is heavier than regular paper—more like light cardboard.

When customers order, they send in the order blank and front panel—and keep the product descriptions and prices as a reminder. (Get lots of these catalog sheets printed, and include one with every order, slip one into every package at the store. It is more reliable to depend on the kindness of customers than that of strangers.)

Sooner or later, though, you'll have to go to a multipage catalog. The easiest way to do this is to plan out the catalog on a series of 8½" x 11" pages folded in half and nested to form a booklet. Each sheet of paper forms 4 pages, so you'll need 8 sheets of paper and a separate cover (maybe heavier paper, or cover stock) to form a 32-page catalog. Of course, the techniques are the same for a longer or shorter catalog, but 32 pages seems a good average: plenty of space, but not heavy enough to cost a fortune to mail.

Type out the copy, or have it set, then make up the mechanicals. Be sure you get the impositions (relationships among pages) correct. For example, in a 32-page booklet made up of 8 pieces of paper, the central piece of paper will have pages 15, 16, 17, and 18 on it. These pages will be printed from 2 mechanicals: one has pages 15 and 18 on it, the other has pages 16 and 17. The bottom sheet of paper (the one closest to the cover) has pages 1 and 2, 31 and 32; on the mechanicals, pages 1 and 32 are on one board, 2 and 31 on another. The best way to keep track of all this is to make a dummy: take 8 pieces of scrap paper, fold each in half, stack them up, and number the pages. Take the dummy apart and unfold the sheets: each side of a sheet gives the page layout for one mechanical. Reassemble the dummy in the correct order, and give it to the printer.

There's another way to make a 32-page catalog: with 2 (17" x 22") sheets, each printed on both sides and folded in eighths. It's cheaper to do it this way, because there are only 4 surfaces to be printed. Throw yourself on the printer's mercy before you do this. There are two ways of making the printing plate ("work and turn" and "work and tumble"), and the mechanicals have to be set up differently for each.

At one time, books were sewn together. Now they're stapled or glued, but the process is still called "stitching." Saddle-stitching means putting staples into the central fold. The advantage is that the pages will open flat; the disadvantage is that, in a thick catalog, the staples will bend and shed the center page (or the cover, depending on which way the staples face). Side-stitching means that the pages are folded into booklets; the booklets are piled up, and the staples go into the side margin from front to back. This is a little stronger than saddle-stitching, but the catalog won't open flat. Perfect-binding is something of a misnomer. The pages are formed into booklets, as for side-stitching. The booklets are glued into the spine. Unless the binding is done carefully, the pages drop like autumn leaves.

In almost all cases, it pays to let the printer do the collating and binding. It costs more than just having the printing done, but the printer has the equipment and experience to do a good job. Anyway, life is too short to stand around stacking and stapling bits of paper.

Your catalog will probably be printed by "sheet-fed offset": the press prints one side at a time of individually inserted sheets of paper. Sheet-fed offset is a good choice for press runs up to 100,000 copies, which should handle your needs just fine. If you ever manage to run 250,000 copies of anything, web-fed offset might be a good choice. A web press uses a continuous roll of paper (a web) rather than separate sheets, and prints both sides at once. Letterpress and rotogravure (processes in use before photo-offset was developed) are still available, but are not really economical unless you have a press run in the hundreds of thousands.

If you're going to the trouble and expense of designing and printing an elaborate catalog, you might as well get decent paper. A heavy (20- or 24-lb) sulphite (all wood pulp, no rag content) paper may do; but for real attractiveness and durability, a rag paper is better. Newsprint is an inexpensive, rough-textured, porous paper. It's hard to print anything on newsprint that doesn't look tacky, but sometimes that's the effect you're aiming for. Newsprint is not very suitable for offset printing; it does better with the older letterpress or rotogravure techniques.

Antique-finish paper is good for offset. This paper has a soft, slightly rough finish, and has a deliberately uneven deckle edge that looks hand-torn, not crisply cut. English-finish paper is also slightly rough, with a nonglare surface. If you want a shiny surface, you want a coated paper; but this slick finish means a sacrifice of durability (no problem if the new catalog comes out in six months). The most common paper for offset printing is called machine finish or offset paper; it's slightly shiny, but not slick. All these finishes are good choices for offset.

The cover can be just another page, or it could be a separate piece of cover stock, so all thirty-two pages can have text. An economical way to introduce a little color is to print the cover in black on colored stock, or in a color on colored stock, leaving the pages inside black-on-white.

After all this trouble, you don't want to have to revise the catalog every time prices or shipping rates go up. One way to keep the catalog current is to keep prices out of the text; insert a separate price sheet inside the cover. That way, you can reprint the price sheets as necessary, at low cost, without making the catalogs obsolete.

Direct Mail

The term "direct mail" covers both orders that are solicited by ads and catalogs, and filled by mail, and orders solicited by letters sent directly to potential customers. Either way, customers must be impelled to buy from you—not a store, not another mail-order house. The mailing piece has to attract attention, demonstrate a benefit to the potential buyer, and provide a clear procedure for ordering.

Both kinds of direct mail are subject to the Federal Trade Commission's rules:

- You must notify the buyer if you can't ship the merchandise within the time you promised in the ad (or within thirty days, if no time was stated); the notice must give customers a chance to cancel the order and get a full refund.
- You have to provide a card or envelope for the cancellation.
- If the customer doesn't respond, you can assume that s/he has agreed to another thirty-day delay.
- If you still can't get the stuff out after a second thirty days, you have to refund the money unless the customer specifically agrees, in writing, to keep waiting.
- If you don't know how long the delay will be, the customer can agree to an indefinite delay, reserving the right to cancel when s/he gets sick and tired of waiting.
- If the customer does throw in the towel, you have seven days to return cash, checks, or money orders, and one billing cycle to straighten out credit accounts.

This FTC rule does not apply to:

- COD sales
- Mail-order services such as photo developing
- Magazine subscriptions *after* the first issue has arrived
- Seeds and plants
- Negative options plans—that is, plans under which customers get merchandise every month unless they say they don't want it

Soliciting customers by mail takes patience, persistence, and a lot of letters; if two percent of the people who get your piece order from you, you're doing unusually well.

A store can develop its own mailing list by sending catalogs to its charge customers; by keeping cards near the cash register for customers to fill out if they want to be on the list; and by asking, when a customer gives his name and address on an order form, if s/he wants to be on the mailing list and if s/he has any friends who'd like to be on the list.

Businesses without stores eventually develop a mailing list of existing customers. In the meantime, you can rent mailing lists from brokers such as:

Alan Drey Co., Inc.
600 Third Avenue
New York, NY 10016

Fred Woolf List Co.
309 Fifth Avenue
New York, NY 10016

Names Unlimited, Inc.
183 Madison Avenue
New York, NY 10016

Fritz S. Hofheimer, Inc.
88 Third Avenue
Mineola, NY 11501

R. L. Polk & Co.
777 Third Avenue
New York, NY 10017

Noma List Services
2544 Chamberlain Road
Fairlawn, OH 44313

A broker can rent you a list of names; for a higher fee, the names can be sorted and characterized (5,000 names in expensive neighborhoods, 2,500 optometrists, 32,000 Lutherans); for another supplement, you can have the addresses delivered on ready-to-use mailing labels.

If you have more time than money, you can assemble your own list. The public library stocks directories of manufacturers, associations, and professional groups. In a small town, your list can come straight from the telephone book. You can send out a mailing to everyone in your neighborhood, or everyone in a good neighborhood. People tend to buy from convenient nearby stores; affluent people tend to buy more than the financially pressed. If your business appeals to a particular ethnic group (saris, sushi, Italian genealogy), you can select likely sounding last names from the telephone directory. In a large city, phone-book strategies are unwieldly.

To simplify the process of getting out a mailing, you can have the printer fold your mailing pieces for you. Get them folded like a business letter, not accordion-folded (Z-shaped), or it will be almost impossible to stuff the envelopes. An operation called a "letter shop" will stuff envelopes (rates are lowest for #10 envelopes, higher for 6" x 9", even higher for 9" x 12", so plan your mailing pieces accordingly. A letter shop will also see that they get sent to the right people, or even create the mailing piece, decide who should get it, and send it out. The cost depends on the extent of the services rendered.

At the other extreme, you can do everything yourself: write and design the mailing piece, make a mechanical, get it photocopied or printed, type the labels or envelopes yourself, and send out the letters or catalogs. A few hints for the hardy, persistent, and destitute:

- If you want a second color, compare prices. It may be cheaper to have colored ink on white paper than black ink on colored paper.
- If you decide to spring for colored paper, you can set up a standard format (for example, your logo and a border on robin's-egg-blue paper), and get lots of blank pages printed up in this format. A long press run is cheaper per unit. Later on, you can bring the bordered paper to the printer and have the text of the letter or announcement printed on it.
- A self-mailer (heavy stock that can be stapled and mailed without an envelope) costs more than a lighter sheet, but it saves the cost of envelopes and the work of stuffing them. The disadvantage is that a self-mailer looks like a direct-mail solicitation; a letter in a business envelope looks as if it *might* be a personal letter, so it has a fighting chance of being opened and read. However, some stores have gotten excellent results with catalogs in self-mailer format. Service businesses do better with communications that seem to be letters.

- If you can't afford to use your regular letterhead envelopes, you might be able to get decent-looking results with thinner, cheaper envelopes that have titanium dioxide (an opaque white chemical) added to the paper.
- Although recycled paper is a worthy idea, it makes lousy envelopes: the paper is soft, absorbs lots of moisture, and bends or glues itself shut before you can get the material inside.
- If you do twenty-five pieces at a time, you'll get the mailing out eventually without drowning in it.

If you have an electronic typewriter or can fit them into an ordinary typewriter, you can even get envelopes in continuous sheets with holes on the side, like computer printouts. You just keep typing, without having to remove one envelope and insert the next. When they've all been typed, you pull off the side tapes with the holes, stuff the top envelope, and go on from there.

Apropos of going on from there, the techniques of copywriting, mailing-list use, and effrontery developed in advertising and direct mail will stand you in good stead in your quest for publicity.

Publicity

The minor factor in getting publicity is the presence of genuine news; the major factor is how badly the local media need material. Your aim is to develop a symbiotic relationship with the press: you provide fascinating stories (and, perhaps, free useful objects or lunches), they inform the public about you, at greater length than you could afford in a paid ad.

If you have personal contacts with journalists or editors, by all means use them. Call in all your IOUs.

Without these contacts, you'll probably have to write a press release, send it out, and follow it up with a well-timed campaign of nagging.

Usually, press releases are typed double-space on one or two sheets of plain paper. That way, a radio announcer can read the press release as it stands, or a writer can file it as a story, unchanged or with minimal alteration. The quid pro quo is publicity for you, traded for the journalist's convenience.

A press release has to have a headline, and the headline has to be interesting enough to keep the person who opens the envelope from discarding the press release unread. Tedium is a relative thing. An announcement of a new kind of squeeze bottle would find little sympathy at *Newsweek,* but might rate a feature article in a trade journal for the packaging industry.

Put a release date in the upper right-hand corner of the paper: either "For Release 9/5/83" or "For Immediate Release." Use a release date if the release is a genuine news item, or if you want the story delayed until some event happens, or until merchandise is actually available. Otherwise, mark it "For Immediate Release." Journalists, even as you and I, procrastinate. A press release with an April date is likely to be discarded when the desk is cleared in December. A "For Immediate Release" could have arrived anytime, and at least calls for a quick skim before incineration.

The body of the press release has to be factual, but has to convey a sense of excitement. The eventual story will displace some other item—even if it's only the cake sale at St. Angela's—so the release must demonstrate interest for the particular audience it's addressed to. If you write only one release for all markets, you have to use follow-up calls to "tailor" the release to particular media. If you're of Hungarian descent, that's the angle for a Hungarian-language newspaper; if you're a woman in a nontraditional occupation, that's the angle for the feminist press, and so on ad infinitum.

By the way, just to be perverse, I send out my press releases single-spaced on letterhead. That way, it's immediately clear who sent the release, and I only have to pay for printing one side, not two.

At the bottom of the press release, give the name and number of the person to be contacted for more information. Usually, you fall into this category. Also ask for copies of the eventual article. Most people won't bother to send you the clips, but at least some will. Save the clips to assemble a clippings book. You can use the existence of these clippings to demonstrate your importance and justify further coverage. You can quote from the articles in your ads. ("The *Hendersonville Herald* says, 'The collection shows a fine sense of style in its handling of supple cashmeres and luscious angora.' ") You can also analyze the clips to see what parts of the release seem worth reproducing; you can reorient future releases in light of this information.

Press releases should always be sent to an identified human being, not a title: Suzanne Bowker, not Editor. For the less important releases (media you don't really expect to pick up the release, or those that you don't expect to generate much business if they do), you can get the names from *Magazine Industry Market Place, Writer's Digest, Standard Rate & Data Service,* or *Editor & Publisher International Year Book.* But because the turnover rate is high, telephone first to get the name if you are particularly interested in a periodical or a radio station. Radio stations chew up material at a furious rate, so they always need more.

If a station picks up your release, what usually happens is that you get a phone call asking if you want to be interviewed—either right away or the next day. The interview itself usually lasts a minute or two, over the phone, on tape delay: the host talks, you talk, and the result emerges from the radio a minute later. The delay gives station personnel a chance to bleep out blasphemy and libel. For a longer interview, you may be invited to the studio to tape. This can less offputting than a telephone interview, or make you more nervous, because you can see your interviewer and perhaps a studio audience; it's an individual reaction. Radio interviews are great for promoting books, because the host often knows what a book is even if s/he's not a reader, and because the audience can remember the title of your book and rush out to a bookstore to get it. Radio is also a good promotion medium for stores, because the store will still be there when listeners get around to visiting it. It's not as good for very new ideas and products, because the host probably won't understand what you're doing and won't be able to ask the right questions; it's downright bad for mail-order products, because the audience won't be able to keep track of prices, shipping fees, and addresses. (Besides, some stations think it's okay to plug a book or a restaurant, but "too commercial" to give prices for mail-order products.)

Normally, to get any results at all from a press release, you have to follow it up. You have to call the people who got the release, persist through a bodyguard of receptionists and secretaries, and sweet-talk the release recipients into running some kind of story. It takes creativity to send out the same press release and find a dozen different angles for covering it; and it takes brass gonads to keep nagging until the material appears in print.

Lacking one or both of these attributes, you may want to hire a publicist. A small expense in PR fees and printing costs can turn a struggling enterprise into a booming success—or add one more useless expense to an already intolerably strained budget. A good publicist is creative and indefatigable in finding angles that make your press release different from any other client's, and indispensable to potential sources of publicity. A good publicist has a wealth of zealously maintained contacts, so s/he can choose a medium and know someone there who will answer the phone. A bad publicist "rounds up the usual suspects" by sending your press release to the same ill-chosen group s/he sends all press releases to, without follow-up.

Promotion

It's easier to get coverage if you create your own event. A designer or clothing store can have a fashion show; an artisan can show crafts; an art gallery can unveil a new show. Press releases, or just invitations to local journalists, are in order to publicize the event. If you can think of something highly creative, or simply out-and-out bizarre, a wire service or local TV or radio station might want to cover it. They always need human-interest stories. However, television calls for stories that are visually dramatic, not just verbally clever.

Sometimes you can use the same quid-pro-quo approach with other businesses: if you're a florist, you can let merchants decorate their shop windows with your flower arrangements, with a discreet yet prominent card in the window saying "Flower Arrangements by . . ." A potter can lend vases to a florist; a photographer can lend wedding photographs to a catering hall; a jewelry designer can lend bracelets to a boutique for the adornment of its mannequins; a painter can lend artwork to a restaurant. (But first, get a written contract specifying when you get the stuff back and who bears the risk of loss or damage; filibuster for adequate insurance coverage, paid for by the borrower.)

Photographers, artists, models, designers, and the like are subjected to go-sees, a tribal rite involving a pilgrimage to art directors and gallery owners. The first step is to get through the perimeter defenses (the receptionist), either to be seen right away or to make an appointment.

When the appointment comes, a small but breathtaking portfolio is more likely to get you jobs than a larger portfolio with a proportion of mediocre work. Try to get the portfolio examined while you wait. If you have to leave it, you can't keep any more appointments until you retrieve it (unless you have a duplicate, which is expensive in any case, and impossible if you get only one tearsheet of an ad or an article), and coffee stains can appear in the interim. It's a very good idea to have a small piece printed up for the potential client to keep: a postcard, a sheet of photographs, a poster. You can send these potential clients a little remembrance every few months; it helps keep your name in their minds.

Consultants, seminar directors, and others who do not have a visible product can use lectures or small-scale demonstrations ("dog and pony shows") to motivate potential clients. You give a short presentation explaining the nature of your work and how it will improve your clients' lives (e.g., higher profits, compliance with federal or local laws), then give a short demonstration—don't give away the store. For example, if you give two-day seminars, you can abstract half an hour that is fascinating but does not preclude the need for the entire seminar.

You can't count on finding a blackboard, so bring your own felt-tip pens and large pad for writing down the points you make. Visual aids (charts, photos, graphs) are often helpful in keeping the audience awake and in illustrating your points. Don't put out the charts before you start talking; the audience will anticipate what you have to say. A 21″ x 28″ chart will be visible from the back of a reasonably sized room, and you'll be able to carry the charts without a forklift. If you can deal with the connotations, a wire tripod used for holding funeral wreaths is a good portable chart-holder.

Whether you choose a direct confrontation method or a more anonymous one (ads, direct-mail letters) depends on your personality and the nature of your business. In any medium, the problem is the same: to find accurate statements that will motivate customers to buy, and to make customers aware of these facts as economically as possible.

CHAPTER TEN

Bells, Whistles, Goodies, and Gadgets: Equipment

WASP, WASP & TOKEN had a word processor. (Indeed, by this time they may have a dozen of them, banked in gleaming rows.) The executives were utterly entranced by the Whizbangatron Omega, and they could hardly wait to make minor, if pervasive, changes in documents so they could be put back on the machine. A favorite use for the Omega was rewriting short letters eight or nine times—in only twice the time it would have taken to retype them on a conventional typewriter. Of course strict rank order was preserved: the most important person's documents were processed first, even if they weren't due for a month. The lesser breeds got whatever time was available on the machine, even if the project was due the next day. Usually, around four o'clock someone would realize that a major deadline was impending, so we'd call a temporary agency. The agency would send an exceedingly well-paid person to work through the night.

My instincts are to condemn all technology out of hand, but that's ridiculous also. The point is not to be seduced by the thought of having the newest, the most sophisticated, the most advanced—the bells and whistles. You may feel the 1932 Rolls-Royce represents the perfection of coachwork, but a 1968 Chevy van would be a better choice for delivering pizzas.

This chapter starts out with some general considerations of what to get in the way of furniture and equipment and continues with a decision of how to get it (buying new merchandise, buying used merchandise, renting, leasing). It finishes with a discussion of where to buy.

What to Get

RESTAURANT AND BAR EQUIPMENT

If you serve liquor, either peripherally or as the focus of your business, you need a bar, banquettes, or tables. A long bar is inviting for customers who come in singly. Groups, especially groups of older people, tend to prefer tables. If you have booths or banquettes, make sure patrons can get in and out of them without undue squirming. You'll need at least two sinks and an automatic glass washer, or three sinks, behind the bar or near the mixing station.

Bar glasses have to be thrown out at the first sign of a chip, so thick rims are helpful. Simple, cheap glasses are less likely to be stolen than fancy ones. You'll need 1- and 2-ounce shot glasses; 4-ounce glasses in several shapes; stemmed cocktail glasses; beer glasses; brandy snifters; tall glasses for iced drinks; and champagne glasses (the flute or tulip shape holds the bubbles better than the flat saucer shape). You'll also need icepicks, paring knives, glass and metal cocktail shakers, a bar mixer, a bar blender, and lots of ashtrays.

The fundamental distinction in barkeeping is between well brands (generic booze, so to speak—the customer orders a scotch on the rocks) and call brands (premium brands ordered by name—a Dewar's on the rocks). Each bartender needs a level surface to mix drinks, ice, a mixing gun for carbonated drinks, and a "speed rack" for keeping the well brands. The bottles should be kept in the same order, so the bartender can grab for the vodka without taking time to read the labels. (Beer taps have individual shapes to identify the brand.) Don't get too loyal to a particular well brand; keep checking the trade catalogs and switch to whatever brand offers you the best "post-off" (quantity discount). The well includes scotch, bourbon, gin, vodka, brandy, rum, mixers, liqueurs used in popular mixed drinks, and bar wine. In some areas, rye and/or tequila go in the well.

Call brands go behind the bar: premium brands of scotch, bourbon, gin, vodka, fancy liqueurs, good brandy. Local custom dictates stocking policy. In a workingman's bar most of the patrons may favor draft beer or boilermakers; preppies drink gin and tonic or Bloody Mary; those who drink amid stained glass and hanging pots of ferns go for white wine spritzers and Black Russians.

Restaurant dishes, like bar glasses, must be cheap, sturdy, and readily available when replacements are needed. Don't put your restaurant's name on things unless you feel the item is inexpensive enough to be sacrificed to souvenir-hunters. Avoid dishes with dirt-collecting ridges or narrow, uncleanable spouts. Try to get china with interchangeable lids for coffee and teapots, covered vegetable dishes, and the like. One of my fixations is that every restaurant worthy of the name should have a pepper mill on every table. On the other hand, those four-foot monsters are harder to steal than pocket pepper mills. Very large plates won't fit into the dishwasher.

In the kitchen, you'll need heavy, easy-to-clean pots and pans, without ridges or crevices to trap dirt; mixing bowls; a professional-quality food processor or slicer, blender, and mixer; spatulas, whisks, salad bowls, and scoops. Scoops for ice cream and salads get larger as the identifying number gets smaller: a #100 scoop is 1⅛″ in diameter, a #6 is 3″ across.

In the preparation area, you'll need a dishwasher with water hot enough to sterilize the dishes; storage space for dishes, pots, and utensils; and convenient, easy-to-clean storage for food. The freezer must maintain 0°F or below. Meat, poultry, milk products, and eggs should be kept at 31°–37°F; fish and seafood should be a little cooler: 29°–33°F.

FACTORY EQUIPMENT

Of course you'll need your production machinery. You'll need storage for parts and inventory: usually open- or closed-back metal shelving, perhaps with individual cardboard bins for separate items. A "pick rack" is a sheet of heavy metal on a trestle base. The surface of the sheet is embossed with projections for hanging individual cardboard or plastic bins. Each bin holds a different item.

You'll need materials-handling equipment: dollies, hand trucks, pallets, forklifts, depending on the scope of your operation and the products involved.

Safety equipment is also essential: hard hats; tape and signs to warn of dangers; grease-resistant, nonconductive rubber floor mats; gas masks. There are four main types of fire extinguisher:

- Type A (marked with a green triangle) is used to extinguish wood and paper fires. Soda acid or plain water extinguishers are Type A.
- Type B (red square): a foam, dry chemical, or carbon dioxide fire extinguisher used to put out oil, grease, or solvent fires.
- Type C (blue circle): carbon dioxide, dry chemical, or bromotrifluoromethane for electrical fires.
- Type D (yellow star): for burning metals; the powder has a sodium chloride base.

All-purpose, A-B-C extinguishers also exist.

Finally, you'll need clean-up equipment: push brooms, shop vacuums, trash barrels, plastic trash bags.

OFFICE FURNITURE

Each person in your firm needs at least a file drawer of his or her own; then there have to be flat surfaces to write on, and there must be someplace to put the typewriter and telephone.

At a higher level of sophistication, you can have an entire desk per person. To economize, you can buy secondhand two-drawer file cabinets, then get half as many flush doors, and put the doors on top of two file cabinets, providing four file drawers per person. As a further refinement of this idea, you can put together two "desks" facing each other, a few inches apart, and wedge a piece of 4' x 6' plywood (on its side) between the two. The plywood (or pegboard or Sheetrock, whatever's handy) provides a certain amount of quiet and privacy. If you attach some felt or cork to the part that sticks up above the "desk," you can tack things up with staples or pushpins.

The acme of luxury is a *real* desk for everyone (an L-shaped desk for everyone with a typewriter). Metal folding chairs are serviceable; swivel chairs on casters can be moved around the office space; orthopedically designed posture chairs help a lot if you have to spend hours doing detail work.

Even if everyone has a personal file cabinet, you'll need file cabinets for the business as a whole. Ordinary file cabinets have the file folders parallel to the front of the cabinet; the drawer pulls outward. File cabinets are not standardized. The variety of heights, widths, and depths is staggering. Unless you have a lot of office space or an exceptional volume of files, get the comparatively shallow file cabinets. The Pendaflex system is a metal framework placed inside a regular file drawer. Pendaflex folders are large pockets that hang from the framework. You put file folders or loose documents into the Pendaflex folders. The advantage is that your file folders won't buckle or get squashed; the disadvantage is that the system costs something, and the temptation to just throw things into the Pendaflex folder (where they will never be found again) is enormous.

Lateral files hold the file folders perpendicular to the front of the cabinet; to reach a file, you flip up the front of the cabinet and pull out the drawer, then turn 90° to search the file. Lateral files are more expensive than regular file cabinets; they need more width but less depth, so they're good for shallow corridors.

When you fill your filing cabinets, you can start throwing out obsolete documents, microfilm older documents, buy more file cabinets, or use transfer files. Transfer files are cardboard cartons with closures of varying degrees of elaborateness, or cardboard file drawers. You put transfer files in a back office, basement or attic, or in a warehouse. Just be sure to label the transfer files, so you don't have to search through a dozen files to get one receipt or letter.

Offices also require other amenities: chairs for visitors or clients or traveling salespersons; someplace to hang coats; bulletin boards; decorations; a refrigerator for the convenience of brownbagging employees; a water cooler; and a coffee machine. Don't overdo these last: Wasp, Wasp & Token had a separate room with a coffeemaker, refrigerator, sink, and kitchen cabinets. The end result was that coffee brewing, coffee consumption, and visits to the bathroom absorbed a fair proportion of the day.

MISCELLANEOUS EQUIPMENT FOR OFFICES AND STORES

Offices can make good use of postage meters if the mail load exceeds a hundred pieces per day. The postage meter weighs the letter or package and prints out a tape showing the correct amount of postage. The Post Office accepts the tape in lieu of stamps: you send the meter to a Post Office, pay for a certain amount of postage (say, $500) and send the meter back for a "refill" when that amount has been used up. If the mail volume is smaller, buy rolls of stamps in various denominations and get a good postal scale.

Calculators come in handy in most kinds of businesses. Most

calculators have a one-year warranty. Features to look for in a plain, ordinary calculator include:

- A large keyboard with clearly marked keys (this is obviously impractical in the ones the size of a credit card)
- An 8-digit display (not 6)
- The ability to add, subtract, multiply, divide, clear a single entry, and compute percentages
- "Automatic constant" figure or a constant key so that you can multiply or divide by the same amount without starting from scratch each time (for example, computing a 3½% price increase on a list of items)
- Memory function, so you can store the result of one calculation and use it to perform further calculations

Financial calculators have been programmed to compute interest, amortization, present value, and other financial concepts. They have special keys for these functions. A programmable calculator can be programmed for financial, scientific, or other purposes: either you do the programming, or you buy chips or other elements to insert into the calculator. Printing calculators print out their results on a strip of paper, either instead of or in addition to a digital display. The paper can be saved as a record of the calculation: very useful if you want to document your sales or other transactions. You can file a tape for each day's receipts; if you deposit a lot of checks at once, the bank may accept the tape in lieu of a deposit slip. If, God forbid, you get audited, you can sort your canceled checks by category and present each bundle to the IRS agent, with a tape showing that the total for telephone bills, travel and entertainment, or whatever, is correct.

If you have a large number of simple transactions to perform and never need the more complicated functions, an adding machine could be a better choice than a calculator. The keyboard of an adding machine is larger than a calculator's keyboard; it's less tiring to use for long stretches of time. Adding machines always produce a tape as a record. Features to look for include:

- 8-digit capacity
- Keys that move freely, without sticking
- A clear indication whether a number is negative or positive (some adding machines print negative numbers in red)
- A repeat button for making a series of similar calculations

- Standard replacement tapes and ribbons. The most common tape width is 2¼″, but widths up to 3⅞″ are used occasionally. Make sure the stationery stores in your area stock the replacement supplies you need.

In its simplest form, a cash register is an adding machine which pops open to receive money. A good cash register produces duplicate tapes (one for the customer, one for your records). The machine should be able to handle tax-free sales, taxable sales, and sales tax. You should be able to get a daily total by ringing the "total" key, then clear the machine with one key to get a $0 balance for the next day's opening. It should be possible to correct errors—but not *too* easy for the employees to make "mistakes" in their own favor. Before you buy a cash register (especially a secondhand one) pretend that it's lunchtime on Christmas Eve: ring up transactions as fast as you can, and see if the keyboard jams or the cash drawer sticks.

Fancy electronic cash registers are called "point of sale systems." They vary in elaboration. Some of them keep a running total of sales as compared to inventory; others handle credit card sales, have typewriter keyboards so a description of the sale can be typed in; others have an electronic eye to read the black-and-white-striped computer code.

TELEPHONE EQUIPMENT

An office—even one at home—should have plenty of telephone jacks, so you can buy your own phones, plug them in, and move them as necessary. Under most circumstances, ordinary dial phones will be sufficient, but Touch-Tone is nice if you make a lot of calls or if you plan to subscribe to a long-distance network (I'll get to that in a minute). If you're very impatient, you can get a gadget that redials numbers that were busy when you dialed the first time. If you need to jot down information as you talk on the telephone, you can get a set that holds the receiver on your shoulder to keep your hands free.

If you have two or more phone lines, a "Hold" button is useful. However, the device that plays tinny music when someone is put on hold is an abomination.

If you have *lots* of phone lines, you may need a switchboard and intercom system. Reconditioned used switchboards are about one third the price of new ones. On the other hand, the newer switch-boards are button-operated and very easy to use; the operator won't need special training.

On a humbler level, a business that can't afford to keep an em-ployee sitting by the phone at all times needs an answering ma-chine. Make sure that the machine is FCC-approved; if it is, the code number will appear somewhere on the machine. You're sup-posed to notify the phone company, and give the FCC number, when you install the machine. There's no extra charge on your phone bill for having an answering machine.

The simplest answering machine just plays back your message and records the caller's message (or beeps on the phone line after the caller hangs up). Greater elaboration can be obtained at higher cost: a dial showing the number of calls you got, extra-long message tapes, the possibility of calling the machine from another phone to get your messages. If you have phone jacks, you can buy a T-adap-tor for about ten dollars, plug it into the jack, and plug the phone and answering machine into the adaptor. If you don't have phone jacks, the telephone company will have to install the machine and charge you for its trouble.

There are several systems for getting "bulk rates" on long-dis-tance telephone calls. The telephone company handles the WATS (wide-area telephone service) system. You get cut rates on long-dis-tance calls, but you have a minimum commitment you must pay each month. WATS lines can rebound. The line is often used by em-ployees for "free" chats with customers, or friends and relatives far, far away. You can minimize this problem by putting all calls through a receptionist or by getting IWATS (incoming collect calls only). The phone company will do a free cost-benefit analysis of the advisability of getting WATS. They're not impartial, but they're not dishonest either. (This was written just after the AT&T antitrust case, which forced the Bell System to sell off its local phone com-panies; the practical repercussions can only be guessed at. Most ob-servers believe that long-distance rates will go down and local rates will rise.)

If this is true, the savings you can get by using a long-distance network rather than the Bell System will diminish. You can get in-formation about private long-distance networks by calling MCI at (800) 243-2140, SPRINT V at (800) 521-4949, and Florist Communi-cations at (301) 363-6322. The three vary in their billing systems and restrictions; usually, you get a code number, then dial a special toll-free number. You tell the operator what your ID number is and what number you are calling. You are billed for the call, or for the total number of long-distance minutes used per month. The disadvantage is the time it takes to dial all those bloody numbers, the frustration of doing all that and getting a busy signal, and the greater frustration of dialing a wrong number after all that fuss.

For the paranoid, or those under surveillance, there is even a plastic device you can use to replace the mouthpiece of your phone. If it turns red, your phone is bugged.

For real-life science fiction, you can use your telephone as part of a modem (modulator-demodulator) so someone else's computer can talk to your copying machine or computer. Devices of this sort are likely to be a bit outside your price range. However, for less exotic copiers . . .

COPIERS AND DUPLICATORS

A copier uses plain or coated paper to make copies directly from an original. A duplicator uses an intermediate medium such as a plate, spirit master, or stencil to make reproductions of the original. You can easily make one copy with a copier; you probably wouldn't bother making fewer than several hundred copies with a duplicator. A copier is one piece of equipment; a duplicator may require a plate maker as well as the duplicator itself. But duplicators are simpler, and usually cheaper, machines than copiers; and the cost per copy is often less. Usually, the quality of duplicated material is lower than the quality of photocopies; but a professional-quality spirit duplicator gives copies that no inexpensive copier can match.

If you don't have the capital available to buy a copier or duplicator, you'll have to take your photocopying to the friendly local copy store, and take long runs or jobs where copy quality must be very high to the friendly local instant offset printer. (They may be the same folks.) There are many advantages to this course of action:

- Your capital investment is nil.
- You don't have to stand there stuffing pages into the machine.
- You can usually get various kinds of paper.
- The store probably has an excellent machine, in good repair.
- If the machine breaks down, it's not your problem (unless the material to be copied is needed right away).

As your face becomes more familiar, you will probably gain the right to pay by check. If you ask nicely, you'll probably be able to open a charge account: you sign for each copying job, then get a monthly bill. Depending on the number of pages copied, the number of copies of each page, and what you want (rag paper, colored paper, and color Xerox cost extra), the cost per copy should be somewhere between three and twenty-five cents; five to seven cents is typical.

With your own copier, assuming that you use coated paper or plain xerographic bond, the cost per copy will be somewhere between two and ten cents; four to six cents is typical. In other words, you are unlikely to save vast amounts of money by getting your own copier. You gain convenience: you can run as many copies as you want, when you want them.

It's hard to figure out how much a copy *does* cost. If you count only direct costs (without figuring out the number of copies the machine will make during its lifetime, dividing the cost by that figure; without accounting for debt service and electricity), you have to consider the cost of the paper, the toner, and any other supplies you will need. You can get a desktop thermographic copier for a couple of hundred dollars, but the special paper costs twenty cents a sheet. At the other end of the spectrum, you can use inexpensive sulphite paper in an expensive plain-paper copier.

The major distinction is between coated-paper copiers which, logically enough, only copy onto special coated paper, and plain paper copiers. (Watch out: some "plain paper" copiers can copy only onto a very limited selection of papers; others onto literally any paper.) The least expensive copiers use heat to develop the image (thermography); copy quality is fairly low, and the machine takes time to warm up, so the "first-copy" time is long. The next step up in price and quality is the coated-paper copier that uses liquid toner; then the coated-paper, dry-toner copier; the plain-paper liquid-toner copier; and the plain-paper dry-toner copier. A desktop copier is any small copier; a console is a larger model.

There's something to be said for getting a lousy copier, or a good one that's hard to use or installed in an inconvenient place. Otherwise you or your staff will be tempted to make endless copies of everything. It costs money to make copies, and it costs money for someone to stand there and make the copies. Often the documents are tossed away unread. If someone takes the time to read them, chances are s/he will fire off a reply to be copied and distributed . . .

As a wholesome discipline, you might insist that, for up to five copies to be distributed within the company, carbons be used. You can get copy sets of four or five pieces of onion skin—with the carbon paper already inserted. It's true that it's hard to correct multiple carbons; but it's an equally wholesome discipline for the person typing the material to bloody well learn how to type.

You can use an inexpensive desktop copier to make six to ten copies for internal distribution; for more copies, you can make a stencil for your mimeograph, rexograph, or hectograph.

If you need a few, high-quality copies for distribution to clients or others outside your organization, a plain-paper copier gives good results. For larger, high-quality runs, your best bet is offset printing. Since you are unlikely to have an offset press on the premises, this means taking the job to an instant-offset place.

Choosing a copier involves consideration of what the copies will be used for, who will make the copies, and the number of copies you need per hour and per month. Small "convenience" copiers are not designed for heavy use, day in and day out.

If you make fewer than 500 copies a month, your best choice is probably a thermographic copier. For 500–2,500 copies, a coated-paper, liquid-toner copier will probably meet your needs best; for 2,500–5,000 copies a month, a dry-toner, coated-paper copier is probably best; and for 5,000–10,000 copies a month, a plain-paper, liquid-toner copier is probably the best choice.

Some copiers require a lot of judgment on the operator's part to make good copies; others are more or less idiotproof. Some copiers jam up or break down fairly often, so a trained "key operator" has to be available. Some machines have lights or buzzers indicating when they need more toner—a very useful feature. The price of paper and toner is an important factor; so is availability. You could run out of toner in the middle of an important project, when it takes three weeks to get the stuff from the one factory (in North Dakota, where the road gets washed out during the summer and snowed in during the winter) that makes it.

Other useful features include a document feeder (so you don't have to lift the copier cover and replace each piece of paper) and a collator (so you don't have to sort out the eight copies of a forty-page report). Some copiers are good at copying book pages, others will accept only single sheets of paper. Some copiers can handle only letter- and/or legal-sized paper; others have a papercutter to prepare copies of any size. A reduction copier produces small copies of large originals.

Check the warranties and service contracts. For example, service contracts for many plain-paper copiers don't cover the photoconductor or the light source used to form the image to be copied: these are expensive items to replace.

For subjective information about copiers, send in the coupons the various manufacturers put in business magazines. The company will send you product literature, and a very persistent salesperson will contact you. You may even be offered a thirty-day free trial of various machines. In the trade, this is called "puppy-dog selling": the hope is that you'll fall in love with the copier and decide to keep it.

For a more objective evaluation, get a copy of the July 1981 issue of *What to Buy for Business,* which rates 154 models of smaller copiers. This expensive ($65.00/year, 12 issues) but superb journal is exhaustive, thorough, and sometimes very funny, though you have to get used to its British spelling ("colourful") and idiom ("Xerox are the pioneers of plain paper copying"). Subscriptions and back issues are available from *What to Buy for Business,* 74 Scotch Pines, PO Box 1783, Fort Collins, CO 80522.

TYPEWRITERS

Backtracking a little: to the equipment you use to produce the material to be copied. It's still possible, though difficult, to get manual typewriters. For all practical purposes, office typewriters are electric. Be sure you get an office model, not a portable designed for home use. With any luck, you'll be pounding out those invoices day and night.

Conventional electric typewriters have a fabric or film ribbon; the letters appear on individual type bars. A film ribbon gives crisper results, but it costs more initially and can only be used once. A fabric ribbon circulates several times before it has to be discarded.

More advanced typewriters use interchangeable elements (they look like Ping-Pong balls) to hold the letters. The advantage is that you can change type styles easily; there are no type bars to jam, so you can type faster. Most of these typewriters use film ribbons, in a

single reel or cartridge form. Some of these machines can use elements with either ten or twelve characters to the inch (ten-pitch or
twelve-pitch). If your typewriter has this potential, make sure the
pitch selector is set for the style you are using at the time; otherwise
the letters will be too crowded or too widely spaced. The newer
Ping-Pong ball typewriters are self-correcting. That is, they have
a special key, which engages a separate spool of white tape. The
tape lifts off the incorrect letter(s), and you retype the correct
letter(s).

The next technical level is the daisy-wheel, a flat disk of plastic
separated into individual rays, each carrying a letter. (Actually, it
looks more like a chrysanthemum.) The daisy-wheel is supposed, in
some way I don't understand, to insure smoothness and high quality
of typed copy.

An electronic typewriter—what name-droppers call an E-
tron—has some or all of these features:

- Electronic wiring, microchips, or other durable substitute for
  moving parts
- Automatic tabs and column layouts
- Self-correction
- "Memory" which permits the machine to recall the last word
  typed, or to type out common phrases ("Sincerely yours, Michael Bowman"); some even have a large enough memory to
  encompass a list of addresses.

A large office equipment store will have many typewriter
models, both new and reconditioned. If you want to buy a newer,
sophisticated typewriter, consider buying it from the manufacturer.
In any event, compare guarantees and service contracts as well as
features of the machine. The service contract is especially important if you get a reconditioned machine; typewriters tend to be
somewhat temperamental until they reconcile themselves to a new
owner.

The purchase price is not the only thing that determines the
cost of a typewriter. First of all, there's the electricity it uses; then
there's the cost of supplies to worry about. The IBM Selectric I, and
similar machines, take a single-spool ribbon that is fairly inexpensive; you can get good-quality Brand X ribbons for these machines.
(I'm partial to Ko-Rec-Type Selectric 71, the ones with the pink
leader, myself.) The Selectric II and III, and the electronic type-

writers, use cartridge or diablo ribbons (which look like a mask with horns) that are much more expensive than the single-spool ribbons. In my experience, the Brand X cartridges for these more complex machines are so unreliable that you are forced to buy the premium-priced, official IBM ribbons—and the cost is substantial.

If the typewriter is self-correcting, you need the spools of white correction tape. If it isn't, you need correction fluid (it's like white paint) and/or correction tabs (my enthusiastic endorsement goes to Executive Ko-Rec-Type). If you own a Selectric I, or something like it, you can get fake self-correcting ribbons with separate plastic tabs to lift off the offending letter. I don't recommend this system, because the ribbon smears and the typed copy looks lousy.

A rubber mat under the typewriter cuts down on noise and keeps the machine from bouncing around on the desk. If noise is a serious problem, you can get a plastic hood that fits over the typewriter, leaving a slot for the paper.

At one end of the spectrum are machines that clearly are typewriters and nothing but. Then there are machines (e.g., the MTST—Magnetic Tape Selectric Typewriter—and MCST—Magnetic Card Selectric Typewriter, also called a "mag card") that use tapes or cards to store memory. They are particularly useful for repetitive projects such as form letters. You type the address and salutation, the machine types the rest. An electronic typewriter carries the memory in its own circuits, blurring the distinction between typewriters and word processors.

WORD PROCESSING

A word processor (WP) has a keyboard with keys like a typewriter, plus other keys (or dials, or switches) for functions such as "move" and "delete." The word processor usually has a screen like a television screen. The "typed" material appears on the screen. The operator can make corrections or changes on the screen. The material is not printed on paper until the operator is satisfied with the copy. The operator can wipe out a single letter or whole lines or pages. (When you shop for a word processor, make sure that the "delete" key isn't too easy to operate. Otherwise a single letter, whole lines, or pages can be wiped out quite accidentally.)

Word processing comes into its own when long documents have to be adapted from earlier documents: an RFP submitted to the Navy is recycled for the Department of Housing and Urban Devel-

opment; Mrs. Santiago's will is much like Mr. Goldfarb's; you send
out a form letter announcing a new product, asking for payment, or
explaining why a shipment is delayed. Again, when shopping, find
out how easy it is to make changes. Some word processors make it
difficult to shorten a page, or to move material from one page to
another.

The software (programming) for word processors is not very
standardized, so it may be difficult or impossible to combine the
products of different companies. Word processors vary greatly in
their memory capacity. The most common memory device is the
"floppy disk," which is made of magnetic tape and looks like a 45-
rpm record interpreted by Salvador Dali. Other word processors
use cassette tapes or hard disks to store memory. The usefulness of
any of these depends on one prosaic factor: how well you label the
sleeves (for disks or floppies, aka diskettes) or boxes (for cassettes),
and how well you index and store them. Otherwise, you'll have
to run through dozens of storage units until you find the material
you need. If you ever use a service bureau to process your
cassettes, disks, or diskettes, make sure they can handle your software.

The lack of standardization can also create problems if you buy
a less popular brand of word processor. It may be hard to get parts
or service. Some word processors are only a little harder to use than
typewriters; others are only a little harder to use than the controls
of a jumbo jet. In the latter event, make sure the person who sells or
rents or leases you the word processor will train your operators.

The machine you do get should fit your present needs and your
projected future needs. If you won't use the WP very often, you
won't need the finest high-speed equipment. If the unit's speed is
given in characters per second, you can figure out the number of
words produced per minute by multiplying by 10: 25 characters per
second is approximately equal to 250 wpm. It's important to distinguish between theoretical speed and use speed—the amount of
work you can really get out of the machine.

Some word processors are programmed to correct spelling and
grammatical errors, to hyphenate words, or to arrange material into
tables. Other WP units can display and print graphs and charts.
Some word processors can "talk" to other word processors, copiers,
or computers with modems. In fact, some word processors can handle numbers (data processing) blurring the distinction between
word processors and . . .

COMPUTERS

A computer is a bunch of on-off switches. Letters and numbers are stored as strings of binary digits, which in turn stand for switches that are on (binary number 1) or off (binary number 0). If you ask a computer a question, the question is translated into binary and the computer rummages around until it finds the correct string(s) of digits.

A computer can give you a list of all your customers whose first or middle name is Irving; it can tell you the number of cans of tomato paste you had in stock on any given date; it can tell you how profitable a new product will be, given certain underlying assumptions. But it can't criticize your assumptions: as the computer aphorism has it, GIGO (Garbage In, Garbage Out).

A computer is not a phallic symbol, or a way of demonstrating your modernity. Used appropriately, a computer is a powerful tool for improving efficiency and profitability. Otherwise, it's a family-size rathole down which you will throw money.

Before you rent, buy, or lease a computer, figure out how often you will use it, and whether you could get the same results another way (e.g., with a programmable calculator). Decide what information the computer will provide; who wants the information; and why. Computers provide millions of pages of useless information every year; and computer printouts on unwieldy sheets take up more space than ordinary useless information on 8½″ x 11″ paper.

One test of a rational need for a computer is an inability to get your receivables out in five days. To decide whether a computer will be cost-effective, list the functions you expect the computer to perform: perhaps general ledger, accounts payable, accounts receivable, inventory, and payroll. Figure out the cost of performing each function using your present methods, and decide the percentage you expect to save by computerization.

Then figure out what the computer will cost. As a rule of thumb, the total cost of a computer system is three times the cost of the hardware (the machinery). The cost of a maintenance contract or service calls is usually about three percent of the overall annual cost of the system.

Next calculate the impact of your computer system: the deductible rental or lease payments, depreciation and investment credit on a system you own. Consider interest payments, and what you would have done with the money had it not been invested in the computer. Of course, it helps to have a computer to do this work.

A computer system consists of a CPU (central processing unit) which contains the memory; an input device (e.g., a keyboard or card reader for putting information into the system); memory storage devices (tapes, hard disks, drums, floppies); and output devices (printers, cathode-ray tubes, terminals—for getting information from the computer out to human beings). The *mainframe* is the body of the computer itself. *Remotes* or *peripherals* are items like terminals and modems that extend the reach of the mainframe. For example, if you participate in time-sharing, the mainframe will be in someone else's office, and one or more terminals will be in your office. Sometimes the output is a display on a CRT (cathode-ray tube—which either looks like a television set or, in an inexpensive computer, is a television set). Sometimes the output comes in the form of *hard copy*—typed or printed copy. A *letter-quality* printer produces results at least as good as a typewriter. A *character printer* (many of them are rebuilt Selectric typewriters) prints one character at a time, and is comparatively slow (say, fifteen characters per second). A *line printer* prints an entire line at a time; not unreasonably, it is faster (say, thirty to fifty-five characters per second). Paper gets into the printer via *tractor feed* (continuous sheets with sprockets on the side) or *cut sheets* (single pages).

Memory is measured in *kilobytes* (K) or *megabytes* (M). A *bit* is a single computer blip, on or off; a *byte*, eight bits, is one letter or number; a *kilobyte* is a thousand bytes, a *megabyte* a million bytes. Therefore, a 64K memory holds sixty-four thousand bytes.

If your computer uses floppy disks, make sure the operator can format the disks (get them ready for use); otherwise, you'll have to buy preformatted disks, which are even more expensive.

Many, many companies make computer equipment of various kinds; you don't have to get all your equipment from the same manufacturer. A peripheral is *plug-compatible* with a mainframe if it can be plugged right in without rebuilding or modification.

A *dedicated* computer is not one that works nights, but one that does only one thing. A *general-purpose* computer is more versatile, but costs more and is harder to set up.

Software comprises programs and other informational resources used to run your computer. *Applications programs* handle a particular task such as accounts receivable or inventory. If you buy all your software prepackaged, you can avoid learning how to program. But if you are independent-minded, or have unusual needs, the service of a programmer will be needed. (See also "Computers: Special Considerations," below.)

Although it will soon be possible to communicate with computers in ordinary human language, right now computers have to be addressed in computer language. The most common language for business computers is BASIC, which has several dialects. Scientific computers tend to use FORTRAN or PASCAL. (Some scientific computers use ADA, a language named for Lord Byron's daughter, who did not invent the digital computer, but not for lack of trying.)

A "home computer" which is designed for video games and an occasional fit of balancing the checkbook probably won't meet your needs. In fact, a system sold as a "small business computer" may not stand up to heavy use day in and day out.

Some of the questions to ask about a computer you may rent, lease, or buy are:

- What is its memory capacity (in Kbytes or Mbytes)?
- How much does the mainframe cost?
- What can it do?
- What peripherals are available?
- What can they do for how much money?
- What other manufacturers' peripherals are plug-compatible with the mainframe? How do their cost and effectiveness compare to this manufacturer's products? (There's an argument that the first-time user should stick to one company's products, buying the best overall system. You have enough problems without mixing equipment.)
- How many terminals can be hooked up to the mainframe at once?
- Can two, four, or eight diskettes be run at once?
- How large is the CRT screen? (Twenty-four lines of eighty characters each is a bare minimum.)
- How fast is the printer?
- What applications programs are available? What do they do? How much do they cost?
- How easy is the system, and its applications programs, to use?
- Will the renter, lessor, or vendor train your personnel?

- How long will it take to get the system set up and working properly ("on-line")?
- How long has the rentor/lessor/vendor been in business? What is its track record? Is it likely to still be in business when you need repairs or new equipment?
- How long are the warranties? What do they cover?
- How reliable is the equipment?
- Can you fix it yourself, or is professional service required?
- What special conditions does the system require? (Most computers are finicky about temperature; some have to be air-conditioned all year.)
- What happens in case of power failure? (For some computers, instant amnesia.)

The commonest mistake new computer owners make is to get rid of the old records as soon as the last digit is input. Then there's a power outage, or an inexperienced operator has hit the "delete" key by mistake, or the wrong entry has been made on a customer's account, and there's nothing to check it against. So keep the old records, at least until the system is working smoothly.

Given the enormous problem of choosing the right kind of equipment, the right software, the right manufacturer, and the right lessor or vendor, many computer users bring the problem down to manageable size by hiring a computer consultant. The consulting profession is less organized (and less subject to licensure) than, say, the legal or medical profession, but these organizations should be able to provide the names of computer consultants in your area:

- Association of Consulting Management Engineers, Inc.
230 Park Avenue
New York, NY 10017
(212) 697-9693

- Association of Data Processing Service Organizations, Inc.
1925 North Lynn Street
Arlington, VA 22209
(703) 522-5055

- Data Processing Management Association
505 Busse Highway
Park Ridge, IL 60068
(312) 825-8124

- Independent Computer Consultants' Association
  PO Box 27412
  St. Louis, MO 63141
  (314) 567-9708

- Institute of Management Consultants, Inc.
  19 West 44th Street
  New York, NY 10036
  (212) 921-2885

Rent? Lease? Buy?

Once you've decided that you need a particular object, be it an electronic typewriter or a company car, the next problem is to decide how to get it: rental, lease, purchase of a new item, purchase of a used item. This section also includes a discussion of time-sharing for computers and other intricacies. The section ends with a short discussion of cost comparisons, but not a discussion of cost-benefit analysis, a discipline for the adepts of accounting, calculus, and other black arts.

RENTALS

Usually a rental is a short-term arrangement. You pay so many dollars a day or month for a particular piece of equipment. Rental works well if you need a piece of equipment rarely: scaffolding for once-a-year paint jobs, for example, or a rented car for the duration of your business trip to Chicago. It's also common to rent copying machines: usually you pay a monthly fee, plus a meter charge (charge per copy made) which decreases as you make more copies.

The advantage of renting is that you pay for the equipment only as long as you have it around. You can upgrade or change your equipment as often as you want. Rental payments are deductible (as long as they are ordinary and necessary business expenses); and you won't get stuck with obsolete equipment. The disadvantage is that the overall cost of rental will be higher than the cost of buying or leasing the same equipment.

LEASING

Usually a lease is a longer-term arrangement than a rental. Sometimes the lease contains an option to buy the item. If so, it is important to distinguish between a lease with an option to buy and a conditional sale (a sale with an option to return the stuff). The accounting and tax consequences of the two are quite different, and you should get skilled professional advice before you sign a lease calling for substantial payments. A sale-leaseback is a special kind of lease: you sell one of your own assets, but continue to use it, making lease payments to the new owner. The advantage is that you get cash for the item, and the lease payments are deductible. Again, professional advice is needed to avoid nasty surprises at the hands of the IRS. The basic rule is that the sale-leaseback must involve a lease term under thirty years and both the sale price and the lease payments must be reasonable about what objective parties would agree on.

Leasing heavy equipment is common, and probably more computer-users lease their hardware than buy it. Often, the "company car" is leased. A closed-end auto lease has a fixed monthly payment. An open-end lease also calls for monthly payments, but your last payment depends on the car's resale value at the lease's end. If you kept the car in good shape, and its value is higher than the amount the lessor projected at the beginning of the lease, you get to keep the difference. If the car is worth less, you have to make up the difference, up to three lease payments' worth.

In general, the advantages of leasing are:

- You don't have to use your capital or borrow money to get the item.
- Financing lasts as long as you have the item; bank loans can run out.
- The lease rate is fixed and won't rise with interest rates.
- As the lease continues, payments are made in cheaper dollars.
- You may be able to exchange obsolete leased equipment for newer models without increasing the payments to intolerable levels.
- The lease payments are currently deductible and come out of operating revenues, not profits.

You can lease equipment either from the manufacturer or seller (e.g., a car dealer) or from an independent leasing company that buys directly from the manufacturer. The usual trade-off is that an independent company will offer a longer lease, at lower rates—but the manufacturer or vendor will provide better service.

It really helps to choose a lessor that will still be in business at the end of the lease term. You want to have a full selection of equipment to choose from, with an opportunity to trade up (or down) as your needs change. Make sure that the price quoted to you is not higher than the normal price or unrealistically low; "lowball" bids will be compensated for by poor service or excessively high service charges. Try to find out the lessor's track record, and try to get a full-service contract, including regular checkups so you can keep the equipment functioning.

BUYING

When you buy a piece of equipment, it's yours. You can do with it as you like, subject to no restrictions; but if it breaks, you have to have a service contract, or find someone to repair it. If a newer, better model comes out, you'd have to sell or trade in the old model to get it.

When you add up the total cost, it almost always costs less, in the long run, to buy an item than to rent or lease it. After all, the rental or leasing company has to make a living too. But if you buy the item, you have to pony up the money. If you can't buy it for cash, you have to take the interest costs into account. Correspondingly, any equipment you have becomes an asset on your balance sheet. The 1981 changes in the tax code encourage investment by shortening the time over which items are depreciated, thus increasing the depreciation deduction that can be taken in each year. And, if you own an item, you may be entitled to an investment credit. (All this was discussed in Chapter Six.)

Sometimes buying used equipment is a splendid idea: if the reconditioned equipment is perfectly tailored to your needs. Sometimes buying used equipment is an appalling mistake: you lumbered yourself with a useless piece of junk that no one is willing to repair (and they couldn't get the parts anyway). If you buy used equipment that is in good condition or reconditioned by an expert mechanic, that was made by a reputable manufacturer in the first place, and was replaced because a better model came along, you'll probably do well. Sometimes private companies sell their old equipment. The prices will be lower than if you bought from a dealer, but you'll have to arrange for service elsewhere. A dealer can provide parts and service, but the price of the equipment will be higher.

Watch out for older, off-brand equipment, because the service problems will be immense. But don't be put off by older standard equipment that is slower or less versatile than the newest model: you probably wouldn't keep the newest model busy anyway.

One thing to watch out for is the kid-in-the-toyshop effect: the desire to make up for the Lionel electric train you never got by stocking your business with the newest and shiniest equipment. You'll have to pay for the stuff somehow, and the sparkling gadgets you boast about today leave you vulnerable to one-upmanship when the other Jaycees buy something even fancier.

COMPUTERS: SPECIAL CONSIDERATIONS

Computers are fast, and even small computers are expensive (though the cost and size of computers have decreased dramatically and presumably are still falling). If you can handle your payroll and accounts in a few hours of computer time a month, it is frustrating to have a computer sitting around costing money the rest of the time. But, having tasted the delights of computerization, it's hard to go back to pencil and paper calculations. One way you can reconcile the conflicting forces is to use an outside computer service bureau. They own the computer; you bring them the work and pay for the time you use.

The least expensive way to do this is batch processing. The service plugs your program into the computer and runs off your work. It usually takes about twenty-four hours between the time you send out the documents (payroll records, for instance) and the time you get back the results (e.g., computer-generated paychecks and withholding tax records). The problem with batch processing is that it's comparatively slow and the records leave your office and can be lost in transit. Remote-batch processing deals with some of these problems by installing a terminal on your premises. You input the information in the central computer and get your results hours or days later.

Time-sharing eliminates more difficulties. Either a group bands together to buy a computer, installing terminals in each office, or various organizations pay for the privilege of tapping into someone else's computer via terminals. Several users can get a response from the computer simultaneously. Time-sharing is more effective than batch processing if you need to use the computer right away: for example, if you interrupt a meeting to get some projections of the effect of price increases for magnesium on next year's profitability. Time-sharing is more flexible than batch processing and therefore costs more.

If you need a computer full-time, you can rent one; rent one with an option to buy (usually you have one to two years to make up your mind, and fifty to seventy percent of your rental payments are applied toward the purchase price); lease a computer, with or without an option to buy; buy a used computer; or buy a new computer.

But that's only one problem. You'll also need software (programs). If your needs are conventional, a good many standard programs already exist for inventory, accounts payable, and the like. For unique needs, you can learn to program, hire a programmer, buy software from a consulting firm, or buy your computer from a systems house. A systems house is a small independent operation which sells computers complete with software tailored to your needs. Systems houses are good at developing software and will give you plenty of personal attention. However, like all small, independent operations, they run a not-inconsiderable risk of going broke. If they do, you will be in the position of one who tries to get parts for his beloved Studebaker.

The most important question in buying a used computer is *why* it is for sale. Perhaps it was owned by a little old lady who used it only to run a short applications program on Sundays. More plausibly, the owner may be trading up to a more sophisticated system, or the computer may be a useless heap of junk. The seller will be more eager to prove the former than the latter.

Ask to see the owner's records. What was the average time between breakdowns? What were the maintenance costs? Don't just bargain on price; try to get the seller to recondition the unit or give you a warranty. Get as much help as you can with installation, training, and software.

COST COMPARISONS

In the end, you have to sit down with pencil and paper, or your financial calculator, or your computer, and figure out the potential cost of each of the alternatives.

For example, if you need a copier, the rental price will probably be \$X per month, plus a meter charge of Y¢ per copy. Or, you might pay a rental fee which includes a certain number of copies and pay a meter charge for copies over that number. Your cost is the rental cost, plus meter charges, plus the cost of supplies. Lease terms may call for a flat payment or a payment plus a meter charge. If you buy a machine, you have to compute interest charges, or the potential earnings of the capital used to buy the machine, then allow for tax costs or tax savings due to deductions and the investment credit.

Although it's arbitrary, you also have to assign a monetary value to the benefits the new equipment will produce. You have to determine, as best you can, the time saving, cost saving, additional sales, or additional profits the new equipment is expected to provide. Then decide how long it will take for the equipment to pay for itself. Three years is an achievable goal.

Where to Buy

If you want new machinery or equipment, follow the ads in general and trade publications. The manufacturers have fleets of salespeople who yearn to explain their products to you. Even if you don't buy from the manufacturer or its authorized distributors, you'll learn which products are available and what their capacities are. The manufacturers and distributors usually have a good service network and often provide rebates, trade-ins, or other incentives. Discounters, of course, discount the merchandise.

If you decide to go with "preowned," "gently used," or "preloved" equipment, make sure that the seller has the capacity, and willingness, to make repairs as needed. Sometimes large corporations maintain a program for selling obsolete equipment. Just because Exxon or Du Pont finds a piece of equipment old hat doesn't mean you will be equally blasé. Industrial auctions and going-out-of-business sales will be advertised in newspapers; trade journals have "For Sale" classified ads. Have the equipment inspected by a knowledgeable person before you buy. Also make sure that the equipment meets safety and pollution-control standards: it may be for sale precisely because of this noncompliance. The Used Computer Exchange, 2329 Hunters Wood Plaza, Reston, VA 22091, and American Used Computer, PO Box 68, Kenmore Station, Boston, MA 02215, match buyers and sellers of used computers.

The stakes are lower if you're buying used office furniture. A forty-five-dollar desk is both cheaper and less critical to your success than a twenty-thousand-dollar injection molding machine or switchboard. And you can probably inspect a desk chair even if you can't evaluate competing models of computers. Goodwill, the Salvation Army, and garage sales are never-ending resources. Going-out-of-business sales usually include office furniture. Fancy office-furniture stores may buy up the old furniture when they redecorate an office; sometimes they sell the old stuff at low prices.

Large cities have low-rent districts in which sellers of used office furniture gather. In New York, for example, Canal Street and West Twenty-third Street are old-desk enclaves. In Washington, D.C., try H. Baum & Son at 616 E Street NW, or Ginn's at 1210 Connecticut Avenue NW. In Atlanta, the Academy Desk Corporation, 338 Peachtree Street NE; Atlanta Office Furniture Company, 1003 Howell Mill Road NW; Wholesale Office Furniture Co., Inc., 699 11th Street NW; or Army Surplus Sales, Inc., 342 Peachtree Street NW. In San Francisco, check the Dorman Co., 550 Mission Street, and Busvan Bonded Dealers, 900 Battery Street; in Los Angeles, Cut/Rate Office Equipment Company, 1228 South Figueroa Street, or the McMahon Brothers Desk Co., Inc., 937 South Alameda. Or look in the Yellow Pages under "Used Furniture" or "Office Furniture and Equipment, Used." Moving and storage companies sometimes have abandoned furniture for sale.

You can save a lot of money by ordering conventional stationery items (pads, ball-point pens, message pads) in bulk. Certain more exotic items (imprinted five-part invoices) are available only from printers or mail-order stationers. If you send away for one of these catalogs, the mailing list will be sold, and you'll get all of them. It does pay to read and compare the catalogs, because each offers a slightly different assortment of products; one catalog can be more expensive for one item but cheaper for another than a rival's catalog.

For stationery, filing equipment, and factory accessories such as parts bins and rubber mats:

* Apple Label
  30–30 Northern Boulevard
  Long Island City, NY 11101

- Fidelity Products Co.
  5601 International Parkway
  PO Box 155
  Minneapolis, MN 55440

- Grayarc
  PO Box 2944
  Hartford, CT 06104

- New England Business Service, Inc.
  North Main Street
  Groton, MA 01450

- Stationery House
  1000 Florida Avenue
  Hagerstown, MD 21740

- TIE Office-Mates
  North Washington Street
  Brownsville, TN 38012

- 20th Century Plastics, Inc.
  3628 Crenshaw Boulevard
  Los Angeles, CA 90016

For office furniture (but watch out that shipping charges don't wipe out any potential savings):

- Business & Institutional Furniture Co.
  PO Box 92069
  Milwaukee, WI 53202

- National Business Furniture
  222 East Michigan Street
  Milwaukee WI 53202;
  905 Mateo Street
  Los Angeles, CA 90021;
  1401 Peachtree Street NE
  Atlanta, GA 30309

For work clothes and uniforms:

- Eastern Wear-Guard
  33 Everett Street
  Boston, MA 02134

GOVERNMENT SURPLUS

The federal government buys a remarkable quantity and variety of merchandise; and sooner or later, much of it is resold. (Don't get your hopes up too high for an Army surplus neutron bomb.)

For military surplus, you can find out what's available by sending for a free copy of "Classes of Surplus Personal Property" from the Defense Property Disposal Service, Box 1370, Federal Center, Battle Creek, MI 49016. You can get on the mailing list for future property sales by writing to the Department of Defense Bidders' Control Office at the same address. The Small Business Administration will also act as a liaison between small businesses and military installations with property to be disposed of.

The General Services Administration's ten regional offices handle civilian property. The addresses are in Appendix B. Again, the SBA can mediate and see that your name is added to the mailing list. If you want to buy strategic materials (e.g., minerals) write to the Minerals and Ores Branch, Office of Stockpile Disposal, General Services Administration, 18th & F Streets NW, Washington, DC 20405.

If the Post Office can't contrive to deliver a parcel, after ninety days the parcel is fair game for auction. To get on the mailing list, write to the Postmaster, Dead Parcel Post Branch, of the nearest regional Post Office. Ask when the next auction will be held. The Post Office also sells former mail trucks at auction. If the quality of mail service is any indication, the trucks were driven very, very slowly.

Surplus property is sold to the highest bidder: either via sealed bids, spot bids on agency forms, or by auction. There is a catalog for each auction, and all surplus materials can be inspected before the sale. (However, you can't inspect the lots at dead-parcel auctions.) Surplus materials are sold as is, so careful inspection is necessary.

Sometimes you need more than that. According to the *Whole Earth Catalog*, a bargain hunter picked up a Naval-surplus metal cabinet of unknown purpose. It was only fifty dollars. When he got it home, he opened up the back and began experimenting with the knobs and switches. He fled when a siren sounded. The cabinet blew up, taking his house with it. It was designed to keep secret documents out of the hands of the enemy by blowing them up when the ship was captured.

CHAPTER ELEVEN

Diving Into the Wreck: Failure and How to Survive It

IT IS THE RECEIVED WISDOM of the business schools that only one out of every fifty-seven new products succeeds. The statistics for new businesses are not quite as grim, but they're nothing to cheer about either. If business reverses come, the best course of action is one that recoups your losses and lets the business continue, stronger than ever. As you can imagine, this doesn't happen very often. Bankruptcy is a less than happy experience, but it's not quite the horror depicted in Victorian novels. If your business does become bankrupt, you want to arrange the bankruptcy as neatly as possible; and you want to be able to step out of the ruins and go on with your own life.

But there are less drastic alternatives. If one product isn't selling, or if your new Whizbangatron isn't cost-effective, you can deal with the individual problem. You can cut back on your business, firing the employees, cutting back (or eliminating) advertising, shortening your hours. Although the law requires business owners to meet their obligations, it does not enforce any particular level of business activity. (Remember, though, that any losses from a "hobby" as distinct from a "business" are not tax-deductible.) If you're an antique dealer, you can close your shop and sell at flea markets. Your restaurant can serve dinners only, saving the cost of a lunch chef, provisions, and waitresses. (But this will not lower your rent or electric bill, while it will limit your potential revenues.)

You can change your methods of operation: if a tactic isn't working, you have nothing to gain by remaining loyal to it. You can

301

get new sources of capital and expertise by taking partners (or more partners), selling stock (or more stock), according to your situation and form of business organization.

But sometimes, no matter what you do, the business is unsalvageable. As Alvie Singer told Annie Hall (in the movie of the same name) a relationship is like a shark: it has to keep moving forward, or else it dies. "Honey, I think what we have on our hands is a dead shark." A business, too, has to change and grow. You can think of this chapter as 101 uses for a dead shark.

Blood in the Water

It takes time for any business to start making money, and you just have to keep your hair on until that time comes. When you started the business, you decided how much money you could afford to lose, or how long you could support both yourself and it. I think you owe it to yourself to give the business at least that much time, and to pour at least that much money down the proverbial rathole. Otherwise you'll spend the rest of your life bemoaning the fact that you coulda been a contender.

But a dramatic change in personal circumstances (divorce, illness in the family) or business circumstances (your best customer goes bankrupt; your product is declared illegal or embargoed; raw materials are unavailable or triple in price) can modify the time frame.

You know you're in trouble when you can't keep current in paying your bills. On the other hand, stalling is an ancient and virtually honorable custom (as you will find out as you try to collect your receivables). Stalling is worthwhile if there is some rational basis for your belief that the situation will improve. For example, if your business is seasonal and the good season is approaching, you probably will be able to settle accounts. But if all you have on your side is wishful thinking, the expenses will have to be limited dramatically and immediately, or the business terminated.

On a higher, if still dismal, plane, you may be paying your expenses but still be unable to take a draw for yourself; or your draw may represent an entirely inadequate return on the capital you invested and the time you put in, with little hope of improvement. You may have been offered a lucrative job. In any of these cases, the most sensible thing to do is to pay your debts and say the hell with the whole thing. Chalk it up to experience.

Losing Propositions

If life gives you a lemon, they say, make lemonade. If a particular item or piece of equipment is a turkey, take your turkey and stuff it . . . no, that didn't come out quite right.

For the sake of argument, assume that your newest product is a garlic-flavored toothpaste called Ail. It has a Unique Selling Proposition: not only does it fight cavities, it repels vampires.

If, after a few months, your entire stock remains in the warehouse, you can do several things:

- Step up your efforts at advertising and promotion. Maybe a good salesperson can induce supermarkets and drugstores to stock your product. Maybe more exposure will induce consumers to demand it.
- Change your advertising. Perhaps the "If he bit you once, will he bite you again?" campaign will do the trick.
- Reposition the product—that is, appeal to a new market segment. Maybe eight- to fourteen-year-olds, or health food enthusiasts, or people over sixty-five will buy the stuff.
- Find new uses for it. Perhaps you can sell it to pizzerias. Maybe Ail will remove the tarnish from jewelry without damaging the delicate stones.

If none of the above work, you can sell the merchandise to a "liquidator" who buys closeouts (look in the Yellow Pages, or in classified ads in the general or business press) or directly to a store selling job lots, odd lots, or closeouts.

If the unsuccessful item is a component part used in manufacturing, you can take out a listing in the Industrial Surplus Locator, Water-Gard Publishing, Box GG, Gainesville, GA 30501. If the unfortunate item is a machine that is no longer needed or has not proved cost-effective, try the McGraw-Hill Equipment Bulletin, Box 900, New York, NY 10020.

If *all* your efforts are unavailing, you can find a complaisant charity and make a donation of the merchandise. At least your deduction for tax purposes will be the market value of the merchandise, either the regular selling price or the closeout price of an item unsalable at regular price. The maximum deductible donation is ten percent of your taxable income, as computed before the charitable deduction or operating loss carrybacks are taken into account. And be sure to get a receipt from the charity.

Contraction

The American ideal of perpetual, burgeoning growth can't always be achieved. At times, as a result of a recession-caused decline in demand, exploding wage and material costs, or simple stupidity and bad management, you will find that your business has expanded to a point that it cannot sustain. Sometimes economic conditions will improve (the rising tide, as they say, lifts all the boats) as you stand around trying to figure out what to do. If this doesn't happen, you will have to do some combination of these:

- Close all branches or additional locations.
- Get advice from a management consultant about correcting your mistakes, redirecting your focus, or whatever is needed to make the business profitable.
- If sales are satisfactorily high and costs within reason, but your cash flow is bad, consider factoring or hiring a collection agency.
- Fire your employees and handle all the work yourself, or with your partner(s) and family.
- Keep your employees, but cut back their hours to part-time status, saving on wages and fringe benefits (but limiting the amount of work they can accomplish).
- Lessen your tax and fringe-benefit payments by using independent contractors rather than employees.
- Stress productivity very hard and cut costs as savagely as you can without jeopardizing the quality of the product.
- Limit the days or hours of business.
- Move to a less expensive location (but moving costs, disruption, and customer confusion have to be taken into account).
- Give up the office/store/factory and work at home/by appointment only/in the garage.

As you have no doubt heard before, conflicting interests must be balanced. If you cut your advertising budget or your working hours, both expenses and potential revenue go down. The determination of which declines more sharply is more difficult and more or less subjective.

Collaboration

If you think it's hard to attract investors for a new business, wait till you try it for a business in difficulties. Still, the task is not necessarily impossible. The investor may be a rich, indulgent relative of yours or a rich nonrelative looking for a tax deduction. Maybe the business problems were caused by technical difficulties that have now been worked out. Maybe the business has great potential for success, but substantial funds are needed for promotion. For example, the Ideal Toy Company spent $1.5 million to promote Rubik's Cube, an unmistakable success.

A sole proprietor can take partners; a proprietorship or partnership can incorporate and issue stock to its new investors. Less conventional collaborations are possible. If your restaurant is in a business district with a strong lunch trade but a few diners, you can close at night and let someone else operate a coffee house or use the kitchen to cater parties or prepare specialty food items. In California, a secondhand bookstore shares quarters with a service that matches potential roommates. You can go away for the month of August (or take a summer job) and let someone sublet your premises—if the lease permits, of course.

Hibernation

Pay your debts, fire the employees, cancel your lease, hold a going-out-of-business sale, or sell the merchandise to a closeout specialist. If you pay your debts, no one will feel sufficient hostility to hassle you, and your credit rating will remain good (or as good as it was, anyway). If a prospective employer, or anyone else, asks you why the business went belly-up, blame the economy or undercapitalization. Even if the problems were the result of your unmitigated stupidity, why embarrass yourself further?

Your first impulse will probably be to terminate the business and forget about the whole sordid incident. There are several reasons to disregard this impulse:

- Orders will continue to dribble in after the formal closing of the business (especially true of mail order). Make sure that would-be customers know where to find you.
- The official mind—and the official computer—is attuned to processing returns and forms with nothing on them except zeroes. City, state, and federal governments will not be distressed by your business' lack of income. But if you *stop* filing returns, or if you try to cancel a doing-business-as registration or sales tax number, someone may pull your file, and real or fancied irregularities may be detected.
- You never know when you'll need a corporation or a DBA registration, or a resale number, so you might as well keep them in force.

When the business is in hibernation, you don't invest any effort or money into making it go. But if a piece of business comes your way, take advantage of it. Later, if you have more money, more energy, or a new, enthusiastic partner, you can reanimate the sleeping enterprise.

Selective Repayment

A Central European monastery owns a tattered scrap of parchment dating back to 1109. It is a letter from a knight to his feudal overlord, dealing with the knight's obligation to produce one Bohemian man-at-arms complete with armor and equipment. The letter begins, "Your Czech is in the mail . . ."

This is the first recorded use of the device, but not the last. No doubt you've heard it from your own customers. There are several approaches (of varying shabbiness) to selective repayment:

- Pay everyone in full, but only after they jump up and down and threaten to have your legs broken.
- Pay everyone a little bit at a time, keeping the unpaid balance below the point at which it becomes worthwhile to sue you.

- Say "sue me" and hope they won't.
- Complain about something to delay the "disputed" payment.
- Pay the most important creditors first.

Crass as it may seem, the most important creditors in this context are those who can do you the most harm—not those to whom you owe the most money. Never stiff the federal government out of withholding taxes, because it can and will put you out of business. If you are in the public relations business, you cannot exist without a telephone, so you must keep on passably good terms with the telephone company. (The printer, however, is not going to repossess your business cards and stationery.) If you own a factory, it will probably be upsetting if your machinery is repossessed. On the other hand, if you have an enormous backlog of inventory and no orders, you can be more philosophical about it. So pick and choose those to be paid carefully.

Dig out all your loan agreements, contracts with suppliers, and lease agreements. A creditor is anyone to whom you owe money. A secured creditor is one who has collateral or security for the debt: that is, the right to repossess and sell something when you default. The simplest form of default is failing to make your payments on time, but other events, such as your bankruptcy or the credit or "deeming itself insecure" can make the entire remaining balance due immediately. If you have trouble finding this month's three-hundred-dollar payment, imagine what it would be like trying to scrape up eight thousand dollars.

The simplest form of collateral is the item you bought: the refrigerator, punch press, or computer. But your creditors may have a security interest in other equipment, in your inventory, your real estate, or your accounts receivable. It depends on what the contract says. In fact, several creditors may have security interests in the same collateral, a situation leading to interesting bar exam questions but less amusing in real life.

Therefore, when the wolf is at the door, figure out who will become hostile if unpaid, and how to conciliate him/her/it. It is an excellent idea to get legal advice about what constitutes default and what happens if you default. I know it seems as if a legal fee is the last thing you need at this point. (Trust me. The eternal curse of the pharaohs descends inexorably on those who stiff their lawyers.) But you may be able to get some of your creditors to be satisfied with partial repayment. This creates no problems if business improvements and a nagging sense of honor impel you to pay all your debts anyway, or if you manage to chug along, paying everyone a little bit at a time. But if you file for bankruptcy, or are driven into it involuntarily, creditors who get twenty-five cents on the dollar receive a "preference" over those who get five cents. Preference transactions can be invalidated by the less fortunate creditors, leaving you without collateral or a source of income, but with bills to pay. So get legal advice about whom to pay, how much, and when.

Selling Things

If the business is going into hibernation and you have something worth selling, you may be able to get enough money to pay your debts by selling off the business equivalent of the family jewels. For example, if your public relations business is closing its office, you probably won't be able to fit the eight-foot teak desk in your studio apartment. If you're not custom-printing T-shirts or manufacturing cut glass or ball-bearings anymore, you won't need the equipment. So, find a willing buyer, get the money, pay your debts, and stroll happily into the sunset, unless:

- You borrowed money to buy the item sold and need the lender's permission to sell the item. Read the security agreement and loan contract before you arrange the sale.
- You got permission, but the lender has first claim on the money, and you paid someone else off first.
- You borrowed money for some other purpose and *that* lender has a claim on all your equipment. Read *all* your loan contracts and accompanying security agreements.
- The sale is part of a bulk sale (I'm getting to that).

Not exactly a problem, but something to be taken into account, are the tax consequences of the sale. In most cases, business equipment you've owned for over six months can be treated as a capital investment, and the sale price minus your basis will be considered a capital gain, so you'll be taxed at capital gain rates, which are lower than ordinary income rates. (The loss will be a capital loss, which is not quite as good as an ordinary loss, if you're so desperate that you sell at less than your basis.) But business inventory, as distinct from equipment, yields ordinary income or loss.

If you chose to expense part or all of the cost of the equipment, that part of the basis will be treated as ordinary income. If this seems particularly cryptic, refresh your recollection in Chapter Six.

If, on the other hand, you used the ACRS method of depreciation and also took the investment credit, and if you sell a car or truck within three years of buying it, or other equipment within five years of buying it, you may have a higher tax bill because the investment credit lowered your basis. (Turn to page 173 for more thrilling details.)

If you're a sole proprietor, it's your decision whether to sell the equipment. In a partnership, the partnership agreement may contain restrictions on sales of equipment and may provide rules for settling disagreements among partners about financial policy. A corporation's charter or Articles of Incorporation and its bylaws will contain provisions mandating approval by a certain percentage of stockholders (e.g., a majority, two thirds) for major sales.

In any event, the money from the sales must be treated as if it were a trust fund for the benefit of the corporation's creditors. You have to manage the money sensibly and use it to pay debts before you distribute anything to the stockholders.

If the entire business, not just its equipment, is being sold, see the sections on selling the business later in this chapter.

Bulk Sales

A bulk sale is a one-time transaction (not ordinary business dealings) that disposes of the majority of your inventory or a substantial part of your equipment *if* the equipment sale is connected with the sale of inventory.

However, a sale of equipment and inventory is *not* a bulk sale if:

- The buyer is a business newly organized to take over your failing business.
- The buyer agrees to assume the business' debts.
- The buyer gets nothing but a (shaky) business and the obligation to pay its debts—no cash, no stock, no property unrelated to the business.
- You publish notices of the transfer, so your creditors know where to send the bills.

The Uniform Commercial Code (UCC) is a series of laws about business transactions. All the states except Louisiana have adopted the UCC, although the states can, and have, made individual changes in the text that apply to each individual state.

Article 6 of the UCC, which deals with bulk sales, is designed to prevent two kinds of fraud committed by debt-burdened businesses: selling off the assets to an accomplice for an unreasonably low figure, then turning this sum over to creditors; or selling the assets to anyone and absconding with the proceeds. Article 6's requirements for bulk sales that are not auctions are:

- The seller must sign and swear to the accuracy of a complete list of creditors, then give this list to the buyer.
- The seller must list the property to be transferred.
- The buyer keeps this list available to creditors for at least six months.
- The buyer must contact each creditor personally, or by registered or certified mail, and tell each creditor:
  —That a bulk transfer will be made
  —Who the buyer and seller are
  —(If the seller is paying debts right away) where to send the bills
  —(If not) where the list of transferred property will be kept.

The creditors must get this notice before the buyer pays for the bulk transfer, or ten days before the merchandise changes hands— whichever is earlier.

If the bulk transfer will be made at an auction, the seller gives the auctioneer a list of the creditors and helps prepare a list of material to be sold. The auctioneer notifies the creditors (in person or by registered or certified mail) that an auction will take place, at least ten days before the auction.

You may need a special permit for a bulk transfer, or sales tax may be due. It depends on state law.

Selling the Business: Practical Aspects

There are certain embarrassing aspects to selling your business when it is unsuccessful. You must either demonstrate to the buyer that you are an outstanding manager and the business is not practicable or show that a great business idea has been driven into the ground by your ineptitude. The latter approach is particularly hazardous if you hope to sell the business to a large corporation and stay on as a salaried manager.

Oh, well, I exaggerate: another possibility is that the business is inherently sound and well managed, but it needs more capital, more depth of management (i.e., someone who knows which end of a balance sheet is up), and affiliation with a company of national reputation.

If you take this latter tack, prepare a professional-looking report, indicating your business' history, current and past income statements, current and past balance sheets. Describe the marketing history and prospects of individual products. The report should be clean and crisp-looking: no carbon smudges or coffee stains. On the other hand, if you produce a gloriously printed masterpiece, with the best photographs this side of Italian *Vogue,* potential buyers will wonder why you have that kind of money to throw around and whether your company is being peddled all over town.

Someday, however, your prince will come, and you will negotiate a *merger* (in which two businesses combine, and one of the original businesses survives) or *consolidation* (in which a new, third business is created) or *acquisition* (a term usually used for the purchase or stock buy-out of a smaller business by a larger one). The distinction between the first two and the third is the difference between becoming someone's spouse and someone's lunch.

To drag out the analogy a little further, you may want to use a broker or finder to make the match. A finder just introduces potential buyers; a broker participates in the negotiation of the entire deal. Be sure to sign a detailed contract with either. The usual custom is to pay the broker or finder a percentage of the sales price and to pony up in cash when you close the deal with the buyer. If the buyer gives you nothing but stock in return for your stock or assets, you will naturally prefer to give some of this to the broker or finder. Specify this in the broker's/finder's contract.

Maybe the buyer will pay this fee. You will find this particularly useful because the broker's or finder's fee is not tax deductible. If you pay it, and the transaction is a taxable sale, you can use the fee to decrease your capital gain or increase your capital loss. But if the transaction is a tax-free reorganization, the fee is an unrecoverable out-of-pocket expense.

PERMISSIONS

If you are a sole proprietor, there is little gap between the will and the deed. Once you have decided to sell the business, and a willing buyer has been lined up, all you need do is sign the necessary documents, take the money, pay your debts, pay your taxes, and wind up your business affairs.

To sell a partnership's business, you need approval of a majority of the partners: a majority in number, not partnership interest— unless the partnership agreement specifies a different arrangement. If one partner disapproves of the sale, it may be possible for the other partners to buy the dissenter's interest and then sell the business.

State corporation law governs the procedure for selling a corporation. Usually, once tentative agreement with a buyer has been reached, contracts are drawn up and the corporation's Board of Directors votes to sign the contracts and follow a plan or merger, consolidation, or participation in an acquisition. Then the stockholders have to approve the plan (e.g., holders of two thirds of the shares in New York, holders of the majority of the shares in Delaware). Once the stockholders approve, the actual sale is consummated, and the newly sold corporation files a certificate proving that there has been a merger or consolidation or acquisition with the state's Secretary of State (or whoever regulates corporate affairs).

At times a corporation gets bought even though its management was not aware of having offered it for sale. The would-be acquirer buys enough of the stock to gain control, then boots out the Board of Directors. This somewhat savage procedure is called a "tender offer": the acquirer offers lots of money to the stockholders who will tender (i.e., hand over) their stock. Resisting a takeover attempt is nerve-wracking, expensive, and fortunately unlikely to happen to a very small business, though it could happen in a family-owned business if the family members hate each other.

PRICES

The immediate impulse is to demand as much as possible for your business. This is not always correct. First of all, an unseemly display of culpable greed will torpedo the negotiations. Second of all, a business can be bought with various combinations of:

- Authentic cash money
- Promissory notes
- The acquiring corporation's stock or bonds
- Another corporation's stock or bonds
- Merchandise
- Business equipment
- *Any* valuable property, from industrial diamonds to Chinese ceramics

Your lawyer and/or accountant must negotiate to get you the combination of payments resulting in the largest possible aftertax income for you, paid on a schedule that suits your needs.

You can get all the money up front (thus preventing default) or get at least one payment after the year of the sale. The latter treatment is called an installment sale (more of this anon) but despite positive tax consequences it can leave you with a fistful of worthless IOUs. If you do take promissory notes, try to get negotiable ones—that is, promissory notes that can be sold to a bank or another investor. You won't get the full face value, but at least you'll get some immediate cash. You can also set a fixed price or let the price depend on conditions such as business performance. For example, an "earnout" is an arrangement under which the original owners of the business get additional money or stock if the business meets certain profit projections after the sale. The earnout is most common when the original owners stay on as employee managers of the business; it gives them a chance to prove that their claims about the business' potential were correct.

As a general rule, a corporation that merges with another corporation or enters into a consolidation is responsible for the acquired corporation's debts and has to perform its contracts. But a corporation that buys another business' (not necessarily corporate) assets for cash or stock or that buys assets at a judicial (bankruptcy) sale, or a stockholder of a corporation that is reorganized by its creditors to keep it out of bankruptcy, is not liable for the failed corporation's debts under ordinary circumstances. The successor corporation can be left holding the bag if the arrangement involves fraud on anyone's part, if the reorganization is a sham instead of a real transaction, or if the acquiring corporation explicitly agrees to be responsible for these debts.

This paragraph raises two points. First of all, if your business has substantial debts, the buyer will probably prefer to buy the assets and leave *you* responsible for the debts. If your business has net operating loss carryovers that it has not used, the buyer has further legal headaches to worry about. Second of all, the legal term "reorganization" has several meanings. In the paragraph above, it means the action of the creditors and stockholders of a failing corporation. They get together to buy the corporation's property, either from the corporation itself or at a bankruptcy sale. Then they run the corporation for their own benefit in an attempt to recoup their losses. However, the term "reorganization" also includes the tax-free sale of a corporation as described on page 315. The legal profession does things like that to keep the peasants out.

If it is not already obvious, selling a business is not a do-it-yourself project. Even if you and the buyers rejoice in unblemished integrity, a handshake deal will not be sufficient. You need a professional appraisal of what your business is really worth. If you bought land or buildings many years before the sale, you may undervalue them in your books. On the other hand, you may put too much value on unsalable inventory or obsolete equipment. You need a written contract specifying not merely how much you'll get, when you'll get it, and the form (money, stock, etc.) you'll get it in. The agreement must also allocate the payment among the various assets.

If you're selling all your corporation's stock, all the assets go along with the stock, and all the money is paid for stock. If you sell the assets of a going business, some of the money pays for your inventory, some for your accounts receivable, some for equipment. The buyer of your business will probably protect against competition by getting you to sign a covenant (agreement) not to compete. You, in turn, will want some money in return for this promise. You will also want some recompense for the reputation your business has developed and for your customers' predilection for buying your merchandise rather than someone else's. These concepts are lumped together under the heading of "goodwill," and it, too, costs something. The tax consequences of each kind of payment are different. (See page 318.) In a tax-free reorganization, it is only good business to allocate the payment; in a taxable sale, it is essential, because without an allocation the IRS can make the calculation that results in the greatest amount of tax due.

As a general rule, if the tax consequences of a particular arrangement are good for you, they're bad for the buyer; so spirited negotiation will be necessary. You may have to take less money, or surrender on another point, to get favorable tax treatment on a particular item.

Selling the Business: Tax Aspects

Let me hurry to state that business taxation is a monstrously complex subject, and that this rapid overview does not tackle the subtleties. For God's sake don't assume that the general rules apply to your particular case unless a knowledgeable person has thought about it.

With that out of the way, we can start with the easy part. There are two kinds of business sales: tax-free reorganizations and taxable sales. There are three major ways to reorganize a corporation without a taxable transaction occurring. (There are four minor methods; please take my word for it that we don't need to go into them here.) The stock, money, or other property paid by the buyer is distributed to the stockholders. In most cases, they get to keep the stuff tax-free.

For reasons to be reached in a moment, a tax-free reorganization is not always the best choice for the selling corporation. A sole proprietorship or partnership sale is always a taxable sale. However, the tax burden can be lightened by making the appropriate allocations. I'll get to that on page 318, and I'm sure you can hardly wait.

TAX-FREE REORGANIZATIONS

The three types we are involved with here are:

- TYPE A REORGANIZATION ("A Reorg"): you and another corporation carry out a merger or consolidation conforming to the laws of any state or the District of Columbia.
- TYPE B REORGANIZATION ("B Reorg"): at least eighty percent of your corporation's stock is exchanged for voting stock of the acquiring corporation. Afterward the acquiring corporation is in control of your corporation. For the reorganization to be tax-free, the stockholders of your corporation can't get anything except voting stock—no money, no non-voting stock. After the transaction, your corporation would

probably become a subsidiary of the acquiring corporation. If you stay on as a manager, and if you have an employment contract, the IRS may challenge the B Reorg, claiming that the employment contract is a way of giving you cash for your stock, not a legitimate employment arrangement. Also, a B Reorg is a problem for Subchapter S corporations, because they lose the benefits of Sub S taxation for the whole year in which the transaction takes place.

- TYPE C REORGANIZATION ("C Reorg"): substantially all of the assets of your corporation (not the corporation's stock) are exchanged for voting stock in the acquiring corporation. This time, you can get up to twenty percent of the fair market value of your assets in money, IOUs, or other forms than voting stock. Usually, after a C Reorg the acquired corporation is liquidated and its stock distributed to its stockholders.

In an A, B, or C Reorganization, the stockholders of the selling corporation won't have to pay tax on their *gain* from the transaction. But if the corporation is a real disaster area, the selling corporation's shareholders won't be able to use their losses on the deal to reduce their other taxable income. Therefore, they will probably prefer a taxable sale.

The acquiring corporation, on the other hand, tends to favor a B or C Reorganization. Whether or not it has plenty of money, it probably has plenty of its own stock. B Reorgs were especially popular in the bull market of the 1960s. Conglomerates were formed by massing small corporations together, and everyone was happy as long as the price of the stock went up. However, both the acquired corporation's stock and the acquiring corporation's stock are restricted: to avoid the need for a complicated and expensive SEC registration, those who get stock must promise that they buy it for investment purposes, and must hold it for at least two years unless special circumstances intervene.

B Reorgs are no longer quite so popular: conglomerates have run into a lot of trouble, and the stock you get today that isn't worth very much per share may be worth even less tomorrow. However, the main problem with a B Reorg is that you get *no* cash and *no* immediately salable stock; you have to wait several years to see any cash from the sale of your business. Make sure the lawyers handling the sale are familiar with the technical changes made by the 1982 Tax Equity and Fiscal Responsibility Act.

A B or C Reorg is more likely to meet your needs if you have other income and want to invest in the acquirer's stock, or plan for retirement, than if you are beset by bills and lack current income. If that's your situation, you would probably be better off with an A Reorg, or even a taxable sale, that provides a lot of cash, or a healthy down payment and annual income. A B Reorg is only possible if holders of eighty percent of the stock will accept the acquiring corporation's stock; if anyone opposes the reorganization, or holds out for cash, a B Reorg is impossible.

Remember I said that, in most cases, the stockholders of the selling corporation don't have to pay tax on their gains? In one of those little ironies that make the law so much fun, a "tax-free reorganization" sometimes subjects the selling stockholders to tax liability. "Boot" is taxable gain: in an A or C Reorganization, money and property other than voting stock is considered boot; in a B Reorg, a selling stockholder has boot if s/he gets stock worth more than the stock s/he gave up. Sometimes boot is taxed as capital gain, sometimes as ordinary income. Should you find yourself in this situation, throw yourself on the mercy of your tax accountant. "Boot" used to mean advantage, which is why in the sonnet, Shakespeare beseeched "deaf heaven with [his] bootless cries"; he didn't leave his galoshes at the Globe.

There are two more pitfalls to worry about. The "continuity of interest" rule says that a reorganization can be tax-free only if the stockholders in the acquired corporation still have an interest in the surviving corporation. This is not a problem in a B or C Reorganization because the stockholders have their voting stock in the acquiring corporation to keep them active and interested. However, if the stockholders in a would-be A Reorganization are paid in money, and they take the money and disperse, the IRS can treat the transaction as a taxable sale. Therefore, good planning dictates that an A Reorganization involve at least fifty percent voting stock.

The second pitfall is the "business purpose" rule that says that the acquirer in a tax-free reorganization must really want to use the acquired corporation to carry out a business. If the acquirer wants the assets or stock for some other purpose (e.g., speculation or buying undervalued assets and selling them at full price), the deal will also be treated as a taxable sale.

TAXABLE SALES

The taxable sale of a proprietorship, or of a corporate business, is treated as several separate sales: the sale of inventory, of real property (if any), of other capital assets, of intangible assets (e.g., patents, copyrights, goodwill). The seller must compute the amount paid for each class of asset, what his/her/its basis is in each class, and what the gain or loss will be. Therefore, it is very important for the sales documents to clarify the amount paid for inventory, leases, equipment, and all the other items included in the sale. A lot of the energy in the negotiations for the sale of a business goes into establishing these allocations.

The buyer wants to get as many tax deductions as possible and wants a high basis for the assets (so the potential tax burden is lower if they are sold or exchanged). The buyer wants to put a high valuation on the inventory, so it will have less taxable gain on the inventory. *You* want a low valuation on the inventory, because your gain from inventory is taxed at ordinary income rates, not capital gain rates. A sale of inventory won't qualify as an installment sale either (see page 319). Both parties stand to benefit by a high valuation on equipment. The seller gets an investment credit and can use ACRS for rapid recovery of the investment. You can pay capital gains rates on the sale (except to the extent that you have to recapture depreciation and investment credit; the recaptured amounts are ordinary income). One problem: if you allocate more than the fair market value to these depreciable assets, you may be slapped with state sales tax. Ask your lawyer, and nag until the appropriate tax returns are filed.

If your accounts receivable are included in the sale, the seller may let you place a high value on them because bad debts are deductible. However, when a very small business (which may have a high percentage of uncollectible accounts) is sold, the custom is for the seller to keep the accounts receivable. Otherwise, the seller would be in a dilemma. The amount allocated to accounts receivable is ordinary income for the seller, who therefore would prefer a low allocation. But this would be a confession that the accounts are, at best, dubious.

The real tug-of-war comes over the goodwill and the covenant not to compete. The buyer wants a high value put on the covenant not to compete, because he/she/it can amortize the cost of the covenant over the number of years it lasts. However, the covenant not to compete yields ordinary income for you as the seller. You want as much as possible to be allocated to goodwill, because you can treat this amount as capital gain. The seller can't deduct, depreciate, or amortize *any* of this amount, unless it can be shown that a specific part of the goodwill payment is attributable to an intangible asset with a definable life: for example, a mailing list which gradually becomes obsolete.

Section 1231 of the Internal Revenue Code gives the seller a break. Gain on "§1231 property," which is to say land, and depreciable or amortizable business property held for more than one year, is treated as long-term capital gain. On the other hand, any loss is treated as an ordinary loss. This is the best of all possible tax worlds.

If the taxable sale is a transfer of stock, the seller usually has a long-term capital gain (or loss). The amount of the gain is the price of the stock minus the stockholder's basis. Usually, the stockholder's basis is the cost of the stock. However, if your corporation had the foresight to make a §1244 election, and the stockholder has the bad luck to lose money, up to $50,000 per stockholder ($100,000 for stockholders who file joint tax returns) can be treated as an ordinary loss, reducing ordinary taxable income.

Stockholders of a "collapsible corporation" can't take advantage of §1244, and must pay ordinary income rates on the price of their stock. A collapsible corporation is one formed to transform ordinary income into capital gains by getting contracts and selling all the stock before the contracts can be performed.

According to Code §741, a partnership interest is a capital asset. A partner who sells his/her interest therefore gets capital gain treatment for most of the proceeds of the sale. The exceptions are funds paid for accounts receivable and inventory whose value has increased substantially. The question of what is "substantial" must be settled on a case-by-case basis.

Many business sellers choose to structure the transaction as an installment sale. The term "installment sale" is something of a misnomer: you can take advantage of these tax provisions even if the payment is a single lump sum—as long as at least one payment is made after the year of the sale. The person or corporation receiving the income pays tax only on the "gross profit percentage." For example, assume that a taxpayer agrees in 1983 to sell stock or business assets with a basis of $75,000. The sales price of $150,000 will be paid $25,000 in 1983, $100,000 in 1984, and $25,000 in 1985. The gross profit percentage is 50% (basis of $75,000 divided by sales price of $150,000), so the taxpayer has $12,500 taxable income in 1983 and 1985, and $50,000 taxable income in 1984. (You should be so lucky.) Installment sale treatment is automatic, unless you choose not to use it. But installment reporting applies only to gains; you can't use this method to spread a loss out over several tax years.

Liquidation

A corporation doesn't lose its charter and right to do business just because it's insolvent (unable to pay its bills). If, however, it is obvious that the corporation will *never* be able to pay its bills, further business activity acts as a fraud on the creditors and must be stopped.

A corporation can throw in the towel, even when it is not insolvent, if the stockholders vote to dissolve the corporation, or if the Board of Directors calls for dissolution and the stockholders approve. (The procedure depends on state law, and on the way the individual corporation is structured.) A corporation that is mismanaged, insolvent, or has failed to pay state taxes or file required annual reports can also be dissolved by court order. Again, the rules vary from state to state.

When a corporation is dissolved either at or against the will of its stockholders, the corporation's property is considered a trust fund. First the creditors have to be paid, in the order set by law. Usually the secured creditors (those who demanded collateral for their loans) get paid. If there isn't enough to go around, the Uniform Commercial Code sets the priorities. If anything is left, the unsecured creditors get paid. If anything remains after that, it is distributed to the stockholders. As a general rule, once the dissolution process begins, the corporation can't undertake any new business, buy new property, or spend any money except to wind up the business. In many states (e.g., California, Colorado, Idaho, Illinois, Kansas, Maine, Missouri, Nebraska, New York, Texas), either the directors are held to the same standard of responsibility as trustees, or the court appoints a trustee to manage the dissolution. A trustee is required by law to be honorable, true, faithful, and in general a mercantile Boy Scout. Another alternative is bankruptcy reorganization, as described on page 324.

Once the corporation adopts a plan of liquidation or dissolution (the demarcation line is blurry)—whether because the corporation has been sold, discontinued, or is insolvent—the IRS gets into the act. We've seen the consequences for the stockholders when there is a tax-free reorganization or taxable sale. When the corporation is liquidated for other reasons, the stockholders usually have a taxable capital gain or loss on whatever they receive for their stock. If they have a gain, they can't use the installment sale provision (see page 319)—even if payments stretch over several years. However, the stockholders can defer paying the tax if the corporation meets the requirements of §333 of the Internal Revenue Code. (That will be dealt with on page 322.)

So much for the stockholders. What is the tax position of the corporation? The corporation has ordinary income if it has to recapture depreciation or investment credit on its property. (Ask your accountant; it's too complicated to go into here.) Otherwise, the corporation does not have to pay federal income tax on the amount it receives for liquidating its assets. On the other hand, no taxable income means no tax-deductible loss; so, if a corporation would have deductible losses, it should be very leisurely about the liquidation process.

There are two major ways to liquidate a corporation: a twelve-month liquidation, as defined by Code §337, and a one-month liquidation under §333. (I bother to mention the Code sections so that you can ask your lawyer which one you're undergoing, and what its effects are.)

Under §337, the corporation adopts a formal plan to liquidate. Then, within twelve months of the date the plan was adopted, the corporation must distribute all of its assets except for those needed to pay debts and other claims against the corporation. The remaining assets are distributed to the stockholders. If everything is distributed in time, the corporation can avoid paying tax on the money obtained for assets that are sold; if the distribution is not finished within the year, the corporation has taxable income. However, if the corporation would have tax-deductible *losses,* it should avoid meeting the §337 criteria, because the losses are also wiped out in a twelve-month liquidation.

A corporation using §337 has thirty days from the adoption of the plan to file Form 966 with the nearest IRS district office. The corporation then files its normal income tax return, attaching this information:

- A copy of the plan of liquidation
- Minutes of the meeting at which the plan was adopted
- A list of the assets distributed, and the date of distribution of each

For each shareholder who gets six hundred dollars or more as a liquidating distribution, the corporation must send the IRS a Form 1099L. All the 1099Ls have to be bundled together with a Form 1096 (which is the IRS equivalent of a cover letter) and sent to the IRS by February 28 of the year after the last distribution.

A collapsible corporation (see page 179) is not allowed to use §337.

To qualify for §333 (a one-month liquidation, with tax benefits for the shareholders):

- Holders of at least eighty percent of the shares must file Form 964 choosing §333 treatment.
- Each shareholder choosing this treatment must mail the form within thirty days of the adoption of the liquidation plan.
- These stockholders must inform the IRS how much stock they own, what property and how much money they received in the liquidation, and what fraction of the corporation's earnings and profits should be attributed to each stockholder.
- The corporation must distribute all its assets to the stockholders within one *month* of the adoption of the plan.

Obviously this will entail some rushing around. It's seldom worth the trouble if the stockholders get money as a liquidating distribution. It may be very worthwhile if they get assets (machinery, stock in other corporations). In that case, they won't have to pay tax on their gain until they sell the assets. The amount of gain depends on the stockholder's individual share of the corporation's earnings and profits. "Earnings and profits" is a technical term that has very little to do with real cash flow. Some corporations have assets but no earnings and profits: for example, a corporation could own three apartment buildings whose depreciation deductions wipe out its earnings and profits, but whose value has increased substantially since the corporation bought them. If the corporation has three stockholders, and each one receives an apartment building as a liquidating distribution, they can avoid paying tax on the buildings' appreciation until they sell the buildings. When they do, their basis is measured by a series of hideously complex rules which I will not even attempt to deal with here.

NONCORPORATION BUSINESSES

Life is much easier for sole proprietors and partners. They terminate the business. A proprietor completes a last Schedule C for the last year of business. A partnership files a final information return (Form 1065), and each partner reports his/her share of gain or loss on Schedule E.

PRACTICALITIES

A dissolved or liquidated business must:

- Surrender its charter or DBA certificate
- Send back its sales tax authorization
- Make a final sales tax return
- Surrender any licenses dependent on maintaining a going business

In general, the process of dissolving a business is the inverse of starting one, so recollect what you did, and contact each agency (e.g., licensing board) and find out what you have to do.

Bankruptcy

One of the problems with being broke is that people keep hassling you for money. If they're not repossessing your office furniture, they're sending you dunning letters or engaging in out-and-out litigation. First of all, this is nerve-wracking for you. Secondly, it is not necessarily productive for the creditors. If there isn't enough money to go around, and you pay the most demanding creditors rather than those with the best legal claims, the creditors will end up suing each other, to the benefit of the legal rather than the business community.

Therefore, the institution of bankruptcy serves several purposes. The debtor is cleared of debt. The creditors are not left at the

mercy of chance; there is an orderly process of distributing the
debtor's assets as far as they will stretch. Bankruptcy is regulated by
federal law: Title 11 of the United States Code. Three of Title 11's
chapters can be used for business bankruptcies:

- Chapter 7: liquidation of a business, creation of a repayment
  plan, and sale of the debtor's assets and distribution of the
  sales proceeds according to the plan.
- Chapter 11: a repayment plan is created, and the business
  continues in operation. Part or all of its future income goes to
  repay the creditors. Either the trustee manages the business
  or the original owner(s) continues to manage the business—
  one hopes more skillfully than before the bankruptcy.
- Chapter 13: a human being (not a corporation, although a
  corporation is treated as a "person" for other legal purposes)
  devotes some or all of his/her post-bankruptcy income to repaying debts. Usually, the plan must provide for repayment
  within 3 years; the court can allow up to 5 years for repayment. Chapter 13 relief is available only if the debtor owes
  less than $100,000 of unsecured debt and/or $350,000 of secured debt.

Chapter 13 is always voluntary; Chapter 7 or 11 bankruptcy can be
voluntary (the debtor asks for relief) or involuntary (creditors demand that the business be liquidated or placed under the control of
a trustee).

A corporation or partnership can't use Chapter 13, although individual partners can. Some bankruptcy courts consider a sole proprietorship a person eligible for Chapter 7 or 11; the courts that
refuse this treatment will allow a troubled proprietorship to incorporate for the specific purpose of going bankrupt. Quite often, the
proprietor will go through Chapter 13 at the same time. A sole proprietor, after all, is personally liable for proprietorship debts, and
they can come and take away the dishwasher, the color TV, or other
goodies even after the proprietorship has been discharged in bankruptcy (has no further obligation to pay debts).

One problem is that Chapter 13 can be used only by individuals
who have stable income or at least a reasonable prospect of stable
income. It takes tolerance on the court's part (bankruptcy cases are
heard in federal District Court) to view an unsuccessful sole proprietor in this light. If the court is less tolerant, the individual may

have to use the stricter Chapter 11 procedure for him/herself as well as for the business.

In all kinds of bankruptcy cases, a petition is filed. There is always a trustee in Chapter 7 and 13 cases; there usually is one in Chapter 11. The trustee must be a responsible person who is not involved in the bankruptcy case. S/he is instrumental in running a Chapter 11 business, and in seeing that the repayment plan is carried out. The trustee has the right to avoid preferential transfers. That is, if the business was insolvent (had liabilities greater than its assets) and if it sold assets or paid bills within ninety days before filing of the bankruptcy petition, and if the recipient got a larger proportion of the money owed than other creditors with legally comparable claims get under the repayment plan, the trustee can get the money or equipment back. The trustee has this power to prevent potential bankrupts from "selling" valuable assets to an accomplice, who then transfers them back to the bankrupt.

Once the petition is filed, *all* of the debtor's creditors have to stop all enforcement and collection efforts. During this cease-fire, the debtor prepares lists of debts and assets. It's very important to make an accurate list. If a creditor is not listed, the debt to that creditor will continue in force even after the debtor is discharged in bankruptcy. *All* business assets are turned over to the trustee. (In a Chapter 11 case with no trustee, the existing management continues to hold the assets.) Chapter 13 debtors are allowed to keep personal, family, and household goods as well as tools of their trades; the rest of the bankrupt individual's assets are turned over to the trustee.

In Chapter 13, only the debtor has the right to devise a repayment plan; the plan must then be approved by the court, and the creditors can give their approval. If they don't approve, various intricate rules apply. I am abjectly grateful that the length and scope of this book prevent me from discussing these rules. The debtor filing a Chapter 7 or 11 petition has one hundred and twenty days after filing to create a plan and submit it for approval. If the debtor can't devise a satisfactory plan, the court, trustee, and creditors work it out.

After the repayment plan has been carried out, the debtor is discharged: s/he/it is no longer responsible for the debts covered by the bankruptcy. Some debts can't be discharged in bankruptcy: taxes, child support, alimony, most student loans, and court judgments based on the debtor's fault (e.g., fraud or products liability). The debtor is free and clear. Ironically, some bankrupts find it easy to get credit. You have to wait seven years between bankruptcies, and some creditors figure they'll get paid somehow, during that time.

CHOICES

An insolvent business can:

- Avoid bankruptcy by getting all creditors to accept partial repayment. However, if bankruptcy does happen, some of these transactions may be declared invalid as "preferences."
- File for Chapter 7 and undergo liquidation.
- File for Chapter 11 and stay in business, usually under supervision of a trustee. A Chapter 11 business is allowed to carry out normal business activities, including borrowing money and selling inventory. Court permission is needed for extraordinary transactions, such as the sale of equipment.

A proprietor, partner, or personally liable director or stockholder may want to get out from under business debts through Chapter 13.

Creditors who do not expect to be repaid have various options. If an insolvent business has fewer than twelve creditors, one or more creditors can file an involuntary bankruptcy petition against the business. If there are more than twelve creditors, at least three, with total claims over five thousand dollars, are needed. The creditors can:

- File an involuntary Chapter 7 petition, demanding liquidation of the business.
- File a Chapter 11 petition. Bankruptcy law protects the creditors by restricting Chapter 11 plans to plans that give the creditors at least as much as they would receive in a liquidation.
- Prevent a corporation's bankruptcy by joining its stockholders in a reorganization of the business. A new management is installed whose primary responsibility is repaying the creditors. A reorganization of this kind is reconsidered a tax-free reorganization, similar to the A, B, and C Reorganizations described on page 315.

The bankruptcy laws make it possible to transfer a case from one classification to another. Liquidation can be staved off by proposing a continuation of the business under Chapter 11. A debt-burdened individual can prevent sale of his or her possessions by devising a Chapter 13 plan. The choice among strategies depends on law (some creditors' rights are superior to the rights of other creditors), the ability to predict the future (the presence or absence of income to satisfy obligations under Chapter 11 or 13), and negotiation skills (what the court and the creditors will go along with).

Summary

The best—and perhaps rarest—solution to business problems is a change in financing or operation methods that turns the business around. It may be necessary to cut expenses and contract operations, or even to pay off all creditors and cease to do business.

Sometimes a business can be sold. The best outcome provides a buyer who will pay the business' debts or enough cash and other property to satisfy the creditors and still leave something for the business owners. If the original owners stay on as salaried managers, they have an assured income (which, to look on the dark side, they may need to file for Chapter 13).

If no buyer appears and the corporation is insolvent, it may be possible to reorganize it. If not, the corporation, like an insolvent proprietorship or partnership, is likely to go through voluntary or involuntary bankruptcy. Bankruptcy will discharge the *business*, and creditors will not be able to sue the business if the bankruptcy plan provides less than one hundred percent repayment. However, a sole proprietor, partner, or corporate director or stockholder who agreed to personal liability will still be liable for these debts—unless s/he also files for bankruptcy. A personal bankruptcy is not the best thing for the ego—or the credit rating.

But why be gloomy? Perhaps you are reading this chapter as a warning rather than a guide to the dangers actually threatening you. Perhaps your business is quite sound and is ready to expand in size or scope. This more optimistic discussion is contained in the next chapter.

CHAPTER TWELVE

Integration and Expansion

AFTER YOU'VE SURVIVED the first shocks, and the enterprise starts to show signs of success, there are several things you can do. You can relax, start taking Sundays off, and begin paying yourself a salary. You can expand your operation by adding new personnel, diversifying your product line, expanding your factory, opening a second store or restaurant. You can merge with another business or buy another business. You can join a barter network and obtain merchandise and services that way. You can get government contracts to use the new capacity; or you can find export markets for your products. In fact, you can even borrow money. This may seem paradoxical: after all, you really *needed* the money when you were getting started, not when the business is going moderately well. But while from the borrower's point of view the criterion is need, the banker looks at the plausibility of repayment.

Expansion

The information derived from starting your business will be necessary, but not sufficient, for expansion. It's very much like having a second child. The experienced parent has a great advantage over the first-timer, but it can be a fatal error to assume that the second offspring will be just like the first.

Sometimes the cost of adding a new location or product will be greater than the cost of the original operation. Due to inflation and other factors, new space and new equipment will probably cost more than the old ones did. Then, too, the operating costs of any going business are lower than those of a brand-new enterprise, because the bugs have been worked out, and goodwill brings repeat business.

But expansion makes it possible to take advantage of economies of scale. If you have several luncheonettes, you can buy caseloads of ketchup; you can advertise a special sale at all three of your car-washes in an ad the same size as the one for the original car-wash.

Expansion means that your management innovations can have more scope, and also that your control will be less absolute, because you can't be in two places at once. You'll be more of a manager, giving orders from afar; less of a hands-on practitioner. You can reward key employees with more responsibility, but you'll have to break up the management team and add new people, who may be dramatically better—or worse—than the first lot.

Proprietorships and partnerships, flushed with success, can consider incorporation; private corporations can think about going public. But these changes in organization are not inevitable consequences of solvency. Sometimes the best thing to do is to retain the old form of organization, but improve working conditions somewhat: buy some firsthand furniture for the office, and get a dental insurance plan.

Adding new products or new manufacturing and sale outlets is called horizontal integration. Starting to manufacture your raw materials instead of buying them, or starting to sell your products directly to the public rather than to wholesalers, is called vertical integration. You can accomplish either kind of integration by starting a completely new business, or by merging with or acquiring an existing business.

As for the problems of starting a business, you've been through that already. A merger joins two businesses into a third, new business (e.g., Nabisco merges with Standard Brands to form Nabisco Brands). In an acquisition, one company buys another company.

A business is a good buy for an acquiring company (or, to look at it another way, a target vulnerable to raiders) if:

- It is profitable, or could be made profitable with better management.
- It has a good reputation.

- The buyer can get immediate control of the company.
- Key employees will stay with the business.
- The business has salable assets which the buyer can convert to cash in case of financial emergency.

Mergers and acquisitions can be structured in many different ways; each way has a unique lineup of financial and tax consequences. For example, the acquiring company can trade its stock for stock of the acquired corporation; or the buyer can buy all of another company's assets, or all of its stock. Many variations can be rung on these comparatively simple themes.

The decision whether or not to expand calls for sophisticated cost-benefit analyses about whether or not the larger operation will be more profitable than the smaller, original operation. Sometimes the gross profit is much greater, but the change in net profit is not great enough to justify the investment and aggravation. The decision whether to merge or acquire another business calls for economic, accounting, and legal sophistication; and a good programmable calculator or a small computer helps a lot.

Whether you expand by replacing outmoded equipment with newer, more productive models, or by acquiring the assets of a bankrupt company, you will certainly need money to undertake the expansion and to keep the fledgling operational until the money starts coming in. Fortunately, you may at last be in a position to get some money.

Financing Expansion

There are several plausible sources of funds for expansion: bank loans, factoring, and venture capital. This chapter also deals with barter, an offbeat way to facilitate expansion.

BANK LOANS

When you apply for a bank loan, you're better off going to the central office of the bank. Your local branch bank may be sympathetic, but it can only "service" loans (collect the payments, figure out what to do if the payments stop), not originate them.

Banks can grant various kinds of loans:

- Short-term (thirty- to sixty-day) loans, usually used to buy inventory. The loans are supposed to be repaid as soon as the inventory is sold. Seasonal businesses (e.g., makers of bathing suits or Christmas-tree ornaments) also use short-term loans to pay bills during the off-season
- A term or intermediate-term loan lasts for one to five years and can be used for expansion, for ordinary business operations, or to buy equipment
- A long-term loan lasts over five years
- If you have a line of credit, the bank determines the maximum amount you can owe at any one time. You borrow as you need, repay when you can. You may have to maintain a compensating balance (i.e., part of the loan must be kept in the bank, reducing the effective amount of the loan, but not the amount you must repay or the amount on which interest is computed); and you will probably be expected to clear up the balance at least once a year, even if you restart the cycle
- Bridge loan: a short-term loan that pays itself off: for example, the bank advances you the money needed to complete a lucrative contract

Loans are also divided into categories based on the kind of collateral the borrower offers. Collateral is property which serves as security for repayment: if you don't pay, the bank can keep or sell the collateral, retaining the amount owed and returning whatever is left over (if anything is left over) to the borrower.

An unsecured loan has no collateral; the bank relies on its trust in the borrower. You can imagine how likely that is these days. Some types of collateral:

- *Liquid assets:* you use your savings account, stocks, or bonds as collateral.
- *Accounts receivable:* you give the bank copies of your accounts receivable. You pay the bank as your customers pay you; the bank monitors carefully to see if you're—ah—*forgetting* anything.
- *Flooring:* you use specific, valuable inventory items (for example, cars or refrigerators) as collateral, and repay part of the loan as each item is sold.
- *Inventory:* smaller inventory items can also be used as collateral. High-style merchandise and custom-made merchandise are not suitable collateral, because the bank will have a hell of

a time selling the stuff. One disadvantage of using inventory as collateral is that the Uniform Commercial Code (a series of laws governing commercial transactions) requires the lender to file an official record of inventory loans. These are public records; if your other creditors see the record, they may conclude that you're in financial trouble and demand immediate repayment. The prophecy then becomes self-fulfilling.

- *Fixed-asset or equipment loans:* the bank holds a mortgage on your plant or machinery.

Read the loan agreement and security agreement (which covers the collateral) very carefully. If it is at all possible, have a lawyer present during the negotiation. At least have a lawyer explain the documents before you sign. Truth-in-Lending and plain-English laws apply only to consumer transactions: the bank can make the documents for business loans as obscure as it likes.

If the bank makes you keep a compensating balance, try to lower the requirement. If you can only get a demand loan (one which gives the bank the right to demand payment at any time), push for a clause that keeps the bank from seizing your assets during the busy season and averts a demand during your slow season. Try to get an extra grace period after the bank notifies you of a default, and before the bank grabs the collateral. The loan agreement may include restrictions on your business operations. You can try to keep these "restrictive covenants" out of the agreement by proving that these provisions damage your business. Whatever you may have seen in Victorian melodrama, banks are far more interested in getting paid than in foreclosures and want your business to continue so you can keep paying. You can try to negotiate more favorable loan terms, but the bank will probably point out that if you don't want the money on the original terms, plenty of other people do.

When you apply for a loan, you'll have to provide a wealth of information, including:

- Your balance sheets and income statements
- A statement of the owner(s)'s personal net worth (The bank doesn't want you to take the money and buy a Bugatti with mink upholstery.)
- An aging statement for your accounts receivable
- An analysis of your leading sources of income
- A detailed explanation of what you're going to do with the money, and how you plan to repay it

This material is pretty well standardized; you can prepare a "canned" version, keep it handy, and update it every few months. Word-processing capacity is very useful, but not indispensable. If you have reasonably current information, in final draft form, available all the time, you can put together a loan application at any time, with minimal trouble and at minimal expense.

Loan agreements contain a dazzling variety of provisions, expressed in stupefying prose. A typical loan agreement spells out:

- Length of the loan term
- Schedule of payments
- Compensating balance required
- Amount of interest
- Collateral
- Amount of other fees, and when they are due
- What the bank will do if you miss a payment
- Restrictions on other loans you can take out during the loan term
- Restrictions on your business (amount of working capital you must maintain; limits on salaries, dividends, and other spending during the loan term)

If interest rates drop dramatically, large businesses satisfy their borrowing needs; if the economy perks up, you may be able to borrow on comparatively favorable terms. But given tight money, and if AT&T, IBM, and other huge corporations are lined up ahead of you at the loan window, you have very little negotiating power.

FACTORING

Factoring is the process of selling your accounts receivable to a financial organization called a factor. Usually this is done by changing your invoice to tell the customer to pay the factor, not you. Discount factoring means that the factor pays you right away (usually 98½% to 99% of the value of the receivables they buy). Maturity factoring means that the factor collects the money first and then pays you, taking out its own share. This may seem charitable, but the factor hopes you will ask for advances. The interest rate for advances is high—usually 3% to 4% above the prime rate. If you let the factor keep the money after it is due to you, the factor will pay *you* interest, but the interest is less than the prime rate.

Most factoring arrangements are on a "notification" basis: the factor does all the bookkeeping and takes the risk of bad debts. However, the factor won't get involved if a customer claims the merchandise was defective: that's your problem. To save money, you can use "nonnotification" factoring: the factor advances you money, you keep the records, collect the money yourself, and then repay the factors for their trouble.

Whether you want to factor your accounts depends on whether the security of knowing you can get immediate return on your accounts receivable is worth the factor's fee. You don't have to handle—or pay for—collections. If you borrow money from a factor, the cost will be higher than a bank loan, but there is no compensating balance requirement; you have effective use of all the money.

Whether a factor wants to deal with *you* depends on the stability of your business and the reliability of your customers. Factors provide a valuable service to the business community, but no one mistakes them for Santa Claus.

VENTURE CAPITAL: THE BUSINESS PLAN

The private investors who told you to go to hell when you needed start-up money may be a little more polite once the business is viable.

The basic tool for extracting money from venture capitalists is the business plan. The business plan is a presentation, as slick as you can make it, of your company's history, financial standing, and future plans. If at all possible, the business plan should be typeset, with some jazzy-looking photographs and drawings. If the budget won't stretch that far, at least experiment with margins, single- and double-spacing, and styles of paper to make the typed page look as good as possible. A business plan is one part research and development, one part finance, and one part show business.

A typical plan for a manufacturer might include:

- Company history
  - Date, place of incorporation
  - Products manufactured: date of introduction and sales trends of each
  - Company's position in the industry
  - Ownership and control
  - Patents held by the company
  - Names, backgrounds, and duties of top executives
  - Amount your company wants to raise

- —Acceptable terms (interest rate, percentage of ownership, payment terms)
- The product to be developed
  - —Origin of product
  - —How it will be manufactured
  - —Cost of research and development
  - —Potential patents
  - —Cost of producing the product
  - —Packaging
- Marketing
  - —Why a market exists for this product
  - —Competitors
  - —Who the potential customers are
  - —How the product serves their needs
  - —Advertising strategies
- Financial background
  - —Balance sheets for past five years (or as long as you've been in business)
  - —Income statements
  - —Cash flow statements
  - —Projected costs
  - —Projected sales
  - —Estimates of the impact of the new product on your financial status

All of this, of course, is given in the greatest possible detail. A service business (e.g., a two-week intensive course in conversational Chinese for business executives) would use a similar format, explaining its creditworthiness, financial history, and projected income from the seminars. A restaurateur would explain why she is offering buttercream pastries to caterers or bakeries, or why she wants to set up a café and retail shop. In any case, the focus is on the financial stability of the enterprise and the glittering potential of the new product or service.

It's well worth the money to hire a nationally known accounting firm to prepare your financial statements. Potential investors sometimes shy away if they see your friendly local CPA's name at the bottom of the statements. The CPA may in fact be a good accountant, but the investors are afraid that s/he:

- Won't know all the legal and administrative requirements for disclosure to potential investors

- Won't be able to pay the judgment if something dreadful
  occurs and you sue for malpractice
- Needs your fees desperately and therefore will overlook any
  improprieties in your finances. (On the other hand, it's been
  said that major accounting firms are too lenient toward the
  major corporations whose executives frequent the same country clubs as the auditors.)

BARTER

Barter, of course, predates money. Barter is being revived in response to inflation, sluggish markets, and high taxes. In simplest
form, you give your accountant one of the refrigerators from your
stock in lieu of a fee. (One of my grandfathers was a lawyer, and
many of his clients were furriers. Apparently it is virtually impossible to get furriers to pay you, with the result that my grandmother
had a phenomenal number of fur coats.) The accountant gets a refrigerator, which s/he needs more than the time required to work
for you; you can provide a refrigerator more easily than a cash fee.

According to the IRS, you have taxable income as a result of the
deal: the value of the accountant's services minus the wholesale cost
of the refrigerator. If the retail cost of the refrigerator is more than
the accountant's normal fee, s/he has taxable income also. Very few
people are sufficiently straight-arrow to report this income; conse-
quently, the IRS dislikes barter intensely.

On the other hand, various complex deals involving stock, oil
and gas leases, bridges, and franchises have been found by various
federal courts to be free of taxable profit. In fact, the Internal Revenue Code includes elaborate provisions for "tax-free reorganizations," some of which are, in effect, ways to buy a company with
barter. The moral is, that just as God is on the side of the big battalions, the Internal Revenue Code is on the side of the big businesses.
The subsidiary moral is that you need professional tax advice to
structure all major transactions: what seems to be a trivial change in
pratical terms can have vast tax consequences.

A more modern development in barter is the barter exchange.
You pay a fee to join (typically somewhere between fifty and two
hundred fifty dollars) and annual dues (say twenty-five to one hundred dollars). The network publicizes what it is you have to exchange: free meals at your restaurant, rental of your typewriters,
space in your industrial park. You decide what you need: the ser-

vices of a pension planning consultant, radial tires for your delivery truck, advertising in a small newspaper. You arrange the transactions through the barter network, which sets up a system of "credits" or "tokens" to make sure it all works out by the end of the month.

Barter networks include:

- American Barter Systems
  202 Westchester Avenue
  White Plains, NY 10601

- Atwood-Richards, Inc.
  99 Park Avenue
  New York, NY 10016

- Barter Systems, Inc.
  4848 North MacArthur
  Oklahoma City, OK 73122

- International Association of Trade Exchanges
  5001 Seminary Road
  Alexandria, VA 22311

- Pfeister Barter
  122 East 42nd Street
  Suite 1700
  New York, NY 10017

- TradeAmerican Card Corporation
  777 South Main Street
  Suite 204
  Orange, CA 92668

- UTX, Inc.
  Lenox Hill Station
  PO Box 369
  New York, NY 10021

The subject of barter is considered here, rather than as a subtopic of capitalization or equipment, because your business has to be operational before you have anything to barter. It also forms a bridge between the topic of getting money for expansion and the even more pleasing topic of earning money through your expanded activities.

EXPORT

The United States, after all, is only one country, in a world full
of people. Some countries have demand for consumer goods and industrial materials that cannot be produced locally.

The advantages of exporting include the opening up of large
markets without large advertising budgets. The disadvantages include tangling with other languages, other laws and customs, fluctuating currency exchange rates, and Customs. You may be able to
manufacture without the constraints imposed on products for the
American market; on the other hand, some countries (e.g., Scandi-
navian nations) have tougher safety and quality restrictions than the
United States.

Whether a product can be exported successfully depends on
local tastes (e.g., Japan is not much of a market for Camembert),
local conditions (e.g., most of Europe uses 240-volt current), and
local laws (e.g., you can undoubtedly make money selling Chivas
Regal in Abu Dhabi, but only if you're very, very careful). It also
helps to understand the local language: Parisians think hamburgers
called "le gros Mac," or "big pimp," are hilarious, and the French
soft drink Pschitt would be hard to advertise in the United States.

You can export directly, by selling to a foreign end-user, a state-
controlled trading company in the Communist countries, or to a
foreign distributor; or indirectly, through a commission agent or an
export management company. A distributor buys the merchandise
from you, and takes title to it. Usually, they get a twenty-five to
thirty percent discount. An agent gets orders for you, but you keep
title to the merchandise and have the responsibility of filling orders.
Typical commissions are in the ten to eighteen percent range. Selling directly is more work; selling indirectly means you have to
place enormous trust in your agent. You will also need explicit contracts with reliable translations into the relevant languages. You
will have to cover all the usual business contract terms (e.g., how
long the contract lasts, its subject matter, how it can be terminated). You will also have problems that are unique to the export
situation. You'll have to decide which nation's laws will govern, and
what court or agency will handle disputes. The contract must include shipping terms: who pays the freight, and at what point ownership (and risk of loss) passes to the buyer. Local tax laws have
their idiosyncrasies; local invoicing practices vary. If you won't get

paid in U.S. dollars, you'll have to figure out how to cope with currency fluctuations. You'll need a cable address, or a (less costly) Telex address, and an understanding banker who can cope with foreign paperwork.

There are enormous advantages to getting paid in advance, but not everyone you deal with will be this trusting. You can open an account for your customers or ship merchandise on consignment, as you would in the United States. Neither is a good idea if the country is likely to undergo a revolution in the near future. Whatever your political views, you will agree that guerrilla warfare and urban terrorism are bad for the business climate. You can buy what is delicately called "political risk" insurance to cover expropriation and expulsion of the infidel.

Certain payment methods are peculiar to exporting: sight drafts, time drafts, delivery orders, and letters of credit. They are too complicated to explain here, but all depend on the processing of certain documents and the approval of various third parties.

Exporting involves a heap of paperwork:

- Export licenses (ask the nearest district office of the Department of Commerce for advice)
- Validated export licenses for strategic materials (apply to the Office of Export Administration in Washington, using Form ITA-622P)
- The Shipper's Export Declaration (Form 7525-V from the Office of Export Administration)
- An invoice in a form acceptable both to you and to the importing country; the importing country may require visas on special forms issued by its consulate
- A Certificate of Origin, if U.S. goods get preferential treatment on import duties
- An inspection certificate, if the importing country demands it
- A Plant Health Certificate from the U.S. Department of Agriculture
- Bills of lading (shipping documents)
- Dock and warehouse receipts
- Export packing lists giving the contents, weight, and dimensions of each package
- Insurance certificates

Either you or the buyer can get "ocean marine cargo insurance" for freight that is literally shipped. The policy can be a blanket one, covering all of a company's shipments, or a special one-time policy covering a single transaction.

Packing merchandise for export is a fascinating multivariable problem. The packaging has to be cheap, light, yet highly protective. Shipping costs may depend on weight (so sawdust or Styrofoam is a good packing material) or size (so smaller, denser packages are better). You'll need explicit markings on the cartons so the merchandise will arrive at the right place and be treated properly; but you don't want to provide information for pilferers or hijackers. Use international shipping and handling symbols; if you use English, you'll be understood at this end but not necessarily at the other.

If the importing country has cheap labor, and if taxes and import duties are based on the value of the incoming shipment, your customers may prefer to buy the components and assemble them. This makes for smaller, easier-to-ship packages. But if the importer is taxed on value added, it will probably prefer to buy finished goods, ready for sale. This is also true if labor in the importing country is very expensive, or if assembly facilities are lacking.

The usual sales terms for export include:

- C.i.f. (cost, insurance, freight) to a particular port: your price includes all charges needed to get the stuff to a port in the importing country
- C & F (cost and freight) to a port: you pay to get the stuff to the port, but you don't pay for insurance
- F.a.s. (free alongside) a U.S. port: your price includes delivery to a ship or plane; the buyer takes it from there
- FOB (free on board): you get it to the FOB point, which can be in this country, on a ship, or in the importing country. The buyer has legal ownership, and assumes the risk of loss, at the FOB point
- *Ex* a port: the price includes only the merchandise. Picking it up, or having it shipped, is the buyer's problem

The Federal Maritime Administration licenses foreign freight forwarders. These useful operations give you advice about packing methods, freight costs, port charges, and legal requirements. The forwarder gets the stuff through Customs, makes sure it is loaded onto the right vessel, and that it leaves on time. Some forwarders will even handle the paperwork. Get estimates from several forwarders before you form a relationship with one: but be sure the estimates all cover the same amount of work. By the way, importers usually pick up the forwarder's fee.

As far as the United States is concerned, you can mail packages worth less than fifty dollars without an export declaration. If the package is worth a bit more than that, go to a large Post Office and get Form 2966 (Customs declaration), Form 2933 (international parcel post sticker), and Form 2972 (dispatch note). Attach one of each to each package.

If you use another method of shipment, you'll have to file an export declaration with the Collector of Customs at the port where the merchandise leaves the United States.

As for the Customs policy of the importing country, ask the agent (if you have one), your lawyer (if s/he knows), or one of the government or private agencies set up to assist exporters.

The Department of Commerce is very active in promoting exports to aid the United States' generally dismal balance of payments. The Department of Commerce has an Export Information Reference Room in its Washington headquarters and in each district office.

Outside the United States, the Department of Commerce's U.S. International Marketing Center produces the U.S. Pavilion at International Trade Fairs; Commerce and the U.S. Foreign Service jointly run the U.S. Trade Centers in other countries. For $25 a day (1982 price), you can use the Center as a temporary "office" in a foreign country; you can hold business meetings there, get clerical help, or get advice from the staff.

The Department of Commerce also provides specific information you can use for market research. The fees quoted here are those for early 1982; they may be higher when you use the services. The Agent/Distributor Service ($90/country) and Trade Opportunities Program (a flat fee of $100) match up exporters and potential representatives and agents in the importing country. The Export Contact List Services ($15 access fee, plus $.25/name) include mailing lists, a Foreign Traders' Index, lists of state-controlled trading companies, geographically sorted lists of firms in particular industries, and lists of firms in developing countries.

The Industry and Trade Administration publishes Market Share Reports each year, analyzing U.S. participation in foreign markets. The ITA also publishes International Economic Indicators quarterly, for eight countries; the United States is one of the countries. The Bureau of the Census issues FT 410 reports each month, ana-

lyzing United States exports by commodity and by country. Prices
for publications vary, but tend to be quite low.

The Department of Commerce has marketing managers who
can give information about the commercial and economic situation
in "their" country. To reach the managers, dial (202) 377- and the
extension for the particular country:

Canada, UK	3415	USSR	4655
Mexico, Central America,		Middle East, Iran,	
Panama	2313	Israel, Egypt	3752
The Caribbean	2995	North Africa	5737
Latin/South America	5427	Sub-Sahara Africa	4927
France, Benelux, Spain,		Australia, New Zealand	3646
Portugal, Switzerland,		Southeast Asia	2522
Yugoslavia	2795	East Asia, Pacific	5401
Germany, Austria	3187	China	3583
Italy, Greece, Turkey	3944	Japan	2896
Eastern Europe	2645		

Dun & Bradstreet's International Marketing Service is head-
quartered at 1 World Trade Center, New York, NY 10048. It publishes the very comprehensive *Exporters' Encyclopaedia,* which is
reissued every year and supplemented twice a month. If you shell
out for the "EE" (the 1982 price is a more-than-negligible $325),
you can use a special hotline number to get information from the
D & B staff. If you can't afford your own copy, maybe you can talk
your lawyer into buying a copy of this extremely useful reference
work.

Sell Overseas America, an association for exporters, can be
found at 5950 Canoga Avenue, Woodland Hills, CA 93167. In exchange for your dues (1982 level: $175/year), Sell Overseas
America will provide exposure to foreign markets by featuring your
products in trade shows and can provide the names of potential foreign customers. Your membership also entitles you to research assistance and management counseling.

The Export-Import Bank of the United States ("Eximbank") has
two programs to help small businesses enter the import field. Eximbank more or less acts as an insurer for the exporter: if there is a revolution, or the importer stiffs the exporter, the Eximbank makes
good the loss. The two programs are called the Commercial Bank
Guarantee Program and the Small Business Export Credit Insurance Policy. Eximbank's address is simply Export-Import Bank of

the United States, Washington, DC 20571; the phone number is (800) 424–5201, (202) 566–8812, and the title of the person who deals with small business is "loan officer."

The insurance program is offered in collaboration with a private organization, the Foreign Credit Insurance Association (1 World Trade Center, New York, NY 10048); the FCIA offers a full range of insurance programs to exporters. OPIC (the Overseas Private Investment Corporation—no relation to you-know-who) offers insurance to United States manufacturers who want to establish factories in less developed countries or who want to enter into joint ventures with investors in those countries. Its address is 1129 20th Street NW, Washington, DC 20527. PEFCO (the Private Export Funding Corporation, 280 Park Avenue, New York, NY 10017) makes Eximbank-guaranteed loans to would-be exporters. You can also get financing for export projects from Eximbank itself, from export management companies, factors, or commercial banks. The application process is about the same as for any business borrowing.

If you can understand the endless detail involved in finding markets abroad, getting your products ready, clearing Customs, and getting your money, you're ready for something *really* complicated: selling to the United States government.

Government Contracting

Budget cuts or no budget cuts, the United States government and state and city governments still buy billions of dollars' worth of goods and services a year. If you manufacture anything from brooms to nuclear ordnance (no, I'm not making this up; the "Commerce Business Daily," discussed later, has a special category for Big Bangs), or if you provide a service from catering to computer programming to English-Urdu, Urdu-English translations, the odds are fairly good that some government agency will pay you to do it.

Small businesses stand an excellent chance of getting government contracts. In fact, the federal government makes a policy of helping small and minority businesses. All contracts under ten thousand dollars are set aside for small businesses; so are certain classes of larger contracts. If a contract involves over half a million dollars (one million for construction), the prime contractor has to have a formal program for using small businesses as subcontractors.

If you do become a subcontractor, make sure that the prime contractor is reasonably honest. If the prime contractor stiffs you, you can't go to the federal government to complain.

If a small business and a larger business are tied for the lowest bid in a competitive situation, the small business will be awarded the contract. Small businesses can ask for progress payments; they can get installment payments as they work on a contract. Larger businesses don't get paid until the job is finished.

For these purposes, a small business is defined as being independently owned and operated (that is, not a subsidiary of a major corporation) and is not a dominant firm in its field. A minority business enterprise is at least fifty percent owned by blacks, Hispanics, Asian-Americans, American Indians, Eskimos, Aleuts, or some combination thereof. If the business is a public corporation, at least fifty percent of its stock must be owned by members of minority groups.

The Small Business Administration's §8(a) Program helps minority-owned businesses get government contracts. The minority enterprise submits its business plan to the local SBA office. If the SBA office thinks the plan is reasonably plausible, it finds suitable federal contracts. The SBA becomes the prime contractor; the minority enterprise becomes the subcontractor, doing the actual work.

The SBA's PASS program (it stands for Procurement Automated Service Systems) is a computerized dating service for small businesses. You get a PASS application from the SBA, and indicate your company's name, address, last year's sales, what you can do, and whether the business is owned by minorities, women, or veterans. You mail the application to the SBA. The information is programmed into the SBA computer and is made available to government agencies and private businesses looking for contractors and subcontractors.

SOLICITATION

The process of finding sellers for "government procurement" is called "solicitation"; they even called it that before Watergate.

There are two major methods of solicitation: advertised procurement and negotiated procurement. Advertised procurement is done by means of IFBs. IFBs (invitations for bids) are used for straightforward purchases: for example, 75,000 #2 pencils with attached erasers, to be packaged in a particular way and delivered on a certain date. You submit a bid, and the lowest bidder gets the contract.

Projects that call for discretion call for RFPs (requests for proposals). The agency publishes its request, and the would-be contractors submit proposals (universally, if inaccurately, referred to as RFPs). Preparing an RFP is an intricate ritual; the steps in the dance will be described below.

The entry into the magical world of government procurement is Form 129, the Bidder's Mailing List Application. You file one with the procurement office of each agency you hope to sell something to. The agency puts you on the mailing list for upcoming solicitations. If you want to sell to the military (about three quarters of procurement dollars go to swords rather than plowshares), you have to attach Form DD 558-1 to your Form 129. The forms are simple (name, address, whether or not the company is a small business, who is authorized to sign an RFP) and won't take much time to complete.

To sell most products (as distinct from services) to government agencies, your output has to be on the agency's "Qualified Products List." To get listed, you review the agency's detailed specifications for the item. If your product conforms, you send a letter (in duplicate) to the agency. Describe what you manufacture, which specification it conforms to, and how you plan to test the product. Ask the agency for its "Provisions Governing Qualification," then submit test reports showing the product measures up. If your product makes the list, you agree not to use this fact as an endorsement; you also agree to tell the agency if and when you modify the product.

The federal government publishes a vital, if extremely tedious, publication called "Commerce Business Daily." The CBD has 75 classifications of goods (13 is ammunition and explosives; 26 is tires and tubes; 71 is furniture) and 19 classes of services (A is research and development; U is training; Y is construction). You check the CBD under your areas of interest, and write or call to ask for the IFB or RFP. You can also get the classification information from the small business specialist in the agency. It pays to cultivate a friendly relationship. Trade associations often supply procurement information to their members. The National Small Business Association (1225 19th Street NW, Washington, DC 20036) has a program called BEAM: Bidders' Early Alert Message. BEAM participants tell the NSBA the kinds of contracts they want to bid on. The NSBA sends participants computer printouts, giving the agencies with similar needs, the contract number, specifications, the last date to get the bid package from the agency, and the last date to submit the completed RFP. All you have to do is contact the agency for the bid package. Some trade associations maintain "bid rooms" in which you can read RFPs and decide whether or not to bid. The federal agencies all have bid rooms, though not necessarily anyplace particularly convenient for you.

The Department of Defense's Defense Logistics Agency gives a preference to firms in "labor surplus areas" whose unemployment rate is twenty percent above the national average. The DLA adds five percent to bids submitted by businesses outside "labor surplus areas," so contractors in disadvantaged areas seem to bid lower.

THE BID PACKAGE

Bid packages are inevitably smeary and hard to read and always have at least a couple of pages printed crooked and/or upside down. The top sheet tells you which agency wants a bid or quotes, what the item is, and what the solicitation number is. The solicitation number is crucial information; so are the name, address, and phone number of the person who will answer questions about the bid package. The second page of the package tells you where to submit the completed bid, and the closing date and time. They are not kidding about these.

The top page is especially important if you're on the agency's mailing list and they sent you the package without a request. If you get a package but don't want to bid, fill out the back of the top sheet ("No response for reasons checked") and mail it back to the agency. If you don't respond at all, the agency will take your name off the mailing list, and you may not hear about solicitations you *would* like to bid on.

The bid package will also tell you whether the contract will be a fixed-price contract (e.g., the agency will pay $128,728.50) or a cost-reimbursement contract (the agency pays the contractor's cost of producing the goods or services, plus a fixed fee or a percentage of the cost: this last is the origin of the cost overrun, one of America's major contributions to civilization).

PREPARING A BID

The key to preparing either an IFB or an RFP is literal-mindedness. You have to fill in all the blanks, get all the required signatures from authorized persons, and show that you have satisfied every requirement of the bid exactly. If you have questions, call or write to the information officer listed in the bid package. Try to get a written answer: minute technicalities matter greatly.

Put the solicitation number and the date and time the bid will be opened on the envelope (for an IFB) or package (for an RFP).

IFBs are fairly simple to prepare: just decide how little you can sell the stuff for and still make a profit. RFPs are a little more cumbersome.

The bid package will give you any special requirements and there are lots of forms to fill out; but the RFP itself usually contains two parts. You have to submit a technical proposal and a cost proposal. Generally, the two volumes will be bound and read separately, so the agency can decide if you can do the work before it considers your price.

The technical proposal contains:

- A statement of the problem
- Specific steps you will take to solve it
- When each step will be completed
- Personnel who will work on the project; enclose a resume for each
- Related projects your company has handled
- Your business' current contracts
- Reports of your current financial status
- Subcontractors you work with

The cost proposal includes:

- Your overall bid
- Direct labor costs for the project
- Overhead
- Other costs (for example, printing, subcontractors)
- General and administrative expenses
- Your fee or profit

As you can see, much of this information is quite general. If you make sure that all employees and consultants update their resumes to include new and impressive accomplishments, and if you write a brief laudatory description of every project your firm completes, and if you keep your financial statements current, you can assemble an RFP quickly. All you have to do is write a glowing, cliché-laden summary of what you will do on this particular project, make a schedule of "milestones" (submit blueprints for agency review; revise blueprints; hire contractors and subcontractors; break ground), and assemble the applicable resumes.

PERT and GANTT charts go over big. If you really want to show that you've been a good boy or girl, and Santa should give you a contract, you can include a response matrix. The response matrix is a chart cross-referencing the requirements in the RFP to your proposal:

Requirement	RFP Page	Our Response	Notes
Adequate ventilation	7	Vol. I, p. 9	
R-32 insulation	8	Vol. I, p. 12	
Barrier-free design	32	Vol. I, p. 19	

You get extra brownie points for providing that column for notes.

If you think the job could be done better another way, you can submit an alternate proposal, but make it entirely separate from the main proposal. Make sure you satisfy all the requirements of the solicitation in the main proposal.

In fact, you can send a completely voluntary, unsolicited proposal if you think an agency should satisfy some need of which it is still unaware. The unsolicited proposal explains in great detail what you want to do for the agency, why you are qualified to do it, if you are a minority or small business, and how much it will cost the agency to have the work done.

EVALUATING THE PROPOSAL

A winning bid has to be responsive: that is, the bidder must agree to deliver precisely what the IFB or RFP calls for, precisely on schedule. The firm must be responsible: it must have enough qualified personnel to do the job, they must be available at the right time, adequate facilities and equipment must be on hand, the business must have enough working capital or credit to stay in business until the job is finished, and must have a satisfactory performance record in related projects.

Usually, the agency goes through all the technical proposals and rejects the nonconforming ones immediately. Then the conforming proposals are examined and evaluated with a point system (for example, twenty points for imagination, ten points for a short completion schedule). If you submit an alternate proposal, it will seldom be considered unless you have a strongly competitive conforming proposal. Finally, the cost proposals are examined, and the low bidder gets the contract. The low bid is calculated by taking any discounts the bidder offers, except the discount for payment within ten days. Everyone knows the government won't pay within ten days. If you have a gambler's temperament, you can count on the fact that most RFPs call for items that will never be used, so you can bid low on these items.

The federal government has the largest and most elaborate procurement program, but states and cities also buy goods and services. The American Bar Association has drafted a Model Procurement Code that has been adopted by eleven states and cities; thirteen more are considering it. You may want to check this Code for guidance in preparing bids.

CHAPTER THIRTEEN

Summary

We are not bound by any iron law of economics to devote our collective efforts as a nation to armpit odors, herbicides, bad breath, cluster bombs, and ring-around-the-collar. We can spend our time and energy in any way we want.—PHILIP SLATER

THIS BOOK HAS BEEN about success, and how to avoid it.

The shelves are choked with books telling you how to work, plan, or claw your way to success—how to become, as one early, satirical manual phrased it, "a four-window girl," one with a large sunny corner office.

The more innocent of these tomes counsel you to adopt the strenuous Dale Carnegie virtues: patience, persistence, belief in yourself and your goals. They tell you how to make lists and card files, and how to chivy the unfortunates so set until they buy cars, insurance, give you a job, or otherwise set your feet on the path to success.

The most pernicious books explain to you that success belongs to the fastest poniard in the West. Machiavelli has been democratized: not only princes can chisel their way to the top.

Princesses, Jewish and otherwise, can also join the struggle. Betty Lehan Harragan's *Games Mother Never Taught You: Corporate Gamesmanship for Women* is rendered even more offensive by Ms. Harragan's good writing. She believes that women will not be able to succeed in corporate hierarchies, because they are unfamiliar with the army and with sports. This is relevant because Ms. Harragan believes that military and sports vocabulary and models of behavior permeate the business world. Perhaps this is true, though the spectacle of grownups mistaking an oil company for a football game is a tragic one.

350

Harragan instructs women that they must respect their place in the hierarchy and must not attempt to assume command until they are promoted (even if the "Gatling is jammed and the Colonel's dead"). At the same time, they must be team players. It's beyond me how you can do both at the same time, because team play requires cooperation among equals.

John Molloy teaches you how to eat with the right fork and speak with the right accent; Michael Korda teaches you how to avoid answering the telephone and how to appropriate territory by having file cabinets painted your ceremonial color. Dozens of experts tell you how to outmaneuver a hostile boss, or make a stupid one look good, how to have a "power desk" with the right bibelots.

However, all these book and articles are extremely self-referential. They assume that the business world is a closed circle—in fact, a circle-jerk—in which the major part of every day is spent in paper shuffling and palace intrigue. Elaborate plots are confected to gain the boss' favor or to make someone else look bad. This may in fact be true—my sojourn at Wasp, Wasp & Token suggests this— but surely we can do a little better.

Thorstein Veblen attributed the malaise of his contemporaries to the shift of American capitalism from "industry," whose central concern was the product, to "business," whose central concern is profit. I think it's gone one step further, to the "rec room," whose central concern is success via game-playing.

In an "industry," the workers can be underpaid and overworked, but they can understand what it is they are producing. In early industrial society, they could understand the necessity of the product (steel to build railways, cloth, mass-produced furniture) and how it benefited those who had the money to buy it. The workers in a business are alienated in a crucial way: the emphasis is on profit, not the product, so good products may be dropped and inferior ones touted. By the time the economy has reached this stage, the workers have been turned into consumers: they have bread, a roof over their heads, and are prepared to listen to people telling them what to buy. When every reasonable want of those with money has been saturated, the business turns into a rec room, and "creative advertising" is used to convince people that some truly demented product is "new," "different," "improved," or the epitome of gracious living. No one is particularly concerned about making the stuff better, or cheaper; they'd rather worry about the relative lushness of another vice-president's carpet, or the comparative coldness of the lunchtime martinis in various expense-account restaurants.

I never believed too deeply in the Smithian free market or the law of supply and demand; however, current "supply side" economics completely violates these shibboleths. At one time, profit was considered the appropriate compensation for risking capital and producing goods and services people wanted and/or needed. Now it seems that profit is a placatory device used to prevent the schoolyard bully from taking his basketball and going home if the other kids won't play his way. Costs are blithely passed along to the customer; big companies scream for tax breaks to sustain ever-increasing profits. (At the same time, they do a virtuoso job of poor-mouthing and bitching about government regulations.)

One of the major delusions propagated in America is that growth can be infinite. Sooner or later, one of the ingredients runs short, or everyone who wants a refrigerator *has* one, or everyone who wants to buy a refrigerator patronizes one of your eighty-three competitors. Costs increase and even if you hand them off to the hapless buyers, some of these buyers will tell you where to put your washer-dryer or your frozen imitation spinach soufflé. Therefore, when profit curves flatten, heads roll and game-playing intensifies to make sure that someone else will be blamed for the debacle.

The delusion is predicated on an earlier delusion: that resources are infinite. There will always be plenty of oil, coal, steel, aluminum; the bloody wogs will always sell us the stuff at a penny a ton; and we can just dump the residue into the river. Perhaps if we finish lunch before three, we may think a little about future supplies or pollution problems.

The success ethic assumes that the business world is a zero-sum game (where the amount of benefits is constant and one wins only to the extent that another loses) or even a negative-sum game (where benefits decrease and cumulative losses are higher than cumulative gains). Therefore, the best strategy is to sabotage someone else's chance for promotion, or make another department look bad. Once again, the customer is nowhere because the effort is intramural, rather than a striving to increase market share by providing a better and/or cheaper product.

For that matter, even if the customers are deliriously happy with the stuff, what if the workers are keeling over from occupational diseases and the producer is using up scarce resources as fast as it discharges toxic effluents? Success means producing more every year—even if the product can only be unloaded by appealing to human snobbishness, greed, and insecurity. Success means when the market can absorb 100,000 units, making 100,000 units and selling 40,000 of them—when your 4 competitors make 100,000 units each and only sell 15,000 apiece.

Success is being too busy to see your family because you're flying to a meeting on the coast or lunching with an important prospect or working up a proposal or getting out the monthly report. Success is being the first one in every morning and the last one out. Success is winning the "I can work harder than you" game—whether or not you can produce more or indeed whether the stuff you produce is worthwhile or even actively harmful.

At first, working hard showed submission to the station in life in which God placed you. Later, justification by works applied to both charitable acts and worldly labors. The Protestants substituted justification by faith in the religious context, but stressed the importance of fulfilling oneself through a calling. Now that religion is a living force in fewer people's lives, something has to take its place. For those opposed to pleasure (especially other people's), there is the grim satisfaction of grinding toil and keeping others up to the mark. For hedonists, there are the pleasures of a job well done or of beating someone else's brains out. For the insecure, there is the assurance that all the *really* top people thrive on a diet of fifteen-hour days, endless convention speeches, and stupefying professional journals. If there's something else you'd rather do, you must be a lazy slob, ill-adjusted, or something.

If you're a woman, you're further criticized for not picking yourself up by your ankle straps. You must have succumbed to traditional feminine conditioning. If you have done this, you have not merely deprived yourself of three-martini lunches and phantom stock plans; you are failing to serve as a role model. If you like being a housewife, nurse, or, God forbid, a secretary, you're letting down the side. It is your duty to generations yet unborn to become the president of General Motors.

It's not that I think women are less qualified to lead giant corporations than men are, or that we bring feminine virtues of tenderness and compassion to the cold corporate world. I know that women can handle anything from backbiting to genocide with aplomb. However, it seems to me that women, as outsiders, have a priceless opportunity to point out the idiocies and suggest that good sense be substituted. A cosmetics company is *not* a football team, and good old Witherspoon is not the quarterback. Women (and other outsiders—blacks, Hispanics, Orientals) can point out that many workers are parents, and that provision of reliable day care is a better fringe benefit than establishing a pension plan that helps only a few top executives. Outsiders can point out that most of the meetings settle nothing, the reports are unread, and if there isn't any real work to do we might as well go to the movies.

Of course, pointing these facts out to the entrenched hierarchy is a fairly efficient method of becoming unemployed. However, a one-person business *has* no entrenched hierarchy; the owner of that business can strive against his or her own imperialistic drives as the business gets larger.

A small business can sometimes provide an excellent income, or even a fortune, for its owner; it can also be a short course in Bankruptcy Self-Taught. But any bureaucratic nonsense, any makework, any Charge of the Light Brigade idiocy is directly attributable to the owner. This is frightening, and indeed the constant presence of someone else to blame is a major corporate fringe benefit. But there is a great deal of satisfaction in determining one's own fate and accepting responsibility. Because the small business owner is at the top of the heap (indeed is often the entire heap) decisions can be changed when this is necessary. The fewer other people around, the less embarrassing it is to admit a mistake has been made and to try something else.

Large businesses have standard operating procedures; small businesses can't afford them. Small businesses (unless they aspire to the status and ossification of large businesses) have to react to what is really happening now—not to what happened ten years ago, or what was projected to happen this quarter. This is not to say that small businesses don't need plans. But large operations can continue to churn out plans blissfully, insulated from the results of last month's ukase. In a boutique, it takes a substantial effort of will to ignore the fact that zero knicker suits, rather than the projected two hundred and twenty-five, have been sold. A large operation can write off a mistake, perhaps endowing the parent organization with a cherished tax loss. A small operation either stops making these mistakes, or stops, period.

A very large business tends to commit itself to generating new products at intervals, whether or not needs have changed or real innovation has occurred. The advertising agency has a budget, and it must be used to produce a certain number of ads. From time to time the agency gets restive and requires new ways to insult the public's intelligence. But all the existing products have vice-presidents and product managers, who will fight to the death to save their jobs. Hence, duplication of product, of effort, and ruinous use of resources to fabricate, package, ship, and promote the product. A small business, unless fueled by a very wealthy person or group, will have to face reality much faster—with a concomitant saving of human and fossil-fuel energy.

While chicanery lurks in both human and corporate hearts, some of the extravagances of bribery and crooked accounting are impossible for small businesses. And, no matter how imperious the entrepreneur is, it's hard to have an executive washroom or oak-paneled executive dining room when there are only two employees.

The executives of large companies in their oaken playpen eat lunch with their confreres, "take" meetings, and "cut" deals, hanging out with their coevals on yachts and golf courses. They will then do business with these buddies—even if a subassembly of equal quality could be bought from an outsider for less. After all, it's not their money. If the cost goes up, it's tax-deductible, and anyway the full amount can be passed on to the customer. If higher prices result in lower sales, blame government regulation and lobby for favorable tax treatment.

The scenario works out a little differently for small businesses. The owners of a start-up business don't have these cushy connections; they must buy, and provide their buyers with, quality at the lowest possible price. They have nothing else to offer—no tradition, no conditioning produced by relentless advertising. This is not to say that small businesses cannot thrive by producing shoddy merchandise or slipshod services—only that *someone* has to like the results.

As John Molloy reminds us, business success hinges on eighty-sixing one's Brooklyn accent and having a good appreciation of Armagnac. A spouse who is sexually hyperactive, alcoholic, or snaps bubble gum will terminate the advancement of a well-qualified sales manager or financial analyst. Thus, many talented people who have bombed out of the corporate world are available for hiring by small businesses.

All of the above may sound as if I believe that all large businesses are infested with vicious pigs and bumbling idiots, and that all small businesses are staffed by a coalition between Thomas

Edison and the Poor Clares. Large businesses (I can't think of an example offhand, but there must be some) can demonstrate superb efficiency in tackling huge projects and making good use of economies of scale. They also have the capital to mobilize behind large projects. (On the other hand, these days labor-intensive, rather than capital-intensive, projects seem to fit the imperatives of a world with many unemployed workers and few unused resources.) Small businesses go under so frequently in part because stupidity, prejudice, and venality are equally distributed even though resources are not.

A new business is a new start. It can devote itself to efficient organization, quality control, waste trimming, resource conservation, and real service to customers. It can provide interesting jobs with identifiable results—not makework—for its employees. It can gather information in response to legal requirements or for practical use in decision-making—not to molder in a file cabinet.

Starting a business can have the same effect on the bank balance that dancing cheek-to-cheek with a vampire has on the hematocrit. Rarely does starting a business lead to great wealth. But for the many businesses in the middle, the owner gets a good living in both senses of the term. The success game is abandoned in favor of a positive-sum game. Everybody wins: good products and services for the customers, interesting jobs at fair wages for the employees, real pleasure, real challenges, and real autonomy for the business owner.

APPENDIX A

Incorporation and Franchise Taxes

KEY

AI   Articles of Incorporation

CI   Certificate of Incorporation

SS   Secretary of State

$50+ means that the filing fee depends on the number or value of shares issued, with a minimum of $50.

A franchise tax is a tax on the privilege of doing business in a state. Franchise taxes can be flat fees (e.g., $100) or may have a minimum amount and a sliding scale.

(1) = based on value of stock

(2) = based on net income earned in that state

(3) = based on stated capital

(4) = based on net worth or assets in that state

In addition to these taxes, you may have to pay license taxes and/or other fees when you incorporate; fees when you amend the Articles of Incorporation; and license, income, and/or excise taxes each year.

same = Franchise tax for a foreign corporation is the same as for a domestic corporation.

State	What to File	Where to File It	Filing Fee (Domestic Corp.)	Filing Fee (Foreign Corp.)	Franchise Tax (Domestic)	Franchise Tax (Foreign)
AL	AI	County Probate Judge of county where business is located	$45	$45	$25+(1)	same
AK	AI	Department of Commerce and Economic Development Pouch D Juneau 99811	$35+	$35+	$100 (every 2 yrs.)	$200 (every 2 yrs.)
AZ	AI	Corporation Commission 2222 West Encanto Blvd. Phoenix 85009	$50	$50	NONE	NONE
AR	AI	SS Corporate Department State Capitol Bldg. Little Rock 72201	$15+	$50+	$11+(1)	same
CA	AI	SS 111 Capitol Mall Sacramento 95814	$65	$550	$200+(2)	same
CO	AI	SS 1575 Sherman Ave. Denver 80203	$22.50	$100	NONE	NONE

CT	CI	SS 30 Trinity St. PO Box 846 Hartford 06115	$50+	$150+	10% of net income	same
DE	CI	SS Dover 19901	$10+	$10+	$20+(1)	$30
FL	AI	SS Charter Section Tallahassee 32304	$35+	$45+	$10	same
GA	AI	SS 225 Peachtree St. NE Atlanta 30303	$15	$100	$10+(2)	same
HI	AI	Department of Regulatory Agencies 1010 Richards St. Honolulu 96813	$50+	$50+	NONE	NONE
ID	AI	SS State House Boise 83720	$60	$60	$20+(2)	same
IL	AI	SS Corporation Division Springfield 62706	$\frac{1}{10}$ of 1% of stated capital	$\frac{1}{10}$ of 1% of stated capital	$25+(3)	same
IN	AI	SS State House #155 Indianapolis 46204	$30+	$30+	NONE	NONE

State	What to File	Where to File It	Filing Fee (Domestic Corp.)	Filing Fee (Foreign Corp.)	Franchise Tax (Domestic)	Franchise Tax (Foreign)
IA	AI	SS Corporations Division Des Moines 50319	$25+	$20	$5+(3)	same
KS	AI	SS Corporation Division Topeka 66612	$50	$50	$20+(1)	same
KY	AI	SS Capitol Bldg. #150 Frankfort 40601	$10+	$35	$10+(3)	same
LA	AI	SS Corporations Division PO Box 44125 Baton Rouge 70804	$10+	$10+	$1.50/ $1,000 stock	same
ME	AI	SS Augusta 04333	$10+	$100	NONE	NONE
MD	Form 1	Department of Assessments and Taxation 301 West Preston St. Baltimore 21201	$20	$20	NONE	NONE

	Articles of Organization				
MA	AI (Form C95)	Secretary of the Commonwealth Corporation Division 1 Ashburton Place Boston 02108	$150	$150+	NONE	NONE
MI	AI	Department of Commerce Corporation Division Box 3004 Lansing 48909	$25	$25	NONE	NONE
MN	AI	SS Corporation Division 180 Senate Office Bldg. St. Paul 55155	$62.50+	$125	NONE	NONE
MS	AI	SS PO Box 136 Jackson 39205	$25+	$25+	$10+(3)	same
MO	AI (Form 41)	SS Jefferson City 65101	$50+	$60+	$25+(1)	same
MT	AI	SS State Capitol Helena 59601	$50+	$50+	$10+(2)	same
NB	AI	SS Corporation Division 2304 State Capitol Bldg. Lincoln 68509	$20+	$20+	$10+(1)	same

Appendix A

State	What to File	Where to File It	Filing Fee (Domestic Corp.)	Filing Fee (Foreign Corp.)	Franchise Tax (Domestic)	Franchise Tax (Foreign)
NV	AI	SS Corporation Division Capitol Bldg., Capitol Complex Carson City 89710	$50+	$50+	NONE	NONE
NH	Record of Organization	SS Concord 03301	$60+	$100	$60+(1)	$150
NJ	CI	SS State House Trenton 08625	$25+	$165	$25+(4)	$50+(4)
NM	AI	State Corporation Commission Corporation and Franchise Tax Departments PO Drawer 1269 Santa Fe 87501	$50+	$100+	$10+(4)	same
NY	CI	SS Division of Corporations 162 Washington Ave. Albany 12231	$10+	$10+	10% net NY income	same

NC	AI	SS Corporations Division 116 West Jones St. Raleigh 27603	$40+	$40+	$10+(1)	same
ND	AI	SS Division of Corporations Bismarck 58505	$25+	$75+	NONE	NONE
OH	AI	SS Division of Corporations 30 East Broad St. Columbus 43215	$50+	$50+	$50+(3)	same
OK	AI	SS State Capitol Bldg., Rm. 101 Oklahoma City 73105	$3+	$18+	$10+(3)	same
OR	AI (Form 11-B)	Corporation Commission Commerce Bldg. Salem 97310	$10	$50	$10+(2)	$200
PA	AI and Registry Statement	Secretary of the Commonwealth of Pennsylvania Corporation Bureau Harrisburg 17120	$75	$150	1¢/$10 stock	same
RI	AI	SS Providence 02903	$80+	$15+	$100+(1)	same

State	What to File	Where to File It	Filing Fee (Domestic Corp.)	Filing Fee (Foreign Corp.)	Franchise Tax (Domestic)	Franchise Tax (Foreign)
SC	AI	SS Box 11350 Columbia 29201	$45+	$45+	$10+ (based on dividends)	same
SD	AI	SS State Capitol Pierre 57501	$40+	$50+	NONE	NONE
TN	Charter	SS Corporation Division Nashville 37219	$10+	$300	$10+(1)	$25+ (based on gross receipts in TN)
TX	AI	SS Corporation Division Sam Houston State Office Bldg. Austin 78711	$100	$500	$55+(3)	same
UT	AI	SS State Capitol Bldg., Rm. 203 Salt Lake City 84114	$25+	$25+	$25+(2)	same
VT	Articles of Association	SS Montpelier 05602	$20+	$60	NONE	NONE

VA	AI	State Corporation Commission Box 1197 Richmond 23209	$20+	$60+	$20+(1)	same
WA	AI	SS Corporation Division Legislative Bldg. Olympia 98504	$50+	$50+	$30+(1)	same
WV	AI	SS Corporation Division Charleston 25305	$30+	$260+	$20+(1)	$35+(1)
WI	AI (Form 2)	SS Corporation Division State Capitol Bldg. Madison 53702	$55+	$55+	2.3% or more of income	same
WY	AI	SS Division of Corporations Cheyenne 82002	$50+	$50+	$10+(4)	same

APPENDIX B

Federal Phone Book

TO GET HELP:

U.S. Department of Commerce, Industry and Trade Administration District Offices:

505 Marquette, N.W., Room 1015, Albuquerque, NM 87102 (505) 766-2386

632 Sixth Avenue, Hill Building, Suite 412, Anchorage, AK 99501 (907) 265-5307

1365 Peachtree Street, N.E., Suite 600, Atlanta, GA 30309 (404) 881-7000

415 U.S. Customhouse, Gay and Lombard Streets, Baltimore, MD 21202 (301) 962-3560

908 South 20th Street, Suite 200-201, Birmingham, AL 35205 (205) 254-1331

441 Stuart Street, 10th Floor, Boston, MA 02116 (617) 223-2312

Federal Building, 111 West Huron Street, Room 1312, Buffalo, NY 14202 (716) 842-3208

3000 New Federal Office Building, 500 Quarrier Street, Charleston, WV 25301 (304) 343-6181, ext. 375

6022 O'Mahoney Federal Center, 2120 Capitol Avenue, Cheyenne, WY 82001 (307) 778-2151

Midcontinental Plaza Building, 55 East Monroe Street, Room 1406, Chicago, IL 60603 (312) 353-4450

10504 Federal Office Building, 550 Main Street, Cincinnati, OH 45202 (513) 684-2944

666 Euclid Avenue, Room 600, Cleveland, OH 44114 (216) 522-4750

Forest Center, 2611 Forest Drive, Columbia, SC 29204 (803) 765-5345

1100 Commerce Street, Room 7A5, Dallas, TX 75202 (214) 749-1515

New Customhouse, 19th and Stout Streets, Room 165, Denver, CO 80202 (303) 327-3246

609 Federal Building, 210 Walnut Street, Des Moines, IA 50309 (515) 284-4224

203 Federal Building, West Market Street, PO Box 1950, Greensboro, NC 27402 (919) 378-5345

Federal Office Building, 450 Main Street, Room 610-B, Hartford, CT 06103 (203) 244-3530

4106 Federal Building, 300 Ala Moana Boulevard, PO Box 50026, Honolulu, HW 50026 (808) 546-8694

2625 Federal Building, 515 Rusk Street, Houston, TX 77002 (713) 226-4321

357 U.S. Courthouse and Federal Office Building, 46 East Ohio Street, Indianapolis, IN 46204 (317) 269-6214

11777 San Vicente Boulevard, Room 800, Los Angeles, CA 90049 (213) 824-7591

147 Jefferson Avenue, Room 710, Memphis, TN 38103 (901) 521-3213

City National Bank Building, 25 West Flagler Street, Room 821, Miami, FL 33130 (305) 350-5267

Federal Building and U.S. Courthouse, 517 East Wisconsin Avenue, Milwaukee, WI 53202 (414) 224-3473

218 Federal Building, 110 South Fourth Street, Minneapolis, MN 55401 (612) 725-2133

Gateway Building, Market Street and Penn Plaza, Fourth Floor, Newark, NJ 07102 (201) 645-6214

International Trade Mart, 2 Canal Street, Room 432, New Orleans, LA 70130 (504) 589-6546

Federal Office Building, 26 Federal Plaza, 37th Floor, New York, NY 10007 (212) 264-0634

Capitol Plaza, 1815 Capitol Avenue, Suite 703A, Omaha, NB 68102 (402) 221-3665

9448 Federal Building, 600 Arch Street, Philadelphia, PA 19106 (215) 597-2850

2950 Valley Bank Center, 201 North Central Avenue, Phoenix, AZ 85073 (602) 261-3285

2002 Federal Building, 1000 Liberty Avenue, Pittsburgh, PA 15222 (412) 644-2850

1220 S.W. Third Avenue, Room 618, Portland, OR 97204 (503) 221-3001

777 West Second Street, Room 120, Reno, NV 89503 (702) 784-5203

8010 Federal Building, 400 North Eighth Street, Richmond, VA 23240 (804) 782-2246

120 South Central Avenue, St. Louis, MO 63105 (314) 425-3302

1203 Federal Building, 125 South State Street, Salt Lake City, UT 84138 (801) 524-5116

Federal Building, 450 Golden Gate Avenue, Box 36013, San Francisco, CA 94102 (415) 556-5860

235 U.S. Courthouse and Post Office Building, 125-29 Bull Street, Savannah, GA 31402 (912) 232-4321, ext. 204

706 Lake Union Building, 1700 Westlake Avenue North, Seattle, WA 98109 (206) 442-5615

U.S. Department of Defense Information Offices

(These offices do not give out procurement contracts; see page 375 for *those* offices.)

Department of Defense Directorate for Small Business and Economic Utilization Policy Office, Undersecretary of Defense (Research and Engineering) Pentagon, Room 2A340, Washington, DC 20310 (202) 697-4912

Department of Defense Directorate for Disadvantaged Business Utilization Policy Office, Undersecretary of Defense (Research and Engineering) Pentagon, Room 2A340, Washington, DC 20310 (202) 697-1481

Director for Small and Disadvantaged Business Utilization Office, Assistant Secretary of the Army (Installations, Logistics and Financial Management) Pentagon, Room 2E577, Washington, DC 20310 (202) 697-2868, -8113

Army Materiel Development and Readiness Command, Office of the Special Assistant for Small Business, Department of the Army, 5001 Eisenhower Avenue, Alexandria, VA 22333 (202) 274-8185

National Guard Bureau, Office of the Legal Advisor, Small Business Specialist, Pentagon, Washington, DC 20310 (202) 697-6652

Director for Small and Disadvantaged Business Utilization Office, Assistant Secretary of the Navy (Manpower, Reserve Affairs, and Logistics) Crystal Plaza 5, Room 124, Washington, DC 20310 (202) 692-7122

Director for Small and Disadvantaged Business Utilization Office, Deputy Chief of Staff, Research, Development, and Acquisition, Department of the Air Force, Washington, DC 20310 (202) 697-4126, -5373

Staff Director for Small and Disadvantaged Business Utilization Headquarters, Defense Logistics Agency, Cameron Station, Room 4B110, Alexandria, VA 22314 (202) 274-6471

Staff Director for Small and Disadvantaged Business Utilization, Defense Contract Administration Services, Cameron Station, Room 8D390, Alexandria, VA 22314 (202) 274-7605

Armed Services Board of Contract Appeals, Small Business Liaison, Hoffman Building #2, 200 Stovall Street, Alexandria, VA 22332 (202) 325-9070

Federal Trade Commission Regional Offices

Region I (Connecticut, Massachusetts, Maine, New Hampshire, Rhode Island, Vermont) 150 Causeway Street, Room 1301, Boston, MA 02114 (617) 223-6621

Region II (New Jersey, New York east of Rochester) 26 Federal Plaza, Room 2243-EB, New York, NY 10278 (212) 264-1207

Region III (Delaware, District of Columbia, Maryland, Pennsylvania east of Pittsburgh, Virginia, West Virginia) 600-C Gilman Building, 2120 L Street, NW, Washington, DC 20037 (202) 254-7700

Region IV (Alabama, Florida, Georgia, Mississippi, North Carolina, South Carolina, Tennessee) 1718 Peachtree Street NW, Room 1000, Atlanta, GA 30309 (404) 881-4836

Region V (Illinois, Indiana, Iowa, Kentucky, Minnesota, Missouri, Wisconsin) 55 East Monroe Street, Suite 1437, Chicago, IL 60603 (312) 353-4423

Region VI (Michigan, New York west of Rochester, Ohio, Pennsylvania west of Pittsburgh) 1339 Federal Office Building, 1240 East 9th Street, Cleveland, OH 44199 (216) 522-4207

Region VII (Arkansas, Louisiana, New Mexico, Oklahoma, Texas) 2001 Bryan Street, Dallas, TX 75201 (214) 749-3056

Region VIII (Colorado, Kansas, Montana, Nebraska, North Dakota, South Dakota, Wyoming) 1405 Curtiss Street, Suite 2900, Denver, CO 80202 (303) 837-2771

Region IX (Arizona, southern California) 11000 Wilshire Boulevard, Room 13209, Los Angeles, CA 90024 (213) 824-7575

and

(Northern California, Hawaii, Nevada) 450 Golden Gate Avenue, Box 36005, San Francisco, CA 94102 (415) 556-1270

Region X (Alaska, Idaho, Oregon, Washington) 915 Second Avenue, 28th Floor, Seattle, WA 98174 (206) 442-4655

Small Business Administration Offices

For a list of free publications, ask for Publication 115A; for publications for which you pay, ask for Publication 115B. The addresses marked with an asterisk (*) administer the PASS Program (see page 344). Phone numbers with an asterisk are PASS numbers.

Region I (Massachusetts, Maine, New Hampshire, Connecticut, Vermont, Rhode Island)

* 60 Batterymarch Street, 10th Floor, Boston, MA 02110 (617) 223-3204; * (617) 223-3162
150 Causeway Street, 10th Floor, Boston, MA 02114 (617) 223-3224
302 High Street, 4th Floor, Holyoke, MA 01050 (413) 536-8770
40 Western Avenue, Room 512, Augusta, ME 04330 (207) 622-6171
55 Pleasant Street, Room 211, Concord, NH 03301 (603) 224-4041
One Financial Plaza, Hartford, CT 06103 (203) 244-3600
87 State Street, Room 204, PO Box 605, Montpelier, VT 05602 (802) 229-0538
40 Fountain Street, Providence, RI 02903 (401) 528-4580

Region II (New Jersey and New York)

* 26 Federal Plaza, Room 29-118, New York, NY 10278 (212) 264-7772; * (212) 264-5270
26 Federal Plaza, Room 3100, New York, NY 10278 (212) 264-4355
35 Pinelawn Road, Melville, NY 11747 (516) 454-0750
970 Broad Street, Room 1635, Newark, NJ 07102 (201) 645-2434
1800 East Davis Street, Camden, NJ 08104 (609) 757-5183
100 South Clinton Street, Room 1073, Syracuse, NY 13260 (315) 423-5383
111 West Huron Street, Room 1311, Buffalo, NY 14202 (716) 846-4301
180 Clemens Center Parkway, Elmira, NY 14901 (607) 733-4686
445 Broadway, Room 236A, Albany, NY 12207 (518) 472-6300
100 State Street, Room 601, Rochester, NY 14614 (716) 263-6700

Region III (Delaware, District of Columbia, Maryland, Pennsylvania, Virginia, West Virginia)

* 231 St. Asaphs Road, Suite 646, West Lobby, Bala Cynwyd, PA 19004 (215) 596-5984; * (215) 596-5988
231 St. Asaphs Road, Suite 400, East Lobby, Bala Cynwyd, PA 19004 (215) 596-5889
100 Chestnut Street, Suite 309, Harrisburg, PA 17101 (717) 782-3840
20 North Pennsylvania Avenue, Wilkes-Barre, PA 18702 (717) 826-6497
844 King Street, Room 5207, Wilmington, DE 19801 (302) 573-6294
8600 LaSalle Road, Room 360, Towson, MD 21204 (301) 962-4392
109 North Third Street, Room 302, Clarksburg, WV 26301 (304) 623-5631

Charleston National Plaza, Suite 628, Charleston, WV 25301 (304) 343-6181

1000 Liberty Avenue, Room 1401, Pittsburgh, PA 15222 (412) 644-2780

400 North Eighth Street, Room 3015, PO Box 10126, Richmond, VA 23219 (804) 771-2617

1030 Fifteenth Street, NW, Suite 250, Washington, DC 20417 (202) 653-6963

Region IV (Alabama, Florida, Georgia, Kentucky, Mississippi, North Carolina, South Carolina, Tennessee)

* 1375 Peachtree Street, NE, Fifth Floor, Atlanta, GA 30367 (404) 881-4963; * (404) 881-4588

1720 Peachtree Street, NW, Sixth Floor, Atlanta, GA 30309 (404) 881-4325

52 North Main Street, Statesboro, GA 30458 (912) 489-8719

908 South 20th Street, Room 202, Birmingham, AL 35205 (205) 254-1344

230 South Tryon Street, Suite 700, Charlotte, NC 28202 (704) 371-6563

215 South Evans Street, Room 206, Greenville, NC 27834 (919) 752-3798

1835 Assembly, Third Floor, PO Box 2786, Columbia, SC 29202 (803) 765-5376

100 West Capitol Street, Suite 322, Jackson, MS 30201 (601) 960-4378

111 Fred Haise Boulevard, Second Floor, Biloxi, MS 39530 (601) 435-3676

400 West Bay Street, Room 261, Box 35067, Jacksonville, FL 32202 (904) 791-3792

600 Federal Plaza, Room 188, PO Box 3517, Louisville, KY 40201 (502) 582-5971

2222 Ponce de Leon Boulevard, Fifth Floor, Coral Gables, FL 33134 (305) 350-5521

700 Twiggs Street, Suite 607, Tampa, FL 33602 (813) 228-2594

701 Clematis Street, Room 229, West Palm Beach, FL 33402 (305) 659-7533

404 James Robertson Parkway, Suite 1012, Nashville, TN 37219 (615) 251-5881

502 South Gay Street, Room 307, Knoxville, TN 37902 (615) 637-9300

167 North Main Street, Room 211, Memphis, TN 38103 (901) 521-3588

Region V (Illinois, Indiana, Minnesota, Michigan, Ohio, Wisconsin)

* 219 South Dearborn Street, Room 838, Chicago, IL 60604 (312) 353-0535; * (312) 353-0438

219 South Dearborn Street, Room 435, Chicago, IL 60604 (312) 353-4528

1240 East Ninth Street, Room 317, Cleveland, OH 44199 (216) 552-4194

85 Marconi Boulevard, Columbus, OH 43215 (614) 469-6860

550 Main Street, Room 5028, Cincinnati, OH 45202 (513) 684-2814

477 Michigan Avenue, Detroit, MI 48226 (313) 226-7241

540 West Kaye Avenue, Don H. Bottom University Center, Marquette, MI 49855 (906) 225-1108

575 North Pennsylvania Street, Room 552, Indianapolis, IN 46204 (317) 331-7000

501 East Monroe Street, Suite 120, South Bend, IN 46601 (219) 232-8163

212 East Washington Avenue, Room 213, Madison, WI 53703 (608) 264-5205

500 South Barstow Street, Room B9AA, Eau Claire, WI 54701 (715) 834-9012

517 East Wisconsin Avenue, Room 246, Milwaukee, WI 53202 (414) 291-3941

100 North Sixth Street, Minneapolis, MN 55403 (612) 725-2358

Four North, Old State Capitol Plaza, Springfield, IL 62701 (217) 955-4200

Region VI (Arkansas, Louisiana, New Mexico, Oklahoma, Texas)

* 1720 Regal Row, Room 230, Dallas, TX 75235 (214) 767-7643; * (214) 749-2447

1100 Commerce Street, Room 3C36, Dallas, TX 75242 (214) 767-0605

100 South Washington Street, Room G-12, Marshall, TX 75670 (214) 935-5257

501 West 10th Street, Room 527, Fort Worth, TX 76102 (817) 334-3971

5000 Marble Avenue NE, Room 320, Albuquerque, NM 87100 (505) 766-3430

500 Dallas Street, Houston, TX 77002 (713) 226-4341

320 West Capitol Avenue, PO Box 1401, Little Rock, AR 72201 (501) 378-5871

1205 Texas Avenue, Room 712, Lubbock, TX 79401 (806) 762-7466

4100 Rio Bravo, Suite 300, El Paso, TX 79902 (915) 543-7586

222 East Van Buren Street, PO Box 2567, Harlingen, TX 78550 (512) 423-8934

3105 Leopard Street, PO Box 9253, Corpus Christi, TX 78408 (512) 888-3331

1001 Howard Avenue, 17th Floor, New Orleans, LA 70113 (504) 589-6685

500 Fannin Street, Room 5B06, Shreveport, LA 71101 (318) 226-5196

200 Northwest Fifth Street, Suite 670, Oklahoma City, OK 73102 (405) 231-4301

333 West Fourth Street, Room 3104, Tulsa, OK 74103 (918) 581-7495

727 East Durango Street, Room A-513, San Antonio, TX 78206 (512) 229-6250

300 East Eighth Street, Austin, TX 78701 (512) 397-5288

Region VII (Iowa, Kansas, Missouri, Nebraska)

* 911 Walnut Street, 23rd Floor, Kansas City, MO 64106 (816) 374-5288;
   * (816) 374-3516
1150 Grande Avenue, Fifth Floor, Kansas City, MO 64106 (816) 374-3416
220 East Commercial Street, Springfield, MO 65803 (417) 864-7670
400 North Main Street, Sikeston, MO 63801 (314) 471-0223
373 Collins Road NE, Cedar Rapids, IA 52402 (319) 366-2411
210 Walnut Street, Room 749, Des Moines, IA 50309 (515) 284-4422
19th and Farnum Streets, Second Floor, Omaha, NB 68102 (402) 221-4691
One Mercantile Tower, Suite 2500, St. Louis, MO 63101 (314) 425-4191
110 East Waterman Street, Wichita, KS 67202 (316) 267-6571

Region VIII (Colorado, Montana, North Dakota, South Dakota, Utah, Wyoming)

* 1405 Curtis Street, 22nd Floor, Denver, CO 80202 (303) 837-5763;
   * (303) 837-3686
721 19th Street, Denver, CO 80202 (303) 837-2607
100 East B Street, Room 4001, PO Box 2839, Casper, WY 82601 (307) 265-5266
657 Second Avenue North, Room 219, PO Box 3086, Fargo, ND 58108 (701) 237-5771
301 South Park Avenue, Room 528, Drawer 10054, Helena, MT 59601 (405) 449-5381
125 South State Street, Room 2239, Salt Lake City, UT 84138 (314) 425-5800
101 South Main Street, Suite 101, Sioux Falls, SD 57102 (605) 336-2980
515 Ninth Street, Room 246, Rapid City, SD 57701 (605) 343-5074

Region IX (Arizona, California, Nevada, Hawaii)

* 450 Golden Gate Avenue, PO Box 36044, San Francisco, CA 94102 (415) 556-7487; * (415) 556-1650
211 Main Street, Fourth Floor, San Francisco, CA 94105 (415) 556-7490
1515 Clay Street, Room 947, Oakland, CA 94612 (415) 273-7790
1229 N Street, PO Box 828, Fresno, CA 93712 (209) 487-5189
2800 Cottage Way, Room W-2535, Sacramento, CA 95825 (916) 484-4726
301 East Stewart, PO Box 7525, Downtown Station, Las Vegas, NV 89101 (702) 386-6611
50 South Virginia Street, Room 114, PO Box 3216, Reno, NV 89505 (702) 784-5268
300 Ala Moana, Room 2213, PO Box 50207, Honolulu, HI 96850 (808) 546-8950

* 350 South Figueroa Street, Sixth Floor, Los Angeles CA 90071 (213) 688-2956; * (213) 688-2946

2700 North Main Street, Santa Ana, CA 92701 (714) 547-5089

3030 North Central Avenue, Suite 1201, Phoenix, AZ 85012 (602) 241-2200

301 West Congress Street, Room 3V, Tucson, AZ 85701 (602) 762-6715

880 Front Street, Room 4-S-29, San Diego, CA 92188 (714) 293-5440

Region X (Alaska, Idaho, Oregon, Washington)

* 710 Second Avenue, Fifth Floor, Seattle, WA 98104 (206) 442-5676; * (206) 442-0390

915 Second Avenue, Room 1744, Seattle, WA 98174 (206) 442-5534

1016 West Sixth Avenue, Suite 200, Anchorage, AK 99501 (907) 271-4022

101 12th Avenue, Box 14, Fairbanks, AK 99701 (907) 452-1951

1005 Main Street, Second Floor, Boise, ID 83701 (208) 334-2200

1220 Southwest Third Avenue, Room 676, Portland, OR 97204 (503) 221-2682

West 920 Riverside Avenue, Room 651, PO Box, 2167 Spokane, WA 99210 (509) 456-5310

To Buy Government Surplus:

The General Services Administration sells civilian government surplus. To get on the bidders' mailing list, contact one of these Business Service Centers:

Region I (Connecticut, Maine, Massachusetts, New Hampshire, Rhode Island, Vermont)
John W. McCormack Building, Boston, MA 02109 (617) 223-2868

Region II (New Jersey, New York)
26 Federal Plaza, New York, NY 10278 (212) 264-1234

Washington, DC Region
7th and D Streets, SW, Washington, DC 20407 (202) 472-1804

Region III (Delaware, Maryland, Pennsylvania, Virginia, West Virginia)
Ninth and Market Streets, Philadelphia, PA 19107 (215) 597-9613

Region IV (Alabama, Florida, Georgia, Kentucky, Mississippi, North Carolina, South Carolina, Tennessee)
1776 Peachtree Street, NW, Atlanta, GA 30309 (404) 881-4661

Region V (Illinois, Indiana, Michigan, Minnesota, Ohio, Wisconsin)
230 South Dearborn Street, Chicago, IL 60604 (312) 353-5383

Region VI (Iowa, Kansas, Missouri, Nebraska)
1500 East Bannister Road, Kansas City, MO 64131 (816) 926-7203

Region VII (Arkansas, Louisiana, New Mexico, Oklahoma, Texas)
819 Taylor Street, Forth Worth, TX 76102 (817) 334-3284
and
Federal Office Building and Courthouse, 515 Rusk Street, Houston, TX
    77002 (713) 226-5787

Region VIII (Colorado, Montana, North Dakota, South Dakota, Utah, Wy-
    oming)
Building 41, Denver Federal Center, Denver, CO 80225 (303) 234-2216

Region IX (Arizona, California, Hawaii, Nevada)
525 Market Street, San Francisco, CA 94105 (415) 556-2122
and
300 North Los Angeles Avenue, Los Angeles, CA 90012 (213) 688-3210

Region X (Alaska, Idaho, Oregon, Washington)
440 Federal Building, 915 Second Avenue, Seattle, WA 98174 (206) 442-
    5556

To Bid on Government Contracts:

Agriculture, U.S. Department of
Agricultural Marketing Service, Procurement and Contracting Section,
    Property and Procurement Branch, 14th Street and Independence
    Avenue, SW, South Building, Room 0758, Washington, DC 20250
    (202) 447-3457

Defense, U.S. Department of, and Military Services
• Defense Logistics Agency, Small Business and Economic Utilization
    Advisor, Cameron Station, Room 4B110, Alexandria, VA 22314 (202)
    274-6471
• Army and Air Force Exchange Service, 3911 South Walton Walker,
    Dallas, TX 75222 (214) 330-2225
• Army Corps of Engineers, U.S. Army Engineer Division Headquarters,
    Pentagon, Washington, DC 20310 (202) 693-0201

- Naval Aviation Supply Office, 700 Robbins Avenue, Building #1, Room 201, Philadelphia, PA 19111 (215) 697-2806
- Veterans Administration Marketing Division, VA Marketing Center, PO Box 76, Hines, IL 60141 (312) 681-6782

Environmental Protection Association, Procurement and Contracts Management Division, Minority Business/Small Business Section, 401 M Street, NW, Washington, DC 20460 (202) 755-0616

Food and Drug Administration, Procurement, Property and Facilities Management Branch, 5600 Fishers Lane, Room 5020, Rockville, MD 20857 (301) 443-3250

Federal Trade Commission, Procurement and Contracting Branch, 633 Indiana Avenue, NW, Washington, DC 20580 (202) 724-1133

General Accounting Office, Procurement Branch, 441 G Street, NW, Room 3130, Washington, DC 20460 (202) 275-3455

Goverment Printing Office, Printing Procurement Department, North Capitol and H Streets, NW, Room C-883, Washington, DC 20401 (202) 275-2265

Health and Human Services, U.S. Department of Office of Grants and Procurement, Office of the Assistant Secretary for Management and Budget, Hubert H. Humphrey Building, 200 Independence Avenue, SW, Room 513D, Washington, DC 20201 (202) 655-4000

Housing and Urban Development, U.S. Department of Office of Procurement and Contracts, Procurement and Grants Division, 451 Seventh Street, NW, 9th Floor, Washington, DC 20410 (202) 724-0036

Internal Revenue Service, Contracts and Procurement Section, Eleventh and Constitution Avenue, NW, Room 1237, Washington, DC 20224 (202) 566-3656

Labor, U.S. Department of
Division of Procurement Office of Administrative Services, 200 Constitution Avenue, NW, Room 51514, Washington, DC 20210 (202) 523-6451

National Institutes of Health, Procurement Branch, Division of Administrative Services, 9000 Rockville Pike, Building 31, Room 3C39, Bethesda, MD 20014 (301) 496-3181

Postal Services, U.S.
Procurement and Supply Program, Plans and Management Division, 475 L'Enfant Plaza West, SW, Washington, DC 20260 (202) 245-5663

Small Business Administration, Procurement and Supply Branch, Imperial Building, 1441 L Street, NW, Room 221, Washington, DC 20416 (202) 653-6639

Bibliography

On the principle that if you can't say something nice, don't say anything, all these books are recommended.

Consciousness-Raising

These books are recommended, not so much for specific tips and techniques, as for ways of thinking about business.

Brown, Deaver. *The Entrepreneur's Guide.* New York: Macmillan, 1980. Good examples, and Brown is an excellent writer.

Grossman, Lee. *Fat Paper: Diets for Trimming Paperwork.* New York: McGraw-Hill, 1976. Not only *are* there specific tips and techniques, but Grossman provokes you to think about what goes on in an office.

Mungo, Raymond. *Cosmic Profit: How to Make Money Without Doing Time.* Boston, MA: Little, Brown, 1980. A charming meditation on the metaphysics of wealth, illustrated with countercultural examples.

Phillips, Michael and Raspberry, Salli. *Honest Business.* New York: Random House, 1981. An explanation of why and how some businesses operate with candor, and without engaging in war on the consumer.

Townsend, Robert. *Up the Organization.* New York: Fawcett, 1970. A thoughtful and often funny discussion of how to manage an organization that produces goods, services, and profit—not one that produces social-climbing and infighting.

Finances

Dlugatch, Irving. *Dynamic Cost Reduction.* New York: John Wiley and Sons, 1979. Some excellent cost-cutting techniques, well-explained.

Follett, Robert. *How to Keep Score in Business: Accounting and Financial Analysis for the Non-Accountant.* New York: Mentor Executive Library, 1978. A fantastic book. Essential to your well-being and peace of mind. Read Kamoroff first (see below), then read this and accounting will become almost comprehensible.

Kamoroff, Bernard. *Small-Time Operator*. Laytonville, CA: Bell Springs Publishing, 1980. Bookkeeping made easy and efficient. Watch out for the tax advice, though; this book was written pre-ERTA.

Stidger, Howe C. and Ruth W. *Inflation Management: 100 Practical Techniques for Business and Industry*. New York: Wiley-Interscience, 1976. Similar to Dlugatch (above); this one reads a little easier.

Legalities

Angel, Juvenal L. *Directory of Professional and Occupational Licensing in the United States*. New York: Simon and Schuster, 1970. A good first step for finding out if you need a license to do whatever you want to do. "First step" because requirements may have changed since the date of writing; Angel gives addresses for the regulatory agencies, so you can ask them.

Hamilton, Harper. *How to Prepare Your Own Partnership Agreement*. Boulder, CO: Hamilton Press, 1978. The agreements are written in standard dinosauresque legal prose, but the explanations are quite good. Better have your lawyer take a look at self-prepared agreements before you sign them, though.

Petersen, Dan. *The OSHA Compliance Manual*. New York: McGraw-Hill, 1975. Occupational safety in words of one syllable, with appropriate forms. Make sure a particular recommendation is current before you follow it.

Sacharow, Stanley. *Packaging Regulations*. Westport, CT: AVI Publishing Co., 1979. A dry but quite comprehensible rundown. Read it (or donate a copy to your lawyer) before you start selling packaged goods.

Particular Business Problems

Barzman, Sol. *Everyday Credit Checking: A Practical Guide*. New York: Thomas Y. Crowell Co., 1973. Good guide to trade credit (e.g., credit to commercial customers—not consumers).

Douglas, F. Gordon. *How to Profitably Sell or Buy a Company or Business*. New York: Van Nostrand Reinhold, 1981. An excellent treatment of the subject in good utilitarian prose.

Hanson, Richard E. *The Manager's Guide to Copying and Duplicating.* New York: McGraw-Hill, 1980. As much information as you'll ever need on the subject; read it before the copier salespeople start working on you.

Holtz, Herman R. *Profit-Line Management: Managing a Growing Business Successfully.* New York: Amacom, 1981. Somewhat repetitious, but it's a good basic introduction to management control systems, and Holtz is a vivid writer. Especially useful for service businesses.

Loffel, Egon W. *Protecting Your Business.* New York: David McKay Co., Inc., 1977. Security devices and precautions.

Lowry, Albert J. *How to Become Financially Successful by Owning Your Own Business.* New York: Simon and Schuster, 1981. Some very useful, specific information—but Lowry posits a rather higher level of capital than you're likely to be working with. Style is quite readable.

Mancuso, Joseph K. *Small Business Survival Guide: Sources of Help for Entrepreneurs.* Englewood Cliffs, NJ: Prentice-Hall, 1980. This is a comprehensive assembly of sources (magazine articles, government agencies, private organizations, venture capital firms) but take it with a grain of salt. Because the listings are comprehensive, heavily padded junk is treated in the same way as more useful material.

Mandell, Mel. *1001 Ways to Operate Your Business More Profitably.* Homewood, IL: Dow Jones-Irwin, 1975. Mandell is a fine utilitarian writer, and the book has some excellent pragmatic suggestions for coping with shortages and high prices—though your business may be too small for a while to use the suggestions.

Martin, Thomas J. and Trahue, Bruce. *Sell More and Spend Less.* New York: Holt, Rinehart and Winston, 1980. Too much filler (this book would make a sensational magazine article) but it's a good basic introduction to marketing.

Smith, Brian K. *The Small Computer in Small Business.* Brattleboro, VT: The Stephen Greene Press, 1981. Nice straightforward text with good discussion of computer fundamentals and when a computer is cost-effective.

Specific Kinds of Business

Anderson, Charles B. and Smith, G. Roysce, editors. *A Manual on Bookselling* (2nd ed.). New York: Harmony Books, 1974. The excellent material on inventory control will also be useful in other types of business.

Brabec, Barbara. *Creative Cash: How to Sell Your Crafts, Needlework, Designs, and Know-How.* Milwaukee, WI: Countryside Books, 1979.

Never mind the cute title and illustrations; there's a great deal of solid, well-focused information here.

Brownstone, Douglass L. *How to Run a Successful Specialty Food Store.* New York: John Wiley and Sons, Inc., 1978. For would-be purveyors of health food, gourmet trifles, or delicatessen.

Clark, Leta W. *How to Open Your Own Shop or Gallery.* New York: St. Martin's Press, 1978. Some overlap with Brabec's book (above), but more focus on retail sales.

Holtz, Herman. *The $100 Billion Market: How to Do Business with the U.S. Government.* New York: Amacom, 1980. Well-handled, detailed information on government procurement.

Kleeman, Elayne J. and Voltz, Jeanne A. *How to Turn a Passion for Food Into Profit.* New York: Rawson, Wade, 1979. For would-be restaurateurs, caterers, and restaurant suppliers.

Kopelman, Arie and Crawford, Tad. *Selling Your Photography: The Complete Marketing, Business and Legal Guide.* New York: St. Martin's Press, 1980. Not as complete as it *could* be, but well written and easy to use.

Miller, Daniel. *Starting a Small Restaurant.* Harvard, MA: Harvard Common Press, 1978. Well-tailored, useful information in good clean prose.

Mooney, Sean and Green, George. *Sean Mooney's Practical Guide to Running a Pub.* Chicago, IL: Nelson-Hall, 1979. A classic of how-to book writing as well as saloon-keeping. It could have a bit more about equipment and decoration, though.

Scott, Michael. *The Crafts Business Encyclopedia.* New York: Harcourt Brace Jovanovich, 1977. Somewhat difficult to use because it's organized as a series of short articles, but plenty of useful information is packed in there.

Reference Books

These are listed by title, not author, because the authors (or, more properly, editors) change from edition to edition. All these books are updated frequently, so be sure you have the most current. If you can't afford the often hefty prices of the reference works you need, check the local library; your patience will often be rewarded.

Blue Book of Photography Prices. Photography Research Institute. Information on cost, hourly rates, and expenses of various kinds of photography; updated every thirty days.

Consultants and Consulting Organizations Directory. Detroit, MI: Gale Research Co. Where to find a systems analyst, OSHA specialist, or management consultant; updated twice a year.

Contemporary Crafts Marketplace. New York: R. R. Bowker. Where to sell crafts items.

Craftworker's Market. Cincinnati, OH: Writer's Digest Books. Similar to the above; watch out for obsolete entries.

Encyclopedia of Associations. Detroit, MI: Gale Research Co. Great for finding appropriate trade organizations—and for compiling mailing lists.

Estimating Manual for Professional Photography. Professional Photographers West. Similar to the *Blue Book*—less complete, but less expensive.

MacRae's Blue Book. The Torrington Co. Five-volume industrial directory, updated each year: one volume lists corporations; three volumes list products and services; one volume reprints manufacturers' catalog sheets. A directory like this is great for locating hard-to-find components, comparing prices, or compiling mailing lists for your own new products.

National Trade and Professional Associations of the United States. Washington, D.C.: Columbia Books, Inc. Another source for groups to join.

O'Dwyer's Directory of Public Relations Films. Updated annually; good place to start if you need a publicist.

Standard Directory of Advertisers. Skokie, IL: National Register Publishing Co., Inc. Three volumes (one by company name, one geographical, one listing advertising agencies)—terrific for compiling mailing lists.

Standard Rate and Data Services. Skokie, IL: Lists consumer and business publications. Where to send your press release. Bring a magnifying glass.

Thomas' Register. New York: Thomas Publishing Co. Sixteen volumes of product information a year: eight of products and services, two of company names and addresses, six of catalog pages. The business equivalent of the Sears Roebuck catalog.

U.S. Industrial Directory. Boston, MA: Cahners Publishing Co. Similar to *Thomas' Register* but shorter: one volume of listings by manufacturers' names, two volumes of product information, a volume of catalog pages.

Index